# INSTRUCTOR'S RESOURCE MANUAL

THE Gregg
Reference
Manual

A MANUAL OF STYLE, GRAMMAR,
USAGE, AND FORMATTING

# INSTRUCTOR'S RESOURCE MANUAL

THE **Gregg Reference Manual**

A MANUAL OF STYLE, GRAMMAR, USAGE, AND FORMATTING

**Tenth Edition**

WILLIAM A. SABIN

McGraw-Hill
Irwin

Boston   Burr Ridge, IL   Dubuque, IA   Madison, WI   New York
San Francisco   St. Louis   Bangkok   Bogotá   Caracas   Kuala Lumpur
Lisbon   London   Madrid   Mexico City   Milan   Montreal   New Delhi
Santiago   Seoul   Singapore   Sydney   Taipei   Toronto

# CONTENTS

## A. GUIDELINES FOR DEVELOPING A COURSE BASED ON *THE GREGG REFERENCE MANUAL*     A–1

## B. USING THE *BASIC WORKSHEETS*      **B-1**

## C. USING THE *COMPREHENSIVE WORKSHEETS*      **C-1**

The section titled "Guidelines for Developing a
Course Based on *The Gregg Reference Manual*"
was written by Elizabeth Kay Anderson,
instructor of English, Fox College, Oak Lawn, Illinois.

 **McGraw-Hill**
**Irwin**

Instructor's Resource Manual to accompany
THE GREGG REFERENCE MANUAL: A MANUAL OF STYLE, GRAMMAR, USAGE,
AND FORMATTING, Tenth Edition
William A. Sabin

1 2 3 4 5 6 7 8 9 0 QPD/QPD 0 9 8 7 6 5 4

ISBN 0-07-293656-8

www.mhhe.com

The **McGraw·Hill** Companies

# GUIDELINES FOR DEVELOPING A COURSE BASED ON *THE GREGG REFERENCE MANUAL*

The following guidelines will show you how to create several different courses based on *The Gregg Reference Manual (GRM)* and one of the two sets of worksheets that accompany the manual—the *Basic Worksheets* or the *Comprehensive Worksheets*.

## COURSE OBJECTIVES

All of these courses are designed to achieve these objectives:

- Sensitize students to the most common mistakes in style, grammar, and usage, and show them how to avoid making these mistakes in the future.

- Introduce students to (1) the evolving changes in style, grammar, and usage and (2) the on-the-job standards and practices that they will be expected to meet.

- Show students several ways to locate answers quickly in *GRM,* and provide them with much-needed practice in applying the appropriate rules correctly.

- Develop students' editing skills so that they can spot errors on their own and correct them with the help of *GRM.*

- Strengthen students' writing skills if time permits, and enhance the quality of the written documents they produce in class and on the job.

## TWO SETS OF WORKSHEETS TO CHOOSE FROM

### Basic Worksheets

This set of worksheets provides carefully sequenced exercises that focus entirely on Sections 1–11 (the sections that deal with punctuation, capitalization, number style, abbreviations, plurals and possessives, spelling, compound words, word division, grammar, and usage). The *Basic Worksheets* focus entirely on the "basic" rules in Sections 1–11—that is, those rules that have been highlighted by means of a red panel over the appropriate rule numbers. In this way students can ignore those rules that deal with fine points of style, and they can concentrate just on those rules that will help them overcome the most common errors in style, grammar, and usage.

### Comprehensive Worksheets

This set of worksheets provides exercises that cover all 18 sections in the manual. These exercises cover a much wider range of rules in Sections 1–11. Moreover, they provide "problem" letters, memos, and other business documents that will help students develop their formatting skills.

**Features of the Worksheets.** Both sets of worksheets have been designed to build three critical skills:

- They will sensitize students to the common problems they are likely to encounter in any written material they have to deal with.

- These worksheets will direct students to the appropriate rules in *GRM* so that later on, when they encounter similar problems in their own work, they will know where to look for answers.

- These worksheets will sharpen students' editing skills so that they can apply the rules correctly under many different circumstances.

Both sets of worksheets begin with a diagnostic survey of each student's editing skills. At the end of the program, students will encounter a parallel survey that will show how much their editing skills have improved. In most of the intervening worksheets, rule numbers are provided alongside the answer blanks so that students can quickly locate the answers they need to complete each set of exercises. Interspersed within this sequence of worksheets are editing exercises and editing surveys that will help your students integrate all the things they learned up to that point.

**Important Note:** If you are using the worksheets for the first time, be sure to familiarize yourself with the material on pages B-2 to B-7 for the *Basic Worksheets* and the corresponding material on pages C-2 to C-7 for the *Comprehensive Worksheets.* This material will give you an overview of how the worksheets are organized along with specific suggestions on how to use them effectively.

## WHICH SET OF WORKSHEETS IS RIGHT FOR YOUR STUDENTS?

### Basic Worksheets

Choose these worksheets if your students do not already possess a solid foundation in language skills. These worksheets allow students to concentrate on mastering the basic rules so that they can avoid making the kinds of errors that most commonly appear in business writing.

## Comprehensive Worksheets

Choose these worksheets if you want to (1) familiarize your students with a wider range of rules involving style, grammar, and usage and (2) teach your students how to format a variety of business documents. The editing exercises that involve these business documents enable your students to apply their newly gained skills in a realistic context.

## ALTERNATIVE CURRICULUM PLANS

The following charts suggest how you can structure a *basic course* (one that uses the *Basic Worksheets* and runs for 10 or 15 weeks) and a *comprehensive course* (one that uses the *Comprehensive Worksheets* and runs for 15 weeks). Because courses vary in length from one institution to another, you will want to adjust these suggested plans to fit the number of weeks that you actually have to work with.

These charts list only the material to be covered in the manual and a set of the worksheets. You should feel free to select as much or as little material as your schedule allows or as your students need. Moreover, you should adjust the workload suggested for each week, depending on the ability level of your students.

**Important Note:** If time permits, you should supplement the use of worksheet exercises by assigning writing exercises. This additional component not only will enhance the value of the course but will strengthen your students' writing and editing skills at the same time.

Suggestions for appropriate writing assignments are provided on pages A-6–A-8.

### BASIC COURSE—10 WEEKS

| Week | Assignment |
|---|---|
| 1 | **Introduction.** Introduce the course. Refer to pages xiv–xvi, "How to Look Things Up." Administer diagnostic survey (Worksheet 1). |
| 2 | **Section 1. Punctuation: Major Marks.** Worksheets 2–4. |
| 3 | **Section 2. Punctuation: Other Marks.** Worksheet 5. |
| 4 | **Sections 3–4. Capitalization and Numbers.** Worksheets 6–7. Use Editing Survey A (Worksheet 8) as a review. |
| 5 | **Sections 5–6. Abbreviations, Plurals, and Possessives.** Worksheets 9–11. |
| 6 | **Sections 7–9. Spelling, Compound Words, and Word Division.** Worksheets 12–15. Use Editing Survey B (Worksheet 16) as a review. |
| 7 and 8 | **Section 10. Grammar.** Worksheets 17–19. |
| 9 and 10 | **Section 11. Usage.** Worksheets 20–21. Use Editing Survey C (Worksheet 22) as a review. Use either Worksheet 23 or 24 as a final exam and the other for reinforcement or as a second chance. |

### BASIC COURSE—15 WEEKS

| Week | Assignment |
|---|---|
| 1 | **Introduction.** Introduce the course. Refer to pages xiv–xvi, "How to Look Things Up." Administer diagnostic survey (Worksheet 1). |
| 2 and 3 | **Section 1. Punctuation: Major Marks.** Worksheets 2–4. |
| 4 | **Section 2. Punctuation: Other Marks.** Worksheet 5. |
| 5 | **Section 3. Capitalization.** Worksheet 6. |
| 6 | **Section 4. Numbers.** Worksheet 7. Use Editing Survey A (Worksheet 8) as a review. |
| 7 | **Section 5. Abbreviations.** Worksheet 9. |
| 8 | **Section 6. Plurals and Possessives.** Worksheets 10–11. |
| 9 | **Section 7. Spelling.** Worksheets 12–13. |
| 10 | **Section 8. Compound Words.** Worksheet 14. |
| 11 | **Section 9. Word Division.** Worksheet 15. Use Editing Survey B (Worksheet 16) as a review. |
| 12 and 13 | **Section 10. Grammar.** Worksheets 17–19. |
| 14 and 15 | **Section 11. Usage.** Worksheets 20–21. Use Editing Survey C (Worksheet 22) as a review. Use either Worksheet 23 or 24 as a final exam and the other for reinforcement or as a second chance. |

# COMPREHENSIVE COURSE—15 WEEKS

| Week | Assignment |
|---|---|
| 1 | **Introduction.** Introduce the course. Refer to pages xiv–xvi, "How to Look Things Up." Administer diagnostic survey (Worksheet 1). |
| 2 and 3 | **Section 1. Punctuation: Major Marks.** Worksheets 2–5. |
| 4 | **Section 2. Punctuation: Other Marks.** Worksheet 6. Use Editing Survey A (Worksheet 7) as a review. |
| 5 and 6 | **Sections 3–5. Capitalization, Numbers, and Abbreviations.** Worksheets 8–12. Use Editing Survey B (Worksheet 13) as a review. |
| 7 | **Sections 6–7. Plurals and Possessives; Spelling.** Worksheets 14–17. |
| 8 | **Sections 8–9. Compound Words; Word Division.** Worksheets 18–19. Use Editing Survey C (Worksheet 20) as a review. |
| 9 and 10 | **Section 10. Grammar.** Worksheets 21–22. Collaborative writing: Have students compose quiz questions based on Section 10. |
| 11 | **Section 11. Usage.** Worksheets 23–24. Use Editing Survey D (Worksheet 25) as a review. |
| 12 | **Section 13. Editing and Proofreading; Letters, Memos, and E-Mail.** Worksheets 26–27. |
| 13 | **Section 13 (continued).** Writing: Use this week to work on the writing assignments for Section 13. Allow students to participate in peer editing. Encourage revising. Editing Practice A (Worksheet 29). |
| 14 | **Sections 14–15. Reports and Manuscripts; Notes and Bibliographies.** Editing Practice B (Worksheet 30). |
| 15 | **Sections 16–18. Tables; Other Business Documents; Appendixes.** Writing: résumé or collaborative writing. Editing Practice C (Worksheet 31). Review using Worksheet 28, Looking Things Up. Use this time for students to revise writing assignments. Editing Practice D (Worksheet 32). |

**Two-Term Program.** If you have the luxury of two terms in which to teach the program, you can distribute the course work a number of ways. Here are two options:

a. Spend the first term working through *GRM* and completing the worksheets. Spend the second term composing business or academic documents that incorporate the lessons from the first term.

b. Integrate composition assignments as you cover each section and assign the corresponding worksheets. In this way you can still follow the suggested schedules but spend more time on each section. Add an extra week to each unit and reserve two weeks for portfolio review, peer editing, and revision sessions.

In either case, do not base a student's final grade only on midterm and final exams that make use of the worksheets. Consider each student's writing portfolio as well.

## GENERAL METHODOLOGY FOR BASIC AND COMPREHENSIVE COURSES

Whether you teach a basic or a comprehensive course, use a variety of approaches tailored to the learning styles and ability levels of your students. Consider using any of the following techniques as time permits.

**Warm-Up Writing Exercises.** Before formally introducing a new series of rules, ask students to write some sentences based on one of those rules and be prepared to read them aloud. This type of exercise is likely to compel students to read the rules more thoughtfully and apply them more carefully, once they know they will have to read their sentences aloud. Students will probably make mistakes in their sentences, but these mistakes create wonderful teaching opportunities.

At the start of each class period, choose a new rule for the warm-up exercise. If your class runs for several hours, consider using a warm-up exercise each time you return from a break. These exercises are most beneficial when completed on a regular basis.

**Sectional Outline of Topics.** When introducing a new section, have students first review the list of topics on the opening pages.

Indicate which rules you consider particularly important and plan to stress.

**Glossary of Grammatical Terms.** Before assigning new rules, remind students to consult this glossary in Appendix D (pages 636–645) if they are unfamiliar with the grammatical terminology used throughout the course.

**PowerPoint Slides and Transparency Masters.** Pages D-1 to D-11 in this resource manual provide detailed suggestions for using these graphic materials to introduce new rules and concepts. To accommodate different learning styles, have students read examples provided by these materials and invite class discussion.

**Group Presentations.** After you have presented a new set of rules, divide students into small groups and assign two rules to each group. Allow time for each group to prepare a brief explanation of the rules and to write new sample sentences on the board. Putting these examples on the board provides an opportunity to reinforce grammatical concepts and invites class discussion.

**Student Journals.** Have students maintain journals in which they record sample sentences taken from current reading assignments, group activities, and their own individual work. Have the students label these sample sentences by rule number.

Especially noteworthy sentences should be read aloud in class and written down in everyone's notebook. While *GRM* itself provides excellent examples, most students require this additional practice to master the concepts thoroughly.

**News Articles.** To promote class discussion, encourage students to bring news articles to class that display three of the rules previously discussed.

**Using the Worksheets.** You can use the worksheets as homework, but you will also find it quite effective to allow class time for students to work on some of the exercise items. This kind of group activity under your guidance decreases the tendency of students to guess rather than look up the rules.

a. At the outset, explain how the worksheets are organized (see pages B-2 to B-5 for the *Basic Worksheets* and C-2 to C-3 for the *Comprehensive Worksheets*), and review the appropriate proofreaders' marks that may have to be used in the various exercises. (See Transparencies 12-3 to 12-8 on pages D-27 to D-32.)

b. On occasion assign parts of certain exercises as a class activity (using an overhead projector if possible), or allow students to work in small groups to complete this assignment.

c. When students have completed all the exercises on a particular worksheet, you can review the answers with the whole class (displaying the correct answers by means of PowerPoint slides or overhead transparencies created from the keys in this resource manual).

d. You may prefer to collect the completed worksheets and correct them yourself. In that case, consider using the following method:

- Circle incorrect responses, but *don't make the corrections yourself.*
- Return the worksheets and tell students that they must return the corrected worksheets for full credit.
- If particular students are having special difficulty with the material, you might reserve 15 minutes at the end of each class period for

tutoring or else set up tutoring time outside of class. Helping these students work through their incorrect answers gives them a better understanding of the underlying concepts.

**Assigning Homework.** If your class meets for three or more one-hour sessions a week, you may want to give one assignment for each night. If your class meets once or twice each week for longer sessions, you may want to give two or more assignments each night. The homework could involve the following types of activities:

a. Ask students to complete the worksheet exercises that were not finished in class.

b. Ask students to revise erroneous sentences from the warm-up exercise.

c. Ask students to write more sample sentences based on your assessment of problem areas.

d. If you have access to a computer lab, reserve lab time for students to work on posted material.

e. Ask students to write a paragraph on a topic you assign. Students should be asked to identify five rules that apply to the sentences in their paragraph.

## INTRODUCING *THE GREGG REFERENCE MANUAL*

1. Briefly explain the importance of reference manuals and handbooks. Explain how the ability to use these resources effectively can have a significant effect on one's ultimate success on the job. If time permits, ask the students which resources they have used in the past, and encourage a brief discussion of their successes and failures.

2. Introduce students to the contents and the format of *The Gregg Reference Manual.* Encourage them to think of *GRM* as a search engine for writers.

   a. Turn to pages vi–vii ("Contents"), and point out the titles of the 18 sections and the 3 major parts.

   b. Turn to pages viii–xi ("Preface"), and call specific attention to the availability of an "Ask the Author" feature on the *Gregg* Web site. Note that the URL appears on the bottom of the back cover.

   c. Turn to pages xiv–xvi ("How to Look Things Up"), and let students know that you will soon return to those pages.

   d. Review the Section 1 list of topics (pages 2–3), and note that each section begins with a comparable list. Point out the structure of numbered headings and subheadings.

   e. Ask students to flip through the manual quickly to get a concrete sense of all that it contains.

   f. Point out the location of the page number, which can sometimes be more helpful than a rule number when trying to locate certain information. Explain that on left-hand pages the boldface paragraph number beneath the page number refers to the first new paragraph at the *top* of that page (rather than to a continuation of a paragraph carried over from the previous page). Explain that on right-hand pages the boldface paragraph number beneath the page number refers to a new paragraph that begins (but may not end) at the *bottom* of that page. If students are not familiar with the paragraph symbol (¶ or ¶¶), explain how it is used in the singular and the plural.

   **g.** Encourage or require students to keep a notebook specifically for this course, in which they can record notes on new things they have learned.

**3.** Acquaint students with the five suggested methods for retrieving information from *GRM*.

   **a.** Look at pages xiv–xvi together, and use Transparencies H-1 to H-6 to facilitate the discussion.

   **b.** In discussing the use of *the printed index*, have the students turn to pages 646–688 and point out the difference in font between rule numbers and page numbers.

   **c.** In discussing the use of *the electronic index*, note that it contains many more entries than the printed index. Indicate where it can be located on the *Gregg* Web site <http://www.gregg.com>, and note that for fast access it can be downloaded on each student's computer.

   **d.** In discussing *the fast-skim approach*, point out the two locations for skimming: the "Quick Guide to Key Topics" on the inside cover and the outline of topics at the beginning of each section. Also note how the marginal tabs can be used to find a particular section in the manual.

   **e.** In discussing *the "play the numbers" strategy*, point out the value of quickly memorizing the name of the topic that each section number refers to.

   **f.** In discussing the need to *look up specific words and phrases*, point out that the electronic index is a far better source than the printed index because it contains so many more entries.

   **g.** Point out the extensive use of cross-references throughout the manual and in the index. Explain the two types of cross-references:
- If the cross-reference begins with "See also," it means that another rule will provide additional information to help the student understand the rule or example at hand, but it is not essential to take this extra step.
- If the cross-reference begins with "See," it means there is another rule containing vital information that the student ought to consult.

## ADMINISTERING THE DIAGNOSTIC SURVEY

Administer the diagnostic survey to determine students' strengths and weaknesses. (Use Worksheet 1 in either set of worksheets.) Allow the students to refer to *GRM* if they wish.

**1.** The diagnostic survey in the *Basic Worksheets* contains 100 items. Because these items are grouped sequentially by section number, it is relatively easy to determine in which areas each student is particularly weak. The chart on page B-6 indicates the correlation between the errors a student has made and the particular worksheets that will help to overcome those errors.

**2.** The diagnostic survey in the *Comprehensive Worksheets* contains 175 items, which are similarly sequenced by section number. The chart on page C-6 indicates the correlation between the errors a student has made and the corrective worksheets. Because the diagnostic survey in the *Comprehensive Worksheets* is much longer and more challenging than the one in the *Basic Worksheets,* it may require more than one class period to complete.

**3.** Before asking students to complete the diagnostic survey, alleviate some of their fears by explaining that the scores on this survey will not count toward their grade but will simply be used to determine which areas the course should highlight.

**4.** Point out the chart of proofreaders' marks that appears both on the inside back cover and on pages 358–359. Focus only on those marks that students will need to use when they complete the diagnostic survey: inserting or deleting punctuation marks (periods, question marks, exclamation points, commas, semicolons, and colons); changing a capital letter to a lowercase letter or vice versa; correcting spelling or changing wording; and indicating how an item should be italicized or underlined.

**5.** Score each student's performance on the diagnostic survey simply to establish a baseline against which to measure the student's performance on a final survey (which is constructed in exactly parallel fashion). For the *Basic* diagnostic survey, which contains 100 items, simply subtract 1 point for each incorrect answer from a total of 100. For the *Comprehensive* diagnostic survey, which contains 175 items, deduct ½ point for each incorrect answer from a total of 100.

**6.** Before you assign a score to each student's survey, you may want to have these surveys checked for errors in class. In that case, you could have students check their own work, but you ought to consider letting students check one another's work, since that will give them helpful proofreading and editing practice and let them see that everyone in the class has weaknesses to overcome.

7. To display the correct answers, create PowerPoint slides or overhead transparencies from the keys for these diagnostic surveys. (See pages B-12 to B-15 for the key to the *Basic Worksheets* survey and pages C-12 to C-18 for the key to the *Comprehensive Worksheets* survey.) After the checking of answers is finished, have the surveys returned to their owners. Allow a few minutes for students to consider how well they did, and encourage them to write in their notebooks any answers that surprised them or any new concepts they learned. If students raise immediate questions about certain answers, try to respond briefly but resist the temptation to use this situation as an occasion for providing basic instruction. Collect these surveys at the end of the class, assign a numerical score to each, and retain this information as a basis for tracking each student's progress throughout the course.

## DESIGNING A SELF-PACED COURSE

1. After you evaluate each student's performance on the diagnostic survey, you may discover that the students' abilities vary so widely that it may make sense for you to provide them with different assignments and let them work at their own pace.

2. If you decide to teach a *self-paced course,* hold individual conferences with each student after you have analyzed that student's strengths and weaknesses.

3. In the course of each individual conference, establish which worksheets the student needs to complete during the course. Turn to the first page in the student's copy of the Worksheets, which presents the table of contents. On that page, circle the number of each worksheet that you are asking each student to complete. Direct the student to initial and date each of the assigned worksheets after he or she completes and scores it.

4. Make a copy of the answer keys available (as indicated on pages B-12 to B-85 for the *Basic Worksheets* and C-12 to C-110 for the *Comprehensive Worksheets* of this resource manual).

5. Let students know that they will be tested on the material to encourage them to take their mastery of the material seriously. You can use portions of the editing surveys as exams.

## TEACHING A TRADITIONAL COURSE

1. Even if you decide to teach the course in a traditional manner and have all students complete the same schedule of assignments, try to make time for an individual conference with each student so that you can discuss that student's particular strengths and weaknesses.

2. These conferences will help you gauge the length of time and amount of work you need to devote to each section in the manual and the related worksheets.

3. If your students as a whole did not perform well on the diagnostic survey, you may find it desirable to have the students work in small groups to complete many of the worksheets.

4. Consult the charts on pages A-2 to A-3 for suggested teaching plans, depending on whether you will be teaching a 10-week basic course, a 15-week basic course, or a 15-week comprehensive course.

## SUPPLEMENTAL WRITING ASSIGNMENTS

### Sections 1–11

The writing assignments described below do not constitute an exhaustive list of projects. They are intended merely to suggest the kinds of assignments you might want to make as you cover the rules in Sections 1–11.

The actual assignments are likely to take different forms, depending on the focus of the course you plan to teach. However, in any writing that students are asked to do, they should be required to incorporate sentences that reflect five rules currently under discussion. (They should also be asked to identify the rule numbers in the margins.)

**Paragraphs and Essays.** You might initially ask students to write a brief paragraph on any topic that interests them or on one that you assign. Then as you present more rules, have students create a second and then a third paragraph on the same theme. In each new paragraph, students should once again be asked to incorporate (and identify) sentences that reflect five new rules currently under discussion.

Then ask students to expand the paragraphs into a three-page essay, adding an introduction and a conclusion. You will probably need to discuss the characteristics of a good essay.

At each stage of the developmental process, have students review one another's work. In the process of finding errors in someone else's writing, students develop the editing skills that will help them spot the errors in their own work and become better writers.

Here are some specific topics that could provide the basis for these assignments. They can be linked to any of the first eleven sections in the manual.

- **Hobbies.** Ask students to write a paragraph describing a favorite hobby or one they'd like to try. When the first paragraph has been reviewed and adequately revised, ask students to create another paragraph in which they discuss a different leisure-time activity. After the second paragraph has been successfully revised, have students write a third paragraph about a hobby they would not like to try or have tried unsuccessfully. Then ask students to convert these three paragraphs into a coherent three-page essay. **Note:** This assignment could be linked to the punctuation rules in Sections 1 and 2.

A-6

- **Travel.** Ask students to write a paragraph describing a place they have already visited and very much enjoyed. When the first paragraph has been reviewed and revised, ask students to create another paragraph in which they discuss a place they would very much like to visit. Then have students write a third paragraph about a trip they took that did not turn out the way they hoped. Finally, ask students to develop these three paragraphs into a three-page essay. **Note:** This assignment could be linked to the capitalization rules in Section 3.

- **Families.** Assign an essay in which students describe their families. Have them start by drawing a family tree showing aunts, uncles, and cousins as well as parents, siblings, and grandparents. From the family tree, students should create a number of paragraphs that can then be expanded to an essay. **Note:** If this assignment is given in conjunction with Section 6, ask students to use possessives when describing various family relationships.

- **Work experience.** Ask students to develop an essay describing jobs they've had and liked, jobs they didn't like, and jobs they hope to have.

- **Academic experience.** Ask students to develop an essay that describes courses they've already taken and that indicates how these courses relate to their long-range goals.

  As a separate assignment, ask students to list the objectives of the courses they are currently taking, following guidelines contained in ¶1081. This project will give students practice in constructing lists with parallel structure.

- **Gender bias.** On the basis of ¶¶1050–1053, ask students to write a brief essay in which they advise new students about the need to avoid gender-biased language in their writing. The essay should provide concrete examples of the kinds of things to avoid.

### Creating Problems That Need to Be Corrected.

The following suggestions call for the students themselves to write paragraphs and sentences with deliberate errors embedded in them. Some of the assignments (for example, creating sentences with dangling constructions) could be more fun if carried out by small groups of students working together. In other cases, students might get more out of an assignment if they had to deal with it on their own.

- On the basis of ¶719, have students create sentences or paragraphs that deliberately misuse words that look alike or sound alike. Then have students exchange this material so that they can each correct the mistakes they find.

- Have students create sentences or paragraphs that deliberately misspell a number of words that are listed in ¶720. Then have students exchange this material so that they can each correct the mistakes they find.

- Have students create sentences that contain dangling constructions that produce a comic or absurd meaning. (See ¶¶1082–1085.) When these materials are exchanged, students will have to rewrite these sentences to overcome the problems they find.

- Have students create sentences or paragraphs that are heavily salted with abbreviations found throughout Section 5. When these materials are exchanged, students will have to rewrite the sentences or paragraphs, decoding these abbreviations in the process.

- Provide a photo or painting that displays lots of activity or detail. Invite students to describe the scene using only passive forms. When these materials are exchanged, students should be asked to (1) change passive verbs to active forms as appropriate and (2) justify the passive constructions they decide not to change.

### Sections 12–18

These sections in the *Gregg* manual deal primarily with the formatting of a wide variety of business documents. If you plan to ask your students to demonstrate their ability to execute these formats correctly, you can enrich these assignments by asking them at the same time to create documents that are personally meaningful.

**Writing Letters.** Ask students to draft letters on a variety of topics. Have them exchange their drafts so that they can get comments and suggestions from a classmate. Then ask students to revise their letters as necessary so that the final version would be good enough to be mailed. In some cases, you may want to suggest that a letter actually should be mailed. Then, if the letter elicits a response—especially a response that delivers the result the writer was hoping to achieve—the writer will know that he or she has been very successful.

Depending on the content of your course, you could have students write (1) a thank-you letter for the excellent service they received, (2) a letter that simply requests some information, or (3) a letter to the editor of a newspaper or a magazine on a topic of current interest. Letting students base the content of these letters on their personal experience is the best way to engage their interest in these letter-writing assignments.

For teaching purposes, however, you may want every student to write a letter based on the same topic. Here is one possible scenario for students to consider:

- You have just purchased $200 worth of books at the college bookstore for the new school term. Your math textbook was supposed to come with a companion workbook. However, when you opened the shrink-wrap, the workbook was not there. You returned to the bookstore to ask for a new one. You were treated rudely by the salesperson, who told you there was nothing he could do. In fact, he implied that you probably had misplaced the workbook. When you asked to speak to the bookstore manager, the salesperson said you would have to come back. You have left three messages for the manager, but she has not called you back. *Your assignment:* Write an effective complaint letter to the manager that gets you the results you want.

As an additional aspect of these letter-writing assignments, you may want to ask students to design a personal letterhead (on the basis of the guidelines in ¶¶1310–1311), which they will then use for the letters they write as individuals. If you plan to create assignments in which the students write letters as the employees of a fictitious organization, you could ask them to design a letterhead for that situation as well. You could also ask that an appropriate envelope be prepared for each letter they write.

**Writing Memos and E-Mail Messages.** Some of the suggestions offered for letter-writing exercises could also be assigned as memos or e-mail messages. Or students could be asked to take a letter they previously wrote and rewrite it as a memo or an e-mail message. That would require students to consider what will be different and what will be the same.

One possible suggestion for a memo or an e-mail message would require students to draft a message to incoming first-year students, explaining how to survive their first week of college.

**Writing Reports.** Although you could ask students to write a new report for your course, it might be equally effective to ask them to bring in a brief report they had written for another class and revise it on the basis of everything previously covered in your course.

**Preparing a Résumé.** If time permits, have each student prepare a current résumé. This assignment will require many revisions but will create a valuable addition to each student's portfolio.

**Preparing Other Business Documents.** If it meets the objectives of your course, ask students to prepare—on a collaborative basis—various documents based on the models in Section 17. Different groups could prepare different documents that could then be critiqued by the class as a whole.

# USING THE *BASIC WORKSHEETS*

# A NOTE TO THE INSTRUCTOR

The *Basic Worksheets* that accompany the tenth edition of *The Gregg Reference Manual* are designed to familiarize your students with the contents and the organization of the first eleven sections of *The Gregg Reference Manual*. When the two components are used together, they will serve as the basis for a short course on English grammar, usage, and style. These materials can be used as a separate unit of instruction where a modular curriculum is in effect, or they can be used as part of a cooperative training class or a course in keyboarding, machine transcription, office procedures, business communications, or document processing. Moreover, they can be effectively used in programs for developmental English, English as a second language, adult education, and workplace education courses for English. (*Note:* If you are looking for a set of worksheets that cover not only grammar, usage, and style but also the techniques and procedures for handling letters, memos, and other types of business communications, consider using the *Comprehensive Worksheets* [ISBN 0-07-293655-X] that also accompany the tenth edition of *The Gregg Reference Manual*. See pages C-2 to C-7 in this *Instructor's Resource Manual*.)

## OBJECTIVES OF THESE WORKSHEETS

The *Basic Worksheets* are designed to build three basic editing skills your students need to possess if they are going to achieve an on-the-job level of proficiency.

1. Your students need to know when they are in the presence of a potential problem. Otherwise, they'll never be tempted to consult a reference manual, even though you put one in their hands. They'll simply assume that whatever they have written, edited, or typed is correct.
2. Even when your students know they have a potential problem, they still need to know where to look in a reference manual to find the appropriate rule. If they aren't properly acquainted with the contents and the organization of a reference manual and if they aren't properly introduced to the various techniques for looking things up, they won't find the answers they need.
3. Even when your students have mastered the skill of looking things up and can find the rule that covers a particular problem, they still need experience in applying the rule correctly. What's more, they need immediate reinforcement that tells them they *have* applied the rule correctly.

How do the *Basic Worksheets* develop these three skills? To begin with, almost every worksheet focuses on one particular section in *The Gregg Reference Manual*—and in all cases focuses on a selected set of rules within that section. (See the chart on page 3 for the primary coverage of each worksheet.) As students progress through a given worksheet, they are forced to confront a number of problems within a specific area—whether punctuation, capitalization, number style, or some other area of potential difficulty. The exercise items on these worksheets do not attempt to cover the fine points of style in the related set of rules. Instead, the exercise items cover the most basic kinds of problems that students are likely to encounter whenever they write, transcribe, type, edit, or proofread. The objective here is to familiarize them with the typical problems that occur in business communications so that later on, in similar situations, they'll possess that editorial "twitch" that alerts them to the possible presence of such problems. They may not remember how to deal with a given problem on the spot. However, the important thing is that they sense that a problem could exist and they are motivated to consult *The Gregg Reference Manual*. If students could develop just this skill alone, most of the errors they make would no doubt disappear.

Knowing how to look things up is not an automatic skill; it, too, has to be worked on. To help students develop this skill, the typical worksheet supplies the appropriate rule number(s) next to each exercise item. In this way students can concentrate on reading the rules and applying them correctly to the specific situation. As students complete each worksheet, a quick review of their answers against the key will tell them which rules may be giving them trouble and need to be reexamined.

To further develop the skill of spotting problems and looking things up on their own, students will encounter a short editing exercise at the end of each typical worksheet. These editing exercises provide no clues to the ten errors embedded in the material and no marginal references to the appropriate rule numbers. Instead, students will have to identify the errors (all based on the preceding exercises in the same worksheet), find the appropriate rules, and make the necessary corrections without any additional help. Moreover, students will from time to time encounter an editing survey worksheet designed to help them integrate what they have learned from earlier worksheets. These editing survey worksheets are also designed to help students achieve the three objectives outlined at the outset: (1) to detect potential problems, (2) to find the appropriate rules, and (3) to apply the rules correctly to solve the problems.

## ORGANIZATION OF THE WORKSHEETS

As the table of contents on page B-4 indicates, Worksheet 1, the Diagnostic Survey, is a four-page pretest that covers the most basic rules in the first eleven sections of *The Gregg Reference Manual.* This pretest contains 100 items grouped in five exercises: Exercise A deals with common punctuation problems (covered in Sections 1 and 2); B with capitalization problems (Section 3); C with problems relating to numbers and abbreviations (Sections 4 and 5); D with problems relating to plurals, possessives, spelling, and compound words (Sections 6–8), and E with problems relating to grammar and usage (Sections 10–11). The Diagnostic Survey will tell your students (and you) how much they already know, how effective they are in looking things up on their own, and what sections of *The Gregg Reference Manual* they need to give special attention to. (See the chart on page B-6.)

Worksheets 2–22 follow this pattern. Worksheets 2–7 each focus on a limited number of rules in Sections 1–4 of the manual (relating to punctuation, capitalization, and number style). The chart on page 3 shows which rules are covered in each worksheet.

Worksheet 8, the first editing survey worksheet, integrates the knowledge and skill that students have been acquiring from Worksheets 2–7. It requires students to rewrite 10 problematic sentences and edit two passages of connected copy (each with 10 errors).

Worksheets 9–15 focus on Sections 5–9 of the manual (relating to abbreviations, plural and possessive forms, spelling, compound words, and word division). Worksheet 16, the second editing survey, is structured like Worksheet 8, except that the first exercise focuses on Sections 5–8 and the remaining two exercises—aiming to increase the range of rules to be covered—involve errors drawn from Sections 1–9.

Worksheets 17–21 focus on Sections 10–11 (relating to grammar and usage). Worksheet 22, the third editing survey worksheet, follows the pattern of the two earlier editing surveys, except that the first exercise focuses on Sections 10–11 and the remaining two exercises cover Sections 1–11. In effect, the three editing surveys provide progressively broader integration of the skills and knowledge acquired in the individual worksheets. In this way students become prepared for the Final Survey (Worksheet 23 or 24) and for a final measurement of their heightened mastery of grammar, usage, and style.

Worksheet 23, the Final Survey, is a four-page posttest that exactly parallels the Diagnostic Survey in coverage and construction. Both the pretest and the posttest should be scored so that you can measure each student's gain in achievement by the end of this unit of instruction. (The discussion entitled "How to Use the Worksheets" on pages B-5 to B-6 provides guidelines on scoring.)

Worksheet 24, which appears only in this *Instructor's Resource Manual* (see pages B-8 to B-11), is a *second* Final Survey that exactly parallels Worksheet 23 in coverage and construction. You may reproduce Worksheet 24 for use in your classroom (1) as an alternative to Worksheet 23 or (2) as a "second chance" for students who did not perform well on Worksheet 23. (For a further discussion of the best ways to use Worksheet 24, see page B-6.)

## ORGANIZATION OF A TYPICAL WORKSHEET

If you look at Worksheet 2 (see pages B-16 to B-17 in this *Instructor's Guide*), you will see how a typical worksheet is organized.

Exercise A covers the most basic rules governing the use of a period, a question mark, and an exclamation point at the end of a sentence. Note that each of the 12 items in Exercise A is clearly labeled so that students with a weak grasp of grammar can easily see what kind of sentence they are dealing with in each case. Also note that the rule numbers alongside the answer blanks fall in numerical order. This was deliberately done so that students can use this exercise as a study guide as they make their way through ¶¶101–119. Exercise B is constructed exactly like Exercise A with one difference: the introductory labels have now been withdrawn; students must now determine on their own what kind of sentence they are dealing with in each case. Exercise C deals with a special problem that involves only two rules (¶¶106–107). Exercise D provides sentences to be rewritten. Rule numbers are provided alongside, but now the problems relate to a much wider range of rules. The final exercise—Exercise E—provides a short editing exercise with ten errors embedded in the copy. The errors all represent problems that students have dealt with in the preceding exercises in this worksheet. Moreover, they call for the students to exhibit mastery of the full range of rules covered in this worksheet—¶¶101–119. However, in this final exercise no rule numbers have been provided; thus students will have to identify the problems and the related rules on their own. However, because of the careful progress in the earlier exercises from the simple to the complex, your students should now be able to cope with the challenge posed by this final exercise in the worksheet.

If you look at Worksheet 3 (see pages B-18 to B-19 in this *Instructor's Resource Manual*), you will see a similar pattern of organization. Exercise A focuses on just one rule—¶122—dealing with the use of commas that set off. Each item in Exercise A is labeled so that students can easily see what kinds of elements they are dealing with. Moreover, the rule numbers alongside the exercise items fall in numerical order so as to lead the student systematically through all the subparagraphs in ¶122. Exercise B is structured just like A, but the labels have now been removed from the exercise items. Exercises C and D cover just two rules—¶¶123–124, dealing with the use of commas that separate. Exercise C provides identifying labels for each exercise item; Exercise D follows the same pattern as C but

---

*Selected rules.

without the identifying labels. Exercise E, the final exercise, is an editing exercise that requires the students to detect the errors and apply ¶¶122–124 on their own.

To take one final example, look at Worksheet 17 (on pages B-54 to B-57 in this *Instructor's Resource Manual*), which deals with the agreement of subjects and verbs. Since many students have difficulty identifying subjects and verbs in sentences, Exercises A and B ask students to construct various verb forms for regular verbs (A) and irregular verbs (B). Now that the students have some experience in constructing and recognizing various verb forms, Exercises C–E expose students to the problems of subject-verb agreement. To help students learn to recognize subjects, the subject in each sentence in these three exercises is given in boldface. Moreover, to help students master the rules of agreement, alternative verb forms are provided in parentheses. In Exercise F, the editing exercise that concludes this worksheet, students should now be able to detect problems in subject-verb agreement and correct them on the basis of their newly acquired skill and knowledge.

## HOW TO USE THE WORKSHEETS

The following suggestions are intended to help you make the most effective use of these worksheets. This resource manual offers a CD-ROM with PowerPoint slides as well as transparency masters designed to be used along with these worksheets. Use the table of contents to identify slides that will help you (1) explain to your students how to look things up in *The Gregg Reference Manual*, (2) introduce many basic rules before your students have to apply them in specific worksheets, and (3) review those rules that students have had difficulty in applying correctly. (See also page B-6 for a further discussion of using these slides and transparencies with the worksheets.)

**Worksheet 1.** Before administering the Diagnostic Survey (Worksheet 1), give the students a brief orientation to *The Gregg Reference Manual*. Point out that certain rule numbers in Sections 1–11 appear in white within a red panel. This graphic device serves to highlight the basic rules that students need to master. Also point out such features as these: the topical index on the inside front cover for fast reference, the detailed 43-page index at the back of the book, the electronic index on the *Gregg* Web site, the detailed outline of headings at the beginning of each section, the rule-numbering system (whereby the first one or two digits of each rule number express the section number), the displayed rule numbers in the upper left and right corners of each two-page spread, and the section number and title displayed at the edge of each page. Have the students skim the preface and the table of contents in

*The Gregg Reference Manual.* Ask them to read the section entitled "How to Look Things Up." Also familiarize your students with the proofreaders' mark they will need to use in the second exercise of Worksheet 1. (These marks—which are shown in the directions for these two exercises—relate simply to the insertion or deletion of punctuation and to changes in capitalization.) When you are satisfied that students have the requisite familiarity with the organization and features of *The Gregg Reference Manual*, ask them to complete Worksheet 1, *referring to the manual as necessary.* (*Note:* To support your discussion of how to look things up, use the corresponding "How to Look Things Up" transparency masters (H-1 to H-6) on pages D-13 to D-18.)

*Scoring Worksheet 1.* As soon as the assignment is completed, have the worksheets corrected and score them as follows: from a total score of 100, deduct 1 point for each item incorrectly answered. Retain this score for later use.

*Diagnosing Each Student's Needs.* More important than assigning a score to each student's performance on Worksheet 1 is a diagnosis of each student's strengths and weaknesses. The chart at the top of page B-6 will help you provide specific prescriptions for each student.

**Worksheets 2–22.** Once the Diagnostic Survey has been completed, you have several choices to pursue: (1) ask each student to complete all the worksheets from 2 through 22 *in sequence;* (2) ask each student to complete Worksheets 2–22 in a sequence that gives priority to those sections in which the greatest number of errors occurred on the Diagnostic Survey; or (3) ask each student to complete *only* those worksheets (between 2 and 22) that deal with sections in which a significant number of errors occurred on the Diagnostic Survey. However you decide to assign these worksheets, ask the students to follow this procedure before starting any worksheet: study the relevant rules as a whole (identified alongside the answer blanks) before proceeding to apply individual rules to the items on the worksheet. In this way students will be better able to grasp the principles of style that underlie and unify the individual rules within that section. If students proceed directly to apply the individual rules in isolated fashion, they may miss the broader rationale. (*Note:* Use the appropriate slides if you plan to introduce specific rules before the students apply them in the worksheet exercises or if you want to review specific rules that students have had difficulty in applying correctly.)

**Editing Survey Worksheets.** All students should complete Worksheets 8, 16, and 22 to ensure that they have an adequate grasp of the wide range of rules each of these editing survey worksheets covers. Since these worksheets require the students, for the first time, to locate the rules entirely on their own, you may want to

| In Worksheet 1, if a student made many errors in the following items: | That student should give special emphasis to the following worksheets: |
| --- | --- |
| 1–20 | Worksheets 2–5 (dealing with punctuation) |
| 21–30 | Worksheet 6 (dealing with capitalization) |
| 31–40 | Worksheet 7 (dealing with number style) |
| 41–50 | Worksheet 9 (dealing with abbreviations) |
| 51–60 | Worksheets 10–11 (dealing with plurals and possessives) |
| 61–70 | Worksheets 12–13 (dealing with spelling and choosing the right word) |
| 71–80 | Worksheets 14–15 (dealing with compounds and word division) |
| 81–90 | Worksheets 17–19 (dealing with grammar) |
| 91–100 | Worksheets 20–21 (dealing with usage) |

have the students reread "How to Look Things Up" before they begin these exercises. Also remind the students of the various features in *The Gregg Reference Manual* that will help them find their way around. (*Note:* To support this discussion, consider using the appropriate slides.)

**Worksheet 23.** Once the students have successfully completed Worksheets 2–22, have them proceed to the Final Survey (Worksheet 23), *again referring to the manual as necessary.* You might suggest that they quickly review their answers on the earlier worksheets as preparation for this posttest. (The worksheets have been three-hole-punched so that after the sheets have been detached, they can easily be kept in a binder for reference.)

*Scoring Worksheet 23.* As on Worksheet 1, use this scoring procedure: From a total score of 100, deduct 1 point for each item incorrectly answered. Since this is an open-book exercise, a student should get no more than 30 items wrong. In effect, the minimum acceptable grade on this test should be 70. Compare each student's score on the Final Survey with the score achieved on the Diagnostic Survey. Assign a final grade on the basis of the gain in performance the student has achieved.

**Worksheet 24.** As noted previously, this alternative Final Survey, which appears only in this *Instructor's Resource Manual* (on pages B-8 to B-11), may be used in

place of Worksheet 23. If you decide to use Worksheet 24 as the posttest, you might want to allow students to use Worksheet 23 as practice for the real thing. On the other hand, if you decide to use Worksheet 23 as the posttest, you could assign Worksheet 24 to those students who did not score well on Worksheet 23. Allowing these students additional time to review the relevant rules in *The Gregg Reference Manual* and then giving them a second chance to apply these rules in Worksheet 24 could help them raise their final scores and boost their sense of achievement as well.

*Scoring Worksheet 24.* Apply the same scoring procedure provided for Worksheet 23 above.

## CHECKING WORK

To provide the necessary reinforcement and ensure that proper learning is taking place, you should make sure that each worksheet is checked and corrected before the student proceeds to the next one. If your students are each working at their own pace, place the worksheet keys in a central location so that all students can check their own work. (Remove the keys to Worksheets 23 and 24, however.) If you prefer, you can check the worksheets yourself or appoint one or more student assistants to help you with the job.

If your students are all doing the same worksheet at the same time, you may wish to read the answers aloud and have all the students check their own (or someone else's) work at the same time. Under any circumstances, be sure to make yourself available to answer the questions of students who have made mistakes on the worksheets but do not understand why these are mistakes.

If you have weak students who are not capable of studying the rules on their own and applying them effectively, consider the following procedure: Before assigning any worksheet, preview the designated set of rules with the whole group and explain any rule or concept that could prove difficult. Then ask the students to complete the worksheet on an individual basis. Finally, critique the answers for the whole group, and resolve any questions or difficulties they have in reference to the correct answers.

## A NOTE ON THE KEYS

Full-size facsimiles of the worksheets are reproduced on pages B-12 to B-85 with the correct answers inserted. Because a number of these errors can be corrected in more than one way, give credit for answers that are acceptable, even though they do not agree with what is specifically shown in the facsimile key.

## USING THE POWERPOINT SLIDES AND TRANSPARENCIES WITH THE WORKSHEETS

This resource manual provides a CD-ROM with nearly 350 PowerPoint slides plus transparency masters of sample documents to help you (1) reinforce the basic rules of grammar, usage, and style and (2) explain the guidelines for formatting letters, memos, and other business documents.

- As you introduce particular rules to your students, use the related slides or transparencies to reinforce the points you want to make.

- Before students begin a particular worksheet or a particular exercise, use the appropriate slides or transparencies to *review* the rules they will have to apply.

- After you score a completed worksheet, use the appropriate slides or transparencies to support your discussion of the problems students may have encountered in completing that worksheet.

*Note:* Pages D-1 to D-7 describe how each sequence of slides and transparencies can be used to support the presentation of a specific set of rules in *GRM*.

# 24  Final Survey

**A. Directions:** The following items deal with problems of punctuation. Correct all errors by inserting or deleting punctuation, using the appropriate revision marks (shown on the inside back cover of *The Gregg Reference Manual*). Circle any changes you make. If a sentence is correct as given, write *C* in the answer column. **References:** Sections 1–2.

1. Will you please specify the color you want _____

2. Will you please let us use your pool _____

3. I asked Lance when he hoped to get his license _____

4. Lance, when do you hope to get your license _____

5. I met the woman, who found my wallet. _____

6. It is, therefore, critical that we vote tomorrow. _____

7. By Thursday March 1 2007 we must come up with the money. _____

8. The Codys are free on that date but the others are not yet sure. _____

9. The food the service and the decor were not as good as we had expected. _____

10. The French Agency offers prompt reliable service. _____

11. To lower the sound turn the left knob to the right. _____

12. When you arrive go directly to my office on the sixth floor. _____

13. In fact I suggested that strategy myself. _____

14. We flew to Seattle and then drove to Vancouver. _____

15. These items are on sale, the others are not. _____

16. The novelist Jane Austen never fails to delight her readers. _____

17. I like your plan for boosting sales, for example, it does not require us to hire additional staff. _____

18. The chapter entitled Taking Charge of Your Life is the best one in the book. _____

19. One of my favorite movies is a musical entitled Singin' in the Rain. _____

20. The Wall Street Journal is publishing a three-part series on the hearings. _____

Name _____ Date _____ Class _____  71

**B. Directions:** The following items deal with problems of capitalization. If an item is correctly capitalized, write *C* in the answer column. Correct any incorrect items as follows: To change a capital letter to a small letter, draw a line through it: *The*. To change a small letter to a capital letter, draw three lines under it: *the*. Circle any changes you make. **References:** Section 3.

21. used to work for the Xerox corporation _____

22. providing aid to the third world _____

23. planned to raft down the River _____

24. the new President of our company _____

25. going into partnership with my Father _____

26. driving across the Bridge to Sausalito _____

27. hoping to move back East next month _____

28. during the early Nineteen Hundreds _____

29. working on a doctorate in Economics _____

30. treated in Appendix A on Page 313 _____

**C. Directions:** The following items deal with problems of number style and abbreviations. If an item is correct as given, write *C* in the answer column. If an item is incorrect, circle the error and write the correct form in the answer column. **References:** Sections 4–5.

31. on or before December twenty-ninth _____

32. only three percent of the defects _____

33. four bus drivers and 87 passengers _____

34. at least eighty-seven thousand dollars _____

35. carries a price tag of only $99.00 _____

36. keep the cost under $.50 a unit _____

37. . . . started last week. 60 days from now. . . _____

38. during the first decade of the 19th century _____

39. over 1/2 of these traffic accidents _____

40. must be sure to leave by 4:00 p.m. _____

41. George Appleby Singleton Junior _____

42. revolutions per minute *(abbreviated)* _____

43. graduated last year from M.I.T. _____

44. will prepare a new demo. disk _____

45. an exciting article by N.W. Hertzog _____

46. was examined by Doctor Warren Fong _____

47. the U.S. Department of Agriculture _____

48. worked for two years in Washington, DC _____

49. 600 gals. @ $15.50 *(on an invoice)* _____

50. consider joining an H.M.O. next year _____

72

B-9

# Final Survey (Continued)

**D. Directions:** The following items deal with problems of plural and possessive forms, spelling, and compound words. If an item is correct as given, write *C* in the answer column. If an item is incorrect, circle the error and write the correct form in the answer column. **References:** Sections 6–8.

51. whether or not taxs should be cut _____

52. need to review our outstanding liabilitys _____

53. a business that is owned by our wifes _____

54. a dinner prepared by my four sister-in-laws _____

55. attended a reception for the alumnuses _____

56. a proposal supported by many CEO's _____

57. purchased several hundred dollar's worth _____

58. bought seven more saving's bonds _____

59. Congress' latest budget proposals _____

60. a fantastic sale on mens' suits _____

61. the flooding that recently occurred _____

62. suffered minor injuries in the accident _____

63. intended to send an acknowledgement _____

64. could not beleive that it happened _____

65. we'll have to conceed the truth of that statement _____

66. needs to use more tack with callers _____

67. and should try to be more discrete _____

68. don't want their help or their advise _____

69. serve as our liason with the steering committee _____

70. a topic that falls in another catagory _____

71. must checkout of our hotel room by noon _____

72. supervising a large crew of workmen _____

73. to air condition this entire office _____

74. proposing tax cuts across-the-board _____

75. needs a machine readable format _____

76. thought his speech was long winded _____

77. the repainting of our reception room was much-needed _____

78. found a new co-author to work on the book _____

79. would be willing to re-employ Ms. Foley _____

80. designing self study programs _____

Name _____ Date _____ Class _____  73

**E. Directions:** The following items deal with problems of grammar and usage. If an item is correct as given, write *C* in the answer column. If an item is incorrect, circle the error and write the correct form in the answer column. **References:** Sections 10–11.

81. Cindy don't like the idea very much. _____

82. One of the calls were for you. _____

83. Are you the one who drunk all the coffee? _____

84. If I was rich, the first thing I'd do . . . _____

85. Chris and me are hoping to go camping for a week. _____

86. The company monitors it's costs zealously. _____

87. The position was offered to Meg and myself. _____

88. We feel badly about your transfer to the main office. _____

89. Which is the best of these two paintings? _____

90. I don't have nothing that I care to add. _____

91. Your visit is not an every day happening. _____

92. These kind of problems always crop up. _____

93. The reorganization plan is all together too complex. _____

94. This change will have no affect on us. _____

95. We just received a large amount of orders. _____

96. Does anyone beside you think that? _____

97. We've had less complaints this year. _____

98. You could of called if you were displeased. _____

99. The pay raise was sure appreciated. _____

100. I use to work in the Virgin Islands. _____

# 1 Diagnostic Survey

**A. Directions:** The following items deal with problems of punctuation. Correct all errors by inserting or deleting punctuation, using appropriate proofreaders' marks (shown on pages 358–359 and on the inside back cover of *The Gregg Reference Manual*). Circle any changes you make. If a sentence is correct as given, write *C* in the answer column.
**References:** Sections 1–2.

1. Will you please indicate your choice below.    _____ 103a

2. Will you please lend me some money?    _____ 103b

3. I asked Jason why he was planning to leave.    _____ 104

4. Jason, why are you planning to leave?    _____ 110a

5. I hired someone/who is quite experienced.    _____ 122 132

6. It is therefore my intention to resign.    C _____ 122 141

7. On Friday, May 1, 2007, we will be moving to Idaho.    _____ 122e 154b

8. Bev will be able to help you, but Tom and Dwayne are tied up right now.    _____ 123a 126a

9. My mother, my sister, and my aunt are planning to attend the wedding.    _____ 123b 162a

10. It promises to be a cold, rainy November.    _____ 123c 168a

11. To get to our office, turn at Exit 54 and go left.    _____ 124 135b

12. Before we move in, we need to replace the roof and waterproof the basement.    _____ 124 130a

13. In my opinion, Mr. Honeywell is not giving us the whole story.    _____ 124b 138b

14. I saw the movie/and agreed with your criticism of the acting.    ; or ⊙    _____ 127b

15. Fran loved the show, Hal and I hated it.    _____ 128 176a

16. The year 2008 will be our sixtieth year in business.    ; or ⊙ For    C _____ 149

17. The location sounds ideal, for example, your children can walk to school.    _____ 181a 187b 187c

18. The article called "No More Violence" appeared in the August issue of *Harper's*.    _____ 240a 242

19. What could the word (syzygy) possibly mean?    _____ 285a

20. My new cookbook, (Stepping Up to the Plate,) was published last year.    _____ 289a

Name _____ Date _____ Class _____    1

**B. Directions:** The following items deal with problems of capitalization. If an item is correctly capitalized, write *C* in the answer column. Correct any incorrect items as follows: To change a capital letter to a small letter, draw a line through it: ~~T~~he. To change a small letter to a capital letter, draw three lines under it: <u>the</u>. Circle any changes you make.
**References:** Section 3.

21. were stranded at the O'Hare
    ~~a~~irport     303 / 331

22. would like to take a tour of the
    <u>white</u> <u>house</u>     305

23. used to work as a consultant for
    our ~~C~~ompany     308 / 321

24. once served as ~~M~~ayor of
    Waldoboro     313c

25. wants to ask my ~~F~~ather for
    advice     319a

26. because of severe fog at the
    ~~A~~irport     331

27. somewhere on the <u>west</u> <u>coast</u>—
    maybe Oregon     338a

28. dropped out of sight during the
    eighties     C     345

29. received a ~~B~~achelor's degree in
    history     352 / 353

30. appears in Chapter 6,
    ~~P~~age 134     359

**C. Directions:** The following items deal with problems of number style and abbreviations. If an item is correct as given, write *C* in the answer column. If an item is incorrect, circle the error and write the correct form in the answer column.
**References:** Sections 4–5.

31. on or before September
    (twelfth)    **12**    401b / 407b

32. has been reduced by over
    (twenty) percent    **20**    401b / 447a

33. 38 students and (three)
    teachers    **3**    402

34. (sixty-nine thousand
    dollars)    **$69,000**    413a

35. will cost over ($500.00) to
    repair    **$500**    415

36. were sold for only ($.30)
    apiece    **30 cents**    418a

37. ... next month. (6) months
    ago    **Six**    421

38. toward the end of the
    twentieth century    **C**    424

39. will affect over (⅓) of our
    customers    **one-third**    427a

40. before we meet at (12:00)
    noon    **12**    440c

41. Jasper A. Throckmorton
    (Junior)    **Jr.**    502b

42. (revolutions per minute)
    *(abbreviated)*    **rpm**    507 / 535a

43. will be audited by the
    (I.R.S.)    **IRS**    508 / 524a

44. on the basis of your (memo.)
    of June 4    **memo**    510

45. consulted with (P.R.)
    Voorhees    **P. R.**    516a

46. get a second opinion from
    (Doctor) Burgos    **Dr.**    517a

47. the (US) Department of
    Education    **U.S.**    525

48. no longer lives in
    Washington, D.C.    **C**    527b

49. 200 (gals.) *(on an
    invoice)*    **gal**    535a

50. will send the purchase order
    (Asap)    **ASAP**    541

2

# Diagnostic Survey (Continued)

**D. Directions:** The following items deal with problems of plural and possessive forms, spelling, and compound words. If an item is correct as given, write *C* in the answer column. If an item is incorrect, circle the error and write the correct form in the answer column. **References:** Sections 6–8.

| | | | |
|---|---|---|---|
| 51. made two copys for your boss | copies | 604 | |
| 52. met with the three attornies | attorneys | 605 | |
| 53. the rescue squad that saved our lifes | lives | 608b | |
| 54. coping with our mother-in-laws | mothers-in-law | 612a | |
| 55. has established only one criteria | criterion | 614 | |
| 56. have invited a large group of VIP's | VIPs | 622a | |
| 57. has left on a three week's trip | weeks' | 627a 646 | |
| 58. ought to open a saving's account | savings | 628a | |
| 59. need to get my boss' approval | boss's | 631 | |
| 60. bought some childrens' toys | children's | 633 | |
| 61. is being transfered to Dallas | transferred | 702 | |
| 62. don't think it will make a difference | C | 704 | |
| 63. using your best judgment | C | 708 | |
| 64. and recieved it only yesterday | received | 712 | |
| 65. will have to procede with Plan B | proceed | 716b | |

| | | | |
|---|---|---|---|
| 66. which maybe quite true | may be | 719 | |
| 67. too much time has past | passed | 719 | |
| 68. written on pale blue stationary | stationery | 719 | |
| 69. will try to accomodate you | accommodate | 720 | |
| 70. asked for seperate checks | separate | 720 | |
| 71. need to follow-up with Paul | follow up | 802 | |
| 72. you can talk to any salesman | salesperson OR salesclerk | 809a | |
| 73. double space this manuscript | double-space | 811a 812a | |
| 74. order something more up-to-date | up to date | 831a | |
| 75. use our toll free number | toll-free | 820a | |
| 76. considered this to be rather old-fashioned | C | 823a | |
| 77. is well-known for her generosity | well known | 824b | |
| 78. counting on your co-operation | cooperation | 835b | |
| 79. was not re-elected for another term | reelected | 835a | |
| 80. needs to build up his self confidence | self-confidence | 836a | |

Name _____ Date _____ Class _____ 3

**E. Directions:** The following items deal with problems of grammar and usage. If an item is correct as given, write *C* in the answer column. If an item is incorrect, circle the error and write the correct form in the answer column. **References:** Sections 10–11.

81. Janice (don't) seem very happy about her new job. — **doesn't** — 1001a

82. One of the printers (are) broken. — **is** — 1008a

83. Joe (done) it all by himself. — **did** — 1032b

84. If I (was) you, I would not go. — **were** — 1040

85. Dennis and (me) already have tickets. — **I** — 1054a

86. The firm treats (it's) employees well. — **its** — 1056e

87. They've invited Samantha and (myself.) — **me** — 1060d

88. I feel very (badly) about what I said to Harriet. — **bad** — 1067

89. Bo is the (best) of the two golfers. — **better** — 1071g

90. I (don't want no) (one) to see this. — **I don't want anyone** OR **I want no one** — 1076a

91. Thanks (alot) for all that you did. — **a lot** — 1101

92. I think it happened (accidently.) — **accidentally** — 1101

93. Do you think this looks (alright?) — **all right** — 1101

94. How will these cutbacks (effect) our sales? — **affect** — 1101

95. A small (amount) of people responded. — **number** — 1101

96. Drive a little (further) on. — **farther** — 1101

97. (Less) people came to this week's shows. — **Fewer** — 1101

98. I must (of) left the report at home. — **have** — 1101

99. We could (sure) use some help. — **surely** — 1101

100. My family (use) to live in Toledo. — **used** — 1101

4

**A. Directions:** Insert the appropriate mark of punctuation at the end of each sentence and circle it. If a sentence is correct as given, write *C* in the answer column. **References:** Consult the rules shown below as you complete this exercise. See Appendix D for the definition of any grammatical terms that you may not be familiar with.

1. **Statement:** We question the need to reduce the size of the staff at this time.    1. _____ 101a
2. **Command:** Send copies to Victoria Hochshield and Jeremy Morgenthal Sr.    2. **C** 101a
3. **Elliptical statement:** Now, to return to the main theme of this presentation.    3. _____ 101b
4. **Polite command:** Will you please let me know whether you need more money.    4. _____ 103a
5. **Favor:** Will you please let me borrow your BMW this weekend?    5. _____ 103b
6. **Indirect question:** I asked Austin why he couldn't play tennis this Saturday.    6. _____ 104
7. **Direct question:** Why can't you play tennis this Saturday?    7. _____ 110a
8. **Rhetorical question:** Why not come into our store and see for yourself?    8. _____ 110b
9. **Elliptical question:** I heard that you're planning to quit. Why?    9. _____ 111a
10. **Direct question:** The only question I have is, When will Joe be told?    10. _____ 115 / 104
11. **Indirect question:** The only question I have is when Joe will be told.    11. _____ 115
12. **Exclamations:** Wow! I think what you did was fantastic!    12. _____ 119a

**B. Directions:** Insert the appropriate mark of punctuation at the end of each sentence and circle it. If a sentence is correct as given, write *C* in the answer column. **References:** Consult the rules shown below as you complete this exercise.

13. Do not speak to anyone from MacroTechnology Inc.    13. **C** 101a
14. I doubt whether I'll be able to take any time off in July.    14. _____ 101a
15. You wanted to know whether we are still accepting applications. Of course.    15. _____ 101a-b
16. May I suggest that you send your résumé directly to Mrs. Hoehn.    16. _____ 103a
17. Will you please call me if you have any further questions.    17. _____ 103a
18. May I get an advance copy of the report you are preparing for your boss?    18. _____ 103b
19. May I ask your assistant for help while mine is on vacation?    19. _____ 103b
20. Why Tina stormed out of here is something I can't explain.    20. _____ 104
21. You asked whether you could take Friday off. By all means.    21. _____ 104 / 101b
22. Do you have any contacts at Cybernautics Inc.?    22. _____ 110a
23. Why not take advantage of this money-back guarantee?    23. _____ 110b
24. Why bother? I don't think there's any point in discussing this further.    24. _____ 111a / 101a
25. We won! We beat them by just one point! It's unbelievable!    25. _____ 119a

Name _____ Date _____ Class _____ 5

**C. Directions:** Insert punctuation as necessary in the following items, and circle any changes you make. If an item is correct as given, write *C* in the answer column. **References:** ¶¶106–107.

26. This technical writing program will help you:

    **a.** Analyze the purpose and the audience for your writing;

    **b.** Develop and organize the content;

    **c.** Edit for clarity and accuracy.

26. _____ 106 107a

27. We can help you improve your sales and marketing operations with the following custom-designed software:

    • Customer information system

    • Product information system

    • Competitive information system

27. **C** 106 107b

**D. Directions:** Rewrite the following sentences to correct all errors in punctuation. Eliminate sentence fragments and adjust the capitalization as necessary. **References:** Consult the rules shown below as you complete this exercise.

28. Have you heard the latest. Our firm is merging with Sigma Inc.. I still don't believe it. **Have you heard the latest? Our firm is merging with Sigma Inc. I still don't believe it!**
110a 101a 119a

29. I plan to buy a new SUV. As soon as I find a better job that pays more. **I plan to buy a new SUV as soon as I find a better job that pays more.**
101c

30. Will you let us use your swimming pool? While you're away. **Will you let us use your swimming pool while you're away?**
101c 103b

31. We would like to ask when you are coming to Omaha? Could you stay with us? For a few days. **We would like to ask when you are coming to Omaha. Could you stay with us for a few days?**
104 101c 110a

32. The big question now is how will we break the news to your parents. **The big question now is, How will we break the news to your parents?**
115

**E. Directions:** Edit the following paragraph to correct all errors in punctuation. Eliminate sentence fragments and adjust the capitalization as necessary. Use appropriate proofreaders' marks (shown on pages 358–359 and on the inside back cover of *The Gregg Reference Manual*) to indicate your corrections. For example, to change a capital letter to a small letter, draw a line through it: *The*. Circle any changes you make. **References:** Consult the appropriate rules in ¶¶101–119.

```
        101c
Is it true? That you sold your house and will be moving up to your cottage      1
        110a          119a
at the lake? Great news! Janet and I have been talking about whether we should   2
        104                           101c
do the same thing. We realize that we can't afford to move? Until we sell the    3
house we live in now.  We have no idea how much our house is worth.  Would you   4
                                        103b
please tell us how much you got for your house? We would also appreciate         5
learning something about:                                                        6
                                         107 a
    1.  The real estate agent who handled the sale for you;                      7
                          107a
    2.  Our new neighbors;                                                       8
                                                      107a
    3.  The availability of affordable housing up at the lake;                   9
                                                        110 a
In any event, congratulations!  When can we get you two over to celebrate?      10
```

6

# 3

## The Comma

**A. Directions:** Insert commas as necessary in the following sentences, and circle any changes you make. If a sentence is correct as given, write *C* in the answer column. **References:** Read ¶122, especially the introductory note. See Appendix D for the definition of any grammatical terms that you may not be familiar with.

|   |   | Answer | Ref. |
|---|---|---|---|
| 1. | **Nonessential expression:** I hired Tom Rae who has a lot of experience. | 1. _____ | 122 |
| 2. | **Essential expression:** I hired someone who has a lot of experience. | 2. **C** | 122 |
| 3. | **Nonessential expression:** We have decided therefore not to accept your offer. | 3. _____ | 122 |
| 4. | **Essential expression:** We have therefore decided not to accept your offer. | 4. **C** | 122 |
| 5. | **Interrupting expression:** Let's meet on Friday or if you wish on Monday. | 5. _____ | 122a |
| 6. | **Afterthought:** You still haven't made your mind up have you? | 6. _____ | 122b |
| 7. | **Transitional expression:** It is true nevertheless that Bob's work is good. | 7. _____ | 122c |
| 8. | **Transitional expression:** It is nevertheless true that Bob's work is good. | 8. **C** | 122c |
| 9. | **Independent comment:** It is certainly our intention to act quickly. | 9. **C** | 122c |
| 10. | **Independent comment:** It is our intention certainly to act quickly. | 10. _____ | 122c |
| 11. | **Descriptive expression:** Thanks for the memo of May 2 in which you . . . | 11. _____ | 122d |
| 12. | **Descriptive expression:** Thanks for the memo in which you . . . | 12. **C** | 122d |
| 13. | **Date:** The concert has been rescheduled for Friday July 6 2007 at 8 p.m. | 13. _____ | 122e |
| 14. | **Names:** Helen Moraga M.D. is moving her practice to Bath Maine in May. | 14. _____ | 122f |
| 15. | **Names (preferences unknown):** John Blake Jr. is joining Pennon Inc. | 15. **C** | 122f |

**B. Directions:** Insert commas as necessary in the following sentences, and circle any changes you make. If a sentence is correct as given, write *C* in the answer column. **References:** ¶122.

|   |   | Answer | Ref. |
|---|---|---|---|
| 16. | Let's interview Simon Perry who worked in this department for over three years. | 16. _____ | 122 |
| 17. | It is therefore essential that we investigate this complaint at once. | 17. **C** | 122 |
| 18. | It is essential therefore that we investigate this complaint at once. | 18. _____ | 122 |
| 19. | It is true isn't it that Marcia will be promoted rather than Tanya? | 19. _____ | 122a |
| 20. | Helen Wu resigned as company treasurer last June if I remember correctly. | 20. _____ | 122b |
| 21. | You must remember however that this situation is only temporary. | 21. _____ | 122c |
| 22. | Our investors in my opinion will not be satisfied with our year-end results. | 22. _____ | 122c |
| 23. | Thank you for your letter of July 9 in which you asked about our discounts. | 23. _____ | 122d |
| 24. | The Board of Directors will meet on Monday August 6 2007 at 10 a.m. | 24. _____ | 122e |
| 25. | Warren Himmelfarb Ph.D. of Medina Ohio will teach this seminar next year. | 25. _____ | 122f |

Name _____ Date _____ Class _____ 7

**C. Directions:** Insert commas as necessary in the following sentences, and circle any changes you make. If a sentence is correct as given, write *C* in the answer column. **References:** ¶¶123–124.

26. **Compound sentence:** I can't meet this Friday‸but I'm free next week.  26. _____ 123a
27. **Series:** I've asked Gloria‸Ted‸and Alison to work on this project with me.  27. _____ 123b
28. **Adjectives:** This tough job calls for a cool‸low-key person.  28. _____ 123c
29. **Numbers:** Homes like this cost between $800‸000 and $1‸200‸000.  29. _____ 123d
30. **Clarity:** Why the production schedule fell apart‸I can't explain.  30. _____ 123e
31. **Introductory word:** Well‸we all make mistakes like that.  31. _____ 124
32. **Introductory phrase:** To understand why the schedule slipped‸ask Tim.  32. _____ 124
33. **Introductory clause:** After the dust settles‸find out what happened.  33. _____ 124
34. **Introductory adverb:** Yesterday we spent the day reviewing budgets.  34. **C** 124b
35. **Introductory phrase:** In the afternoon we'll have more time to talk.  35. **C** 124b
36. **Transitional expression:** In any case‸it's too late to change course.  36. _____ 124b
37. **Independent comment:** In my judgment‸we should not say anything more.  37. _____ 124b

**D. Directions:** Insert commas as necessary in the following sentences, and circle any changes you make. If a sentence is correct as given, write *C* in the answer column. **References:** ¶¶123–124.

38. I've spoken to Amy and Dave‸but I can't reach Mike‸Betty‸or Dru.  38. _____ 123a / 123b
39. We could use a restful vacation after our long‸hard winter.  39. _____ 123c
40. How I lost (\$40‸000) on that investment‸I'll never understand.  40. _____ 123d / 123e
41. Yes‸I can readily understand why you feel as you do.  41. _____ 124
42. To learn more about this offer‸call 1.800.555.3261.  42. _____ 124
43. As soon as our CEO returns‸we should be able to resolve this problem.  43. _____ 124
44. On the weekend I may be able to start painting our bedroom.  44. **C** 124b
45. On the other hand‸I may want to go skiing at Devil's Gorge.  45. _____ 124b

**E. Directions:** Edit the following paragraph to correct all errors in the use of commas. Use appropriate proofreaders' marks (shown on pages 358–359 and on the inside back cover of *The Gregg Reference Manual*) to indicate your corrections. Circle any changes you make. **References:** ¶¶122–124.

```
        124
    Well‸guess who got stuck with organizing Henry Richmond's retirement     1
                                 123a
party?  I don't know why I was chosen‸but I know that I can't handle it      2
                                              122
myself.  That's why I'm asking for help from colleagues‸who have had         3
                                              124
experience in managing such affairs.  To get to the point‸I hope that you,   4
                                              123b
Fred Fox, and Nan Shea will agree to share the joy, the honor‸and the burden 5
                              124
of working with me on this event.  If we all pitch in‸the planning should go 6
              122c                                              122c
smoothly.  The problem‸however‸is that we don't have much time.  It is‸       7
          122c
therefore‸critical that we meet tomorrow to agree on a distribution of       8
                   124b
labor.  In my opinion‸you would be the best person to organize the           9
                      123c
presentations.  Given your warm‸ingratiating manner, you should have no      10
trouble lining people up.                                                    11
```

8

# **4** The Comma (Continued)

**A. Directions:** Correct the following sentences by inserting missing commas, striking out inappropriate commas, and supplying any other punctuation that may be needed. Circle any changes you make. If a sentence is correct as given, write *C* in the answer column. **References:** Consult the rules shown below as you complete this exercise. For the definition of any grammatical terms that you may not be familiar with, see Appendix D.

1. **Compound sentence:** I finished the Garvey ads last week and I am now working on Garvey's catalog.

   1. _____ 126a 127a

2. **Compound predicate:** I finished the Garvey ads last week and am now working on Garvey's catalog.

   2. _____ 127b

3. **Run-on sentence:** I finished the Garvey ads last week I am now working on Garvey's catalog.

   3. _____ 128

4. **Compound sentence:** Please call Brian and ask whether he is free for lunch next Monday.

   4. **C** 127c 129

5. **Introductory dependent clause:** Before you watch the videotape you should scan the script.

   5. _____ 130a

6. **Essential dependent clause:** We need updated sales data when we meet with the managers.

   6. **C** 131a

7. **Nonessential dependent clause:** We need updated sales data by Monday when we meet with the managers.

   7. _____ 131b

8. **Nonessential dependent clause:** I want to explore the ancient ruins of Greece for I have a deep interest in archaeology.

   8. _____ 131b 132

9. **Introductory phrase:** In 2008 my wife and I will celebrate our fortieth wedding anniversary.

   9. **C** 135c

10. **Introductory phrase:** In reviewing your application I noticed a few significant omissions.

    10. _____ 135c

**B. Directions:** Correct the following sentences by inserting missing commas, striking out inappropriate commas, and supplying any other punctuation that may be needed. Circle any changes you make. If a sentence is correct as given, write *C* in the answer column. **References:** Consult the rules shown below as you complete this exercise.

11. Either we cut our prices sharply or we watch our competitors steal our customers.

    11. _____ 126a 127a

12. Not only was the pianist excellent but the orchestra was in fine form as well.

    12. _____ 126a 127a

13. Paul passed his California bar exams last month and is now practicing in Palo Alto.

    13. _____ 127b

Name _____ Date _____ Class _____        9

14. Bert will write the in-house announcement; or : I will handle the press release and the media interviews.

14. _____ 128
127c

15. Check with Sheila and see what she thinks about the plan.

15. _____ 129

16. If Sid can't join us on Saturday, ask whether he can send someone in his place.

16. _____ 130a

17. If possible, let us have your decision on the revised contract terms by next Wednesday.

17. _____ 130b

18. The person who sold us that equipment no longer works for FaxCo.

18. _____ 131a

19. Vera Suggs, who sold us that equipment, no longer works for FaxCo.

19. C _____ 131b

20. I would not recommend Doug for that job, even though I like him personally.

20. _____ 131b
132

21. Having watched you build the business from scratch, I'm truly proud of your success.

21. _____ 135a

22. To understand what Steve is recommending, you have to read his full report.

22. _____ 135b

23. At the time the hearing was going on, Bob was still churning out new data.

23. _____ 135c

24. Our efforts to increase our market share are working quite well.

24. _____ 137a

25. Our main goal this year, to increase our market share, will be achieved.

25. C _____ 137b

**C. Directions:** Insert commas as necessary in the following items, and circle any changes you make. If an item is correct as given, write C in the answer column. **References:** Consult the rules shown below as you complete this exercise.

26. In short, I think we should cancel the program in spite of the time and money already invested.

26. _____ 138a
139a

27. Thus I felt it was pointless to try to reconcile my differences with Don Springer.

27. C _____ 139b

28. You asked whether I thought you were qualified to take over the opening in Finance. Of course you are.

28. C _____ 139c

29. Sales and profits should begin to pick up in the fourth quarter, in my opinion.

29. _____ 140

30. It is certainly true that the manager of the Purchasing Department should have used better judgment.

30. C _____ 141

31. It is true, certainly, that the manager of the Purchasing Department should have used better judgment.

31. _____ 141

32. I had hoped to get more money for our house; however, let's accept the best offer that we get in the next month.

32. _____ 142a

33. If we receive your contest entry form by March 31, you can be a winner too.

33. C _____ 130a
143a

10

# The Comma (Continued)

**34.** You too can be a winner if we receive your contest entry by March 31.

**34.** _____ 143b

**35.** The corporation purchased the Goldmark estate in 1994 for $2,500,000 if I remember correctly.

**35.** _____ 144a

**36.** Joe along with Sybil and Ned is setting up a training program to help managers make better use of their computers.

**36.** _____ 146a

**37.** Greta rather than Hal will be representing the company at the small business conference in Washington.

**37.** _____ 147

**38.** On Friday August 12 we are starting off on a tour of Europe.

**38.** _____ 148

**39.** The term *muffin-choker* refers to a bizarre item that you read in the morning paper as you eat your breakfast.

**39.** C 149

**40.** The book *Networking to the Top* sold over 50,000 copies in the first month of publication.

**40.** C 149

**41.** Jake's new book *Networking to the Top* sold over 50,000 copies in the first month of publication.

**41.** _____ 149

**42.** My husband Ralph feels that our business would do much better if we moved to southern California.

**42.** _____ 150

**43.** My older sister Fay Boyarski says that Ralph is much too pessimistic about business conditions here on the East Coast.

**43.** _____ 150

**44.** I myself felt that you did the right thing by refusing to modify your recommendations.

**44.** C 150

**45.** Many thanks for your memo of May 2 in which you offered to cover for Tony Parsons while he was on paternity leave.

**45.** _____ 152

**D. Directions:** Insert commas as necessary in the following items, and circle any changes you make. If an item is correct as given, write *C* in the answer column. **References:** Consult the rules shown below as you complete this exercise.

**46.** After December 31 2007 please use the new address and telephone number shown on the enclosed card.

**46.** _____ 154a

**47.** On Friday February 23 2007 I plan to give notice of my intention to resign and return to college for an advanced degree.

**47.** _____ 154b

**48.** The May 2008 issue of *The Atlantic Monthly* contains an article on how to consolidate school districts to make them more cost-effective.

**48.** C 155a

**49.** Did you know that Ronald Foley Jr. *(style preference unknown)* has been made a senior vice president?

**49.** C 156

**50.** Phyllis Horowitz Ph.D. will be the main speaker at a program designed for direct marketing consultants.

**50.** _____ 157

Name _____ Date _____ Class _____ 11

**51.** Writen Inc. *(style preference unknown)* announced today that it would move its headquarters back to New York City.

**51.** _C_  159

**52.** I'm planning to move from Klein Texas to Xenia Ohio.

**52.** _____ 160a

**53.** We offer a number of different product lines for children teenagers and adults.

**53.** _____ 162a

**54.** I've been told that Vail Fox & Bly *(style preference unknown)* is an excellent law firm.

**54.** _____ 163

**55.** Computer terms  such as *bug, glitch,* and so on are often . . .

**55.** _____ 164

**56.** Coffee, tea, and soda are the only things I plan to serve.

**56.** _____ 165

**57.** The same error appears in all of our ads and brochures and catalogs released this month.

**57.** _C_  166

**58.** A town meeting on the topic of weeknight curfews should be of great interest to teenagers and adults.

**58.** _____ 167

**59.** You have prepared an effective well-written report.

**59.** _____ 168a

**60.** You have prepared an effective annual report.

**60.** _C_  169

**61.** A number of important new Supreme Court decisions were handed down at the end of this year's session.

**61.** _____ 170

**62.** You'll have to negotiate a narrow, twisting, two-lane road in order to reach our house.

**62.** _____ 171

**63.** The fact is we have many more competitors than we used to.

**63.** _____ 172b
123e

**64.** First come first served.

**64.** _____ 172d

**65.** Now now don't worry about it.

**65.** _____ 175c

**E. Directions:** Edit the following paragraph to correct all errors in the use of commas. Use appropriate proofreaders' marks (shown on pages 358–359 and on the inside back cover of *The Gregg Reference Manual*) to indicate your corrections. Circle any changes you make. **References:** Consult the appropriate rules in ¶¶126–175 as you complete this exercise.

```
                   148            150
     Next Friday July 18 my wife Sally and I are starting a      1

two-week bicycle tour through New England. We will be part of a  2
     126a/127a
group tour but the tour offers us some private time and some    3
                  138a / 143a      131a / 132
personal flexibility too. The company that runs the tour has    4
                  169                          138a/ 139a
booked us into charming country inns each night. Moreover our   5

daily cycling itinerary brings us to points of historical in-   6
       127b                                        162a
terest and allows time for frequent rest stops, picnic lunches  7

and gourmet snacks. The feature of the tour that I like best is 8

the van that accompanies us wherever we pedal. Whenever my      9
              130a
energy gives out I know the van will carry me and my bicycle to 10

the next stop on the tour.                                      11
```

# 5

# Other Marks of Punctuation

**A. Directions:** Each of the following sentences consists of *two independent clauses.* Insert a semicolon, colon, or period between the clauses. Change the capitalization as necessary. Circle any changes you make. **References:** ¶¶176, 187. See Appendix D for the definition of any grammatical terms that you may not be familiar with.

1.  My partner wants us to open a second store this year; *or* : I think that would be a big
    mistake.                                                                                    176a

2.  Many thanks for your memo of July 2; the data you requested can be assembled in
    less than a week.                                                                           176b

3.  Your new cottage sounds perfect : *or* . It's it's right on the lake and has a private room and
    bath just for me.                                                                           187a–c

4.  Your new cottage sounds perfect; *or* . Mine mine is not on the lake and has no extra rooms for
    guests.                                                                                     187b–c

5.  Your new cottage sounds perfect; *or* . For for example, the lakeside location is ideal for
    swimming, boating, and ice skating.                                                         187b–c

**B. Directions:** Each of the following sentences contains a **boldface** phrase or clause. Correct the punctuation before, after, and within each boldface expression, and change the capitalization as necessary. Circle any changes you make. **References:** Consult the rules shown below as you complete this exercise.

6.  I think we should take my father to a doctor; *or* . However, **however my brother thinks that we
    should not interfere.**                                                                     178

7.  My sisters agree with my brother; *or* . Hence **hence I have said nothing more about my
    concerns.**                                                                                 178

8.  The offer from Bromley & Finch is quite attractive; *or* . For **for example they are willing
    to meet our price.**                                                                        178
                                                                                                181a

9.  I have only one other question: **namely, how quickly can we transfer
    ownership?**                                                                                178
                                                                                                181b
                                                                                                188

10. Do not use periods in acronyms; **for example, NASDAQ (not N.A.S.D.A.Q.).**                 178
                                                                                                182a

11. There is only one more step we need to take: **namely, get my boss to okay the
    terms of the contract.**                                                                    178
                                                                                                182b

12. In my office we transfer electronic data by means of *sneakernet*—**that is, by
    carrying a diskette from one computer to another.**                                         178
                                                                                                182c

13. Some of our suppliers—**for example, Wynn**—may be raising prices soon. *(No special
    treatment required.)*                                                                       178
                                                                                                183

14. Some of our suppliers—**for example, Wynn, Place, and Shaw**—may be raising
    prices soon. *(Emphasize phrase.)*                                                          183
                                                                                                202

Name _____ Date _____ Class _____        13

B-24

15. Some of our suppliers, **for example, Wynn, Place, and Shaw**, may be raising
    prices soon. *(De-emphasize phrase.)*

183
219b

16. Replacement parts for this equipment are manufactured only in our **Carbondale**,
    **Pennsylvania**, factory.

219a

17. Please send us, 1) your résumé, 2) samples of your work, and 3) a list of
    **references we can contact.**

222a

18. Please call me by **Friday, (October 3)** if you want us to proceed with the market
    research.

224a
221
225a–c
220

19. You will find a detailed analysis of this topic in **Chapter 4 (see pages 98–112).**

226

20. You will find a detailed analysis of this topic in **Chapter 4. (See pages 98–112.)**

220

**C. Directions:** In each of the following sentences, correct the capitalization of the word following the colon as necessary. Use appropriate proofreaders' marks (shown on pages 358–359 and on the inside back cover of *The Gregg Reference Manual*) to indicate your corrections. Circle any changes you make. If a sentence is correct as given, write *C* in the answer column. **References:** Consult the rules shown below as you complete this exercise.

21. You need the following qualifications for this job: A college degree and
    some retailing experience.

21. _____ 196

22. I think Nan should head the group: She's good with people and she
    understands the key issues.

22. _____ 197

23. My china shop operates on a simple principle: If you break it, you've
    bought it.

23. **C** _____ 198

24. Please keep the following things in mind: a project of this size will have a
    lot of last-minute details. There will not be enough "last minutes" in which
    to deal with them.

24. _____ 199a

25. Caution: do not enter this room when a red light is flashing.

25. _____ 199d

**D. Directions:** Correct the punctuation before, after, and within the boldface elements in the following sentences. Change the capitalization as necessary. Use appropriate revision marks to indicate your corrections. Circle any changes you make. If a sentence is correct as given, write *C* in the answer column. **References:** Consult the rules shown below as you complete this exercise.

26. **Direct quote:** Mr. Potter said, **I want it done. And I want it done now**

26. _____ 227

27. **Indirect quote:** Mr. Potter said that **he wanted action taken**
    **immediately**

27. _____ 228a

28. **Article title:** I've just submitted an article entitled **Finding a Job in**
    **Today's Market**

240a
242

28. _____

29. **"So-called" expression:** If you consider the reduced size of the new box,
    their **so-called price cut** is really a price increase.

29. _____ 240b

# Other Marks of Punctuation (Continued)

30. Quoted statement: "Let's call Sam Hathaway and get his advice," Jerry suggested.

30. _____ 253a / 247a

31. Quoted question: "Why should we consider such a disappointing offer?" Marian asked.

31. _____ 254 / 249a

32. Quoted statement: Mr. Kelly's previous boss said, "He's a lot smarter than he looks."

32. _____ 256a / 247a

33. Quoted question: The defense attorney asked, "What is your evidence for this accusation?"

33. _____ 256a / 249a

34. Quoted statement: Did Louise really say, "I'm going to hand in my resignation"?

34. _____ 256a / 249b

35. Quoted statements: Here's what Louise actually said, "I've made up my mind. I won't work for that bozo."

35. _____ 256b–c / 247a

**E. Directions:** Insert underlining or quotation marks as appropriate for the boldface expressions in the following sentences. Use appropriate proofreaders' marks to indicate your corrections. Circle any changes you make. If a sentence is correct as given, write *C* in the answer column. **References:** Consult the rules shown below as you complete this exercise.

36. What do the words **newbie** and **newsgroup** mean?

36. _____ 285a

37. The Germans would use the word **gemütlich** to describe the atmosphere of this restaurant.

37. _____ 287

38. Richard, my nerdy brother, is graduating **summa cum laude** from the University of North Dakota.

38. **C** 287

39. You'll enjoy an article entitled **Human Rights for Motorists** in a recent issue of **BusinessWeek.**

39. _____ 242 / 289a

40. I urge you to read this book **Electronic Networks: A Surfer's Guide, Second Edition.**

40. _____ 289a, f

41. What does the phrase **surfing the Net** actually mean?

41. _____ 290a, c

42. I always seem to make a mistake when I try to use **affect** or **effect.**

42. _____ 285a / 290c

43. How would you define the terms **landscape orientation** and **portrait orientation?**

43. _____ 285a / 290a, c

44. Have you read **Newsweek's** article on the influence of corporate lobbyists on federal legislation?

44. _____ 289a / 290d

45. I think his writing contains too many **howevers** and not enough **therefores.**

45. _____ 290d

**F. Directions:** Edit the following paragraph to correct all errors in punctuation and capitalization. Use appropriate proofreaders' marks to indicate your corrections. Circle any changes you make. **References:** Consult ¶¶176–199 and the appropriate rules in Section 2 as you complete this exercise.

I've been collecting material about new computer terms for        1

some time. Writing a book rather than an article on this sub-      2

ject appeals to me for two reasons. (1) 1 already have enough       3

material for a book. (2) 1 could use the extra space to analyze     4

the people who dream up these terms. I wouldn't bother with         5

ordinary words like bit and byte. The kinds of words I have         6

in mind for example, *notwork*, *vaporware*, and *sneakernet*, re-  7

flect the wacky, offbeat humor of computer programmers and          8

users. (In case you're interested, *notwork* refers to a network    9

that does not live up to its advance billing, *vaporware* refers   10

to software that is being heavily promoted, even though it has     11

serious developmental problems that could doom its eventual        12

release. I would also deal with abbreviations that have ac-        13

quired crazy pronunciations for example, SCSI (pronounced          14

*scuzzy*). I've sent a proposal to a San Mateo California          15

publishing house that issued a successful book entitled           16

The Internet for Dummies. Maybe the editors will see             17

another winner in my idea.                                         18

# 6 Capitalization

**A. Directions:** Correct the capitalization as necessary in each of the following items. Use appropriate proofreaders' marks (shown on pages 358–359 and on the inside back cover of *The Gregg Reference Manual*) to indicate your corrections. Circle any changes you make. If an item is correct as given, write *C* in the answer column. **References:** Consult the rules shown below as you complete this exercise. See Appendix D for the definition of any grammatical terms that you may not be familiar with.

| | | |
|---|---|---|
| 1. your news is great! Congratulations! | 301a 301b | |
| 2. Jen then asked, "Who cares?" | 301c | |
| 3. The question is, Who will do it? | 301d | |
| 4. the red Cross | 303 | |
| 5. the internet | 303 | |
| 6. The Statue of Liberty | 303 | |
| 7. a congressional hearing | C | 304 |
| 8. a good Samaritan | 305 | |
| 9. roman numerals | C | 306 |
| 10. a few Senators | 307 | |

| | | |
|---|---|---|
| 11. our Company | 308 | |
| 12. the Post Office | 309a | |
| 13. Fifth and Sixth avenues | 309a | |
| 14. Danish pastry | C | 309b |
| 15. Governor Elect Paderewski | 312a 317 | |
| 16. as president of the United States | 312b | |
| 17. the governor of Virginia | 313b | |
| 18. the Mayor of their town | 313c | |
| 19. let's talk to Mother about it | C | 318 |
| 20. let's talk to my Mother about it | 319a | |

**B. Directions:** Correct the capitalization as necessary in each of the following items. Use appropriate proofreaders' marks to indicate your corrections. Circle any changes you make. If an item is correct as given, write *C* in the answer column. **References:** Consult the rules shown below as you complete this exercise.

| | | |
|---|---|---|
| 21. the Kmart Corporation | 320a | |
| 22. this corporation | C | 321 |
| 23. The House of Representatives | 325 | |
| 24. our local Police Department | 327 | |
| 25. Federal tax regulations | 328 | |
| 26. every state in the union | 330a | |
| 27. the Hotel *(referring to the Plaza)* | 331 | |
| 28. moved to the big apple | 333a | |
| 29. the City of Fort Lauderdale | 334 | |
| 30. the state of North Carolina | C | 335a |
| 31. moved to the west coast | 338a | |
| 32. the west coast of the island | C | 338b |
| 33. Southern politicians | C | 340 |
| 34. the Southern half of Idaho | 340 | |
| 35. northern New Hampshire | C | 341 |

| | | |
|---|---|---|
| 36. the fourth of July | 342 | |
| 37. the American revolution | 344a | |
| 38. the Space Age | 344b | |
| 39. throughout the Nineties | 345 | |
| 40. took the fifth amendment | 346a | |
| 41. medicare patients | C | 347a |
| 42. native Americans | 348a | |
| 43. God in his glory | C | 349b |
| 44. the ten commandments | 350a | |
| 45. come down to Earth | 351 | |
| 46. two courses in Economics | 352 | |
| 47. a Bachelor's degree | 353 | |
| 48. met at the Laundromat | C | 356a |
| 49. chapter 6 | 359 | |
| 50. won the Nobel prize | 364 | |

Name _____  Date _____  Class _____  17

**C. Directions:** Correct the capitalization of the boldface elements as necessary in the following sentences. Use appropriate proofreaders' marks to indicate your corrections. Circle any changes you make. If a sentence is correct as given, write *C* in the answer column. **References:** Consult the rules shown below as you complete this exercise.

51. **From a company memo:** When we next meet, we need to:
    - **invite the general managers** to talk about their goals.
    - **review the Company's** commitment to the **City's** redevelopment
      plans.
    - **discuss** our upcoming presentation to the **board of directors.**

    51. _____
    301e
    313d
    321
    334
    322

52. Call the **Marketing Director** of Worknet—**Her** name is Amy Fong, I believe—and ask about her experience with **Powerpoint.**

    52. _____
    313d-e
    302a
    366a
    313a

53. Bernard Lisker, the **President** of our **Company,** is attending a **white house** conference on the role of the **Federal Government** in international trade.

    53. _____
    308
    305
    329
    308

54. Let's ask the **Doctor** if **Penicillin** would stop this infection.

    54. _____
    356

55. Last **Fall,** at the start of my **Junior** year, I decided to major in **Art.**

    55. _____
    343
    354
    352
    360

56. **An article title:** "The **new tax bill: is it** to **be** a **bonanza** or a **disaster?**"

    56. _____
    361

57. **An article title:** "**a follow-up** on **e-mail—how** to **make it work for you.**"

    57. _____
    360a–b
    361
    363
    313e

58. I applied for the job of **Programmer** in their **systems department.**

    58. _____
    322

59. This booklet (**see Pages 16–18**) discusses **Social Security benefits.**

    59. _____
    302a
    359
    347a

60. Enclosed is a **xerox** copy of a list of **realtors** from the **yellow pages.**

    60. _____
    356

**D. Directions:** Edit the following paragraph to correct all capitalization errors. Use appropriate proofreaders' marks to indicate your corrections. Circle any changes you make. **References:** Consult the appropriate rules in Section 3 as you complete this exercise.

Early last Winter, in the middle of my junior year in college, the pro-  1
fessor who taught my Political Science seminar invited me to help him with a  2
book he is writing. The assignment has required me to gather information from  3
key officials in the federal government as well as from the Governors from  4
every State in the Union. We are trying to assess the financial impact of  5
Federal environmental protection laws on the states in the course of the  6
twenty-first Century. My Father is quite proud of what I'm doing. He keeps  7
asking me, "When are you going to Washington to interview the president?" I  8
keep reminding him that I am only the Research Assistant and not the author.  9

# 7 Numbers

**A. Directions:** Circle all errors in number style in each of the following items, and write the correct form in the answer column. Follow the *figure style.* If an item is correct as given, write *C* in the answer column. **References:** ¶¶401–403.

| | | |
|---|---|---|
| 1. eight messages | **C** | 401a |
| 2. about (twelve) phone calls | **12** | 401a |
| 3. over (two thousand) words | **2000** | 401a |
| 4. April (fourth) | **4** | 401b |
| 5. (seven dollars) | **$7** | 401b |
| 6. (nine) a.m. | **9** | 401b |
| 7. a score of (seven to six) | **7 to 6** | 401b |
| 8. got a (sixty) on the exam | **60** | 401b |
| 9. (four) percent | **4** | 401b |
| 10. (six) ft | **6** | 401b |

| | | |
|---|---|---|
| 11. a 6-month research study | **C** | 401b |
| 12. found on page (eight) | **8** | 401b |
| 13. a 5-year loan | **C** | 401b |
| 14. over (20) years ago | **twenty** | 401d |
| 15. (6) people showed up. | **Six** | 401d |
| 16. our (15th) anniversary | **fifteenth** | 401d |
| 17. one-fourth of my income | **C** | 401d |
| 18. six men and (10) women | **ten** | 402 |
| 19. (six) men and 12 women | **6** | 402 |
| 20. (four million dollars) | **$4 million** | 403a |

**B. Directions:** Circle all errors in number style in each of the following items, and write the correct form in the answer column. Follow the *word style.* If an item is correct as given, write *C* in the answer column. **References:** ¶¶404–406.

| | | |
|---|---|---|
| 21. (12) e-mail messages | **twelve** | 404a |
| 22. more than (50) visitors | **fifty** | 404a |
| 23. at least (75) friends | **seventy-five** | 404a |
| 24. over (500) get-well cards | **five hundred** | 404a |
| 25. over 550 get-well cards | **C** | 404a |

| | | |
|---|---|---|
| 26. 126 yeses and (forty) nos | **40** | 405 |
| 27. 200 yeses and 145 nos | **C** | 405 |
| 28. two million years ago | **C** | 406 |
| 29. (two and a half) million | **2.5 OR 2½** | 406 |
| 30. (20,000,000) | **twenty million** | 406 |

**C. Directions:** Circle all errors in number style and related punctuation in each of the following items, and write the correct form in the answer column. Follow the *figure style* unless another style is called for. If an item is correct as given, write *C* in the answer column. **References:** Consult the rules shown below as you complete this exercise.

| | | |
|---|---|---|
| 31. **Formal style:** the (3d) of May | **third** | 407a |
| 32. **Emphatic style:** the 3d of May | **C** | 407a |
| 33. June (eighth) | **8** | 407b |
| 34. the (tenth of August,) 2007 | **August 10,** | 408d |
| 35. the (October, 2006,) issue | **October 2006** | 410 |

| | | |
|---|---|---|
| 36. (twenty thousand dollars) | **$20,000** | 413a |
| 37. bills for ($27.00) and $49.50 | **$27** | 415 |
| 38. ($2) to $4 million | **$2 million** | 416d |
| 39. costs only ($.25) | **25 cents** | 418a |
| 40. $2 million to (4 million) | **$4 million** | 419 |

**D. Directions:** Circle all errors in number style in each of the following items, and write the correct form in the answer column. Follow the *figure style* unless another style is called for. If an item is correct as given, write *C* in the answer column. **References:** Consult the rules shown below as you complete this exercise.

| | | |
|---|---|---|
| 41. . . . now (6 to 12) years ago | **Six to twelve** | 421 |
| 42. several (1000) brochures | **thousand** | 423 |

| | | |
|---|---|---|
| 43. in the (1st) century | **first** | 424 |
| 44. two-thirds of the voters | **C** | 427a |

Name _____ Date _____ Class _____ 19

| | | | | |
|---|---|---|---|---|
| 45. a ½ hour later | **half** 427a | 48. pensions at the age of 60 | **C** | 433 |
| 46. Technical style: (six) feet | **6** 429a | 49. my four-year-old niece | **C** | 434 |
| 47. Technical style: 9ʹ × 12ʹ | **9ʹ × 12ʹ** OR | 50. on my (50th) birthday | **fiftieth** | 435 |
| | **9ʹ × 12ʹ** 432 | | | |

**E. Directions:** Circle all errors in number style and related punctuation in each of the following items, and write the correct form in the answer column. Follow the *figure style* unless another style is called for. If an item is correct as given, write *C* in the answer column. **References:** Consult the rules shown below as you complete this exercise.

| | | | | |
|---|---|---|---|---|
| 51. a bill payable in 3 months | **C** 436a | 59. (30)-40% | **30%** | 453b |
| 52. vacation (2) weeks from now | **two** 437 | 60. in (2002 16) new outlets | **2002, 16** | 456 |
| 53. (20th-century) music | **twentieth-** 424 **century** 438 | 61. 250 (8-page) brochures | **eight-page** | 457 |
| 54. during the (90's) | **ʹ90s** OR **nineties** 439a | 62. (37500) units in stock | **37,500** | 461a |
| 55. opens at (nine) a.m. | **9** 440a | 63. (3,905) Morgan Street | **3905** | 462 |
| 56. closes at (5:00) p.m. | **5** 440c | 64. Word style: (51,000) | **fifty-one thousand** | 465 |
| 57. **Emphatic style:** (six) o'clock | **6** 441a | 65. Word style: (1100) | **eleven hundred** | 466 |
| 58. only (one) percent | **1** 447a | 66. a wad of (twentys) | **twenties** | 467 |

**F. Directions:** Rewrite the following sentences to correct any errors in number style and related punctuation. Follow the *figure style*. **References:** Consult the appropriate rules in Section 4 as you complete this exercise.

67. On March 8th, 1993 we were married. In 2008, we will celebrate our 15th anniversary.  **On** 408a / 410
   **March 8, 1993, we were married. In 2008 we will celebrate our fifteenth anniversary.** 424

68. The January, 2008, issue of *Workaholic* describes the routines of fourteen women, ten men,
   and one married couple. **The January 2008 issue of *Workaholic* describes the routines of 14 women,** 410
   **10 men, and 1 married couple.** 402

69. 15 to 20 percent of the students we interviewed said that they rarely did more than ½ hour of
   homework each night. **Fifteen to twenty percent of the students we interviewed said that they** 421
   **rarely did more than a half hour of homework each night.** 427a

70. On April 15 eighteen callers expressed interest in our offer to sell a few 100 acres. **On April 15,** 410 / 456 / 401a
   **18 callers expressed interest in our offer to sell a few hundred acres.** 423

**G. Directions:** Edit the following paragraph to correct any errors in number style and related punctuation. Follow the *figure style*. If a figure needs to be in words, supply the spelled-out form. Use appropriate proofreaders' marks (shown on pages 358–359 and on the inside back cover of *The Gregg Reference Manual*) to indicate your corrections. Circle any changes you make. **References:** Consult the appropriate rules in Section 4 as you complete this exercise.

```
        (twenty-first) 424        (5) 407b                    (thousand) 423
On my 21st birthday, March fifth, I will inherit several 1000 dollars (50) 447a    1
                                    (four) 401d/437
from the estate of my grandfather, who died 4 years ago. I plan to use fifty         2
                                              (Two) 421
percent of my inheritance to pay off part of my tuition loans. 2 months from          3
          (half) 427a                                          (six) 401a
now, with the other 1/2 of my inheritance, I may take a tour that covers 6           4
                    461a  ($) 413/419
countries in four weeks and costs between $2000 and 3000. If my inheritance           5
is over $10,000, I may buy a new car instead.                                         6
```

B-31

# Editing Survey A

**A. Directions:** Rewrite the following sentences to correct all errors in punctuation, capitalization, and number style. Follow the *figure style* for numbers. **References:** Consult the appropriate rules in Sections 1–4 as you complete this exercise.

1. Our Company is expanding its export business, and will be opening new, shipping facilities in Portland, Oregon on July first.

   **Our company is expanding its export business and will be opening new shipping facilities in**

   **Portland, Oregon, on July 1.**

   308
   127b
   169
   160a
   401b
   407b

2. Would you please let my son borrow your van. He needs to bring about twelve boxes of books and clothes home from College.

   **Would you please let my son borrow your van? He needs to bring about 12 boxes of books and**

   **clothes home from college.**

   103b
   401a
   309a

3. In 2006, our company published between ten and 15 books on the subject of Computer Technology. Don't you think that's rather impressive.

   **In 2006 our company published between 10 and 15 books on the subject of computer technology.**

   **Don't you think that's rather impressive?**

   135c
   410
   402
   352
   110a

4. My Mother and my sister, Anne, opened their consulting business on January 31, 2005. A date that none of us in the family will ever forget.

   **My mother and my sister Anne opened their consulting business on January 31, 2005, a date that none**

   **of us in the family will ever forget.**

   319a
   149
   150
   154a
   122e
   101c

5. I would like to ask whether it is legally permissible for me to xerox eighty-five copies of an article entitled *Ethical Considerations in Business Decisions?*

   **I would like to ask whether it is legally permissible for me to Xerox 85 copies of an article entitled**

   **"Ethical Considerations in Business Decisions."**

   303
   356a
   401a
   242
   360a
   247a
   104

Name _____ Date _____ Class _____ 21

6. This request for a ten percent salary increase will have to be approved by 1) the general manager, 2) the director of finance and 3) the President.

This request for a 10 percent salary increase will have to be approved by (1) the general manager, (2) the director of finance, and (3) the president.

401b
447a
222a
123b
162a
313d–e

7. 24 people responded to our ad for a room clerk but more than ¾ of the applicants had no previous Hotel experience. Unbelievable

Twenty-four people responded to our ad for a room clerk, but more than three-fourths [OR three-quarters] of the applicants had no previous hotel experience. Unbelievable!

421
123a
126a
401d
427a–b
308
331
119a

8. Thank you for your letter of March 9th in which you asked for the location of our branch offices in the State of Maryland.

Thank you for your letter of March 9, in which you asked for the location of our branch offices in the state of Maryland.

401b
407b
122d
148
152
335a

9. For a good analysis of business trends in the 90's read chapter 7 (See page 121 in particular.) in a book entitled "The Outlook for Emerging Markets".

For a good analysis of business trends in the '90s [OR nineties], read Chapter 7 (see page 121 in particular) in a book entitled *The Outlook for Emerging Markets.*

439a
135c
359
224
289a

10. It is, nevertheless, true that we are facing an $80000 shortfall in sales this Summer, therefore I am scheduling a managers' meeting for nine a.m. tomorrow.

It is nevertheless true that we are facing an $80,000 shortfall in sales this summer. Therefore, [OR summer; therefore,] I am scheduling a managers' meeting for 9 a.m. tomorrow.

122c
141
461a
343
128
178
440a

# Editing Survey A (Continued)

**B. Directions:** Edit the following paragraphs to correct all errors in punctuation, capitalization, and number style. Follow the *figure style* for numbers. Use appropriate proofreaders' marks (shown on pages 358–359 and on the inside back cover of *The Gregg Reference Manual*) to indicate your corrections. Circle any changes you make. **References:** Consult the appropriate rules in Sections 1–4 as you complete this exercise.

```
      Are you one of those people who think that all New Yorkers      1

are cold hostile people  Well, it may not be true.  The New York      2

Times  recently carried a story about a doctor who was living in      3

Manhattan and practicing across the river in New Jersey. On a        4

bitterly cold winter morning, he discovered that his car            5

(parked on the street overnight) would not start. "How will I        6

get to my morning appointments?" he wondered.                        7

      As he sat there, another New Yorker hovered alongside in        8

his car, waiting for the doctor to give up his parking space.        9

After one more futile attempt to start the car the doctor got       10

out and told the waiting driver to look for another parking          11

space. Then he went on to say, "I have an even bigger               12

problem  I don't know how I'm going to get to my patients           13

in New Jersey today."                                               14

      The hovering driver asked, "What time do you get back          15

to your apartment here in the city                                  16

      "Oh, about 5:30," said the doctor.                            17

      "Look," said the driver. "You don't have a car. I don't       18

have a parking space. Take my car today. You can return it          19

to me right here about 5:30 this afternoon."                        20

      The doctor and the driver shook hands on the deal and         21

went their separate ways. What do you think of that?                22
```

Handwritten annotations: 168a, 110a, 289a, 169, 343, 124/130a, ⊙ or ⊙ 128/187, 334, 249a, 127b

Name _____ Date _____ Class _____ 23

**C. Directions:** Edit the following paragraphs to correct all errors in punctuation, capitalization, and number style. Follow the *figure style* for numbers. Use appropriate revision marks to indicate your corrections. Circle any changes you make.
**References:** Consult the appropriate rules in Sections 1–4 as you complete this exercise.

122c/138a/139a   122/131a/132
305/333a   8:30  440a
⑥407b

On the other hand there are some New Yorkers who think the
worst of their neighbors in the big apple. About eight-thirty
a.m.--I think it was June sixth--a lawyer named Paul Cronin was

standing inside a subway car, waiting for the train to pull out
of the station. Standing right next to him was a well-dressed,
professional-looking man. Just as the train was getting ready to

130a
leave the well-dressed man bolted for the closing door bumping   137b
into Paul in the process. Paul instinctively felt for his
wallet and realized at once that it was not there. He ran after   127b

the pickpocket and caught him by the lapel just as the door was
closing. In fact, when the door closed, Paul's hand was extended
outside the door and was still clutching the pickpocket's lapel.
As the train started to move, the horrified pickpocket had no
choice but to run alongside, because Paul was gripping his
lapel. Then the lapel came off the man's jacket.

Paul drew his hand back into the subway car, proudly
holding the lapel aloft. He didn't get his wallet back but he   123a/126a
had a trophy to show for his vigorous attempt to assert and
defend his rights. The passengers in the subway car all
applauded Paul for his brave efforts to stand up to a criminal.
Paul's colleagues at his law firm were equally admiring. Then
Paul's wife called.

"Darling, I don't want you to be worried," she said. "You
left your wallet on top of the dresser this morning.   247a/252

1
2
3
4
5
6
7
8
9
10
11
12
13
14
15
16
17
18
19
20
21
22
23
24

# 9 Abbreviations

**A. Directions:** Provide the correct abbreviation, contraction, or short form for each of the following items. If an item is correct as given, write *C* in the answer column. **References:** ¶¶501–514. See Appendix D for the definition of any grammatical terms that you may not be familiar with.

| | | | | | | | |
|---|---|---|---|---|---|---|---|
| 1. | Mister | **Mr.** | 502b | 11. | it is | **it's** | 505d |
| 2. | Junior | **Jr.** | 502b | 12. | Wednesday | **Wed.** | 506a |
| 3. | Incorporated | **Inc.** | 502b | 13. | miles per hour | **mph** | 507 |
| 4. | Part | **C** | 502e | 14. | Post Office | **P.O.** | 508 |
| 5. | continued | **cont.** | 503 | 15. | United States of America | **U.S.A.** | 508 |
| 6. | kilobyte | **KB** | 503 | 16. | National Football League | **NFL** | 508 |
| 7. | fiscal year | **FY** | 504 | 17. | doctor of philosophy | **Ph.D.** | 509 |
| 8. | department | **dept.** | 505a | 18. | limousine | **limo** | 510 |
| 9. | does not | **doesn't** | 505b | 19. | District of Columbia | **D.C.** | 514 |
| 10. | let us | **let's** | 505b | 20. | electronic mail | **e-mail** | 514 |

**B. Directions:** Circle any word or abbreviation that is incorrectly styled, and write the correct form in the answer column. If a sentence is correct as given, write *C* in the answer column. **References:** ¶¶501–514.

| | | | |
|---|---|---|---|
| 21. | Send the bill to the father—Roy Fox (Senior)—and not to his son. | **21. Sr.** | 502b |
| 22. | You have to read only (Pt.) One, not the complete book. | **22. Part** | 502e |
| 23. | (Its) about time that we decided whether to buy or lease a new car. | **23. It's** | 505d |
| 24. | Dr. Juanita Scott will represent us at the (A.M.A.) convention. | **24. AMA** | 508 |
| 25. | Last month Heather Dillingham moved to Washington (D.C..) | **25. D.C.** | 512 |

**C. Directions:** Provide the correct abbreviation or symbol for each of the following items. **References:** Consult the rules shown below as you complete this exercise.

| | | | | | | | |
|---|---|---|---|---|---|---|---|
| 26. | Ruth A. Goodman | **RAG** OR **R.A.G.** | 516b | 36. | February | **Feb.** | 532 |
| 27. | Esquire | **Esq.** | 518a | 37. | Wednesday | **Wed.** | 532 |
| 28. | [John Dellums] the Third | **III** | 518d | 38. | inches | **in** | 535a |
| 29. | Certified Public Accountant | **CPA** | 519g | 39. | ounces | **oz** | 535a |
| 30. | Internal Revenue Service | **IRS** | 520a | 40. | gram | **g** | 537a |
| 31. | Corporation | **Corp.** | 520b | 41. | kilometer | **km** | 537a 538a |
| 32. | World Health Organization | **WHO** | 524a | 42. | chief executive officer | **CEO** | 541 |
| 33. | Los Angeles | **L.A.** | 526 | 43. | shipping and handling | **S&H** | 541 |
| 34. | North America | **N.A.** | 528a | 44. | 48 pounds | **48#** | 543 |
| 35. | Southeast | **SE** | 531 | 45. | World Wide Web | **WWW** | 544a |

Name _____ Date _____ Class _____  25

**D. Directions:** Circle any word or abbreviation that is incorrectly styled, and write the correct form in the answer column. If a sentence is correct as given, write *C* in the answer column. **References:** Consult the rules shown below.

| | | |
|---|---|---|
| 46. | Please schedule a meeting with (E.G.) Cavatelli. | **46.** E. G.  516a |
| 47. | (Doctor) Chang is the best heart surgeon in the state. | **47.** Dr.  517a |
| 48. | I wish (Gov.) Haas would state her position on the budget. | **48.** Governor  517d |
| 49. | Please refer this matter to my attorney, (Mr. Eugene Dill, Esq.) | **49.** Eugene Dill, Esq.  518c |
| 50. | My primary physician is (Dr. Nancy J. Wolfson, M.D.) | **50.** Dr. Nancy J. Wolfson OR Nancy J. Wolfson, M.D.  519c |
| 51. | Have you seen the results of the latest (C.N.N.) poll? | **51.** CNN  523 |
| 52. | He is campaigning throughout the (U.S.) | **52.** United States  525 |
| 53. | A friend of mine from Oberlin, (Oh.,) just moved to Seattle. | **53.** Ohio  527b |
| 54. | I usually fly to (Ft.) Lauderdale rather than to Miami. | **54.** Fort  529 |
| 55. | Their new offices are located at 227 (N.) Fullerton Avenue. | **55.** North  530b |

**E. Directions:** Rewrite the following sentences to correct any errors in abbreviation style. **References:** Consult the rules shown below as you complete this exercise.

56. Dr. Marie Gallagher, Ph. D., has been named C.E.O. of Parametrics, Incorp. **Marie Gallagher,**  519c 519a 541 520b
**Ph.D., [OR Dr. Marie Gallagher] has been named CEO of Parametrics Inc.**

57. Whenever I try to get cash from an A.T.M. machine, I always forget my P.I.N. number. **Whenever**  508 522a 522e
**I try to get cash from an ATM, I always forget my PIN.**

58. Doctor P.J. Malone has been elected to the board of the N.A.A.C.P. **Dr. P. J. Malone has been**  517a 516a 508
**elected to the board of the NAACP.**

59. According to Ms Sokolov's memo., the meeting scheduled for 3 PM on the 2nd of June has been  517a 533 510 503
canceled. **According to Ms. Sokolov's memo, the meeting scheduled for 3 p.m. on the 2d of June**
**has been canceled.**

60. Prof. Jon Lund II. is moving to Saint Petersburg after his retirement. **Professor Jon Lund II**  517d 518d 529b
**is moving to St. Petersburg after his retirement.**

**F. Directions:** Edit the following paragraph to correct any errors in abbreviations and contractions. Use appropriate proofreaders' marks (shown on pages 358–359 and on the inside back cover of *The Gregg Reference Manual*) to indicate your corrections. Circle any changes you make. **References:** Consult the appropriate rules in Section 5 as you complete this exercise.

```
If you want to participate in the experimental drug study now being              1

undertaken by the National Institute of Mental Health, I suggest you ask your    2

doctor to write to Dr. R.G. Valdez, M.D., who is setting up research sites       3

throughout the U.S. The N.I.M.H. is based in Rockville, Maryland, but Doctor     4

Valdez works out of a lab in Washington, D.C. Prof. George Y. Petrus Junior,     5

who lives here in town, knows Dr. Valdez personally, so he may be able to put    6

you in touch with her. I don't have his phone number, but his office is         7

located at 212 E. Mountain Avenue.                                               8
```

# 10 Plurals

**A. Directions:** In the answer column, provide the correct plural form for each of the following items. **References:** Consult the rules shown below as you complete this exercise. See Appendix D for the definition of any grammatical terms that you may not be familiar with.

| | | | | | | | |
|---|---|---|---|---|---|---|---|
| 1. | idea | **ideas** | 601 | 11. | thief | **thieves** | 608b |
| 2. | business | **businesses** | 602 | 12. | woman | **women** | 609 |
| 3. | search | **searches** | 602 | 13. | child | **children** | 610 |
| 4. | fax | **faxes** | 602 | 14. | photocopy | **photocopies** | 611 |
| 5. | policy | **policies** | 604 | 15. | sister-in-law | **sisters-in-law** | 612a |
| 6. | attorney | **attorneys** | 605 | 16. | hang-up | **hang-ups** | 612b |
| 7. | stereo | **stereos** | 606 | 17. | finder's fee | **finder's fees** | 612d |
| 8. | weirdo | **weirdos** | 607a | 18. | alumnus | **alumni** | 614 |
| 9. | potato | **potatoes** | 607b | 19. | criterion | **criteria** | 614 |
| 10. | belief | **beliefs** | 608a | 20. | crisis | **crises** | 614 |

**B. Directions:** Circle any word that is misspelled or misused, and write the correct form in the answer column. If a sentence is correct as given, write *C* in the answer column. **References:** Consult the rules shown below.

| | | | | |
|---|---|---|---|---|
| 21. | We can't base important decisions on Larry Cresskill's (hunchs.) | 21. | **hunches** | 602 |
| 22. | How many (copys) do you want us to distribute? | 22. | **copies** | 604 |
| 23. | I'll get back to you as soon as I've heard from my (attornies.) | 23. | **attorneys** | 605 |
| 24. | My two (brother-in-laws) think they have the answer to every problem. | 24. | **brothers-in-law** | 612a |
| 25. | Getting the job done right is the only (criteria) we need to meet. | 25. | **criterion** | 614 |

**C. Directions:** In the answer column, provide the correct plural form for each of the following items. **References:** Consult the rules shown below.

| | | | | | | | |
|---|---|---|---|---|---|---|---|
| 26. | menu | **menus** | 601 | 36. | Mr. and Mrs. Rossi | the **Rossis** | 615a |
| 27. | crash | **crashes** | 602 | 37. | Mr. and Mrs. Jones | the **Joneses** | 615b |
| 28. | company | **companies** | 604 | 38. | Mr. and Mrs. Marx | the **Marxes** | 615b |
| 29. | journey | **journeys** | 605 | 39. | Mr. and Mrs. Kenny | the **Kennys** | 615c |
| 30. | memo | **memos** | 607a | 40. | No. | **Nos.** | 619 |
| 31. | hero | **heroes** | 607b | 41. | ft | **ft** | 620a |
| 32. | shelf | **shelves** | 608b | 42. | p. (for *page*) | **pp.** | 621a |
| 33. | rule of thumb | **rules of thumb** | 612a | 43. | M.D. | **M.D.s** | 622a |
| 34. | phenomenon | **phenomena** | 614 | 44. | 1990 | the **1990s** | 624a |
| 35. | analysis | **analyses** | 614 | 45. | do and don't | **dos and don'ts** | 625a |

Name _____ Date _____ Class _____ 27

**D. Directions:** Circle any word that is misspelled or misused, and write the correct form in the answer column. If a sentence is correct as given, write *C* in the answer column. **References:** Consult the rules shown below as you complete this exercise.

46. I have received job offers from three agencys.

46. agencies    604

47. We have no one to blame but ourselfs.

47. ourselves    608b

48. Paul St. Germain is an alumni of The Johns Hopkins University.

48. alumnus    614

49. Yesterday's solar eclipse is one phenomena I will never forget.

49. phenomenon    614

50. Have you done an analyses of our sales for the first half of the year?

50. analysis    614

51. We have managed to get through worse crisises in the past.

51. crises    614

52. We invited Mr. and Mrs. Murphy, but the Murphies were away.

52. Murphys    615c

53. How many Ph.D.'s do we have in our Research Department?

53. Ph.D.s    622a

54. Our business grew tremendously during the 90s.

54. '90s    624a

55. I can't stand the weather when the temperature climbs into the 90s.

55. C    624a

**E. Directions:** Rewrite the following sentences to correct any errors in plural forms. **References:** Consult the rules shown below as you complete this exercise.

56. My bookshelfs are crammed with studys analyzing different types of taxs. **My bookshelves are crammed with studies analyzing different types of taxes.**

611
604
602

57. Please correct all the typoes in this memo, and change all the dashs to parenthesis. **Please correct all the typos in this memo, and change all the dashes to parentheses.**

607a
602
614

58. (For a list of the runner-ups, see p. 26-28.) **(For a list of the runners-up, see pp. 26–28.)**

612a
621a

59. Two of our committees have gone to great lengthes to review the pro's and con's of your plan. **Two of our committees have gone to great lengths to review the pros and cons of your plan.**

601
625a

60. My son has five parking summons and ten alibies for not paying them. **My son has five parking summonses and ten alibis for not paying them.**

602
601

**F. Directions:** Edit the following paragraph to correct any errors in plural forms. Use appropriate proofreaders' marks (shown on pages 358–359 and on the inside back cover of *The Gregg Reference Manual*) to indicate your corrections. Circle any changes you make. **References:** Consult the appropriate rules in ¶¶601–626 as you complete this exercise.

```
        The head of our HMO is planning a reception for the three new M.D.'s and          1
their wifes -the Jones, the McCarthies, and the Hastings. If the temperature              2
does not drop into the 70s, the reception will be held outdoors at the home               3
of Mr. and Mrs. Harvey Fox. The Foxs are going all out to make this a special             4
occasion. (No one could ever accuse them of being couch potatos.) They are                5
considering different menus and making arrangements for musical entertain-                6
ment. Many VIP will be invited. There is only one criteria for this event--               7
to do whatever is necessary to make the newcomers feel welcome.                           8
```

# 11

# Possessives

**A. Directions:** For each singular noun in the first column, provide the correct form for the singular possessive, the plural, and the plural possessive. **References:** Consult the rules shown below as you complete this exercise. See Appendix D for the definition of any grammatical terms that you may not be familiar with.

| SINGULAR | SINGULAR POSSESSIVE | | PLURAL | | PLURAL POSSESSIVE | |
|---|---|---|---|---|---|---|
| 1. company | company's | 630a | companies | 604 | companies' | 632a |
| 2. attorney | attorney's | 630a | attorneys | 605 | attorneys' | 632a |
| 3. hero | hero's | 630a | heroes | 607b | heroes' | 632a |
| 4. alumna (f.) | alumna's | 630a | alumnae | 614 | alumnae's | 633 |
| 5. Mr. and Mrs. Bono | Mr. and Mrs. Bono's | 630a | the Bonos | 615a | the Bonos' | 632a |
| 6. woman | woman's | 630a | women | 609 | women's | 633 |
| 7. child | child's | 630a | children | 610 | children's | 633 |
| 8. Mr. French | Mr. French's | 630a | the Frenches | 615b | the Frenches' | 632a |
| 9. actress | actress's | 631a | actresses | 602 | actresses' | 632a |
| 10. Mr. Van Ness | Mr. Van Ness's | 631a | the Van Nesses | 615b | the Van Nesses' | 632a |
| 11. homeowner | homeowner's | 634 | homeowners | 611 | homeowners' | 635a |
| 12. vice president | vice president's | 634 | vice presidents | 612a | vice presidents' | 635a |
| 13. daughter-in-law | daughter-in-law's | 634 | daughters-in-law | 612a | daughters-in-law's | 635b |
| 14. CPA | CPA's | 638 | CPAs | 622a | CPAs' | 638 |
| 15. M.D. | M.D.'s | 638 | M.D.s | 622a | M.D.s' | 638 |

**B. Directions:** Circle all errors in possessive forms in each of the following sentences, and write the correct form in the answer column. If a sentence is correct as given, write *C* in the answer column. **References:** ¶¶627–633.

16. My husband and I are going on a two weeks cruise to Alaska.
16. weeks'  — 627 / 629 / 632a

17. I'm opening a saving's account for my new granddaughter.
17. savings — 628a

18. Would you be willing to raise funds for the boys hockey team?
18. boys' — 628a / 632a

19. When we went to Mr. and Mrs. Smith's house, we met the Smith's sons.
19. Smiths' — 629 / 632a

20. I'm moving to Iowa. What do you know about Des Moines's schools?
20. C — 630b

21. Before you apply for a leave, you will need to get your boss okay.
21. boss's — 631a

22. We take real pride in Massachusetts' historical struggle for freedom.
22. C — 631b

23. Have you ever walked through New Orlean's French Quarter?
23. New Orleans' — 631c

24. Burke & Feldman is having a sale on womens and children's clothing.
24. women's — 633

25. The two eyewitness's statements don't agree on many key points.
25. eyewitnesses' — 635a / 632b

Name _____  Date _____  Class _____  29

**C. Directions:** Rewrite the following sentences to eliminate all errors in possessive forms and awkward expressions. **References:** Consult the rules shown below as you complete this exercise.

26. My sons-in-law's business will require me providing a lot of financial support. **The business owned by my sons-in-law will require my providing a lot of financial support.**

635b
647a

27. If this wallet is not her's, who's is it? **If this wallet is not hers, whose is it?**

636

28. I got a great price on these Levis at Blue Genius Inc.s end-of-winter sale. **I got a great price on these Levi's at Blue Genius Inc.'s end-of-winter sale.**

640a
644
639

29. Do you think Frank's and Arnold's partnership will last? They don't respect each others' views. **Do you think Frank and Arnold's partnership will last? They don't respect each other's views.**

643a
637

30. The organizers of our local farmer's market think this year's sales are twice as good as last year. **The organizers of our local farmers' market think this year's sales are twice as good as last year's.**

652
644

31. We've been invited to a New Years' Eve party at the Russos. **We've been invited to a New Year's Eve party at the Russos'.**

650a
644

32. I asked for fast delivery of several hundred dollars worth of kitchen equipment, but the shipment is now three week's overdue. **I asked for fast delivery of several hundred dollars' worth of kitchen equipment, but the shipment is now three weeks overdue.**

646
647a

33. What did your boss think about you asking for two week's vacation during the August sale? **What did your boss think about your asking for two weeks' vacation during the August sale?**

627
629
632a

34. One of my author's manuscript has been accepted by a publisher, but I don't like the contract's terms. **The manuscript written by one of my authors has been accepted by a publisher, but I don't like the terms of the contract.**

648c
645

35. Did you read Ms. Fox, the producer's comments about our doctor's son's acting career? **Did you read the comments of Ms. Fox, the producer, about the acting career of our doctor's son?**

641
649

**D. Directions:** Edit the following paragraph to correct any errors in possessive forms. Use appropriate proofreaders' marks (shown on pages 358–359 and on the inside back cover of *The Gregg Reference Manual*) to indicate your corrections. Circle any changes you make. **References:** Consult the appropriate rules in ¶¶627–652 as you complete this exercise.

```
Do you remember me telling you about Pam and Marsha's shop going out of        1

business? They had a fantastic sale last week on womens clothes. This year's    2

prices were even lower than last year. I found a new dress for the Rosses       3

anniversary celebration next month. (I like it very much, but I don't think     4

it's as nice as yours.) Then I remembered wanting new clothes for the one       5

week trip to Orlando this spring. The shop had a wonderful price on Levis,      6

so I scooped up three pairs. Before I knew it, I had bought several hundred     7

dollars worth of clothes I probably don't need. I'm going to have to dip deep   8

into my savings account to pay for this wild shopping spree. I hope there is     9

something left to pay for the trip to Orlando.                                  10
```

# 12 Spelling

**A. Directions:** Combine the base word with the suffix for each of the following items, and provide the correct spelling in the answer column. **References:** ¶¶701–709. See Appendix D for the definition of any grammatical terms that you may not be familiar with.

| | | | | | | | |
|---|---|---|---|---|---|---|---|
| 1. | ship + ing | **shipping** | 701 | 11. | cheer + ful | **cheerful** | 705 |
| 2. | mad + en | **madden** | 701 | 12. | equip + ment | **equipment** | 705 |
| 3. | control + ing | **controlling** | 702 | 13. | trust + worthy | **trustworthy** | 706 |
| 4. | occur + ed | **occurred** | 702 | 14. | move + able | **movable** | 707a |
| 5. | prefer + ence | **preference** | 702 | 15. | mile + age | **mileage** | 707a |
| 6. | ship + ment | **shipment** | 703 | 16. | ice + y | **icy** | 707b |
| 7. | mad + ness | **madness** | 703 | 17. | manage + able | **manageable** | 707c |
| 8. | cancel + ing | **canceling** | 704 | 18. | like + ly | **likely** | 708 |
| 9. | total + ed | **totaled** | 704 | 19. | nine + th | **ninth** | 708 |
| 10. | program + ing | **programming** | 704 | 20. | lie + ing | **lying** | 709 |

**B. Directions:** Circle all spelling errors and write the correct forms in the answer column. If a sentence is correct as given, write *C* in the answer column. **References:** ¶¶701–709.

| | | | |
|---|---|---|---|
| 21. | The number of students cutting classes is (begining) to decrease. | 21. **beginning** | 701 702 |
| 22. | Swimming at the beach is (forbiden) when lifeguards are not present. | 22. **forbidden** | 701 702 |
| 23. | The shipment of relief supplies was (cancelled) without any explanation. | 23. **canceled** | 703 704 |
| 24. | The (uncloging) of traffic on Route 101 has benefited all commuters. | 24. **unclogging** | 702 704 |
| 25. | Eyewitnesses (differed) in their accounts of how the accident occurred. | 25. **differed** | 702 704 |
| 26. | Has anyone profited from the (biassed) reporting about the election? | 26. **biased** | 704 705 |
| 27. | Todd and Jeff are (argueing) about whose car gets better mileage. | 27. **arguing** | 707a |
| 28. | Finding knowledgeable workers in this field is not (easey). | 28. **easy** | 707b 707c |
| 29. | Good management requires excellent judgment. | 29. **C** | 708 |
| 30. | I said that Eve was dyeing her shoes; I did not say that she was (dieing). | 30. **dying** | 707a 709 |

**C. Directions:** If any of the following words are misspelled, write the correct spellings in the answer column. If a word is correct as given, write *C* in the answer column. **References:** Consult the rules shown below.

| | | | | | | | |
|---|---|---|---|---|---|---|---|
| 31. | worryed | **worried** | 710a | 36. | weird | **C** | 712 |
| 32. | shyly | **C** | 710a | 37. | recieve | **receive** | 712 |
| 33. | delayed | **C** | 711 | 38. | thier | **their** | 712 |
| 34. | sayed | **said** | 711 | 39. | probible | **probable** | 713a |
| 35. | beleif | **belief** | 712 | 40. | possable | **possible** | 713b |

Name _____ Date _____ Class _____ 31

| | | | | | | | |
|---|---|---|---|---|---|---|---|
| **41.** | persistant | **persistent** | 714 | **46.** | advertize | **advertise** | 715b |
| **42.** | resistant | **C** | 714 | **47.** | analise | **analyze** | 715c |
| **43.** | assistence | **assistance** | 714 | **48.** | supercede | **supersede** | 716a |
| **44.** | relevance | **C** | 714 | **49.** | procede | **proceed** | 716b |
| **45.** | realise | **realize** | 715a | **50.** | precede | **C** | 716c |

**D. Directions:** Circle all spelling errors and write the correct forms in the answer column. If a sentence is correct as given, write *C* in the answer column. **References:** Consult the rules shown below as you complete this exercise.

| | | | | |
|---|---|---|---|---|
| **51.** | What is the likelyhood that this fad will spread countrywide? | **51.** | **likelihood** | 710a |
| **52.** | I don't have a weight problem; I have a hieght problem. | **52.** | **height** | 712, 713b |
| **53.** | Do you think the defendent's testimony is credible? | **53.** | **defendant's** | 714 |
| **54.** | They do a better job of advertising thier merchandise than we do. | **54.** | **their** | 712, 715 |
| **55.** | You will have to concede that the existing proceedure is not working. | **55.** | **procedure** | 716b–c |

**E. Directions:** If the boldface word in each of the following items is misspelled, write the correct form in the answer column. If the item is correct as given, write *C* in the answer column. **References:** ¶720.

| | | | | | |
|---|---|---|---|---|---|
| **56.** | happy to **accomodate** you | **accommodate** | **66.** | plan an **itinery** | **itinerary** |
| **57.** | to make your **aquaintance** | **acquaintance** | **67.** | serve as the **liason** | **liaison** |
| **58.** | is **basicly** all right | **basically** | **68.** | a **momento** of the occasion | **memento** |
| **59.** | need to check the **calender** | **calendar** | **69.** | that's your **privaledge** | **privilege** |
| **60.** | falls in the second **catagory** | **category** | **70.** | order a large **quanity** | **quantity** |
| **61.** | to achieve a **concensus** | **consensus** | **71.** | maintain **seperate** accounts | **separate** |
| **62.** | wants a **definate** answer | **definite** | **72.** | find something **similiar** | **similar** |
| **63.** | **elimanate** the frills | **eliminate** | **73.** | need to regain your **strenth** | **strength** |
| **64.** | on the 14th of **Febuary** | **February** | **74.** | a drop in the **temperture** | **temperature** |
| **65.** | reach his full **heighth** | **height** | **75.** | meet every **Wensday** | **Wednesday** |

**F. Directions:** Edit the following paragraph to correct any spelling errors. Use appropriate proofreaders' marks (shown on pages 358–359 and on the inside back cover of *The Gregg Reference Manual*) to indicate your corrections. Circle any changes you make. **References:** Consult the appropriate rules in Section 7 as you complete this exercise.

```
    Whenever my wife and I discuss vacation arrangements, we often conclude
that we should plan seperate itineries. Basicly, the problem is this: she
likes cold weather and I become miserable when the tempeture drops into the
30s. I have tried to accomodate her preferrences, but we start argueing
nevertheless. Last year we agreed on a trip and then cancelled it at the last
minute. I keep thinking that it should be possable to find a vacation spot
that will satisfy both of us, but I realise that it's not going to be easy.
```

# 13 Choosing the Right Word

**A. Directions:** If the boldface word in each of the following items is misspelled or misused, write the correct form in the answer column. If an item is correct as given, write *C* in the answer column. **References:** ¶719.

| # | Item | Answer | # | Item | Answer |
|---|------|--------|---|------|--------|
| 1. | denied **excess** to the files | access | 16. | to **disperse** company funds | disburse |
| 2. | looking for good **advise** | advice | 17. | ten **discreet** groups of voters | discrete |
| 3. | worked as a health **aid** | aide | 18. | need a **disinterested** observer | C |
| 4. | found **alot** of errors | a lot | 19. | damage **dew** to moisture | due |
| 5. | your **assistants** was helpful | assistance | 20. | to **illicit** many opinions | elicit |
| 6. | more pressure than I can **bare** | bear | 21. | an **imminent** politician | eminent |
| 7. | step on the **breaks** | brakes | 22. | an unsealed **envelop** | envelope |
| 8. | take a deep **breathe** | breath | 23. | was not **phased** by the insult | fazed |
| 9. | that **can not** be true | cannot | 24. | a very courageous **feet** | feat |
| 10. | to **cease** the opportunity | seize | 25. | displayed a **flare** for writing | flair |
| 11. | choose a **cite** for the new office | site | 26. | to **flout** one's possessions | flaunt |
| 12. | a member of the town **counsel** | council | 27. | to **forego** my right to protest | forgo |
| 13. | make daily entries in a **dairy** | diary | 28. | I **formally** taught math | formerly |
| 14. | will not tolerate any **descent** | dissent | 29. | went **fourth** to help others | forth |
| 15. | to **differ** a decision for a week | defer | 30. | their stories do not **gibe** | jibe |

**B. Directions:** If the boldface word in each of the following items is misspelled or misused, write the correct form in the answer column. If an item is correct as given, write *C* in the answer column. **References:** ¶719.

| # | Item | Answer | # | Item | Answer |
|---|------|--------|---|------|--------|
| 31. | eat more **healthy** foods | healthful | 46. | to **pour** over the printouts | pore |
| 32. | had not **herd** the news reports | heard | 47. | make one's **presents** felt | presence |
| 33. | it's **holy** understandable | wholly | 48. | my **principle** goal in life | principal |
| 34. | marched down the **isle** | aisle | 49. | is **quiet** happy with her job | quite |
| 35. | to be **libel** for the damage | liable | 50. | a starring **roll** in the play | role |
| 36. | to be afraid of **lightening** | lightning | 51. | to find the best **root** to Denver | route |
| 37. | I'm **loathe** to take on that job | loath | 52. | to make a **seen** in public | scene |
| 38. | Sue **maybe** the one we hire | may be | 53. | uses expensive **stationary** | stationery |
| 39. | a **miner** irritation | minor | 54. | takes a different **tact** | tack |
| 40. | these bills are **overdo** | overdue | 55. | the ropes must be **taught** | taut |
| 41. | a lot of time has **past** | passed | 56. | make a **through** search | thorough |
| 42. | at the **peek** of his career | peak | 57. | worked much **to** hard | too |
| 43. | need to resist **pier** pressure | peer | 58. | applied **undo** pressure | undue |
| 44. | get at the **plane** truth | plain | 59. | to **wave** your rights | waive |
| 45. | conduct a **pole** of local voters | poll | 60. | to protect **you're** property | your |

Name _____ Date _____ Class _____ 33

**C. Directions:** Select the correct form in parentheses for each of the following sentences, and write your answer in the answer column. **References:** ¶719.

61. Should we (accede, exceed) to Pamela Butler's request for a transfer?

61. <u>accede</u>

62. If you don't like my idea, do you have an (alternate, alternative) to offer?

62. <u>alternative</u>

63. To whom should these purchases be (billed, build)?

63. <u>billed</u>

64. Helena is the (capital, capitol, Capitol) of Montana.

64. <u>capital</u>

65. We have ordered a five-(coarse, course) meal for Ms. Noriega's banquet.

65. <u>course</u>

66. I can no longer cope with Mr. Whitman's (continual, continuous) complaints.

66. <u>continual</u>

67. We need to (device, devise) a fallback plan in case this plan doesn't work.

67. <u>devise</u>

68. This problem needs to be referred to a (higher, hire) level of management.

68. <u>higher</u>

69. Pretending not to understand was very (ingenious, ingenuous) on Carl's part.

69. <u>ingenuous</u>

70. Under the circumstances it was the (leased, least) that we could do.

70. <u>least</u>

71. At this point what do we have to (loose, lose)?

71. <u>lose</u>

72. It's not a good idea to (medal, meddle) in Christopher's affairs.

72. <u>meddle</u>

73. Because of the heavy fog we (missed, mist) the turnoff to the lake.

73. <u>missed</u>

74. A doctor with a good bedside manner exhibits a lot of (patience, patients).

74. <u>patience</u>

75. There is a (perspective, prospective) buyer for our house.

75. <u>prospective</u>

76. What is the best way for us to (precede, proceed)?

76. <u>proceed</u>

77. Harry's requests must take (precedence, precedents) over everyone else's.

77. <u>precedence</u>

78. The predictions of (profits, prophets) are often disregarded by their contemporaries.

78. <u>prophets</u>

79. The Friday afternoon meetings are always a (waist, waste) of time.

79. <u>waste</u>

80. Eating two boxes of cookies at one sitting is not a good (way, weigh) to diet.

80. <u>way</u>

**D. Directions:** Edit the following paragraph to correct any errors in spelling and usage. Use appropriate proofreaders' marks (shown on pages 358–359 and on the inside back cover of *The Gregg Reference Manual*) to indicate your corrections. Circle any changes you make. **References:** ¶719.

```
If my friend Tom could be more discreet and use more tact in his dealings      1
with people, he would be more popular with his colleagues at work. I've tried   2
to give him a lot of advise along these lines, but Tom says that he cannot      3
bare to listen to me any longer. I think he's lost patience with me, and I'm    4
sure that he is reluctant to get some perspective on the way he appears to      5
other people. It maybe true that I have come on too strong in the past.         6
However, I believe that Tom is loathe to change his behavior. In fact, I        7
suspect that he is actually quiet satisfied with things as they are.            8
```

# 14 Compound Words

**A. Directions:** If a boldface item in the following list should be written as a solid word, insert the "delete space" mark (for example, **by law**). If a boldface item should be hyphenated, use the "insert hyphen" mark (for example, **mix up**). If a boldface item should be written as separate words, use the "insert space" mark (for example, **crackdown**). Circle any changes you make. If an item is correct as given, write C in the answer column. **References:** ¶¶801–808.

| | | | | | | |
|---|---|---|---|---|---|---|
| 1. | in a spirit of **good will** | | 801a | 11. | when negotiations **breakdown** | 802 / 803b |
| 2. | need to use some **good sense** | C | 801a | 12. | need to **check in** by 6 o'clock | C / 802 803c |
| 3. | time to say **good-bye** | | 801a | 13. | and watch sales **takeoff** | 802 803f |
| 4. | cut down on the **paper work** | | 801a | 14. | to **takeover** the company | 802 803g |
| 5. | who invented the **paper clip** | C | 801a | 15. | engaged in a **free for all** | 804a |
| 6. | to **follow up** on his progress | C | 802 | 16. | get down to the **nitty gritty** | 804b |
| 7. | do a **follow up** on his memo | | 802 | 17. | ask the **editor in chief** | C / 804c |
| 8. | we need to get a **go ahead** | | 802 | 18. | good at **problem solving** | C / 805a |
| 9. | can we now **go ahead** | C | 802 | 19. | had to go for an **X ray** | 807 |
| 10. | cannot **makeup** their minds | | 802 / 803a | 20. | write to a **vice president** | C / 808c |

**B. Directions:** If any of the following expressions are considered unacceptable, write an appropriate alternative in the answer column. If an expression is acceptable, write C in the answer column. **References:** Consult the rules shown below as you complete this exercise.

| | | | | | | | |
|---|---|---|---|---|---|---|---|
| 21. | layman | **layperson*** | 809a | 26. | Chairman Paul Foy | C | 809d |
| 22. | salesmen | **salespeople** | 809a | 27. | woman doctor | **doctor** | 810 |
| 23. | mankind | **people** | 809a | 28. | stewardess | **flight attendant** | 840a |
| 24. | workmen's comp | **workers' comp** | 809a | 29. | authoress | **author** | 840a |
| 25. | workmanship | C | 809c | 30. | heroine | C | 840a |

***Other answers may be acceptable for items 21–30. See ¶¶809–810, 840.**

**C. Directions:** Edit the boldface element in each of the following items to correct any misspellings. Use appropriate revision marks to indicate your corrections. Circle any changes you make. If an item is correct as given, write C in the answer column. **References:** ¶¶811–812.

| | | | | | | | |
|---|---|---|---|---|---|---|---|
| 31. | to **high light** the key points | | 811a | 36. | to **double space** the report | | 811a |
| 32. | to **baby sit** for a neighbor | | 811a | 37. | to leave a **double space** | C | 812a |
| 33. | to **short change** a customer | | 811a | 38. | an **air conditioned** house | | 812a |
| 34. | to **spot check** the answers | | 811a | 39. | **air conditioning** is essential | C | 812a |
| 35. | **spot checking** the price list | | 812a | 40. | **air conditioning** my bedroom | | 812a |

Name _____  Date _____  Class _____  35

B-46

**D. Directions:** Edit the boldface element in each of the following sentences to correct any misspellings. Use appropriate proofreaders' marks to indicate your corrections. Circle any changes you make. If a sentence is correct as given, write *C* in the answer column. **References:** Consult the rules shown below as you complete this exercise.

41. A **well known** consultant will be helping us develop our **long range** plans.  
41. _____ 813 / 814 / 814

42. I know that this is **high tech** equipment, but is it really **up to date?**  
42. _____ 813

43. Everything said at this **high level** conference is **off the record.**  
43. _____ 815a

44. Even though these goods are **high priced,** they are **tax exempt.**  
44. _____ 815b

45. I'm enrolled in an **all day** program, so I can work only **part time.**  
45. _____ 816a

46. I'm getting hit with a **7.5 percent** increase on my **$400 a month** apartment.  
46. _____ 817a / 817a

47. I've requested a **three month** extension for the filing of my **income tax** return.  
47. _____ 818a / 818a

48. Jack Egan is now an important **real estate** agent with **Park Avenue** clients.  
48. **C** 819a / 818a

49. Pam runs a **mail order** business targeted at **African American** women.  
49. _____ 818d / 820a

50. Phone us **toll free** if you want to take advantage of our **store wide** sale.  
50. _____ 820c / 820c

51. This raincoat is not really **water proof** but it is **water repellent.**  
51. _____ 820a / 821b

52. The level of our **health care related** costs is truly **mind boggling.**  
52. _____ 821a / 822a

53. Under a **long standing** agreement, they send us the **best qualified** people.  
53. _____ 822b / 822a

54. Your dog may be **friendly looking,** but his effect on me was **hair raising.**  
54. _____ 821a / 823a

55. No one would ever accuse our **long winded** speaker of being **close mouthed.**  
55. _____ 823c / 824b

56. The next speaker is **well known** for his **highly focused** presentations.  
56. **C** 824a / 825a

57. Her speech was a **very trying** experience, because it lacked a **clear cut** focus.  
57. _____ 824b

58. Perhaps their demands will be **scaled down** during this **cooling off** period.  
58. _____ 826 / 827d

59. We get **red hot** results by using **tried and true** techniques.  
59. _____ 827b

60. I like Bob's **can do** spirit, but I'm taking a **wait and see** approach.  
60. _____ 828a / 829a

61. I just got a **get well** card from my **ten year old** nephew.  
61. _____ 831a / 831a

62. This **up to date** procedure is actually more **time consuming** than the old one.  
62. _____ 821d

63. Fill out a **change of address** form if this information is not **up to date.**  
63. _____ 831a / 831b

64. A **trial and error** approach won't work; it's time for a **go/no go** decision.  
64. _____ 831d / 832a

65. Use **8½ by 11 inch** paper, and type it **single or double spaced.**  
65. _____ 812a

**E. Directions:** Edit the following paragraph to correct any errors with compound words. Use appropriate proofreaders' marks to indicate your corrections, and circle any changes you make. **References:** ¶¶801–832.

```
    I just heard about Sam Perez's accident. I'm glad you sent him out for          1
 x-rays. If you handle the medical paper work, I'll follow up with the woman       2
 doctor at our clinic. Sam's in for some high priced treatment, but I'm sure       3
 his injury will be covered by workmen's comp. In the meantime, try to get a       4
 part time replacement for Sam for at least a three to four week period. I         5
 will send out a company wide memo telling the staff about Sam's accident and      6
 asking them to start picking out get well cards.                                  7
```

# 15 Using the Hyphen in Compounds and Word Division

**A. Directions:** For each of the following items combine the elements to form a word, and write the properly spelled word in the answer column. Use hyphens as necessary. **References:** Consult the rules shown below as you complete this exercise. See Appendix D for the definition of any grammatical terms that you may not be familiar with.

| | | | | | | | |
|---|---|---|---|---|---|---|---|
| 1. | audio + visual | audiovisual | 833a | 11. | co + operate | cooperate | 835b |
| 2. | multi + purpose | multipurpose | 833a | 12. | co + owner | co-owner | 835b |
| 3. | non + discriminatory | nondiscriminatory | 833a | 13. | re + elect | reelect | 835a |
| 4. | non + civil service | non-civil service | 833c | 14. | pre + eminent | preeminent | 835a |
| 5. | mid + afternoon | midafternoon | 833a | 15. | self + evident | self-evident | 836a |
| 6. | mid + thirties | mid-thirties | 833a 844 | 16. | self + less | selfless | 836b |
| 7. | mid + March | mid-March | 838 844 | 17. | three + fold | threefold | 833a |
| 8. | anti + theft | antitheft | 833a | 18. | thirty + ish | thirtyish | 833a |
| 9. | anti + inflationary | anti-inflationary | 834 | 19. | senator + elect | senator-elect | 808b |
| 10. | anti + American | anti-American | 838 | 20. | ex + husband | ex-husband | 808b |

**B. Directions:** Edit the boldface elements in each of the following sentences to correct any spelling errors. Use appropriate proofreaders' marks (shown on pages 358–359 and on the inside back cover of *The Gregg Reference Manual*) to indicate your corrections. Circle any changes you make. If a sentence is correct as given, write *C* in the answer column. **References:** Consult the rules shown below as you complete this exercise.

21. This is a specially designed **pre/test** for **pre-high/school** students.　　21. _____ 833a 833c
22. Everyone should bring an **extra warm** sweater for **him or herself.**　　22. _____ 833a 836c 836a
23. Our clinic offers **self help** programs for **over and under weight** people.　　23. _____ 832d 833 837
24. We can't decide whether to **release** our apartment or buy a **coop.**　　24. _____ 835b 837
25. Please **resign** the contracts and return them in the **self addressed** envelope.　　25. _____ 836a

**C. Directions:** In each of the following items the diagonal indicates where the item has been divided at the end of a line. In the answer column provide the number of the rule that explains why each word or phrase *should not* be divided in this way. **References:** ¶¶901–906 for items 26–35; ¶¶907–918 for items 36–45; ¶¶919–922 for items 46–55.

| | | | | | | | | | | |
|---|---|---|---|---|---|---|---|---|---|---|
| 26. | ship-/ ped | 902 | 36. | 85,-/ 000 | 915 | 46. | pas-/ sing | 922a | | |
| 27. | stra-/ ight | OR 901c 902 | 37. | self-as-/ surance | 908 | 47. | beginn-/ ing | 922b | | |
| 28. | AM-/ VETS | 905 | 38. | hidea-/ way | 907 | 48. | mill-/ ion | 922c | | |
| 29. | are-/ n't | 906 | 39. | oper-/ ator | 913 | 49. | Mrs./ Sanchez | 919 | | |
| 30. | a-/ cross | 903a | 40. | radia-/ tor | 914 | 50. | May/ 21, 2007 | 920a | | |
| 31. | tho-/ ugh | OR 901c 902 | 41. | su-/ pernatural | 909 | 51. | page/ 42 | 919 | | |
| 32. | chew-/ y | 903a | 42. | responsi-/ ble | 910 | 52. | Ellen/ T. Mann | 920d | | |
| 33. | let-/ up | 904 | 43. | hope-/ lessness | 911 | 53. | 415/ Grove Street | 920b | | |
| 34. | pres-/ sed | 902 | 44. | undercur-/ rent | 912 | 54. | three people/—Jay, | 920k | | |
| 35. | stere-/ o | 903a | 45. | read-/ dress | 912 | 55. | as follows: (1)/ the | 920j | | |

Name _____　　Date _____　　Class _____　　37

**D. Directions:** Rewrite the following sentences to correct all spelling errors and to remove all sexist expressions. **References:** Consult the rules shown below as you complete this exercise.

56. Please send an inter-office memo to all the salesmen, setting the date when they'll be asked to run-through their sales presentations. **Please send an interoffice memo to all the sales representatives, setting the date when they'll be asked to run through their sales presentations.**

833a
809a
802

57. The woman lawyer who is representing my father in law has asked him to pin-point any discrepancies in the statements of the eye witnesses. **The lawyer who is representing my father-in-law has asked him to pinpoint any discrepancies in the statements of the eyewitnesses.**

810
804c
811a
801a

58. Marilyn is the co-author of a number of 60 to 90 hour self study courses designed for businessmen who want to expand their operations. **Marilyn is the coauthor of a number of 60- to 90-hour self-study courses designed for business owners who want to expand their operations.**

835b
832b
836a
809a

59. Please follow-up on the progress made by the newly-hired employees who recently completed our on the job training program. **Please follow up on the progress made by the newly hired employees who recently completed our on-the-job training program.**

802
824a
831a

60. Please ask Ms. Washington to turnover all of the up to date production reports to George Gangi, our new vice-president. **Please ask Ms. Washington to turn over all of the up-to-date production reports to George Gangi, our new vice president.**

802
831a
808c

**E. Directions:** Edit the following paragraph to correct any errors involving compound words and division of word groups. Use appropriate proofreaders' marks to indicate your corrections, and circle any changes you make. **References:** Consult the appropriate rules in Sections 8 and 9 as you complete this exercise.

```
Janice Darden and I are coowners of a small publishing company that      1
specializes in self-help books for people like you and me--in other words,  2
the typical layman. We'd like to sign up a well-known authoress named Fay    3
V. Fox. She's writing a book that tells people how to prepare their own      4
income tax returns and avoid the annual attack of mid-April blues. Janice    5
thinks we'll have no trouble getting a go-ahead from Fay's agent, but        6
I feel she's being overconfident. The agent has sent us a list of demands,   7
many of which we can't agree to. When we meet with the agent on October      8
23, I'm afraid our contract negotiations will quickly breakdown.             9
```

B-49

**A. Directions:** Rewrite the following sentences to correct all errors relating to abbreviations, plurals, possessives, spelling, and compound words. **References:** Consult the appropriate rules in Sections 5–8 as you complete this exercise.

1. Pt. Two (p. 94-162) analises the long term consequences of the environmental legislation past by Congress last year.

   **Part Two (pp. 94–162) [OR (pages 94–162)] analyzes the long-term consequences of the**    502e
   621a
   **environmental legislation passed by Congress last year.**    715c
   816a
   719

2. We are having a store wide sale during the month of Febuary in all of our branchs across the U.S.— with special discounts on womens' clothing.

   **We are having a storewide sale during the month of February in all of our branches across**    820c
   720
   **the United States—with special discounts on women's clothing.**    602
   525
   633

3. Please enclose a self addressed envelop if you would like to recieve copys of Dr. Ross' speeches at this years' AMA convention.

   **Please enclose a self-addressed envelope if you would like to receive copies of Dr. Ross's**    836a
   720
   **speeches at this year's AMA convention.**    604
   631a–b
   632b

4. The temperture in Washington, D. C., last winter never went below the '30s, according to our real-estate agent, Mrs. Galsworthy's letter.

   **The temperature in Washington, D.C., last winter never went below the 30s, according to the**    720
   508
   527b
   **letter from our real estate agent, Mrs. Galsworthy.**    624a
   818a
   641

5. P.V. Hunsinger is well-known for her analysises of various poles designed to measure consumer's confidence in the economy.

   **P. V. Hunsinger is well known for her analyses of various polls designed to measure consumers'**    516a
   824b
   **confidence in the economy.**    614
   719
   632b

6. The company's attornies have advised our C.E.O. to take a wait and see attitude until the Supreme Court hands down it's judgement in the Sampson case.

**The company's attorneys have advised our CEO to take a wait-and-see attitude until the** _____    605
   541
   828a
**Supreme Court hands down its judgment in the Sampson case.** _____    636
   708
   720

7. On the basis of faxs from our salesmen in the field, this year's orders for our line of stationary products are not likely to excede last year.

**On the basis of faxes from our sales representatives [OR salespeople] in the field, this year's** _____    602
   809a
**orders for our line of stationery products are not likely to exceed last year's.** _____    719
   716b
   644

8. From a long range prospective there maybe to many PhD's graduating over the next ten years and not alot of job opportunitys opening up for them.

**From a long-range perspective there may be too many Ph.D.s graduating over the next ten** _____    814
   719
**years and not a lot of job opportunities opening up for them.** _____    519a
   622
   604

9. Please set-up an all day meeting to discuss ways to elemenate several million dollars worth of expenses incurred by our agencys in Chicago and Saint Louis.

**Please set up an all-day meeting to discuss ways to eliminate several million dollars' worth** _____    802
   816a
   720
**of expenses incurred by our agencies in Chicago and St. Louis.** _____    646
   604
   529b

10. There is only one clear cut criteria for success in this business: how well you accomodate your customer's preferrences, no matter what they maybe.

**There is only one clear-cut criterion for success in this business: how well you accommodate** _____    824b
   614
   720
**your customers' preferences, no matter what they may be.** _____    632b
   702
   719

     B-51

# Editing Survey B (Continued)

**B. Directions:** Edit the following paragraphs to correct all errors. Use appropriate proofreaders' marks (shown on pages 358–359 and on the inside back cover of *The Gregg Reference Manual*) to indicate your corrections. Circle any changes you make. **References:** Consult the appropriate rules in Sections 1–8 as you complete this exercise.

~~123a/126a~~

I don't have answers to all the problems that one faces but        1

I can tell you about a technique that can get you through some        2

of life's difficult moments. I learned this technique from a        3

brief anecdote that appeared in the *Reader's Digest* a number        4    *289a*

of years ago.        5    *122/131a*

A woman who was traveling to see her grandchildren found        6

herself stranded at O'Hare Airport in Chicago because of bad        7

weather. All flights had been cancelled since mid-afternoon,        8    *704*   *833a*

and hundreds of unhappy travelers were waiting all over the air-        9    *423/624b*  *309a/331*

port. Every seat had been taken. Travelers were now sitting        10

and lying on the floor, all suffering that terrible frustration        11

that comes from not being able to control one's situation.        12

Nearby was a young mother with a five-year-old child squirming        13

in her lap, whining and whimpering and being altogether impos-        14

sible. The mother was a model of saintly patience. She simply        15

crooned, "There, there, Nancy. It's going to be all right. In a        16

little while you'll be home. You'll have a nice bath and then        17

put on a fresh nightgown and slip into bed for a good nights        18    *630a/632b*

sleep." Over and over she crooned, "There, there, Nancy."        19

About 7 PM the weather started to clear. The grandmother        20    *p.m.*  *533*

heard the boarding announcement for her plane. As she was about        21

to leave the area she felt the impulse to speak to the young        22    *124/130a*

mother. "I want to tell you," she said, "that I think you are        23

the most wonderful mother I have ever seen. Your patience is        24

remarkable. I love the way you talk to your daughter Nancy."        25

The mother looked up with surprise. "Oh," she said, "her        26

name is Emily. My name is Nancy."        27

28

Name _____ Date _____ Class _____        41

**C. Directions:** Edit the following paragraphs to correct all errors. Use appropriate proofreaders' marks to indicate your corrections. Circle any changes you make. **References:** Consult the appropriate rules in Sections 1–9 as you complete this exercise.

|  |  |
|---|---|
| According to one disgruntled author, editors winnow out the | 1 |
| wheat from the chaff and publish the chaff. Perhaps the reason | 2 |
| that editors are so often disliked is that they so often speak with | 3 |
| a sharp tongue. Doctor Samuel Johnson, the great 18th-century | 4 |
| author and critic, offered this comment on a writer's manuscript: | 5 |
| "What you have written is both good and original. Unfortunately, | 6 |
| the parts that are good are not original, and the parts that are | 7 |
| original are not good." Charles Dickens also possessed a sharp | 8 |
| tongue. After reviewing an unpublished collection of poems en- | 9 |
| titled "Orient Pearls at Random Strung," he gave the following | 10 |
| verdict: "Too much string." | 11 |
| Is it possible that some children are destined to become | 12 |
| editors from an early age? It certainly seems that way with | 13 |
| our's. When our son Christopher was four, he announced that | 14 |
| Alpha-Bits was his favorite cereal. He said that he liked it | 15 |
| because the cereal was "made out of letters." Kate, his six- | 16 |
| year-old sister, corrected him. "No, Chris," she said, "it's | 17 |
| the cereal that's made *into* letters." He punched her, re- | 18 |
| vealing that the instinct to strike back at one's editor starts | 19 |
| early. | 20 |
| The editorial tradition in our family seems to be con- | 21 |
| tinuing into the next generation. Our son John was preparing | 22 |
| breakfast for his three-year-old daughter. As he started to | 23 |
| spread jam on her toast, he realized that she wanted to be- | 24 |
| come more directly involved in the process. He said, "do | 25 |
| you want to put the jam on yourself?" "No, Daddy," she re- | 26 |
| plied. "I want to put it on the toast." | 27 |
| I'm afraid that you cannot change editors, that's just the | 28 |
| way they are. | 29 |

# 17

# Grammar: Subjects and Verbs

**A. Directions:** First review how the principal parts of regular and irregular verbs are formed (see ¶1030 and ¶1035). Then, for each boldface verb in the following sentences, write the specified tense of the verb in the answer column. **References:** Consult the rules shown below as you complete the exercise. See Appendix D for the definition of any grammatical terms that you may not be familiar with.

1. **Present tense:** Alan always **do** an excellent job of summarizing our discussions.

   1. does    1031b / 1035b

2. **Future tense:** Natalie **finish** the statistical analysis that you started.

   2. will finish    1031c

3. **Past tense:** Mr. Porter **go** to Chicago last week to meet with his lawyers.

   3. went    1032a / 1030b

4. **Present perfect tense:** I **have see** the review of your new book on telecommunications.

   4. have seen    1033a / 1030b

5. **Present progressive tense:** We **are issue** new directives to our staff this week.

   5. are issuing    1034a / 1030a

6. **Past progressive tense:** Jan **was cancel** her credit cards all during the week.

   6. was canceling    1034b / 1030a

7. **Present perfect progressive tense:** Our sales **have been slip** continually.

   7. have been slipping    1034d / 1030a

8. **Present passive tense:** I **am expect** to do the work of two people.

   8. am expected    1036 / 1030a

9. **Past passive tense:** Charlie **was choose** to head the Eastern Region's sales staff.

   9. was chosen    1036 / 1030b

10. **Present perfect passive tense:** They **have been transfer** to the Boston office.

    10. have been transferred    1036 / 1030a

**B. Directions:** If any of the boldface verbs are incorrectly used in the following sentences, write the correct form in the answer column. If a sentence is correct as given, write *C* in the answer column. **References:** ¶¶1030–1033.

11. **Past tense:** I liked the movie *Burnt by the Sun* so much that I **seen** it four times.

    11. saw    1032b / 1030b

12. **Past tense:** Christopher **done** the whole report without any help from others on staff.

    12. did    1032b / 1030b

13. **Past tense:** Timothy **brung** me the news about your graduating with honors.

    13. brought    1032b

14. **Past tense:** We **begun** the board meeting without waiting for Mrs. Farragut.

    14. began    1032b

Name _____ Date _____ Class _____ 43

15. **Past tense:** This sweatshirt **shrank** about two sizes after only one washing.

16. **Present perfect tense:** The temperature **has rose** to 90°F every day this week.

17. **Present perfect tense:** My neighbor, John Forest, **has broke** my lawn mower for the last time.

18. **Present perfect tense:** I **have wrote** only two job application letters so far this month.

| | | |
|---|---|---|
| 15. | C | 1032b |
| 16. | has risen | 1033 |
| 17. | has broken | 1033 |
| 18. | have written | 1033 1030b |

**C. Directions:** The subject of an independent or dependent clause appears in boldface in each of the following sentences. Select the correct verb form in parentheses, and write your answer in the answer column. **References:** Consult the rules shown below as you complete this exercise.

19. It is essential that these **orders** (are, be) shipped by the end of the week.

20. It is urgent that **Molly** (prepare, prepares) a revised draft of the report.

21. I wish **I** (was, were) more at ease during my weekly meetings with Mrs. Hennessey.

22. If **I** (was, were) better coordinated, I would take up cross-country skiing.

23. If **I** (had, would have) been asked to speak, I would have gladly done so.

24. Phil acts as if **he** (was, were) the greatest computer programmer in the world.

25. Sarah said that **she** (is, was) planning to return to college this fall.

| | | |
|---|---|---|
| 19. | be | 1038a |
| 20. | prepare | 1038b |
| 21. | were | 1039a |
| 22. | were | 1040 |
| 23. | had | 1040 |
| 24. | were | 1042 |
| 25. | was | 1047 |

**D. Directions:** The subject of an independent or dependent clause appears in boldface in each of the following sentences. Select the verb form in parentheses that agrees with the boldface subject, and write your answer in the answer column. **References:** Consult the rules shown below as you complete this exercise.

26. **I** (am, is) the only person who can manage to get along with clients like Mr. Henderson.

27. Only **you** (has, have) the full confidence of all the members of the board.

28. **Jennifer Waterman** (doesn't, don't) handle incoming calls as well as she should.

29. **We** (was, were) quite disappointed by the company's performance last year.

| | | |
|---|---|---|
| 26. | am | 1001a |
| 27. | have | 1001a |
| 28. | doesn't | 1001a |
| 29. | were | 1001a |

44

# Grammar: Subjects and Verbs (Continued)

30. **They** (has, have) been devising a new organization for the entire company.

30. have        1001a

31. **Tom and Greg** (is, are) going to attend the conference in London with me.

31. are        1002a

32. Every **car, van, and truck** (is, are) on sale during the next two weeks.

32. is        1002c

33. **Either Helen or her mother** (has, have) walked off with the keys to my condo.

33. has        1003

34. **Neither Ms. Welling nor the Silbers** (is, are) planning to attend the reception.

34. are        1005

35. The **invoice** for these laptop computers (contains, contain) many errors.

35. contains        1006a

36. The **CEO,** along with his top managers, (is, are) leaving for Tokyo tomorrow.

36. is        1006a 1007

37. **One** of the photocopiers (is, are) going to be taken out of service again.

37. is        1008a

38. Each **strategy** that you have proposed (has, have) to be carefully evaluated.

38. has        1009a

39. **Everybody** in the audience (seems, seem) enthusiastic about the performance.

39. seems        1010

40. **Many** of us (was, were) not asked to provide our reactions to the new ad campaign.

40. were        1012

**E. Directions:** The subject of an independent or dependent clause appears in boldface in each of the following sentences. Select the correct verb form in parentheses, and write your answer in the answer column. **References:** Consult the rules shown below as you complete this exercise.

41. **All** of the proceeds from this campaign (is, are) being donated to the United Way.

41. are        1013a

42. **None** of the applicants (was, were) hired for this job opening. *(General usage)*

42. were        1013b

43. The **criteria** (has, have) been revised by the executive compensation committee.

43. have        1018a 614

44. The **jury** (has, have) finally agreed on a verdict.

44. has        1019a

45. **A number** of employees (has, have) signed up for the grammar seminar.

45. have        1023

Name _____ Date _____ Class _____    45

46. **The number** of employees who signed up (was, were) not as large as I had hoped.

46. <u>was</u>      1023

47. **Two-thirds** of the community (supports, support) the plan to build a new high school.

47. <u>supports</u>    1025a

48. **Two-thirds** of the voters (supports, support) the plan to build a new high school.

48. <u>support</u>    1025b

49. What actions (am, are) **I** supposed to take on the basis of Jim Farley's memo?

49. <u>am</u>    1027a

50. Before we can make a decision, there (is, are) many **factors** that need to be weighed.

50. <u>are</u>    1028a

**F. Directions:** Edit the following paragraph to correct any errors. Use appropriate proofreaders' marks (shown on pages 358–359 and on the inside back cover of *The Gregg Reference Manual*) to indicate your corrections. Circle any changes you make. **References:** Consult the appropriate rules in ¶¶1001–1047 as you complete this exercise.

```
                                                                 1
     I wish I was a better athlete. Unfortunately, my body
                                                                 2
don't respond extremely well to the directions issued by my
                                                                 3
brain.  My problems started early. I crashed my tricycle into a
                                                                 4
car, and my collarbone was broke as a result. I done the same
                                                                 5
thing to my collarbone the following year. My roller skates
                                                                 6
came apart as I began to go down a slight incline. One of my
                                                                 7
friends have reminded me of the time when I, along with some
                                                                 8
classmates, were cutting through a gas station on a bicycle. On
                                                                 9
that occasion I flew headfirst over the handlebars into an ele-
                                                                10
gant pyramid of oilcans. There is probably some extremely good
                                                                11
explanations for my lack of coordination, but none of those
                                                                12
explanations interest me. A number of my neighbors has tried
                                                                13
to get me to go jogging with them, but I always respond with the
                                                                14
words of Robert Maynard Hutchins: "Whenever I feel like exercise,
                                                                15
I lie down until the feeling passes."
```

Edits marked: line 1 "was" → **were** 1039a; line 2 "don't" → **doesn't** 1030b/1031b/1001a/1035b; line 4 "broke" → **en** 1036/1033, "done" → **did** 1032b/1030b; line 6 insert **a** 1032b; line 7 "have" → **has** 1008a; line 8 "were" → **was** 1006a/1007; line 10 "is" → **are** 1028a; line 12 "interest" → **s** 1013b, "has" → **have** 1023

# 18 Grammar: Pronouns

**A. Directions:** In the answer column write the correct pronouns for the boldface words in the following sentences. If a sentence is correct as given, write *C* in the answer column. **References:** Consult the rules shown below as you complete this exercise. See Appendix D for the definition of any grammatical terms that you may not be familiar with.

1. **Subject:** Betty and **me** can make all the necessary arrangements ourselves.

   1. I _____ 1054a

2. **Subject:** I thought that Bob and **her** did an especially nice job on the annual report.

   2. she _____ 1054a

3. **Subject:** The Boyles and **us** have theater tickets for this Saturday night.

   3. we _____ 1054a

4. **Subject:** The Pavlicks and **them** can't seem to agree on the terms of the contract.

   4. they _____ 1054a

5. **Direct object:** They have invited Mr. Worthington and **I** to the reception for the new CEO.

   5. me _____ 1055a

6. **Indirect object:** We sent the Rossis and **they** bouquets from our garden.

   6. them _____ 1055a

7. **Object of preposition:** This matter concerns no one except you and **I**.

   7. me _____ 1055b

8. **Subject of infinitive:** Jane asked Frank and **I** to keep her decision a secret.

   8. me _____ 1055c

9. **Possessive:** I thought that this copy of the long-range plan was **her's**.

   9. hers _____ 1056c

10. **Possessive:** Did you think that this copy of the long-range plan was really **yours'**?

    10. yours _____ 1056c

11. **Possessive:** The corporation was not very happy about **us** talking to the reporters.

    11. our _____ 1056d

12. **Possessive:** Our company would like **it's** employees to participate in the drive.

    12. its _____ 1056e

13. **Following** *than:* Mary Lee can speak Spanish much more fluently than **me**.

    13. I _____ 1057

14. **Following** *as:* I have never been able to cope with these crises as well as **her**.

    14. she _____ 1057

15. **Compound personal pronoun:** Cynthia and **myself** drafted the memo to Ms. Ruby.

    15. I _____ 1060

Name _____  Date _____  Class _____  47

B-58

**B. Directions:** The antecedent of each pronoun appears in boldface in each of the following sentences. Select the correct pronoun forms in parentheses, and write your answers in the answer column. **References:** ¶¶1049, 1054–1056.

16. **Gloria** feels that (she, her) should be allowed to set (her, hers) own hours.

16. <u>she . . . her</u>   1049a
1054
1056b

17. **I** have (my, mine) own opinion of Tim's behavior, just as **you** have (your's, yours).

17. <u>my . . . yours</u>   1049a
1056

18. **We** need to plan (our, our's) response when the **investigators** release (their, they're) report.

18. <u>our . . . their</u>   1049a
1056

19. **Rita and Fran** said (she, they) were eager to offer (her, their) services.

19. <u>they . . . their</u>   1049b
1054
1056

20. **Neither Rita nor Fran** said (she, they) wanted to offer (her, their) services.

20. <u>she . . . her</u>   1049c
1056

**C. Directions:** If any of the boldface words are incorrectly used in the following sentences, write the correct form in the answer column. If a sentence is correct as given, write *C* in the answer column. **References:** ¶1056e.

21. Do you think **its** a good idea to revise our schedule of prices and discounts?

21. <u>it's</u>

22. Every component of this computer has **it's** own design and manufacturing standards.

22. <u>its</u>

23. Do you think that the company can afford to increase **its** dividend this year?

23. <u>C</u>

24. After all, **its** your money and you can spend it in any way that you want.

24. <u>it's</u>

25. I heard that **your** moving to North Carolina later this year.

25. <u>you're</u>

26. Do you plan to sell **you're** house before you move?

26. <u>your</u>

27. I think **your** off to a great start in developing a business plan.

27. <u>you're</u>

28. **Their** buying a larger house to accommodate their rapidly growing family.

28. <u>They're</u>

29. **Theirs** no use complaining about things that can't be fixed.

29. <u>There's</u>

30. My ideas on how to cut taxes and government spending are different from **their's**.

30. <u>theirs</u>

# Grammar: Pronouns (Continued)

**D. Directions:** First read ¶¶1050–1052 carefully. Then edit the following sentences, applying the technique suggested by the rule number in each case. Use appropriate proofreaders' marks (shown on pages 358–359 and on the inside back cover of *The Gregg Reference Manual*) to indicate your corrections. Circle any changes you make. **References:** ¶¶1050–1053, 1060.

31. Every good writer of fiction has his *(or her)* own distinctive way of portraying human experience.  1052a

32. *All* ~~Every~~ good writer *(‑s)* of fiction ~~has his own~~ *(have their)* distinctive way of portraying human experience.  1052b

33. *All* ~~Every~~ parent wants *(‑s)* ~~this~~ *(their)* children to have access to the best schools and the best teachers.  1053a / 1052b

34. Neither one of the ads created the additional sales that ~~they were~~ *(it was)* supposed to.  1053a

35. If anyone does not understand this procedure, ~~you~~ *(he or she)* should speak to ~~me~~ ~~myself~~ at once.  1053d / 1060

**E. Directions:** Each item below contains two sentences. The first sentence requires you to select the correct pronoun in parentheses and write your answer in the answer column. The second sentence—in parentheses—should help you make the correct selection in each case. **References:** ¶¶1061–1063.

36. (Who/Whom) did you say was waiting to see me? (You said **she** was waiting to see me.)  36. <u>Who</u>  1061c

37. Please give this package to (whoever/whomever) asks for it at the front desk. (**She** asks for it.)  37. <u>whoever</u>  1061c

38. Mr. Fogel, (who/whom) you spoke to last week, has called again. (You spoke to **him** last week.)  38. <u>whom</u>  1061d

39. I need a financial planner (who/whom) I can rely on. (I can rely on **her.**)  39. <u>whom</u>  1061d

40. (Who/Whom) are you going to vote for? (You are going to vote for **him.**)  40. <u>Whom</u>  1061d

41. (Who's/Whose) the author of this new book on computer technology? (**He is.**)  41. <u>Who's</u>  1063

42. (Who's/Whose) umbrella is this? (This umbrella is **hers.**)  42. <u>Whose</u>  1063

Name _____  Date _____  Class _____  49

**F. Directions:** Circle the errors in the use of pronouns in the following sentences, and write the correct pronoun forms in the answer column. If a sentence is correct as given, write *C* in the answer column. **References:** ¶¶1061–1063.

43. You can give all of my business management textbooks to
    (whomever) wants them.

43. **whoever**          1061c

44. (Whom) do you think will be nominated for vice president at the
    forthcoming convention?

44. **Who**          1061c

45. (Whom) shall I say is interested in seeing the Watson property?

45. **Who**          1061c

46. (Who) did you say you ran into yesterday?

46. **Whom**          1061d

47. Whom would you like to speak with today?

47. **C**          1061d

48. She's the person (who) I want to hire as Mark Halston's replacement.

48. **whom**          1061d

49. (Who's) idea was it to double-space all the tables in this manuscript?

49. **Whose**          1063

50. Who's the main speaker at the fund-raiser you're holding on Friday
    night?

50. **C**          1063

**G. Directions:** Edit the following paragraph to correct any errors in the use of pronouns. Use appropriate proofreaders' marks to indicate your corrections. Circle any changes you make. **References:** Consult the appropriate rules in ¶¶1049–1063 as you complete this exercise.

Just between you and ⟨me⟩ 1055b I've been seeing a family therapist          1

lately. The fact is, our teenage sons and daughters are driving          2

my husband and me crazy. The therapist says that, among other          3

things, Peter and ⟨I⟩ 1054a have to establish some clear guidelines for          4

the use of our two cars. However, ⟨it's⟩ 1056e not a job that Peter and          5

⟨I⟩ 1060 look forward to. The first task will be deciding ⟨whom⟩ 1061c          6

gets to use the cars each night. The problem is this: everybody          7

thinks his ⟨or her⟩ 1052a needs for transportation always have the highest          8

priority. Then ⟨there's⟩ 1056e the question of ⟨whose⟩ 1063 going to pay for          9

gas. Gina and Kathy are willing to contribute, but neither          10

Craig nor Brad thinks it's ⟨his⟩ 1049c responsibility. I wish I could          11

get some good advice from whoever has successfully dealt with ⟨1061c⟩          12

this problem.          13

# 19

## Other Grammar Problems

**A. Directions:** Select the correct form in parentheses in each of the following sentences, and write your answer in the answer column. **References:** Consult the rules shown below as you complete this exercise. See Appendix D for the definition of any grammatical terms that you may not be familiar with.

1. We had a (real, really) nice time at the Abramowitz party on Saturday night.
2. We were hurt very (bad, badly) by the increases in oil prices in the international market.
3. We felt very (bad, badly) about the way your departure from the company was handled by the media.
4. I looked (careful, carefully) at all the statistical analyses you provided before making a decision.
5. We don't want to come (late, lately) to the reception for the Australian ambassador.
6. You need to play (fair, fairly) with all your investors and not just the heavy hitters.
7. I drive (faster, more fast) than my son (and that's much too fast).
8. I thought it was the (terriblest, most terrible) film that I had ever seen.
9. He's feeling (better, more better), now that the effects of his operation have subsided.
10. Although everyone in my family came down with the flu, my symptoms were the (baddest, worst).

| | | |
|---|---|---|
| 1. really | 1065 |
| 2. badly | 1066 |
| 3. bad | 1067 |
| 4. carefully | 1067 |
| 5. late | 1068a |
| 6. fair | 1068c |
| 7. faster | 1071a |
| 8. most terrible | 1071c |
| 9. better | 1071d–e |
| 10. worst | 1071e |

**B. Directions:** Edit the following sentences to correct the errors in grammar. Use appropriate proofreaders' marks (shown on pages 358–359 and on the inside back cover of *The Gregg Reference Manual*) to indicate your corrections. Circle any changes you make. If a sentence is correct as given, write *C* in the answer column. **References:** ¶¶1071–1073.

11. Of the two candidates, we think that Harkavy is the ~~best~~ *(better)* person for the job.
12. Of all the remedies that people suggested, yours seemed to work ~~better~~ *(best)*.
13. Of all the remedies that people suggested, yours seemed to work better than anyone else's.
14. Philadelphia is larger than any *(other)* city in the commonwealth of Pennsylvania.
15. My partner, Margaret Costanza, is more productive than anyone *(else)* in the office.
16. This month's sales in the Western Region were 22 percent higher than last month *(s)*.
17. I have *(almost saved)* $5000 for the down payment on a new pickup.

| | | |
|---|---|---|
| 11. | 1071g |
| 12. | 1071g |
| 13. C | 1071h |
| 14. | 1071h |
| 15. | 1071h |
| 16. | 1071i |
| 17. | 1072 |

Name _____ Date _____ Class _____ 51

**18.** When will the cost-benefit analyses of a new water filtration system be finished ~~up?~~   **18.** _____1073_____

**19.** Let's continue ⟨on⟩ to fund the research study on air pollution for another six months.   **19.** _____1073_____

**20.** I believe that our best strategy now is to return ~~back~~ to our core business.   **20.** _____1073_____

**C. Directions:** First read ¶¶1074–1075 carefully. Then edit the following sentences to eliminate double negatives. Use appropriate proofreaders' marks to indicate your corrections. Circle any changes you make. **References:** Consult the rules shown below as you complete this exercise.

**21.** The board members have ~~not accused~~ ⟨anyone⟩ no one on this panel of conflict of interest.   1076a

**22.** I have not been able to find ⟨anything⟩ ~~nothing~~ wrong with this spreadsheet software.   1076a

**23.** No one on the Executive Committee likes ~~neither~~ reorganization plan.   1076b

**24.** I don't have the time ⟨or⟩ ~~nor the patience to listen to Beverly Hellman's problems.~~   1076c

**25.** There is no rhyme ⟨or neither rhyme nor reason⟩ ~~nor reason to Mr. Honeycutt's new~~ compensation policy.   1076c

**D. Directions:** If any of the boldface words or phrases are incorrectly used in the following items, write the correct form in the answer column. If an item is correct as given, write *C* in the answer column. **References:** ¶¶1077–1080.

**26.** How does your new summer home in Maine compare **to** the one you used to own in New Hampshire?   **26.** with _____1077_____

**27.** I'm afraid that this copy does not correspond **with** the material I gave you.   **27.** to _____1077_____

**28.** The manager of the Reprographics Department maintains that this copy conforms **to** the original.   **28.** C _____1077_____

**29.** I've just learned that my salary increase is retroactive **from** January 1.   **29.** to _____1077_____

**30.** If you're free for lunch next Wednesday, let's plan to meet **at about** noon.   **30.** at OR about _____1078_____

**31.** If you're coming to see Ralph Featherstone, you'll find that his office is **opposite to** mine.   **31.** opposite ~~to~~ _____1078_____

**32.** If I can get a 25 percent discount, I'd be willing to order a **couple** cases.   **32.** couple of _____1079_____

**33.** You may disagree with me, but I don't like that **type** design.   **33.** type of _____1079_____

**34.** The company plans to launch this year's models with extensive ads on TV, **radio,** and in magazines.   **34.** on radio _____1079_____

**35.** As if our problems weren't already bad enough, we now have something new to worry **about.**   **35.** C _____1080_____

52

# Other Grammar Problems (Continued)

**E. Directions:** Rewrite the following sentences to correct all errors in sentence structure. **References:** Consult the rules shown below as you complete this exercise.

36. I thought your article was thought-provoking, insightful, and it was well balanced in its approach. **I thought your article was thought-provoking, insightful, and well balanced in its approach.**

    1081a

37. Ann Rowe is not only a talented writer, but she is also a skillful photographer. **Ann Rowe is not only a talented writer but also a skillful photographer.**

    1081b

38. Having now completed a review of your manuscript, some questions need to be raised. **Having now completed a review of your manuscript, I need to raise some questions.**

    1082a

39. To get more information about our products, this toll-free number should be called. **To get more information about our products, call this toll-free number.**

    1082b

40. In testing this database management program, a number of bugs were found by our staff. **In testing this database management program, our staff found a number of bugs.**

    1082c

41. If purchased by July 1, alterations will be made on these suits at no charge. **If these suits are purchased by July 1, alterations will be made at no charge. [OR . . . they will be altered at no charge.]**

    1082d

42. I saw two cars collide in the parking lot while racing for the train. **While racing for the train, I saw two cars collide in the parking lot.**

    1082
    1083

43. As the main speaker at our convention, we feel that you should focus on the issues that most concern you. **We feel that as the main speaker at our convention, you should focus on the issues that most concern you.**

    1082
    1084a

44. This memo contains some valuable advice on how to protect your computer files from our technical experts on staff. **This memo from our technical experts on staff contains some valuable advice on how to protect your computer files.**

    1082
    1086

45. A woman's wallet was reported stolen from her desk by the head of our corporate security department. **The head of our corporate security department reported that a woman's wallet was stolen from her desk.**

    1082
    1086

Name _____  Date _____  Class _____  53

**F. Directions:** Edit the following paragraph to correct any errors in grammar. Use appropriate proofreaders' marks to indicate your corrections. Circle any changes you make. **References:** Consult the appropriate rules in ¶¶1065–1088 as you complete this exercise.

```
        I'm not what you would call a decisive type ⟨of⟩1079 person. Last        1

week I thought I had found a real ⟨-ly 1065⟩ nice van. It was only two          2

years old, ⟨it was 1081a⟩ very well equipped, and it had less than 20,000 miles  3
1082/1083

on it. I spotted another van that is almost identical with the                  4

one I saw last week ⟨2⟩ while I was driving to work today. It has a    1077       5

much better sound system compared ~~to~~ ⟨with⟩ the first van, but is it          6

really ~~worth~~ the extra money? I honestly can't decide which one             7

I like ~~best~~ ⟨better⟩1071g. My brother Joe is more knowledgeable about cars    8

than anyone ⟨else⟩1071h in my family. I've asked him for advice, but I've        9

[ not heard ~~nothing~~ ⟨anything⟩1076a from him so far. I do need a new set of  10

wheels very bad ⟨-ly 1066⟩ but maybe I should wait for a few months on          11

the chance that next year's prices will be lower than this                     12

year ⟨'s 1071i⟩. Who knows?                                                      13
```

or ⟨I've heard nothing⟩

# 20 Usage

**A. Directions:** Select the correct form in parentheses in each of the following sentences, and write it in the answer column. **References:** Section 11, pages 311–332, of *The Gregg Reference Manual.* The individual entries are listed alphabetically. If you have difficulty finding an entry, consult the list at the start of Section 11 (on pages 308–310).

1. Jan has made (a, an) unreasonable request for time off this month.

2. Environmental pollution is (a, an) universal problem that affects us all.

3. Thanks (alot, allot, a lot) for your help on the Farnsworth project.

4. I (accidently, accidentally) dropped the keys to your car somewhere in the parking lot.

5. My brother Sylvester is (adverse, averse) to getting up before ten o'clock.

6. The new legislation has had little (affect, effect) on our business operations.

7. Will stricter regulations (affect, effect) the way we deal with our distributors?

8. The new CEO has (affected, effected) a big change in the number of middle management positions.

9. Christopher D'Alessandro, (age, aged) 11, is already a champion tennis player.

10. A large (amount, number) of voters turned down the proposal for a new stadium.

11. We will (appraise, apprise) you of any new developments in the hearings.

12. Marsha felt very (bad, badly) about your decision to take another job.

13. Timothy stood (beside, besides) me when I really needed advice and support.

14. The Blumenthal estate will be divided (between, among) the three grandchildren.

15. Terry (don't, doesn't) understand why I am so angry about her comments.

16. I drove a hundred miles (farther, further) yesterday than I had intended.

17. We have received (fewer, less) complaints about our service this year.

18. Frank was (indifferent, in different) to the recommendations that Joan offered him.

19. As a rule, I (lay, lie) down every afternoon for a thirty-minute nap.

20. Yesterday afternoon I (lay, laid) down and slept for more than two hours.

1. **an** _____
2. **a** _____
3. **a lot** _____
4. **accidentally** _____
5. **averse** _____
6. **effect** _____
7. **affect** _____
8. **effected** _____
9. **aged** _____
10. **number** _____
11. **apprise** _____
12. **bad** _____
13. **beside** _____
14. **among** _____
15. **doesn't** _____
16. **farther** _____
17. **fewer** _____
18. **indifferent** _____
19. **lie** _____
20. **lay** _____

Name _____ Date _____ Class _____ 55

B-66

**B. Directions:** If any of the boldface words or phrases are incorrectly used in the following items, write the correct form in the answer column. If an item is correct as given, write *C* in the answer column. **References:** Section 11, pages 311–332.

21. Do you think **a** FBI investigation is warranted in a case of this type?

22. What sort **a** tasks are involved in this software development project?

23. My partners and I have taken an **averse** view of Jefferson's invitation to join his firm.

24. We're convinced that everything will be **alright** once we get a new CEO.

25. I want to reassure you that the first draft of the quarterly report is **all most** completed.

26. Everything was supposed to be **already** to be shipped last Friday.

27. It's been **all together** too long since the four of us have gotten together.

28. We need to explore **all ways** in which we can boost our sales and profits.

29. We're very **anxious** to get started on the market research and the field tests.

30. I certainly won't do business with that wholesaler **any more.**

31. I will be glad to reschedule our meeting at **anytime** in the future.

32. You can have the office decorated and furnished **anyway** you want.

33. I will personally **assure** that the work is completed according to your specifications.

34. Samantha has decided to postpone her trip to the Middle East for **awhile.**

35. I think you **better** tone down your reply to Ed's memo.

36. Isn't it strange that the sketches done by Ron and Steve are **both alike?**

21. an _____
22. of _____
23. adverse _____
24. all right _____
25. almost _____
26. all ready _____
27. altogether _____
28. C _____
29. eager _____
30. anymore _____
31. any time _____
32. any way _____
33. ensure _____
34. a while _____
35. had better _____
36. ~~both~~ alike _____

B-67

# Usage (Continued)

37. I don't doubt **but what** she'll be promoted to executive vice president.

38. I **couldn't hardly** understand what Fred was suggesting at the board meeting.

39. A visit by the President is not an **every day** occurrence in our town.

40. The general manager notified everyone **except Val and I** about the company's plans to relocate.

41. I will not **graduate** college until I rewrite my senior thesis and have it accepted.

42. When the CEO asked you to sharpen the focus of your proposal, he wanted you to **hone** in on a competitive analysis.

43. Are you **inferring** that Marshall Estabrook lied on the witness stand?

44. Paul just flew **into** visit his parents during the Christmas holidays.

45. I'm writing **in regards to** your fax of June 2, in which you requested our proposal.

46. We have not been **indirect** contact with Helen Morrison for over a year.

47. The new process **insures** that customers will receive faster service.

48. **Irregardless** of what you think, I intend to reorganize the division.

49. My wife and I have never cared much for those **kind** of movies.

50. Who made off with the printouts that were **laying** on top of my desk?

37. that _____

38. could hardly _____

39. everyday _____

40. except Val and me _____

41. graduate from _____

42. home _____

43. implying _____

44. in to _____

45. in regard to _____

46. in direct _____

47. ensures _____

48. Regardless _____

49. kinds _____

50. lying _____

Name _____  Date _____  Class _____  57

**C. Directions:** Rewrite the following sentences to correct all errors in usage. Some (but not all) of the errors appear in boldface. **References:** Section 11, pages 311–332.

51. **Incidently,** the large (amount) of orders that came in yesterday have (all ready) been processed. _____
    **Incidentally, the large number of orders that came in yesterday have already been processed.**

52. **Additionally,** I would **appreciate** if you would write once in **awhile** to keep me (appraised) of any new developments. **In addition, I would appreciate it if you would write once in a while to keep me apprised of any new developments.**

53. I just applied to (a) HMO that is supposed to be **equally as good** as the one I currently belong to, but I have received no response, **however.** **I just applied to an HMO that is supposed to be just as good as the one I currently belong to, but I have received no response. [OR . . . belong to; I have received no response, however.]**

54. **Firstly,** you will need to demonstrate your proficiency in languages such as Japanese, Chinese, Korean, etc. **First, you will need to demonstrate your proficiency in languages such as Japanese, Chinese, and Korean.**

    _____

55. I doubt **if** the plane will take off on schedule **due to** the (averse) weather conditions at the airport. _____
    **I doubt whether the plane will take off on schedule because of the adverse weather conditions at the airport.**

56. Fran was supposed to arrive **at about** 10 o'clock. **Being that** the traffic is backed up for miles, I **doubt** (that) she will arrive before noon. **Fran was supposed to arrive at [OR about] 10 o'clock. Since the traffic is backed up for miles, I doubt whether she will arrive before noon.**

57. Between you and (I,) I was **kind of** surprised that Tim **enthused over** the architect's sketches. **Between you and me, I was rather surprised that Tim was enthusiastic about the architect's sketches.**

58. **In regards to** the **last** version of the agenda for tomorrow's meeting, I left a copy (laying) on your desk. **In regard to the latest version of the agenda for tomorrow's meeting, I left a copy lying on your desk.**

59. The attorneys are (anxious) to assure that the two companies do not sue **one another.** **The attorneys are eager to ensure that the two companies do not sue each other.**

60. Please do not schedule (anymore) meetings for me this week, **as** I am already overcommitted. **Please do not schedule any more meetings for me this week, because I am already overcommitted.**

**D. Directions:** Edit the following paragraph to correct any errors in usage. Use appropriate proofreaders' marks (shown on pages 358–359 and on the inside back cover of *The Gregg Reference Manual*) to indicate your corrections. Circle any changes you make. **References:** Section 11, pages 311–332.

```
      If our computer training program is moved to the school in Fall Brook,        1
a lot of us would be seriously affected. I would have to drive at least five         2
miles farther to school, and many students besides me would have to spend           3
all together too much time everyday traveling back and forth. Ms. Gray, the         4
program director enthused over the advantages of moving the program, but I          5
couldn't hardly understand her reasoning. I seriously doubt whether the move        6
will really take place, but I know that I'll feel very badly if it does.            7
```

was enthusiastic about

# 21

# Usage (Continued)

**A. Directions:** Select the correct form in parentheses in each of the following sentences, and write it in the answer column. **References:** Section 11, pages 332–345, of *The Gregg Reference Manual.* The individual entries are listed alphabetically. If you have difficulty finding an entry, consult the list at the start of Section 11 (on pages 308–310).

1. I was (learned, taught) by someone who is an expert in spreadsheet software.  1. **taught**
2. (Leave, Let) me see whether your notes from the conference agree with mine.  2. **Let**
3. It now looks (like, as if) the storm will last through the entire weekend.  3. **as if**
4. (Like, As) I said before, I can't get authorization to travel for the rest of the year.  4. **As**
5. (May, Can) I speak with you next week about my request for a six-month leave of absence?  5. **May**
6. What advertising (media, medium) does the most to increase your sales?  6. **medium**
7. Bret must (of, have) been the one who spread the story about the Mertzes.  7. **have**
8. Am I to believe that this Waterford pitcher just rolled (off, off of) the table by itself?  8. **off**
9. Sue was (real, really) disappointed that you couldn't be present at her party.  9. **really**
10. I'll call (someday, some day) next week to try to set up a lunch date.  10. **someday**
11. Let's meet (sometime, some time) soon to review all the alternatives we have.  11. **sometime**
12. We managed to spend (sometime, some time) together at the convention last month.  12. **some time**
13. Weren't you (supposed, suppose) to notify the media about our plans to relocate?  13. **supposed**
14. I can (sure, surely) use some good advice about which printer to buy.  14. **surely**
15. You need to take another (tack, tact) with Henry if you want him to change his mind.  15. **tack**
16. Today's performance came off much better (than, then) yesterday's.  16. **than**
17. My husband and I (used to, use to) take a two-mile walk every day.  17. **used to**
18. I'm afraid that all of us here are caught in a vicious (circle, cycle).  18. **circle**
19. It's a long (way, ways) from northern New Hampshire to southern California.  19. **way**
20. I (would have, would of) been glad to help you if only you had asked me.  20. **would have**

Name _____  Date _____  Class _____  59

**B. Directions:** If any of the boldface words or phrases are incorrectly used in the following items, write the correct form in the answer column. If an item is correct as given, write *C* in the answer column. **References:** Section 11, pages 332–345.

21. I have a nosy neighbor who claims that she can **literally** hear the grass grow.

21. ~~literally~~ OR **almost**

22. Jennifer's company **maybe** sending her to an international sales conference in Singapore.

22. **may be**

23. **Most all** our clients are self-employed, and many of them work out of their homes.

23. **Almost all** OR **Most of**

24. Please ask your guests not to drive **on to** our lawn.

24. **onto**

25. After the Butterfield case Victoria went **onto** do bigger and better things.

25. **on to**

26. Please be sure to follow **upon** Sid's progress on a regular basis.

26. **up on**

27. I look **up on** my grades for this semester as a total disaster.

27. **upon** OR **on**

28. Only a small **percent** of the voters favored the two propositions on the ballot.

28. **percentage**

29. What was the **principle** reason for our loss of market share?

29. **principal**

30. Mrs. Butterworth told me that she is **reticent** to file a complaint with the commission.

30. **reluctant**

31. Ask all visitors to **sit** their luggage down in the reception room closet.

31. **set**

32. I thought I made it clear that no one except me was to use **this here** computer.

32. **this** ~~here~~

33. The windows behind my desk look out **towards** the Washington Monument.

33. **C** (OR **toward**)

34. I think we should **try and** negotiate a better price for these supplies.

34. **try to**

35. If the sale of the Kastendorf property goes through, Joe and I will **divide up** the profits equally.

35. **divide** ~~up~~

# Usage (Continued)

**C. Directions:** Rewrite the following sentences to correct all errors in usage. Some (but not all) of the errors appear in boldface. **References:** Section 11, pages 332–345.

36. **More importantly,** you should (of) brought the problem to my attention (sometime) ago.  **More important, you should have brought the problem to my attention some time ago.**

37. The **reason** for the delay in processing telephone orders **is because** we are still not (use) to the new procedures. **The reason for the delay in processing telephone orders is that we are still not used to the new procedures.**

38. It was (sure) nice of you to (learn) me how to use **these kind** of spreadsheet applications. **It was very nice of you to teach me how to use these kinds of spreadsheet applications.**

39. **Per your request,** I will try (and) set up a luncheon with Ross Potter for (someday) next week. **As you requested, I will try to set up a luncheon with Ross Potter for some day next week.**

40. (Can) I borrow your lecture notes this weekend (like) we agreed last Wednesday? **May I borrow your lecture notes this weekend as we agreed last Wednesday?**

41. I need to catch (upon) the latest developments in the Cavatelli case, **plus** I need to report **same** to the members of the board. **I need to catch up on the latest developments in the Cavatelli case, and I need to report those developments to the members of the board.**

42. **Who ever** prepared this analysis **doesn't scarcely** understand why our company is in so much trouble profit**wise**. **Whoever prepared this analysis scarcely understands why our company is in so much trouble in terms of profit.**

43. Be **sure and** remind the staff that we must all do a better job of **servicing** our clients **then** we have in the past. **Be sure to remind the staff that we must all do a better job of serving our clients than we have in the past.**

44. If the customer's claim about scalding soup is valid, it looks (like) we are (literally) in the soup ourselves. **If the customer's claim about scalding soup is valid, it looks as if we are almost in the soup ourselves.**

45. After our stay in Chicago, we (maybe) traveling (onto) Fort Worth and Albuquerque. **After our stay in Chicago, we may be traveling on to Fort Worth and Albuquerque.**

Name _____ Date _____ Class _____  61

**D. Directions:** Edit the following paragraph to correct any errors in usage. Use appropriate proofreaders' marks (shown on pages 358–359 and on the inside back cover of *The Gregg Reference Manual*) to indicate your corrections. Circle any changes you make. **References:** Section 11, pages 332–345.

I'm not real happy about the decision to ~~leave~~ let the vice    1

president appoint who ever flatters her to a managerial    2

position. It would be more appropriate to let the entire com-    3

mittee share in this kind of decision, ~~like~~ as we have done in the    4

past. I suppose I should ~~of~~ have raised an objection at our last    5

meeting, but I guess I wasn't thinking very clearly then. I'm    6

surprised that nobody else raised any objection, because we use ed    7

to make these sort s of decisions as a group. I ~~don't~~ scarcely    8

know what action to take now, ~~plus~~ and it may be too late to over-    9

turn the vice president's action.    10

# 22 Editing Survey C

**A. Directions:** Rewrite the following sentences to correct all errors in grammar and usage. **References:** Consult the appropriate rules in Sections 10–11 as you complete this exercise.

1. Schuyler and myself use to work on the Phillips case, but one of the other lawyers have been handling it alone for sometime now.  **Schuyler and I used to work on the Phillips case, but one of the other lawyers has been handling it alone for some time now.**

    1060
    1101
    1008a

2. Phyllis *says* that she is real sorry for what she done, but if she was sorry, she would of apologized much more fast than she did.  **Phyllis *says* that she is really sorry for what she did, but if she *were* sorry, she would have apologized much faster than she did.**

    1065
    1032b
    1040
    1101
    1071a

3. None of the department managers has given Sharon and I the expense projections that we need to finish up the budget analyses.  **None of the department managers have given Sharon and me the expense projections that we need to finish the budget analyses.**

    1013b
    1055a
    1073

4. Between you and I, it looks like our contract negotiations with Jim Fortunato has broke down all together.  **Between you and me, it looks as if our contract negotiations with Jim Fortunato have broken down altogether.**

    1055b
    1101
    1006a
    1033

5. The number of new subscriptions have rose alot faster than any of us could have foreseen.  **The number of new subscriptions has risen a lot faster than any of us could have foreseen.**

    1023
    1033
    1101

Name _____ Date _____ Class _____ 63

**6.** Mrs. Abernathy, the person (who's) car I (accidently) backed into, (maybe) (adverse) to settling her claim for damages out of court. **Mrs. Abernathy, the person whose car I accidentally backed into, may be averse to settling her claim for damages out of court.**

1063
1101

**7.** If Mr. Pendleton is (inferring) that the products of our competitors are better than (our's), he obviously (don't) know that we get a lot (less) complaints from purchasers than they do. **If Mr. Pendleton is implying that the products of our competitors are better than ours, he obviously doesn't know that we get a lot fewer complaints from purchasers than they do.**

1101
1056c
1001a
1101

**8.** My partners and (me) plan to wait for (awhile) before we go any (farther) with our plans to take over the Kendall Corporation and reinvest (it's) assets. **My partners and I plan to wait for a while before we go any further with our plans to take over the Kendall Corporation and reinvest its assets.**

1054a
1101
1056e

**9.** I feel very (badly) about (him) deciding to return (back) to his old job when he had (all ready) done such good work for us. **I feel very bad about his deciding to return to his old job when he had already done such good work for us.**

1066
1056d
1073
1101

**10.** There (was) so many good reasons why the jury (were) suppose to rule against the defendant that neither the judge nor the lawyers (was) expecting a hung jury. **There were so many good reasons why the jury was supposed to rule against the defendant that neither the judge nor the lawyers were expecting a hung jury.**

1028a
1019a
1101
1005

64

# Editing Survey C (Continued)

**B. Directions:** Edit the following paragraphs to correct all errors. Use appropriate proofreaders' marks (shown on pages 358–359 and on the inside back cover of *The Gregg Reference Manual*) to indicate your corrections. Circle any changes you make. **References:** Consult the appropriate rules in Sections 1–11 as you complete this exercise.

```
      There are still some Bostonians who consider their city the        1

center of the world.  One of my father-in-laws' favorite stories         2
                                          634
concerns a European traveller arriving at Boston's Logan Airport          3
                     704/720                                or seventies  439a
in mid-December sometime back in the 70's.  Coming out of the             4
              he found  1082a                                             5
airport, an empty cab was waiting to take him to his hotel in
     334                        130a                                      6
the city. As they drove along the passenger asked the driver
                                                     814/816a             7
whether he could recommend some sights that a first-time visitor
                                                                          8
to Boston should see.
         All #  1101                                                      9
      "Alright," said the driver. "Let's see. You certainly
                                ie  604              508                   10
ought to visit our great universitys--Harvard and M/I/T/-and at
                                                                          11
this time of year you ought to go to the planetarium. There is
                                                                          12
an exhibit showing how the stars were arranged in the sky on the
                                                                          13
night that Jesus was born."

      "Over Bethlehem?" asked the visitor.                               14

      "No," said the driver with some exasperation. "Over Bos-          15

ton, of course."                                                        16
```

Name _____ Date _____ Class _____   65

**C. Directions:** Edit the following paragraphs to correct all errors. Use appropriate proofreaders' marks to indicate your corrections. Circle any changes you make. **References:** Consult the appropriate rules in Sections 1–11 as you complete this exercise.

There is an exclusive country club located in one of Bos- 1

ton's *630a* more affluent suburbs. It's *505d/1056e* so exclusive that guests who 2

are brought there by members are considered "visitors" if they 3

live within ten miles of the club and "strangers" if they live 4

farther *a 1101* away. To approach the club, you drive between imposing 5

stone pillars, you cross part of the golf course, you drive 6

past *719* a squat, owlish-looking security guard *123a/126a* and you come to an 7

oval where all the club facilities are located. 8

On a lovely spring *343* day--I believe it was in May *410* 1989--a 9

late-model Mercedes driven by a well-dressed *824b* man was only one of 10

a large number of cars that streamed past the guard. About an 11

hour after the Mercedes left, the manager of the golf shop dis- 12

covered that while he had been at lunch, someone had broken in *on 1033* 13

and stolen a good deal of sports equipment. When the police 14

came to investigate, the guard urged them to track down the man 15

in the Mercedes. He even supplied them with the license plate 16

number of the car. When the police intercepted the car a short 17

time later, they discovered all of the stolen items in the 18

trunk. 19

The police immediately returned to ask the guard what had 20

made him suspect a well-dressed man in an expensive car. The 21

guard replied, "It was obvious. The man smiled and waved at me 22

as he drove in. I knew at once that he was not a member of the 23

club. *247a* 24

**A. Directions:** Correct all errors in punctuation in each of the following items. Use appropriate proofreaders' marks (shown on pages 358–359 and on the inside back cover of *The Gregg Reference Manual*) to indicate your corrections. Circle any changes you make. If an item is correct as given, write *C* in the answer column. **References:** Consult the appropriate rules in Sections 1–2 as you complete this exercise.

1. Will you please sign your name below.                    103a

2. Will you please let me borrow your BMW?                  103b

3. We asked Tim when he planned to retire.                  104

4. Tim, when are you planning to retire?                    110a

5. You need someone who writes good ad copy.               122
                                                           132

6. It is, therefore, essential to act now.                 122
                                                           141

7. On Friday, May 4, 2007, I will be forty years old.      122e
                                                           154b

8. I can help you paint this weekend, but Eileen and Gail have a number of other commitments.   123a
                                                           126a

9. My lawyer, my accountant, and I are trying to untangle my tax problems.   123b
                                                           162a

10. We had a frank, open discussion about her work.        123c
                                                           168a

11. To get the best service, call 555-4825.                124
                                                           135b

12. Before you leave, make sure that Mr. Thomas gets a copy of your report.   124
                                                           130a

13. In my judgment, the buyout offer from Chadwick is not worth considering.   124b
                                                           138b

14. I took your suggestion, and found that it solved the problem.   127b

15. Monday and Wednesday are good for me; Friday is ᵒʳ ⊙ not.   128
                                                           176a

16. The name Floyd Fowler doesn't ring a bell.    **C**    149

17. The dealer's terms seem fair; ᵒʳ ⊙ For for example, he's giving you a good price on your car.   181a
                                                           187b
                                                           187c

18. The chapter called "Glued to the Tube" is one of the best in the book.   240a
                                                           242

19. What does the word *muffin-choker* mean?              285a
                                                           290e

20. My next book, *Second Wind,* will be published early next year.   289a

**B. Directions:** Correct the capitalization as necessary in each of the following items. Use appropriate revision marks to indicate your corrections. Circle any changes you make. If an item is correct as given, write *C* in the answer column. **References:** Consult the appropriate rules in Section 3 as you complete this exercise.

21. graduated from Stanford
    university _____ 303

22. a speech given by the first
    lady _____ 305

23. must discuss it with my
    Doctor _____ 308  321

24. a ruling by the state
    Attorney General _____ 313c

25. an exhibit of my Mother's
    paintings _____ 319a

26. check out of the Hotel by
    10 a.m. _____ 331

27. a strong reaction from west
    side voters _____ 338a

28. a surprising trend during the
    Nineties _____ 345

29. a master's degree in Physical
    Therapy _____ 352  353

30. the data shown in Table 4 on
    page 128 **C** 359

---

**C. Directions:** Circle all errors in number style and abbreviations in each of the following items, and write the correct form in the answer column. If an item is correct as given, write *C* in the answer column. **References:** Consult the appropriate rules in Sections 4–5 as you complete this exercise.

31. starting January
    fifteenth **15** 401b  407b

32. a lot more than six
    percent **6** 401b  447a

33. eight lawyers and
    12 paralegals **8** 402

34. forty-five thousand
    dollars **$45,000** 413a

35. was priced at
    $299.00 **$299** 415

36. costs only $.79
    a dozen **79 cents** 418a

37. . . . last year. 12
    weeks later . . . **Twelve** 421

38. in the first decade
    of the 21st century **twenty-first** 424

39. more than ¾
    of the voters **three-fourths**  **OR**  **three-quarters** 427a

40. will not end until
    5:00 p.m. **5** 440c

41. Harvey O. Genther
    Senior **Sr.** 502b

42. miles per gallon
    *(abbreviated)* **mpg** 507  535a

43. ought to notify the
    F.B.I. **FBI** 508  524a

44. hire a temp. for
    two weeks **temp** 510

45. write to M.F.
    Noonan **M. F.** 516a

46. waiting to see
    Doctor Katzenbach **Dr.** 517a

47. the US Treasury
    Department **U.S.** 525

48. moved to Oberlin,
    Oh. last year **Ohio** 527b

49. 550 lbs. *(on an
    invoice)* **lb** 535a

50. discuss it with your
    Ceo **CEO** 541

68

---

B-79

# Final Survey (Continued)

**D. Directions:** Circle all errors dealing with plural and possessive forms, spelling, and compound words in the following items. Write the correct form in the answer column. If an item is correct as given, write *C* in the answer column.
**References:** Consult the appropriate rules in Sections 6–8 as you complete this exercise.

| | | | | |
|---|---|---|---|---|
| 51. received four faxs yesterday | **faxes** | 602 | 66. we can not forgo our rights | **cannot** 719 |
| 52. rethink our company policys | **policies** | 604 | 67. sited a recent consumer poll | **cited** 719 |
| 53. will need three more shelfs | **shelves** | 608b | 68. in the fourth faze of the project | **phase** 719 |
| 54. talked with my two brother-in-laws | **brothers-in-law** | 612a | 69. planning separate itineries | **itineraries** 720 |
| 55. an extraordinary phenomena | **phenomenon** | 614 | 70. ordered a similar quanity | **quantity** 720 |
| 56. consulted several M.D.'s | **M.D.s** | 622a | 71. plan to get-together soon | **get together** 802 |
| 57. a six month's leave of absence | **months'** | 627a / 646 | 72. form a committee of laymen | **laypersons** 809a |
| 58. talk to the sale's manager | **sales** | 628a | 73. need to spot check her work | **spot-check** 811a |
| 59. review the witness' testimony | **witness's** | 631 | 74. got her training on-the-job | **on the job** 831a |
| 60. a sale on womens' sportswear | **women's** | 633 | 75. a cost effective approach | **cost-effective** 820a |
| 61. prefered to use my own tools | **preferred** | 702 | 76. should be more broad minded | **broad-minded** 823a |
| 62. offered to pay for the tickets | **offered** | 704 | 77. chose someone not well-known | **well known** 824b |
| 63. we thought it was wholely acceptable | **wholly** | 708 | 78. to co-ordinate our efforts | **coordinate** 835b |
| 64. all of us felt greatly releived | **relieved** | 712 | 79. need to re-emphasize that | **reemphasize** 835a |
| 65. exceded the weight limit | **exceeded** | 716b | 80. a self addressed envelope | **self-addressed** 836a |

Name _____ Date _____ Class _____ 69

**E. Directions:** Circle all errors dealing with grammar and usage in the following items, and write the correct form in the answer column. If an item is correct as given, write *C* in the answer column. **References:** Consult the appropriate rules in Sections 10–11 as you complete this exercise.

81. Bob (don't) have very much imagination. — **doesn't** — 1001a

82. One of my clients (are) going to sue me. — **is** — 1008a

83. We (begun) this ad campaign on October 1. — **began** — 1032b

84. If I (was) free, I'd go with you. — **were** — 1040

85. Sandy and (me) have decided to get married. — **I** — 1054a

86. The firm has improved (it's) sales. — **its** — 1056e

87. The assignment was given to Doug and (myself.) — **me** — 1060d

88. I feel (badly) about the way you were treated. — **bad** — 1067

89. Which is the (best) of the two plans? — **better** — 1071g

90. (Don't) tell (no one) about my idea. — **anyone OR ~~Don't~~** — 1076a

91. I planned (an) European vacation. — **a** — 1101

92. I used to see Paul once in (awhile.) — **a while** — 1101

93. We are (already) to test the software. — **all ready** — 1101

94. How will this (effect) our profits? — **affect** — 1101

95. We got a large (amount) of calls. — **number** — 1101

96. It's more trouble (then) it's worth. — **than** — 1101

97. Try to express your thoughts in (less) words. — **fewer** — 1101

98. Joan should (of) called by now. — **have** — 1101

99. Fran did a (real) nice job, didn't she? — **really** — 1101

100. Who is (suppose) to take your place? — **supposed** — 1101

# 24

## Final Survey

Basic Worksheets on
Grammar, Usage, and Style for
*The Gregg Reference Manual*
Tenth Edition

**A. Directions:** The following items deal with problems of punctuation. Correct all errors by inserting or deleting punctuation, using the appropriate revision marks (shown on the inside back cover of *The Gregg Reference Manual*). Circle any changes you make. If a sentence is correct as given, write *C* in the answer column. **References:** Sections 1–2.

1. Will you please specify the color you want.          _____ 103a

2. Will you please let us use your pool?          _____ 103b

3. I asked Lance when he hoped to get his license.          _____ 104

4. Lance, when do you hope to get your license?          _____ 110a

5. I met the woman, who found my wallet.          _____ 122 132

6. It is, therefore, critical that we vote tomorrow.          _____ 122 141

7. By Thursday, March 1, 2007, we must come up with the money.          _____ 122e 154b

8. The Codys are free on that date, but the others are not yet sure.          _____ 123a 126a

9. The food, the service, and the decor were not as good as we had expected.          _____ 123b 162a

10. The French Agency offers prompt, reliable service.          _____ 123c 168a

11. To lower the sound, turn the left knob to the right.          _____ 124 135b

12. When you arrive, go directly to my office on the sixth floor.          _____ 124 130a

13. In fact, I suggested that strategy myself.          _____ 124b 138b

14. We flew to Seattle and then drove to Vancouver. ; or . The          c    127b

15. These items are on sale; the others are not.          _____ 128 176a

16. The novelist Jane Austen never fails to delight her readers.          c    149

17. I like your plan for boosting sales; for example, it does not require us to hire additional staff.  for or . For          _____ 181a 187b 187c

18. The chapter entitled "Taking Charge of Your Life" is the best one in the book.          _____ 240a 242

19. One of my favorite movies is a musical entitled Singin' in the Rain.          _____ 285a 290e

20. The Wall Street Journal is publishing a three-part series on the hearings.          _____ 289a

Name _____   Date _____   Class _____          71

B-82

**B. Directions:** The following items deal with problems of capitalization. If an item is correctly capitalized, write *C* in the answer column. Correct any incorrect items as follows: To change a capital letter to a small letter, draw a line through it: ~~T~~he. To change a small letter to a capital letter, draw three lines under it: <u>t</u>he. Circle any changes you make. **References:** Section 3.

21. used to work for the Xerox corporation     303

22. providing aid to the third world     305

23. planned to raft down the River     308 / 331

24. the new President of our company     313a / 321

25. going into partnership with my Father     319a

26. driving across the Bridge to Sausalito     331

27. hoping to move back East next month     **C**   338a

28. during the early Nineteen Hundreds     345

29. working on a doctorate in Economics     352 / 353

30. treated in Appendix A on Page 313     359

**C. Directions:** The following items deal with problems of number style and abbreviations. If an item is correct as given, write *C* in the answer column. If an item is incorrect, circle the error and write the correct form in the answer column. **References:** Sections 4–5.

31. on or before December twenty-ninth   **29**   401b / 407b

32. only three percent of the defects   **3**   401b / 447a

33. four bus drivers and 87 passengers   **4**   402

34. at least eighty-seven thousand dollars   **$87,000**   413a

35. carries a price tag of only $99.00   **$99**   415

36. keep the cost under $.50 a unit   **50 cents**   418a

37. . . . started last week. 60 days from now. . .   **Sixty**   421

38. during the first decade of the 19th century   **nineteenth**   424

39. over 1/2 of these traffic accidents   **one-half OR a half**   427a

40. must be sure to leave by 4:00 p.m.   **4**   440c

41. George Appleby Singleton Junior   **Jr.**   502b

42. revolutions per minute (abbreviated)   **rpm**   507 / 535a

43. graduated last year from M.I.T.   **MIT**   508 / 524a

44. will prepare a new demo. disk   **demo**   510

45. an exciting article by N.W. Hertzog   **N. W.**   516a

46. was examined by Doctor Warren Fong   **Dr.**   517a

47. the U.S. Department of Agriculture   **C**   525

48. worked for two years in Washington, DC   **D.C.**   527b

49. 600 gals. @ $15.50 (on an invoice)   **gal**   535a

50. consider joining an H.M.O. next year   **HMO**   541

# Final Survey (Continued)

**D. Directions:** The following items deal with problems of plural and possessive forms, spelling, and compound words. If an item is correct as given, write *C* in the answer column. If an item is incorrect, circle the error and write the correct form in the answer column. **References:** Sections 6–8.

| | | | |
|---|---|---|---|
| **51.** whether or not (taxs) should be cut | **taxes** 602 | **66.** needs to use more (tack) with callers | **tact** 719 |
| **52.** need to review our outstanding (liabilitys) | **liabilities** 604 | **67.** and should try to be more (discrete) | **discreet** 719 |
| **53.** a business that is owned by our (wifes) | **wives** 608b | **68.** don't want their help or their (advise) | **advice** 719 |
| **54.** a dinner prepared by my four (sister-in-laws) | **sisters-in-law** 612a | **69.** serve as our (liason) with the steering committee | **liaison** 720 |
| **55.** attended a reception for the (alumnuses) | **alumni** 614 | **70.** a topic that falls in another (catagory) | **category** 720 |
| **56.** a proposal supported by many (CEO's) | **CEOs** 622a | **71.** must (checkout) of our hotel room by noon | **check out** 802 |
| **57.** purchased several hundred (dollar's) worth | **dollars'** 646 | **72.** supervising a large crew of (workmen) | **workers** 809a |
| **58.** bought seven more (saving's) bonds | **savings** 628a | **73.** to (air condition) this entire office | **air-condition** 811a |
| **59.** (Congress') latest budget proposals | **Congress's** 631 | **74.** proposing tax cuts (across-the-board) | **across the board** 831a |
| **60.** a fantastic sale on (mens') suits | **men's** 633 | **75.** needs a (machine readable) format | **machine-readable** 820a |
| **61.** the flooding that recently occurred | **C** 702 | **76.** thought his speech was (long winded) | **long-winded** 823a |
| **62.** (suffered) minor injuries in the accident | **suffered** 704 | **77.** the repainting of our reception room was (much-needed) | **much needed** 824b |
| **63.** intended to send an (acknowledgement) | **acknowledgment** 708 | **78.** found a new (co-author) to work on the book | **coauthor** 835b |
| **64.** could not (beleive) that it happened | **believe** 712 | **79.** would be willing to (re-employ) Ms. Foley | **reemploy** 835a |
| **65.** we'll have to (conceed) the truth of that statement | **concede** 716b | **80.** designing (self study) programs | **self-study** 836a |

Name _____ Date _____ Class _____ 73

**E. Directions:** The following items deal with problems of grammar and usage. If an item is correct as given, write *C* in the answer column. If an item is incorrect, circle the error and write the correct form in the answer column. **References:** Sections 10–11.

81. Cindy don't like the idea very much.

doesn't — 1001a

82. One of the calls were for you.

was — 1008a

83. Are you the one who drunk all the coffee?

drank — 1032b

84. If I was rich, the first thing I'd do . . .

were — 1040

85. Chris and me are hoping to go camping for a week.

I — 1054a

86. The company monitors it's costs zealously.

its — 1056e

87. The position was offered to Meg and myself.

me — 1060d

88. We feel badly about your transfer to the main office.

bad — 1067

89. Which is the best of these two paintings?

better — 1071g

90. I don't have nothing that I care to add.

anything OR ~~don't~~ — 1076a

91. Your visit is not an every day happening.

everyday — 1101

92. These kind of problems always crop up.

kinds — 1101

93. The reorganization plan is all together too complex.

altogether — 1101

94. This change will have no affect on us.

effect — 1101

95. We just received a large amount of orders.

number — 1101

96. Does anyone beside you think that?

besides — 1101

97. We've had less complaints this year.

fewer — 1101

98. You could of called if you were displeased.

have — 1101

99. The pay raise was sure appreciated.

surely — 1101

100. I use to work in the Virgin Islands.

used — 1101

# Using the Comprehensive Worksheets

# A NOTE TO THE INSTRUCTOR

The *Comprehensive Worksheets* that accompany the tenth edition of *The Gregg Reference Manual* will do more than familiarize your students with the contents and the organization of *The Gregg Reference Manual*. When the two components are used together, they will serve as the basis for a short course on English grammar, usage, and style, as well as on the techniques and procedures for handling letters, memos, and other types of business communications. These materials can be used as a separate unit of instruction where a modular curriculum is in effect, or they can be used as part of a cooperative training class or a course in keyboarding, machine transcription, office procedures, business communications, or document processing. (*Note:* If you are looking for a shorter set of worksheets that deal only with grammar, usage, and style, consider using the *Basic Worksheets* [ISBN 0-07-293654-1] that also accompany the tenth edition of *The Gregg Reference Manual*. See pages B-2 to B-7 in this *Instructor's Resource Manual*.)

## OBJECTIVES OF THE *COMPREHENSIVE WORKSHEETS*

The *Comprehensive Worksheets* are designed to build three basic editing skills your students need to possess if they are going to achieve an on-the-job level of proficiency.

1.  Your students need to know when they are in the presence of a potential problem. Otherwise, they'll never be tempted to consult a reference manual, even though you put one in their hands. They'll simply assume that whatever they have written, edited, or typed is correct.

2.  Even when your students know they have a potential problem, they still need to know where to look in a reference manual to find the appropriate rule. If they aren't properly acquainted with the contents and the organization of a reference manual and if they aren't properly introduced to the various techniques for looking things up, they won't find the answers they need.

3.  Even when your students have mastered the skill of looking things up and can find the rule that covers a particular problem, they still need experience in applying the rule correctly. What's more, they need immediate reinforcement that tells them they *have* applied the rule correctly.

How do the *Comprehensive Worksheets* develop these three skills? To begin with, almost every worksheet focuses on one particular section in *The Gregg Reference Manual*—and in most cases focuses on only a selected set of rules within that section. (See the chart on pages C-4 to C-5 for the primary coverage of each

worksheet.) As students go through a given worksheet, they are forced to confront a wide range of problems within a specific area—whether punctuation, capitalization, number style, or some other area of potential difficulty. The exercise items on these worksheets do not attempt to cover every minute point of style in the related set of rules. Instead, the exercise items cover the most common kinds of problems that students are likely to encounter whenever they write, transcribe, type, edit, or proofread. The objective here is to familiarize them with the typical problems that occur in business communications so that later on, in similar situations, they'll possess that editorial "twitch" that alerts them to the possible presence of such problems. They may not remember how to deal with a given problem on the spot. However, the important thing is that they sense that a problem could exist and they are motivated to consult *The Gregg Reference Manual*. If students could develop just this skill alone, most of the errors they make would no doubt disappear.

Knowing how to look things up is not an automatic skill; it, too, has to be worked on. To help students develop this skill, Worksheets 2–28 (with the exception of four editing survey worksheets) supply the appropriate rule number(s) next to each exercise item. In this way students can concentrate on reading the rules and applying them correctly to the specific situation. As students complete each worksheet, a quick review of their answers against the key will tell them which rules may be giving them trouble and need to be reexamined.

To further develop the skill of spotting problems and looking things up on their own, the students will from time to time encounter an editing survey worksheet designed to help them integrate what they have learned from earlier materials. Now, instead of correcting isolated sentences, the students will have to edit long passages of connected copy. Without the help of rule numbers in the margin, they will have to identify potential errors, consult *The Gregg Reference Manual*, and make any necessary corrections.

When students get to the concluding worksheets (29–33), they will find that all rule numbers have been completely withdrawn. Moreover, they will find that the exercises in these final worksheets draw on all sections of *The Gregg Reference Manual*. Yet because of the training they have had up to this point, they should now be able to (1) recognize the potential problems that occur in Worksheets 29–33, (2) find the relevant rules on their own, and (3) apply these rules correctly to each situation.

## ORGANIZATION OF THE WORKSHEETS

As the table of contents on pages C-4 to C-5 indicates, Worksheet 1, the Diagnostic Survey, is a four-page pretest that covers all the key rules in *The Gregg Reference Manual*. These are the rules, in the judgment of the author, that all office workers should be able to apply correctly. The first page of Worksheet 1 covers Sections 1–3; the second page covers Sections 4–9; the third page covers Sections 10–11; and page 4 provides a full-page letter that covers Section 13 as well as all the preceding sections. This pretest will tell your students (and you) how much they already know, how effective they are in looking things up on their own, and what sections of *The Gregg Reference Manual* they need to give special attention to. (See the chart on page C-6.)

Worksheets 2–28 focus on specific sets of rules within each section. (The chart on pages C-4 to C-5 shows which rules are covered in each worksheet.) As indicated previously, rule numbers appear alongside the answer blanks in these worksheets so that students will be guided to the appropriate rule in each case.

Within the sequence of worksheets from 2 to 28 come the four editing survey worksheets. After the students finish Worksheets 2–6 (which focus on the proper use of punctuation), they will encounter an editing survey in Worksheet 7 that requires them to draw on the full range of rules in Sections 1–2 while they edit copy without the customary guidance in the margin. In the same way, the editing survey in Worksheet 13 will ask them to apply the rules in Sections 3–5 (on capitalization, numbers, and abbreviations), which they were gradually introduced to in Worksheets 8–12. The editing survey in Worksheet 20 deals with the problems covered in Sections 6–9 and Worksheets 14–19. Finally, the editing survey in Worksheet 25 deals with the rules presented in Sections 10–11 and applied in Worksheets 21–24.

Worksheets 26–28 offer students experience in looking things up whenever questions arise about formatting letters, memos, and other business documents. Worksheets 29–32 then provide a number of editing assignments: five letters (executed in three different styles), a continuation page of a letter, an envelope, a memo with a table, and a page from a business report. These four worksheets require the student to study and apply a number of the rules in Sections 13–16 of *The Gregg Reference Manual.* Moreover, they require the student to identify and resolve a wide range of problems drawn from Sections 1 through 13 and already covered in the earlier worksheets. Because no rule numbers are supplied in these worksheets, students must now concentrate on looking things up without special help.

Worksheet 33, the Final Survey, is a four-page posttest that exactly parallels Worksheet 1, the Diagnostic Survey, in coverage and construction. Both the pretest and the posttest should be scored so that you can measure each student's gain in achievement by the end of this unit of instruction. The four intervening editing surveys may also be scored as a means of measuring the student's incremental progress. (The following section provides guidelines on scoring.)

Worksheet 34, which appears only in this *Instructor's Resource Manual* (see pages C-8 to C-11), is a *second* Final Survey that exactly parallels Worksheet 33 in coverage and construction. You may reproduce Worksheet 34 for use in your classroom (1) as an alternative to Worksheet 33 or (2) as a "second chance" for students who did not perform well on Worksheet 33. (For a further discussion of the best ways to use Worksheet 34, see page C-7.)

## HOW TO USE THE WORKSHEETS

The following suggestions are intended to help you make the most effective use of these worksheets. This resource manual offers a CD-ROM with PowerPoint slides as well as transparency masters designed to be used along with these worksheets. Use the table of contents to identify slides that will help you (1) explain to your students how to look things up in *The Gregg Reference Manual,* (2) introduce many basic rules before your students have to apply them in specific worksheets, and (3) review those rules that students have had difficulty in applying correctly. (See also page C-7 for a further discussion of using these slides and transparencies with the worksheets.)

**Worksheet 1.** Before administering the Diagnostic Survey (Worksheet 1), give the students a brief orientation to *The Gregg Reference Manual.* Point out that certain rule numbers in Sections 1–11 appear in white within a red panel. This graphic device serves to highlight the basic rules that students need to master. Also point out such features as these: the topical index on the inside front cover for fast reference, the detailed 43-page index at the back of the book, the electronic index on the *Gregg* Web site, the detailed outline of headings at the beginning of each section, the rule-numbering system (whereby the first one or two digits of each rule number express the section number), the displayed rule numbers in the upper left and right corners of each two-page spread, and the section number and title displayed at the edge of each page. Have the students skim the preface and the table of contents in *The Gregg Reference Manual.* Ask them to read the section entitled "How to Look Things Up." Also familiarize your students with the proofreaders' marks they will need to use in the first exercise of Worksheet 1. (These marks—which are shown in the directions for this exercise—relate simply to the insertion or deletion of punctuation and to changes in capitalization.) When you are satisfied that students have the requisite familiarity with the organization and features of *The Gregg Reference Manual,* ask them to complete Worksheet 1, *referring to the manual as necessary.* If time permits and equipment is available, ask the students to retype the letter that they edit on the fourth page of this worksheet. (*Note:* To support your discussion of how to look things up, use the corresponding "How to

| Worksheet Number | Worksheet Title | Primary Coverage | For Keys See Page |
|:---:|:---|:---|:---:|
| 1 | Diagnostic Survey | First page: Sections 1–3 (punctuation and capitalization) | **C-12** |
| | | Second page: Sections 4–9 (numbers, abbreviations, plurals, possessives, spelling, compounds, and word division) | **C-14** |
| | | Third page: Sections 10–11 (grammar and usage) | **C-15** |
| | | Fourth page: Sections 1–13 (modified-block letter arrangement plus all sections on style, grammar, usage, and editing and proofreading techniques) | **C-16** |
| 2 | The Period, the Question Mark, and the Exclamation Point | ¶¶101–121 | **C-19** |
| 3 | The Comma | ¶¶122–125; 126–137 | **C-21** |
| 4 | The Comma *(Continued)* | ¶¶138–175 plus 122–137 | **C-23** |
| 5 | The Semicolon, the Colon, and the Comma | ¶¶176–199 plus 122–175; 176–199 plus 101–175 | **C-25** |
| 6 | Other Marks of Punctuation | ¶¶201–226 plus 299; 227–299 | **C-27** |
| 7 | Editing Survey A | Sections 1–2 (punctuation) | **C-29** |
| 8 | Capitalization | ¶¶301–330 | **C-31** |
| 9 | Capitalization *(Continued)* | ¶¶331–366; 301–366 | **C-33** |
| 10 | Numbers | ¶¶401–428; 461; 465 | **C-35** |
| 11 | Numbers *(Continued)* | ¶¶429–470 plus 401–406; 401–470 | **C-37** |
| 12 | Abbreviations | ¶¶501–550 | **C-39** |
| 13 | Editing Survey B | Sections 3–5 (capitalization, numbers, and abbreviations) | **C-41** |
| 14 | Plurals | ¶¶601–626 | **C-43** |
| 15 | Possessives | ¶¶630–638 plus 601–626; 627–652 | **C-45** |
| 16 | Spelling | ¶¶701–711; 712–718; 719–720 | **C-47** |
| 17 | Choosing the Right Word | ¶719; 719–720 | **C-49** |
| 18 | Compound Words | ¶¶801–812; 813–847; 801–847 | **C-51** |
| 19 | Word Division | ¶¶901–922; 915–920 | **C-53** |

Look Things Up" transparencies—H-1 to H-6 on pages D-13 to D-18.)

*Scoring Worksheet 1.* As soon as the assignment is completed, have the worksheets corrected and score them as follows: From a total score of 100, deduct a half point for each item incorrectly answered. Retain this score for later use. (*Note:* There are 125 items on the first three pages and another 50 errors in the letter given on the fourth page. If, out of the total of 175 items, a student got 60 wrong, you would deduct 30 points from 100 and give the test a score of 70.)

*Diagnosing Each Student's Needs.* More important than assigning a score to each student's performance on Worksheet 1 is a diagnosis of each student's strengths and weaknesses. The chart at the bottom of this page will help you provide specific prescriptions for each student.

**Worksheets 2–28.** Once the Diagnostic Survey has been completed, you have several choices to pursue: (1) ask each student to complete all the worksheets from 2 through 28 *in sequence;* (2) ask each student to complete Worksheets 2–28 in a sequence that gives priority to those sections in which the greatest number of errors occurred on the Diagnostic Survey; or (3) ask each student to complete *only* those worksheets (between 2 and 28) that deal with sections in which a significant number of errors occurred on the Diagnostic Survey. However you decide to assign these worksheets, ask the students to follow this procedure before starting any worksheet: study the relevant rules as a whole (identified in the directions) before proceeding to apply individual rules to the items on the worksheet. In this way students will be better able to grasp the principles of style that underlie and unify the

individual rules within that section. If students ceed directly to apply the individual rules in isc fashion, they may miss the broader rationale. Use the appropriate slides if you plan to introduc cific rules before the students apply them in the sheet exercises or if you want to review specific that students have had difficulty in applying corre

**Editing Survey Worksheets.** All students s complete Worksheets 7, 13, 20, and 25 to ensure they have an adequate grasp of the wide range of each of these editing survey worksheets covers. these worksheets require the students, for the time, to locate the rules entirely on their own, you want to have the students reread "How to Look T Up" before they begin these editing assignments. remind the students of the various features in *The ( Reference Manual* that will help them find their around. (*Note:* To support this discussion, consider Transparencies H-1 to H-6 on pages D-13 to D-18.)

*Scoring Editing Survey Worksheets.* Each ed survey worksheet contains two full-page passa There are 30 errors in each complete passage a total of 60 errors in each worksheet. For each erro uncorrected or improperly corrected and for any error introduced by the student, deduct 1 point fr total score of 100. Since this is an open-book exer the minimum acceptable grade on each editing su worksheet should be 80.

**Worksheets 29–32.** All students should comp Worksheets 29–32, even if they were exempted some of the earlier worksheets. If time permits equipment is available, ask the students to retype edited materials in Worksheets 29–32.

| In Worksheet 1, if a student made many errors in the following items: | That student should give special emphasis to the following worksheets: |
|---|---|
| 1–30 | Worksheets 2–9 (dealing with punctuation and capitalization) |
| 31–42 | Worksheets 10–11 (dealing with numbers) |
| 43–50 | Worksheet 12 (dealing with abbreviations) |
| 51–65 | Worksheets 14–15 (dealing with plurals and possessives) |
| 66–80 | Worksheets 16–17 (dealing with spelling and choosing the right word) |
| 81–95 | Worksheet 18 (dealing with compounds) |
| 96–100 | Worksheet 19 (dealing with word division) |
| 101–125 | Worksheets 21–24 (dealing with grammar and usage) |

**Worksheet 33.** Once the students have successfully completed Worksheets 29–32, have them proceed to the Final Survey (Worksheet 33), *again referring to the manual as necessary*. You might suggest that they quickly review their answers on the earlier worksheets as preparation for this posttest. (The worksheets have been three-hole-punched so that after the sheets have been detached, they can easily be kept in a binder for reference.) If time permits and equipment is available, ask the students to retype the letter at the end of this worksheet.

*Scoring Worksheet 33.* As on Worksheet 1, use this scoring procedure: From a total score of 100, deduct a half point for each item incorrectly answered. (There are 125 items on the first three pages plus 50 errors in the letter on the fourth page.) Since this is an open-book exercise, a student should get no more than 40 items wrong. In effect, the minimum acceptable grade on this test should be 80. Compare each student's score on the Final Survey with the score achieved on the Diagnostic Survey. Assign a final grade on the basis of the gain in performance the student has achieved.

**Worksheet 34.** As noted previously, this alternative Final Survey, which appears only in this *Instructor's Resource Manual* (on pages C-8 to C-11), may be used in place of Worksheet 33. If you decide to use Worksheet 34 as the posttest, you might want to allow students to use Worksheet 33 as practice for the real thing. On the other hand, if you do use Worksheet 33 as the posttest, you could assign Worksheet 34 to those students who did not score well on Worksheet 33. Allowing these students additional time to review the relevant rules in *The Gregg Reference Manual* and then giving them a second chance to apply these rules in Worksheet 34 could help them raise their final scores and boost their sense of achievement as well.

*Scoring Worksheet 34.* Apply the same scoring procedure provided for Worksheet 33.

## CHECKING WORK

To provide the necessary reinforcement and ensure that proper learning is taking place, you should make sure that each worksheet is checked and corrected before the student proceeds to the next one. If your students are each working at their own pace, place the worksheet key in a central location so that all students can check their own work. (Remove the keys to Worksheets 33 and 34, however.) If you prefer, you can check the worksheets yourself or appoint one or more student assistants to help you with the job.

If your students are all doing the same worksheet at the same time, you may wish to read the answers aloud and have all the students check their own (or someone else's) work at the same time. Under any cir-cumstances, be sure to make yourself available to answer the questions of students who have made mistakes on the worksheets but do not understand why these are mistakes.

If you have weak students who are not capable of studying the rules on their own and applying them effectively, consider the following procedure: Before assigning any worksheet, preview the designated set of rules with the whole group (using the appropriate transparencies) and explain any rule or concept that could prove difficult. Then ask the students to complete the worksheet on an individual basis. Finally, critique the answers for the whole group, and resolve any questions or difficulties they have in reference to the correct answers.

## A NOTE ON THE KEYS

Full-size facsimiles of the worksheets are reproduced on pages C-12 to C-110 with the correct answers inserted. The letters and other materials that are to be edited in Worksheets 1 and 29–34 are keyed in several ways: first with corrections noted on the original version; then with a detailed, line-by-line commentary that explains each error and gives the appropriate rule number; and finally with a completely retyped and corrected version. Because a number of these errors can be corrected in more than one way, give credit for answers that are acceptable, even though they do not agree with what is specifically shown in the facsimile key.

## USING THE POWERPOINT SLIDES AND TRANSPARENCIES WITH THE WORKSHEETS

This resource manual provides a CD-ROM with nearly 350 PowerPoint slides plus transparency masters of sample documents to help you (1) reinforce the basic rules of grammar, usage, and style and (2) explain the guidelines for formatting letters, memos, and other business documents.

- As you introduce particular rules to your students, use the related slides or transparencies to reinforce the points you want to make.

- Before students begin a particular worksheet or a particular exercise, use the appropriate slides or transparencies to *review* the rules they will have to apply.

- After you score a completed worksheet, use the appropriate slides or transparencies to support your discussion of the problems students may have encountered in completing that worksheet.

*Note:* Pages D-1 to D-7 describe how each sequence of slides and transparencies can be used to support a specific set of rules in *GRM*.

# 34

## Final Survey

**Directions:** Correct the punctuation and capitalization in each sentence below. If the punctuation is incorrect, draw a line through it: *an old winter coat.* If new punctuation is to be inserted, circle it: *I too hope so.* To change a small letter to a capital letter, draw three lines under it: *Christmas.* To change a capital letter to a small letter, draw a line through it: *Enough.* If a sentence is correct as given, write *C* in the answer column. **References:** Sections 1–3.

1. Carole Paula and I have rented a handsome sun-filled house for the summer      1. _____
2. May I please use your transparencies for my presentation next Tuesday May 9      2. _____
3. I've just received your note of May 1 in which you asked whether you could borrow my transparencies of course      3. _____
4. The Marketing Director of Galway industries asked how much the demo cost      4. _____
5. Did you really take top honors in the photo competition my warmest congratulations      5. _____
6. It's strange isn't it that so many nice people turn into ogres when they drive      6. _____
7. Did the person whom I interviewed last monday, submit samples of her work      7. _____
8. In my opinion the Company's stock will not split before the year 2008      8. _____
9. If you have some free time would you please comment on the attached proposal      9. _____
10. We could stop in Hampton New Hampshire and if you like go on to Camden Maine      10. _____
11. It is essential therefore that we notify their Treasurer Tom Bray of the new plan      11. _____
12. Please fill in the following boxes Your date of birth your address your phone number      12. _____
13. Ken Foy LL.D. spoke today to the Company's managers, and will return this Spring      13. _____
14. Did last week's oil spill draw the attention of Federal, and State, regulators      14. _____
15. After we moved down south last Winter we decided to open a small, antique shop      15. _____
16. Forrest's investment in Apple must be over $2000000 by now don't you think      16. _____
17. We must therefore reject your buyout offer even though your terms are attractive      17. _____
18. The lawsuit was filed last May but the case will not be tried until june 3 2008      18. _____
19. Phil have you heard that Jane Seidel the Mayor of Warren will not run again      19. _____
20. In 2004 Ray Twomey Jr. stepped down as the head of Zodiac Creations Inc.      20. _____
21. To leave a message record after the tone, to speak with an operator dial 0      21. _____
22. If you ask Mona for help she always smiles and says what needs to be done      22. _____
23. (See chapter 4 a time to be born in going with the flow      23. _____
24. The locations of our stores are: Tulsa Oklahoma Tyler Texas and Tempe Arizona      24. _____
25. I like the overall design however the Marketing Director wants a brighter color      25. _____
26. Is the Television Bureau Of Advertising really located on Madison avenue      26. _____
27. Nan's field is european history, and literature in the twentieth century for example she has taught courses on the Nineteen-Forties and the holocaust      27. _____
28. After I retired I moved to Northern Vermont but I miss my house in Rye New York      28. _____
29. Martha along with her children is taking a cruise to celebrate mother's day      29. _____
30. An ad hoc committee was created in April 2003 or was it 2004      30. _____

Name _____ Date _____ Class _____      71

**Directions:** The following items deal with problems in number style, abbreviations, plural and possessive forms, spelling, compound words, and word division. (*Note:* The symbol / is used in items 96–100 to show word division at the end of a line.) If an item is correct as given, write *C* in the answer column. If an item is incorrect, circle the error and show the correct form in the answer column. **References:** Sections 4–9.

| | | |
|---|---|---|
| 31. | 18 yeses and six noes | _____ |
| 32. | before December 15th | _____ |
| 33. | on sale for only $99.00 | _____ |
| 34. | cost only $.79 apiece | _____ |
| 35. | . . . our ad. 16 callers | _____ |
| 36. | in the 19th century | _____ |
| 37. | 1/3 of the way through | _____ |
| 38. | in fifty-gallon drums | _____ |
| 39. | my son turned three | _____ |
| 40. | a ninety-day warranty | _____ |
| 41. | nearly 30 years ago | _____ |
| 42. | closes at five P.M. | _____ |
| 43. | wrote to H.H. Green | _____ |
| 44. | Doctor Singh's visit | _____ |
| 45. | approved by the F.D.A. | _____ |
| 46. | US State Department | _____ |
| 47. | lives in Washington, D.C. | _____ |
| 48. | 200 bbls @ $85 | _____ |
| 49. | weighed about 75 km. | _____ |
| 50. | found a good H.M.O. | _____ |
| 51. | too many liabilitys | _____ |
| 52. | made many journies | _____ |
| 53. | a cat with nine lifes | _____ |
| 54. | my two son-in-laws | _____ |
| 55. | more than one criteria | _____ |
| 56. | visited the Kennedies | _____ |
| 57. | throughout the 1990's | _____ |
| 58. | an actress' ambition | _____ |
| 59. | bought Ella Jame's car | _____ |
| 60. | both company's CEOs | _____ |
| 61. | mens' suits are on sale | _____ |
| 62. | it's ours, not your's | _____ |
| 63. | Ed and Jan's shoes | _____ |
| 64. | several dollars worth | _____ |
| 65. | do you mind me asking | _____ |

| | | |
|---|---|---|
| 66. | transfered the deed | _____ |
| 67. | profitted from the sale | _____ |
| 68. | used good judgment | _____ |
| 69. | whatever I recieved | _____ |
| 70. | resistent to infection | _____ |
| 71. | will not interceed | _____ |
| 72. | copy my resume | _____ |
| 73. | this passed week | _____ |
| 74. | I can not tell you why | _____ |
| 75. | that maybe impossible | _____ |
| 76. | was accidently broken | _____ |
| 77. | in a large quanity | _____ |
| 78. | on the nineth or tenth | _____ |
| 79. | something similar | _____ |
| 80. | was a real privaledge | _____ |
| 81. | a true master piece | _____ |
| 82. | to cover-up mistakes | _____ |
| 83. | over 200 hand-outs | _____ |
| 84. | needs skill-building | _____ |
| 85. | type it double spaced | _____ |
| 86. | a high level meeting | _____ |
| 87. | a ten-year's loan | _____ |
| 88. | word-processing center | _____ |
| 89. | a cost effective plan | _____ |
| 90. | very eye catching | _____ |
| 91. | looks old fashioned | _____ |
| 92. | a highly deserved raise | _____ |
| 93. | brought me up to date | _____ |
| 94. | would re-employ him | _____ |
| 95. | the fact is self evident | _____ |
| 96. | I plan-/ ned to leave | _____ |
| 97. | it is imper-/ ative | _____ |
| 98. | try media-/ tion | _____ |
| 99. | retell-/ ing an old story | _____ |
| 100. | controll-/ ing our costs | _____ |

72

C-9

**Directions:** Underline all errors and write the correct forms in the answer column. If a sentence is correct as given, write *C* in the answer column. **References:** Sections 10–11.

101. Every marketing manager and copywriter <u>have</u> seen the new logo.    101. _____

102. Only one of the service representatives <u>are</u> available on weekends.    102. _____

103. <u>Does</u> any of the plans meet the goal of higher sales and lower costs?    103. _____

104. Our criteria for granting parental leave <u>needs</u> to be updated.    104. _____

105. The number of uninsured drivers are high and continuing to grow.    105. _____

106. Nora is one of those people who <u>spends</u> time to say they have no time.    106. _____

107. None of the passengers <u>was</u> seriously injured, but the car was totaled.    107. _____

108. I wish I <u>was</u> going to the convention in Bermuda with the rest of you.    108. _____

109. How long can the company maintain <u>their</u> share of the market?    109. _____

110. Attendance is mandatory for everyone except you and <u>I</u>.    110. _____

111. Maria is so much better at dealing with angry customers than <u>me</u>.    111. _____

112. Jan and <u>myself</u> will move to Utah, even if my transfer is not okayed.    112. _____

113. <u>Whom</u> do you think will get the Oscar this year for best actress?    113. _____

114. It was <u>real</u> nice of you to cover for me while I was in the hospital.    114. _____

115. We feel very bad about your decision to take early retirement.    115. _____

116. I've reviewed your proposal carefully, and I don't have <u>nothing</u> to add.    116. _____

117. How will the proposed increase in the sales tax <u>effect</u> your business?    117. _____

118. Mayor Fry's budget cuts have angered a large <u>amount</u> of voters.    118. _____

119. I need to consider my options for <u>awhile</u> before I make my next move.    119. _____

120. Why do <u>less</u> people attend the Friday concerts than those on Monday?    120. _____

**Directions:** Rewrite the following sentences to correct all errors. **References:** Primarily Sections 10–11.

121. Every congressman should continuously monitor the views of his constituents. _____

_____

122. We not only discussed this years' sales projections but also next year. _____

_____

123. Neither the professors nor the dean is happy about the impact of funding cuts on his programs. _____

_____

124. When applying for a loan, this form should be filled out and brought back. When you come for an interview. _____

_____

125. The new law's provisions have been reviewed by everyone of us lawyers. _____

_____

**Directions:** On the reverse side of this sheet you will find a letter to **Dr. Margaret P. Jensen** (typed in modified-block style—standard format with standard punctuation). Correct all errors in style, grammar, and format; also look for errors in typing and content. Circle all changes you make within the lines or out in the margins; if you prefer, show all changes on a separate sheet, identified by line number. If time permits, retype the corrected letter on a plain sheet of paper, using 1.25-inch side margins and positioning the date on the first line below a 2-inch top margin. **References:** Section 13 plus Sections 1–12. See also pages 358–359 or the inside back cover of *The Gregg Reference Manual* for a chart showing how to indicate corrections on typed material.

Name _____ Date _____ Class _____    73

# Caribbean Cruises

**1200 BISCAYNE BOULEVARD**
**MIAMI, FLORIDA 33132**
**(305) 555-2800**

October 14th 2008

Dr. Margaret P. Jensen M.D.
1523 S. Madison St.
Appleton Wisconsin 54915

Dear Dr. Jenson

Thank you for your letter of October seventh in which you asked for
for information about our Winter cruises to the Carribean. I can well
understand of course why you are thinking about a warmer place a few months
from now. Since I grew up in Northern Minnesota. Let me try to provide
some answers to the questions you raised in you letter.

1. From December 15-March 21 we are offerring a wide selection of cruises.
There are frequent sailing dates to fit every schedule, and prices to fit
every budget.

2. If your time is limited, you maybe most interested in our seven-day
cruises, which stop in 3 ports (for example, Nassau, San Juan and Antigua.

3. If your in a position to take a longer voyage you might consider our
11 day cruises which stop in six ports. Better yet our 16-day cruise sails
from Miami through the Panama canal to Los Angeles

4. Prices start at $1950.00, and includes round trip airfare between
Chicago and Miami (and Los Angeles if you decide on our longest cruise.)

I'm enclosing three brochures, that describe in detail each of our there
types of cruises. Regardless of the one you choose you can expect gourmet
dining, oversized cabins, and an attentive crew to spoil you. If you want
to escape this winter into a warm wonderful world of luxury and excitement,
why not ask your travel agent about reservations.

Sincerely Yours

Mr. Edward J. Cantwell,
Director Of Customer Services

aem
Enclosure 1

13
14
15
16
17
18
19
20
21
22
23
24
25
26
27
28
29
30
31
32
33
34
35
36
37
38
39
40
41
42
43
44
45
46
47
48
49
50
51
52
53
54
55
56
57

74

C-11

# 1  Key
# Diagnostic Survey

**Directions:** Correct the punctuation and capitalization in each sentence below. If the punctuation is incorrect, draw a line through it: *an old / winter coat.* If new punctuation is to be inserted, circle it: *I too hope so.* To change a small letter to a capital letter, draw three lines under it: *Christmas.* To change a capital letter to a small letter, draw a line through it: *Enough.* If a sentence is correct as given, write C in the answer column. **References:** Sections 1–3.

1. Dawn Sam and I now use lightweight compact camcorders in our training sessions        1. _____
2. Could I please ask you to evaluate my manuscript by this Friday July 6?        2. _____
3. I've just read your memo of March 2 which describes your committee's progress in updating the corporate guidelines on sexual harassment many thanks        3. _____
4. The General Manager of the Accounting department asked how much your new iMac cost        4. _____
5. Did we really win the bid for converting the old mill into condos fantastic!        5. _____
6. It's funny isn't it how people with a push-button phone still listen for a dial tone?        6. _____
7. Did the TV reporter who called friday night leave her name and phone number?        7. _____
8. In my opinion the company's sales will triple by the year 2008        8. _____
9. While you're traveling next month could I please make use of your office?        9. _____
10. I'm opening a fast-food outlet in Boise Idaho and if feasible one in Baker Oregon        10. _____
11. It is critical therefore that their President Rob Kidd cut out lavish corporate perks        11. _____
12. Sort the sales data as follows By product type customer class and ZIP Code        12. _____
13. Sarah Hess M.B.A. has joined the company but will not relocate here until fall        13. _____
14. Does the State have jurisdiction or must the case be tried in a Federal court?        14. _____
15. When we went out West last Summer we stayed in an old mining town        15. _____
16. Joe's holdings in the company must be worth at least $1 350 000 wouldn't you say?        16. _____
17. We have therefore decided not to sell even though we got some good bids        17. _____
18. The partners tried to save the business but it folded on june 15 1999        18. _____
19. Is it true Ron that Harvey Snow the Chairman of CMP will run for public office?        19. _____
20. In 2003 we almost hired Wim VanVliet Jr. of Tubbins Inc. for the job of CFO  [commas not needed]        20. **C**
21. To operate the equipment turn the key to the right to stop it press the red panel        21. _____
22. After he accepted the settlement Gary said why didn't I ask for more!?        22. _____
23. (See chapter 3 the man with the gun in the book a time to be saved)        23. _____
    [or: ...me. However, please...]
24. The new officers are Sue Fox President Rob Henry Secretary and Jon Poe Treasurer        24. _____
25. Your figures look okay to me however please get the finance department's approval        25. _____
26. Is the Institute of Management Consultants near Grand Central station?        26. _____
27. She has written articles on american history and politics in the twentieth century  [or: ...century. For...]
    for example her thesis was on the great depression and the thirties        27. _____
28. After I lost my job I went back to Southern Ohio but I miss Washington D.C.        28. _____
29. Tony Nye along with his family flew to Rome to celebrate new year's eve        29. _____
30. An ad hoc committee was formed in June 2003 or was it 2004?        30. _____

Name _____  Date _____  Class _____  1

# 1

## *Rule Numbers*
# Diagnostic Survey

**Directions:** Correct the punctuation and capitalization in each sentence below. If the punctuation is incorrect, draw a line through it: *an old winter coat.* If new punctuation is to be inserted, circle it: *I too hope so.* To change a small letter to a capital letter, draw three lines under it: *christmas.* To change a capital letter to a small letter, draw a line through it: *Enough.* If a sentence is correct as given, write *C* in the answer column. **References:** Sections 1–3.

1. Dawn Sam and I now use lightweight compact camcorders in our training sessions   `123b/162a`   `168a`   `101a`   1. _____

2. Could I please ask you to evaluate my manuscript by this Friday July 6   `148`   `103b`   2. _____

3. I've just read your memo of March 2 which describes your committee's progress in updating the corporate guidelines on sexual harassment many thanks   `131b/152`   `101a/301b`   `101b`   `313d`   `309/322`   3. _____

4. The General Manager of the Accounting department asked how much your new iMac cost   `104`   4. _____

5. Did we really win the bid for converting the old mill into condos fantastic   `110a`   `301b`   `119`   5. _____

6. It's funny isn't it how people with a push-button phone still listen for a dial tone   `114a/122a`   `131a`   `114a`   `110a`   6. _____

7. Did the TV reporter who called friday night, leave her name and phone number   `342`   7. _____

8. In my opinion the Company's sales will triple by the year 2008   `124b/139a, 321`   `149`   `101a`   8. _____

9. While you're traveling next month could I please make use of your office   `130a`   `103b`   9. _____

10. I'm opening a fast-food outlet in Boise Idaho and if feasible one in Baker Oregon   `160`   `122a/144`   `160`   `101a`   10. _____

11. It is critical therefore that their President Rob Kidd cut out lavish corporate perks   `122c/141`   `312b`   `148`   `101a`   11. _____

12. Sort the sales data as follows. By product type customer class and ZIP Code   `189`   `196`   `123b/162`   `101a`   `343`   `101a`   12. _____

13. Sarah Hess M.B.A. has joined the Company, but will not relocate here until Fall   `157`   `309/321`   `127b`   13. _____

14. Does the State have jurisdiction or must the case be tried in a Federal court   `335b`   `123a/126a`   `328`   `110a`   14. _____

15. When we went out West last Summer we stayed in an old mining town   `338`   `343`   `130a`   `169`   `101a`   15. _____

16. Joe's holdings in the company must be worth at least $1250000 wouldn't you say   `123d`   `114/122b`   `114`   16. _____

17. We have therefore decided not to sell even though we got some good bids   `122c/141`   `131b/132`   `342`   `143`   `101a`   17. _____

18. The partners tried to save the business but it folded on june 15 1999   `123a/126a`   `148`   `313d`   `148`   `110a`   18. _____

19. Is it true Ron that Harvey Snow the Chairman of CMP will run for public office   `145`   `156`   `159`   `101a`   19. _____

20. In 2003 we almost hired Wim VanVliet Jr. of Tubbins Inc. for the job of CFO   `135c`   `128/176a`   `136a`   `101a`   20. _____

21. To operate the equipment turn the key to the right to stop it press the red panel   `135b`   `130a`   `256a/227/301c`   `249a/227/257`   `101a`   21. _____

22. After he accepted the settlement Gary said why didn't I ask for more   `130a`   `256a/227/301c`   `249a/227/257`   22. _____

23. (See chapter 3 the man with the gun in the book a time to be saved   `359`   `148/242`   `360/361a`   `148/247a`   `289a/290/360/361a`   `101a/220`   23. _____

24. The new officers are: Sue Foy President Rob Henry Secretary and Jon Poe Treasurer   `191c`   `148/313d`   `184`   `148/313d`   `184`   `148`   `313d`   `101a`   24. _____

25. Your figures look okay to me however please get the finance department's approval   `178`   `142a`   `322`   `101a`   25. _____

26. Is the Institute Of Management Consultants near Grand Central station   `303`   `331`   `110a`   26. _____

27. She has written articles on american history, and politics in the twentieth century for example her thesis was on the great depression and the thirties   `304`   `352`   `125t`   `345`   `181a`   `344a`   `345`   `101a`   `142a/181a`   `160`   `101a`   27. _____

28. After I lost my job I went back to Southern Ohio but I miss Washington D.C.   `130a`   `341`   `133/177c`   28. _____

29. Tony Nye along with his family flew to Rome to celebrate new year's eve   `146a`   `342`   `101a`   29. _____

30. An "ad hoc" committee was formed in June 2003 or was it 2004   `287`   `155`   `207`   `110a`   30. _____

Name _____   Date _____   Class _____   1

**Directions:** The following items deal with problems in number style, abbreviations, plural and possessive forms, spelling, compound words, and word division. (*Note:* The symbol / is used in items 96–100 to show word division at the end of a line.) If an item is correct as given, write *C* in the answer column. If an item is incorrect, circle the error and show the correct form in the answer column. **References:** Sections 4–9.

| # | Item | Answer | Ref |
|---|------|--------|-----|
| 31. | six tapes and 15 CDs | 6 | 402 |
| 32. | no later than March 21st | 21 | 407b |
| 33. | priced under $100.00 | $100 | 415 |
| 34. | more than $.15 apiece | 15 cents | 418 |
| 35. | . . . said yes. 12 said no. | Twelve | 421 / 424 |
| 36. | early in the 21st century | twenty-first | 438 |
| 37. | nearly 2/3 occupied | two-thirds | 427 |
| 38. | sold in eight-ounce cans | 8 | 429a |
| 39. | until I turned five | C | 434 |
| 40. | a 15-year mortgage | C | 436a |
| 41. | more than 20 years ago | twenty | 437 / 440 |
| 42. | starts at seven P.M. | 7 p.m. | 453a |
| 43. | heard from B.J. Malone | B. J. | 516a |
| 44. | referred by Doctor Milano | Dr. | 517a |
| 45. | an F.B.I. investigation | FBI | 524a |
| 46. | US Department of Labor | U.S. | 525 |
| 47. | works in Washington, D.C. | C | 527 |
| 48. | 8 yds. @ $2.75 | yd | 535 |
| 49. | a tolerance of 2 mm. | mm | 538b |
| 50. | an IRS audit | C | 522 |
| 51. | not many vacancys | vacancies | 604 |
| 52. | talk to my attornies | attorneys | 605 |
| 53. | built additional shelfs | shelves | 608b |
| 54. | both my brothers-in-law | C | 612a |
| 55. | use only one criteria | criterion | 614 |
| 56. | called the Peabodies | Peabodys | 615c |
| 57. | throughout the 1990's | 1990s | 624a |
| 58. | can't read my boss' notes | boss's | 631a |
| 59. | bought Ed Jones's house | Jones's | 631a,c |
| 60. | both agencies' assets | C | 632a |
| 61. | womens' compensation | women's | 633 |
| 62. | it's Daisy's, not our's | ours | 636 |
| 63. | Mark and Tom's allergies | Mark's | 642a |
| 64. | bought six dollars worth | dollars' | 646 |
| 65. | talk about us buying a car | our | 647a |
| 66. | prefered to relocate | preferred | 702 |
| 67. | credited my account | credited | 704 |
| 68. | used sound judgement | judgment | 708 |
| 69. | felt quite releived | relieved | 712 |
| 70. | required assistence | assistance | 714 |
| 71. | is now superceded | superseded | 716a |
| 72. | retype your resumé | résumé | 718a |
| 73. | the details don't jibe | C | 719 |
| 74. | more then we need | than | 719 |
| 75. | it's to far to go | too | 719 |
| 76. | look for a concensus | consensus | 720 |
| 77. | after next Febuary | February | 720 |
| 78. | serve as liason | liaison | 720 |
| 79. | discussed publically | publicly | 720 |
| 80. | just read the summery | summary | 720 |
| 81. | too much paperwork | C | 801a |
| 82. | I'll follow-up on it | follow up | 802 |
| 83. | review these print-outs | printouts | 803d |
| 84. | time for decision making | C | 805a |
| 85. | likes it single spaced | single-spaced | 812a / 813 |
| 86. | high risk investments | high-risk | 816a |
| 87. | a nine-month's schedule | nine-month OR nine months' | 817 |
| 88. | a real estate syndicate | C | 818a |
| 89. | a tax exempt purchase | tax-exempt | 820a |
| 90. | becomes habit forming | habit-forming | 821a |
| 91. | too high priced for me | high-priced | 823a |
| 92. | a clearly written draft | C | 824a |
| 93. | is this up-to-date | up to date | 831a |
| 94. | need to re-emphasize | reemphasize | 835a |
| 95. | is rather self serving | self-serving | 836a |
| 96. | they plan-/ ned poorly | planned | 902 |
| 97. | sim-/ ilar conditions | simi-/ lar | 913 |
| 98. | contin-/ uous motion | continu-/ ous | 914 |
| 99. | recall-/ ing the past | C | 922a |
| 100. | compell-/ ing reasons | compel-/ ling | 922b |

2

**Directions:** Underline all errors and write the correct forms in the answer column. If a sentence is correct as given, write *C* in the answer column. **References:** Sections 10–11.

| | | | |
|---|---|---|---|
| 101. | Every videocassette and compact disc <u>are</u> now on sale. | 101. | is    1002c / 1009b |
| 102. | Not one of the photocopiers <u>are</u> working properly. | 102. | is    1006a / 1008a |
| 103. | <u>Does</u> any of the orders call for out-of-stock items? | 103. | Do    1013a |
| 104. | Some criteria on eligibility for outplacement services <u>has</u> to be established. | 104. | have    1006a / 1018a |
| 105. | The number of responses to our mail campaign <u>were</u> unusually high. | 105. | was    1023 |
| 106. | Diane is one of those managers who always <u>resolves</u> problems quickly. | 106. | resolve    1008b |
| 107. | None of the bidders have handled this big a project before. | 107. | C    1013a |
| 108. | I wish I <u>was</u> free to work with you on the Henderson case. | 108. | were    1039a |
| 109. | Can the company maintain <u>their</u> dominant position in the marketplace? | 109. | its    1020 / 1049a |
| 110. | Apparently, everyone on staff has been notified except you and <u>I</u>. | 110. | me    1055b |
| 111. | You obviously know a good deal more about this new technology than <u>me</u>. | 111. | I    1057 |
| 112. | Valerie and <u>myself</u> are the only ones who still report to Mrs. Lee. | 112. | I    1060d |
| 113. | <u>Whom</u> do you think is going to get the Hong Kong assignment? | 113. | Who    1061 |
| 114. | We had a <u>real</u> nice going-away party for Celia Frazier. | 114. | really    1065 |
| 115. | I felt very <u>badly</u> about George's decision to retire. | 115. | bad    1067 |
| 116. | I don't see <u>nothing</u> wrong with the plan you have devised. | 116. | anything    1076 |
| 117. | What <u>affect</u> will the increased sales tax have on your firm? | 117. | effect    1101 |
| 118. | We've had a great <u>amount</u> of calls on the basis of one ad. | 118. | number    1101 |
| 119. | I'm afraid we won't have more stock on Model 364-A for <u>awhile</u>. | 119. | a while    1101 |
| 120. | You need to work for greater precision and <u>less</u> mistakes. | 120. | fewer    1101 |

**Directions:** Rewrite the following sentences to correct all errors. **References:** Primarily Sections 10–11.

121. Every businessman should review his objectives continuously.   **All business managers should review their objectives continually.**
  *(1053a   809a   1052a / 1053a   719)*

122. They not only plan to audit this years' records but also last year.   **They plan to audit not only this year's records but also last year's.**
  *(1081b   630a   644 / 1071)*

123. Neither the salesclerks nor the sales manager has received his bonus check.   **Neither the sales manager nor the salesclerks have received their bonus checks.**
  *(1005   1049c)*

124. When taking a trip, money can be saved. If reservations are made in advance.   **When taking a trip, you can save money if you make reservations in advance.**
  *(1082   101c   1037b)*

125. The contract's terms have been carefully reviewed by everyone of us.   **Every one of us has carefully reviewed the terms of the contract.**
  *(645   1037b   1010, note)*

**Directions:** On the reverse side of this sheet you will find a letter to **Ms. Gina A. Hodgkins** (typed in modified-block style—standard format with standard punctuation). Correct all errors in style, grammar, and format; also look for errors in typing and content. Circle all changes you make within the lines or out in the margins; if you prefer, show all changes on a separate sheet, identified by line number. If time permits, retype the corrected letter on a plain sheet of paper, using 1.25-inch side margins and positioning the date on the first line below a 2-inch top margin. **References:** Section 13 plus Sections 1–12. See also pages 358–359 or the inside back cover of *The Gregg Reference Manual* for a chart showing how to indicate corrections on typed material.

Name _____ Date _____ Class _____    3

# Seco Valley Inn

Post Office Box 151 - Sonoma, California 95476
Telephone: (707) 555-9850 - Fax: (707) 555-9867 E-Mail: svi@aol.com

August
~~Aug.~~ 7, 2007

Ms.
Gina A. Hodgkins
Director of administrative services
Robb, Steele & Baggett
Suite 1950
612 W. 6th St. → West Sixth Street
Los Angeles, CA 90017

Dear Ms. ~~Hodgekin,~~ Hodgkins:

Thank you very much for your letter of August 2nd, in which you expressed an interest in bringing the partners in your law firm to Seco Valley Inn for their annual retreat later this fall. We would be delighted to serve you and your associates in anyway that we can. Let me try to answer the questions you asked in your letter.

1. It will take you about an hour or two to drive from the Airport South of San Francisco to the inn, depending on the time of day you come across the Golden Gate bridge.

2. A 16-hole golf course surrounds the inn. Also readily accessible are eight all-weather tennis courts, a fully equipped exercise room and in and outdoor swimming pools.

3. Room service is available from 6:00 am to 11:00 pm. The Coffee Garden provides a causal menu throughout the day and the Elbow Room offers an elegant award-wining menu for lunch and dinner.

I am enclosing a brochure that describes all our facilities in greater detail. Also enclosed ~~is~~ a schedule of our room rates and a reservation form on which you can indicate the accomodations you want. All of us here at Seco Valley Inn look forward to serving you.

Sincerly yours,

Lyle A. Montoya
General Manager

Enclosures 3
gad

4

13
14
15
16
17
18
19
20
21
22
23
24
25
26
27
28
29
30
31
32
33
34
35
36
37
38
39
40
41
42
43
44
45
46
47
48
49
50
51
52
53
54
55
56
57

# NOTES ON WORKSHEET 1, PAGE 4

**Line 13:**
1. Change *Aug.* to *August.* [1313a]
2. Separate the day and the year with a comma *(August 7, 2007).* [1313a]

**Line 17:**
3. Insert *Ms.* before *Gina A. Hodgkins.* [1321a]

**Line 18:**
4. Capitalize *Administrative Services.* [1324c]
5. Omit the comma after *Services.* [1308b]

**Line 20:**
6. Omit the comma in the suite number *(1950).* [462]

**Line 21:**
7. Spell out *West.* [1330a]
8. Spell out *Sixth.* [1329b]
9. Spell out *Street.* [1328c]

**Line 22:**
10. Omit the comma before the ZIP Code. [161, 1332a]

**Line 24:**
11. Change *Hodgekin* to *Hodgkins* (as in the inside address and the directions). [1202c, 1338f]
12. Change the comma to a colon. [194a, 1338b]

**Line 26:**
13. Change the second *you* to *your* (a typographical error). [1202b]
14. Change *2nd* to *2* in the date. [407b]
15. Insert a comma after *2* (a nonessential clause follows). [122d, 152]

**Lines 26–27:**
16. Do not divide *expressed* before *ed* (*pressed* is one syllable). [901c]

**Line 28:**
17. Do not capitalize *fall.* [343]

**Line 29:**
18. Spell *any way* as two words. [1101]

**Lines 32, 36, 40:**
19. Insert a period after *1, 2,* and *3* in the enumeration. [106, 1345d]

**Line 32:**
20. Spell out *two.* [401a, 404a]
21. Do not capitalize *airport.* [308]
22. Do not capitalize *south.* [338b]

**Lines 33–34, 37–38, 41–42:**
23. Align the turnovers in the displayed enumeration with the first word in the first line. [1345d]

**Line 33:**
24. Change *San Fransisco* to *San Francisco.* [720]

**Line 34:**
25. Capitalize *Bridge.* [331]

**Line 36:**
26. Hyphenate *36-hole.* [817a]

**Line 37:**
27. Hyphenate *all-weather.* [814, 816a]
28. Do not hyphenate *fully equipped.* [824a]
29. Insert a series comma after *room.* [123b, 184]
30. Insert a suspending hyphen after *in* (*in- and outdoor swimming pools*). [832d]

**Line 40:**
31. Omit the colon and the zeros from *6* and *11.* [440c]
32. Insert periods in *a.m.* and *p.m.* [507]
33. Replace the hyphen with *to* in the phrase *from 6 a.m. to 11 p.m.* [459b]

**Line 41:**
34. Change *causal* to *casual.* [719]
35. Insert a comma after *day* (to separate two independent clauses connected by *and*). [123a, 126a]

**Line 42:**
36. Insert a comma after *elegant.* [168a]
37. Hyphenate *award-winning.* [821a]
38. Change *wining* to *winning.* [701]

**Line 44:**
39. Do not indent the first line of a paragraph in a letter typed in modified-block style—standard format. [1302a(1)]
40. Omit the comma before *that* (introducing an essential clause). [131a, 132]
41. Change *facilitys* to *facilities.* [604]

**Line 45:**
42. Change *is* to *are* to agree with the plural subject that follows *(schedule* and *reservation form).* [1027a]

**Line 46:**
43. Change *accomodations* to *accommodations.* [720]

**Line 47:**
44. Change *foreward* to *forward.* [719, 1203a]

**Lines 49, 53–54:**
45. Begin the complimentary closing and the signature block at the center, aligned with the date line. [1346a]

**Line 49:**
46. Spell *Sincerely* with two *e*'s. [708, 720]
47. Omit the apostrophe from *yours.* [1056c, 1346d]
48. Insert a comma after *Sincerely yours.* [1346c]

**Line 56:**
49. Change *Enclosure 1* to *Enclosures 3* or a similar expression (to agree with lines 44–46 in the letter). [1203e, 1358a]

**Lines 56–57:**
50. The reference initials should precede the enclosure notation. [1355a, 1358b]

Final copy with
1.25" side margins

August 7, 2007

Ms. Gina A. Hodgkins
Director of Administrative Services
Robb, Steele & Baggett
Suite 1950
612 West Sixth Street
Los Angeles, CA 90017

Dear Ms. Hodgkins:

Thank you very much for your letter of August 2, in which you expressed an interest in bringing the partners in your law firm to Seco Valley Inn for their annual retreat later this fall. We would be delighted to serve you and your associates in any way that we can. Let me try to answer the questions you asked in your letter.

1. It will take you about an hour or two to drive from the airport south of San Francisco to the inn, depending on the time of day you come across the Golden Gate Bridge.

2. A 36-hole golf course surrounds the inn. Also readily accessible are eight all-weather tennis courts, a fully equipped exercise room, and in- and outdoor swimming pools.

3. Room service is available from 6 a.m. to 11 p.m. The Coffee Garden provides a casual menu throughout the day, and the Elbow Room offers an elegant, award-winning menu for lunch and dinner.

I am enclosing a brochure that describes all our facilities in greater detail. Also enclosed are a schedule of our room rates and a reservation form on which you can indicate the accommodations you want. All of us here at Seco Valley Inn look forward to serving you.

Sincerely yours,

Lyle A. Montoya
General Manager

gad
Enclosures 3

# 2  The Period, the Question Mark, and the Exclamation Point

**Directions:** Supply the appropriate mark of punctuation at the end of each sentence and circle it. If no additional punctuation is required, write *C* in the answer column. **References:** ¶¶101–121.

1. I want to thank you for the fine job you did on the Miller-Jacobs study⊙    1. _____ 101a
2. May I please get your thoughts on how the seminar should be structured ⊙    2. _____ 103a
3. May I invite outside speakers to participate in the seminar?    3. _____ 103b
4. I doubt whether you can find a flight that leaves before 6:30 a.m.    4. **C** 101a
5. Does the CEO really expect the staff to buy that story? Incredible!    5. _____ 119a
6. Would you please have the bill sent to my home address⊙    6. _____ 103a
7. Would you please take care of my cats while I'm away for a month?    7. _____ 103b
8. Why don't you shift your advertising account to Bell, Buch, and Kendall Inc.?    8. _____ 110a
9. The only remaining question is, Do the benefits justify the risks?    9. _____ 115
10. The only remaining question is whether the benefits justify the risks ⊙    10. _____ 115
11. Be sure to verify any figures that Harry Hanks comes up with⊙    11. _____ 101a
12. May I suggest that you talk to your lawyer before signing this contract ⊙    12. _____ 103a
13. I would like to ask why the Bolling project is 50 percent over budget ⊙    13. _____ 104
14. What do you make of this phrase—"at a date to be specified"?    14. _____ 110a
15. I can rely on your support at the board meeting, can't I ?    15. _____ 114a
16. I question the wisdom of doing business with a company called Quality Ltd.    16. **C** 101a
17. To obtain a copy, would you please send us a stamped, self-addressed envelope ⊙    17. _____ 103a
18. Would you let me keep the battery of your BMW charged while you're gone?    18. _____ 103b
19. The sales manager has asked when Model GRX-10 will be back in stock ⊙    19. _____ 104
20. When do you expect to receive your M.B.A.? Next year?    20. _____ 111
21. Now, to return to the main point of my argument ⊙    21. _____ 101b
22. Would you please let us know whether we can do anything more to help you ⊙    22. _____ 103a
23. Could you please arrange to have all the papers ready for me by Friday?    23. _____ 103b
24. You need to deal with the question of how much money you can afford to risk ⊙    24. _____ 115
25. Why not consult your accountant and ask her for her opinion?    25. _____ 110b
26. Where the newspaper got its information will be revealed in tomorrow's issue ⊙    26. _____ 104
27. Has anyone thought about the page design? the font? the type size?    27. _____ 117
28. The action we need to take is obvious; the question is how to break it to the members of the staff ⊙    28. _____ 104
29. We still have the right, do we not, to terminate the agreement in thirty days?    29. _____ 114a
30. We just read about your graduating *summa cum laude.* Congratulations!    30. _____ 120

Name _____ Date _____ Class _____    5

**Directions:** Rewrite the following sentences to correct all errors in punctuation and to eliminate sentence fragments. Change the capitalization as necessary. **References:** ¶¶101–121. Also see ¶101c for a brief discussion of sentence fragments.

**31.** Be sure to proofread the originals carefully. Before you run off 250 copies. __Be sure to__ __proofread the originals carefully before you run off 250 copies.__ 101a 101c

**32.** Did you actually tell your boss that you didn't want the promotion, why? __Did you actually tell__ __your boss that you didn't want the promotion? Why?__ 110a 111

**33.** Is it true that you're planning to move back East, when, where? __Is it true that you're planning__ __to move back East? When? Where?__ 117

**34.** Why don't you call the box office? To see whether there are any seats left. __Why don't you call__ __the box office to see whether there are any seats left?__ 110a 101c

**35.** You can estimate, can't you?, how many units you expect to sell this year. __You can estimate,__ __can't you, how many units you expect to sell this year?__ 114a

**Directions:** Supply missing periods, question marks, and exclamation points. Change the capitalization as necessary. Circle all changes you make. **References:** ¶¶101–121.

**36.** The objectives of this special exercise program are:

1. To teach you new techniques of relaxation. 106
2. To restore your energy and your sense of well-being. 107

**37.** *Illustration caption:* Figure 2-6. Federal Reserve Discount Rate Changes 108

**38.** I bought a quilt in your store about a week ago. However, it doesn't go with the color scheme in my bedroom. Will you please refund my money when I return it? 101a 103b

**39.** You asked whether I would consider forming a partnership with you and your two brothers. By all means. [OR: !] 104 101b 119a

**40.** Jack reports that we did twice as much business this year at the jewelry show as we did last year. Unbelievable! How do you account for it? 101a 119a 110a

**41.** How we can get our candidate elected is the big question. We can count on your backing, can't we? 116 114a

**42.** Why not rent a videocassette from our extensive collection of new releases? Better yet, buy one outright. Our prices are so low that they'll seem unbelievable! [OR: .] 110b 101a 119

**43.** Will you please make sure that all the managers attend the special meeting set for this Friday. I want to ask how we can cut costs without affecting quality. 103a 104

**44.** I want Martha Bradley to have the divisional sales reports as soon as possible. Will you please send her a copy of the printouts by messenger. Many thanks. 101a 103a 101b

**45.** May we ask for your help? Would you be willing to contribute $20 to send a city child to camp this summer? Think about it, won't you? 103b 110a 114a

**46.** I hear that Anne Bonney has seen an advance copy of my new book. What did Mrs. B. think of the coverage? the organization? my writing style? 101a 109a 117

[OR: ... The coverage, the organization, and my writing style?]

# 3

# The Comma

**Directions:** Supply missing commas and strike out inappropriate commas in the following sentences. Circle all changes you make. If a sentence is correct as given, write *C* in the answer column. **References:** ¶¶122–125 (the basic comma rules).

1. The new warehouse has to be completed as I understand it by the end of the year. Your people can finish the job by then can't they?

   1. _____ 122a 122b

2. It is obvious however that you cannot complete the work by December 31. We are therefore proceeding to cancel the contract.

   2. _____ 122c

3. *Newsweek* carried a review of your wife's new book *Managing Your Spouse* in the past month or so. The issue was dated September 17 2007 I believe.

   3. _____ 122d 122e 122b

4. Dean Morgan Hennessy Ed.D. will be speaking at an educational symposium in Knoxville Tennessee on stress and teacher burnout in the classroom.

   4. _____ 122f 125f

5. Luke Wharton II has been named to the newly established position of vice president and creative director of R. U. Kidd Inc.

   5. **C** _____ 122f

6. Marla and I have already signed up for the Caribbean cruise but Sandy Peg and Bud are still mulling the trip over.

   6. _____ 123a 123b

7. A lot of creativity and time and hard work went into developing all these handsome imaginative layouts.

   7. _____ 123b 123c

8. Only $24 000 is required on the signing of the contract; $216 000 on the completion of the project.

   8. _____ 123d 123e

9. When I graduated from business school in 2001 I hung out my shingle as a corporate turnaround expert. In order to deal with the extraordinary demand for my services I had to hire three associates in the very first year.

   9. _____ 124

10. You see I've worked with that pair on a number of projects. How they ever got their reputation for competence I'll never know.

    10. _____ 124a 123e

11. In 2002 we established a new set of terms from credit card purchases. In my judgment those terms are now outdated and need to be rethought.

    11. _____ 124b 122a

12. Our whole staff, I am sure will appreciate your kind words.

    12. _____ 125a

13. Margaret Pierce always turns in competent, well-written research papers. Obviously she is ready for bigger things.

    13. _____ 125c 124b

14. I'm sure I heard the commissioner say "These rate increases will be approved." However his assistant says that he did not.

    14. _____ 125b 124b

15. We hope that you will find the meeting facilities satisfactory and that you will tell us about any special needs. Our staff of course is always on call.

    15. _____ 125f 122c

Name _____ Date _____ Class _____ 7

**Directions:** Supply missing commas and strike out inappropriate commas in the following sentences. Correct run-on sentences (see ¶128) by changing punctuation and capitalization as necessary. Circle all changes you make. If a sentence is correct as given, write *C* in the answer column. **References:** ¶¶126–137 plus the basic comma rules (¶¶122–125).

16. Either the contract must be renegotiated or we must find another supplier.
    16. _____ 126a

17. We must either renegotiate the contract or find another supplier.
    17. **C** _____ 127b

18. Give Jamie whatever data you've assembled and let her finish the analysis.
    18. _____ 127c

19. You handle the names from A to M; I'll take care of N to Z. [OR: ⊙]
    19. _____ 128

20. I handle creative assignments and my partner runs the business.
    20. **C** _____ 129

21. If the meeting starts at 8 a.m. I will have to fly in the night before.
    21. _____ 130a

22. However you want to organize the all-day meeting will be fine with me.
    22. **C** _____ 130c

23. My accountant warned me that before I accepted the financial settlement, I had better consider the tax implications of the arrangement.
    23. _____ 130d

24. This policy applies to employees who have less than six months of service.
    24. **C** _____ 131a

25. Jason Argonne whom I met on a flight to Warsaw turns out to be the uncle of the young woman who is engaged to marry your son.
    25. _____ 131b / 131a

26. Most customers when asked to take a blindfold test could not distinguish the taste of one cola from another.
    26. _____ 131c

27. I sense that Ben Frost is trustworthy even though I have never dealt with him before.
    27. _____ 132 / 122f

28. This year's convention takes place in Portland Maine at the end of May but if you come a week early we can easily work in a trip to Nova Scotia.
    28. _____ 133 / 132 / 130a

29. Having observed how Joe handles the bids I think I can cover for him.
    29. _____ 135a

30. Finding an affordable apartment in this city is not easy.
    30. **C** _____ 135a

31. To receive our highest discount you must order a minimum of 500 units.
    31. _____ 135b

32. In all the years I worked for Mrs. Stebbins I never saw her smile.
    32. _____ 135c

33. On weekdays we are open till 8 p.m.; on Saturdays we close at 6 p.m. [OR: ⊙ On]
    33. _____ 135c / 128

34. The president has announced that out of respect for the memory of Mr. Zucherman the office will be closed on Friday.
    34. _____ 136a

35. What you should do in the meantime is review for the exam.
    35. **C** _____ 137a / 122c

36. What you should do in my opinion is review for the exam. [OR: ⊙ After]
    36. _____ 137b

37. We would like you to speak for about thirty minutes; after a coffee break there will be time for questions and answers. [comma not necessary]
    37. _____ 128 / 135c / 136a

38. At the meeting in Dallas I ran into Ben Hurly who is now with Gasport and spent a few hours recalling old times.
    38. _____ 135c / 131b

39. While I was in graduate school I had to struggle to get through my courses whereas my roommate seemed to coast toward his doctorate.
    39. _____ 130a / 132

40. I'd be willing to meet next week but considering the amount of work you need to do in advance why don't we get together sometime in the following week?
    40. _____ 126a / 127a / 127d / 136a

8

C-22

# 4

# The Comma (Continued)

**Directions:** Supply missing commas and strike out inappropriate commas in the following sentences. Circle all changes you make. If a sentence is correct as given, write *C* in the answer column. **References:** ¶¶138–175 plus the basic comma rules (¶¶122–125) and the rules on clauses and phrases (¶¶126–137).

1. As a rule we can go from the drawing board to the marketplace in less than a year. There are times of course when it takes a little longer.

    1. _____ 139a / 141 / 139b

2. Thus you can now afford an in-ground swimming pool too.

    2. **C** 143a

3. The advertising director along with the marketing managers will present next year's plans on Monday November 5 at 2 p.m.

    3. _____ 146a / 148

4. The word *parameter* is often misused by people who should know better.

    4. **C** 149

5. Thank you for your letter of December 12 in which you expressed a number of reservations about my new book *After the Millennium.*

    5. _____ 152 / 148 / 149

6. Doris Morley according to our personnel files served as promotion director from May 2002 until June 30 2004 the date she resigned.

    6. _____ 122a / 155a / 154a

7. Honorary degrees were awarded yesterday to Wilford B. Williams Esq. and Sarah Kennedy Millstein trustees of Collingwood University.

    7. _____ 157 / 148

8. If you want to reach me while I'm on vacation write to me at this address: Arrowhead Inn 106 Mason Road Durham North Carolina 27712.

    8. _____ 130a / 161 / 167

9. Two aspirin and some strong black coffee always fix me up.

    9. _____ 168 / 139a

10. To sum up these marketing strategies need to be rethought.

    10. _____ 175a

11. In short I think Marianne Yates has the appropriate skills and experience and in my opinion she ought to be promoted.

    11. _____ 139a / 126a / 142b / 124b

12. Well he is the shrewdest, although not the pleasantest person I know.

    12. _____ 144a

13. Dr. Eileen Fahey head of the Halston Health Clinic will retire this year.

    13. _____ 148

14. A parenthetical or nonessential expression should be set off by appropriate punctuation that is by two commas within a sentence or by one comma at the beginning or end of a sentence.

    14. _____ 151 / 148

15. On April 21 2006 we initiated discussions with Llewellyn Perkins of the Micropro Company in Irvine California concerning the acquisition of his software business.                                                     [OR: ⊙]

    15. _____ 154a / 153 / 160

16. Hastings-McConnell Inc. will hold a dinner-dance at the Glen Ridge New Jersey Country Club in honor of Weldon Wright Jr.'s retirement. *(Both the*
    [OR: ⊙] *company and Mr. Wright use commas in their names.)*

    16. _____ 159 / 160 / 156

17. However you want to reorganize your group is entirely your decision.

    17. **C** 139a

Name _____ Date _____ Class _____

18. Senators Allen Barlow and Cantor all agree that the state's methods for financing public education are unfair that the way funds are distributed is inequitable and that a special panel should investigate fairer approaches.

18. _____    162a

19. The more Mr. Felker attacks the plan the more Mrs. Ketcham seems to endorse it. I think that we ought to get Mr. Glenn rather than Mr. Felker to point out the disadvantages of the plan to her. And the faster the better.

19. _____    172d
      147
      172d

20. I'd like to recommend Fred that you recruit a new controller. The auditors I am sorry to say have discovered serious lapses in Don Springer's performance.

20. _____    145
      144

21. My wife Monica and I myself were part of the ecstatic crowd that gave the tenor Thomas Hampson a standing ovation for his performance as Figaro.

21. **c** _____    150
      169

22. Our long-term financial situation now looks much much better than it did a few short months ago.

22. _____    171
      175c
      169

23. A great many ambitious career-minded employees have signed up for Mrs. Horowitz's popular English communications seminar.

23. _____    170

24. The first three letters should be referred to Customer Service for handling; the other five to the Accounts Receivable Department.

24. _____    172a

25. Jim now feels that whatever he does does not count for anything with the people he reports to.

25. _____    175b
      143b

26. You, too, can qualify for this low-cost, easy-to-obtain automobile insurance if you are over 25 and have a clean driving record for the past three years.

26. _____    170
      171
      125f
      167
      169

27. I am pleased to be able to tell you Mr. Berger that the camcorder which you ordered is finally back in stock. You can pick one up at the store or if you prefer have it delivered to your home.

27. _____    145
      131a
      122a

28. If however you and your partner Louis Meltzer prefer to lease the property rather than buy it outright I think I can persuade the owners to agree to that kind of arrangement.

28. _____    142c
      148
      130a

29. On a trip to London Ontario I met an old friend of yours Roy Galt III who is the managing director of Cheswick and Forster Ltd. *(Styling preferences of Galt and the firm Cheswick and Forster are unknown.)*

29. _____    160a
      148
      156
      159

30. Please remember a team of five people has already invested many many hours not to mention thousands of dollars in studying the commercial applications of this new compound.

30. _____    124a
      175c
      144

31. To scrub the project at this time when the first useful data is being uncovered would come as a crushing disappointment.

31. _____    148
      169

32. We would therefore recommend that the present vacation policy be extended until we can investigate what other companies in our industry are doing.

32. _____    141
      132

10

# 5 The Semicolon, the Colon, and the Comma

**Directions:** Supply missing punctuation and strike out or correct inappropriate punctuation in the following sentences. Change the capitalization as necessary. Circle all changes you make. If a sentence is correct as given, write *C* in the answer column. **References:** ¶¶176–199 (on the semicolon and the colon) plus ¶¶122–175 (on the comma).

1. My wife thinks we should move to Maine; myself prefer to stay where we are.
   1. _____ 176a

2. We need to resolve our differences within the next ten days; otherwise I'll take [OR: ⊙ Otherwise...] our business to another order fulfillment company.
   2. _____ 178

3. We have a number of objections to the draft of the agreement; for example it fails [OR: ⊙ For...] to state by what date you will complete the construction.
   3. _____ 181a

4. As a rule, I don't take on malpractice cases, but given the facts as you present them, I would be pleased to represent you.
   4. **C** _____ 139a / 177c / 136a

5. The entire labor dispute boils down to one issue: namely who will set the standards of productivity?
   5. _____ 181b

6. Watch out for words that contain silent letters; for example *autumn mortgage subpoena ophthalmologist*.
   6. _____ 182a

7. Three of our biggest accounts namely Fearoff-Lyon the Porterry Co. and Worth & Worth have submitted strong protests about our plans to close the distribution center in their state.
   7. _____ 183

8. I plan to call on clients in the following locations: Shawnee Mission Kansas; La Crosse Indiana and Fond du Lac Wisconsin.
   8. _____ 189 / 160a / 184

9. The Vreeland property looks like a good buy; the asking price seems in line with the assessed value and the buildings have all been maintained in excellent condition.
   9. _____ 187 / 197 / 167

10. The Vreeland property looks like a good buy; however I'd like more data on the [OR: ⊙ However] zoning laws and the tax rates before I make an offer.
    10. _____ 178 / 182b

11. We need only one final piece to the puzzle: namely the source of the rumor.
    11. _____ 188

12. Those representatives in the Southern Region who exceeded their sales goals by more than 10 percent were Amanda Collins Sue Ellen Mobley and Paul Cox.
    12. _____ 191c / 162a / 187

13. The consultants each identified the same problem: we are understaffed.
    13. _____ 197

14. In short here is what the management consultant told me: the business will need a cash infusion of $200,000 at once; the business also needs an experienced manager to oversee the day-to-day operations. [OR: ; the]
    14. _____ 139a / 187 / 199a / 176

C-25

**Directions:** Supply missing commas, semicolons, and colons as well as the appropriate punctuation at the end of each sentence. Change any incorrect punctuation already supplied. Change the capitalization as necessary. Circle all changes you make. **References:** ¶¶176–199 plus ¶¶101–175.

15. Thank you for your get-well card. I am still confined to bed, but I have been assured that the hip replacement was a complete success. I expect to be up and about in another week, and to be calling on customers within a month. [OR: ; On]
    176b / 126a / 101a / 125f / 101a

16. The Gephardt estimate is not as high as it looks; on the contrary, the amount Gephardt is asking is about the same as the estimate from Kitchens Inc. In fact, if you analyze the estimates closely, Gephardt's is better because of the longer guarantee. [OR: ; Yet...]
    178 / 139a / 130a / 101a

17. Natalie's memo explains why we ran out of stock; yet it does not address the question of how we can avoid running out of stock again.
    179 / 104

18. As it happens, I have a number of reservations about the Hepler Associates market survey; for example, why did they send questionnaires only to people who own their own homes? [OR: . For..]
    130a / 181a / 110

19. I'll be traveling first to Klamath Falls, Oregon; then I'll be going on to Bellingham, Washington. If the negotiations go faster than I've been assuming, I may drive up to visit friends in Prince George, British Columbia. [OR: ; Then]
    160a / 128 / 178 / 101a / 130a

20. Mr. Workman from The Furniture Recyclers wants to know whether you are selling the desks and chairs individually or as a total package; whether the stockroom shelves, the lighting fixtures, and the filing cabinets are also for sale; and whether his drivers can come to collect any of these items before Wednesday, September 28.
    186 / 162a / 148 / 104

21. When selecting a format for a report, consider the following factors:
    130b
    1. For whom are you writing the report?
    189
    2. What outcome do you hope to achieve?
    106 / 107
    3. What is the existing mind-set of your reader?
    110

22. Dear Mrs. Warnecke:

    Thank you for sending us your proposal for a book entitled *How to Start a Successful Business: A Practical Guide for Entrepreneurs.* Would you be able to send us two sample chapters that we can evaluate? Moreover, could you please tell us how long the complete manuscript is likely to run?
    194a / 195a / 101a / 110 / 139a / 103a

23. Why don't we discuss this matter at lunch at 12:30 on Monday, the 14th of April?
    192 / 148 / 110

24. I'll proceed to make reservations for us at Thai Won An, a charming restaurant at 19 Pacific Avenue; do let me know if you prefer some other arrangement, won't you?
    148 / 101a / 114a

25. I'll be glad to reschedule our lunch if that proves necessary; however, I should note that since I'll be leaving the following day on a two-week business trip, I won't be able to see you until after the first of May.
    132 / 101a / 139a / 130d / 101a

12

# 6

# Other Marks of Punctuation

**Directions:** Supply missing punctuation and strike out or correct inappropriate punctuation in the following sentences. Change the capitalization as necessary. Circle all changes you make. **References:** ¶¶201–226 (on the dash and parentheses) and ¶299. For guidance on how to show corrections in these sentences, see the chart on pages 358–359 or the inside back cover of *The Gregg Reference Manual.*

1. Here's a year-round vacation house that's ideal for you and your family/and at a price you can afford!                                          207

2. Chapter 8 discusses the techniques that can make regional marketing work for your company (see pages 86–89). [OR: ⊙ (See pages 86-89⊙)]                   220

3. Family that's what justifies the struggle to make this business succeed.                   210

4. On all expense account items over $25, please be sure to provide (a) a dated receipt and (b) an explanation of the business purpose served by the expense.                   222a

5. Three parts of olive oil, one part of vinegar, and one part of pure maple syrup that's all you need to make an outstanding salad dressing.                   211b

6. Al Riesman (He's the marketing guru we frequently consult) thinks that the approach we're taking in our new advertising campaigns is a total disaster.                   224b 224c

7. Enclosed are the layouts for the catalog/—just the way you wanted them.                   213

8. I thought we had agreed on a formula for compensation in the event the project is terminated before completion. (See your letter dated June 11.)                   226c

9. We will need the large meeting room we had last year—you will surely remember the one I mean; otherwise, we will have to break into two groups. [OR: ⊙ Otherwise...]                   215c

10. In two weeks—October 4, to be exact—the President's panel is expected to release its recommendations on a national health insurance plan.                   216a 299

11. Once a week (on Thursday nights we stay open) until 9 o'clock.                   218

12. At least three people in the company Ed Reidinger, Gertrude Flanagan, and Hope Crawley have volunteered to donate O positive blood.                   202 219

13. In about three months from now say, November 30 why don't we meet to review the committee's progress in drafting guidelines for an internal recycling program?                   211a

14. Attached are the notes I made during each session at the management seminar (except the session on reducing employee absenteeism, which I missed).                   225a

15. Timothy Noonan, the head of our Chapel Hill North Carolina operations, may be taking over as manager of the Mount Vernon New York office.                   219

16. Ella Garner—She used to work in your legal department, didn't she?—has a good chance of being appointed a federal judge in the Ninth Circuit.                   214b

Name _____  Date _____  Class _____   13

C-27

**Directions:** Supply missing punctuation and strike out or correct any inappropriate punctuation in the following sentences. Change the capitalization as necessary. Circle all changes you make. **References:** ¶¶227–299 (primarily on quotation marks and the use of italics or underlining).

17. All he would say to the reporters was "I have no comment to make at this time."

256a
247a

18. Please forward any mail marked "Personal" otherwise, hold everything else until I return to the office. [OR: Otherwise...]

248a

19. What was the meaning you intended to convey in the phrase "must be completed within a reasonable time"?

249b

20. I think you ought to read Chapter 5, "Managing Your Problem-Solving Time" in Right on Time!: The Complete Guide for Time-Pressured Managers.

242
247a
289a

21. I've been given carte blanche on the design and packaging of our new cologne.

287

22. All personnel evaluation memos must be labeled "Confidential."

247a

23. All Beverly would say was this: "If you want to get to the bottom of the matter, why don't you ask Terry?" [OR: say,]

256b
249a
256a

24. Why would Gina say, "I'm going to start updating my résumé"?

257

25. The term infer means to draw a conclusion from someone else's words or actions; the term imply means to suggest something by your own words or actions.

286
248a
247a

26. "How will we explain this decision to the shareholders?" I asked.

254

27. How did you like Hank's latest article, "Are Happy Days Really Here Again?"

258

28. In her memo of June 3 Hazel says, "I'll keep you appraised [sic] of our progress in improving language skills throughout the organization."

283
296a

29. The real question is, Should we be expanding into areas where we have no in-house expertise?

229

30. Altschuler's speech to the financial analysts was well received. (His later comments to the press [see the December 13 issue of The Wall Street Journal] created quite an uproar, I understand.)

296b
289a

31. How many of our employees have read The Art of Getting Things Done?

290a

32. What this company needs is an ombudsman, someone who would represent our customers' interests and make sure that their complaints were fairly resolved.

287

33. Harry Halpin, the noted financial analyst, says, "In my experience . . . these short-term fluctuations in stock prices mean nothing."

274

34. Here are the procedures one authority recommends for typing messages on postcards:

   "First, set the left and right margins at 0.5 inch.

   "Next, type the date on the third line from the top of the card, beginning at the center.

   "Omit the name and address of the person to whom the card is being sent."

265b

35. "I would like to urge you all," said the speaker, Nancy Ellington, "to read an article entitled "The Salvation of Our Cities" in this month's issue of The Atlantic."

262
245a
289a

# 7  Editing Survey A

**Directions:** Supply missing punctuation and strike out or correct any inappropriate punctuation in the following **personal letter.** Change the capitalization as necessary. Circle all changes you make. **References:** Sections 1–2.

Dear Mark, [194a]                                                                                    **1**

When you came to visit last Sunday with Sally and the kids, you were obviously brooding about [124/130a]   **2**

your "dead-end job as a corporate accountant." Yesterday, I came across an article in The New [247a] [124b] [290a]   **3**

York Times that might provide the solution to your problem. (I seem to have mislaid the article, [290a] [123a/126a]   **4**

but I'll send it along, as soon as it turns up.) [133] [226]                                          **5**

Have you considered becoming a CMA? "What's that," I hear you asking? Well, you know that [110a] [?] — 254 — [o] [124]   **6**

a CPA is a certified public accountant — someone who (1) works for a variety of clients and (2) has [216a] [222a] [222a]   **7**

passed a number of required courses and exams administered by the American Institute of          **8**

Certified Public Accountants. To become a CMA, you have to work within a corporation, have at [124/135b]   **9**

least two years of managerial accounting experience, and meet all the certification requirements of [162a]   **10**

the Institute of Management Accountants.                                                           **11**

"Big deal," I can hear you thinking. "Why bother?" According to the article, (which has to be [253a] [263] [224a] [149]   **12**

around here somewhere), top corporate executives are looking for management accountants, who [124/224a]   **13**

can play a bigger part in shaping corporate strategies in an age of intensified global competition, [125f]   **14**

and rapid technological changes. Because these top executives recognize the value of certification,  **15**

corporate accountants with a CMA rating are more likely to get the higher-level, management [169/170] [OR: o For...]   **16**

accounting jobs. Moreover, the CMA designation typically commands a higher salary; for example, [138a/139a] [181a]   **17**

CMAs in your age group (30–39) earn about $10,000 more than people with the same experience     **18**

but without the certification.                                                                     **19**

If you want to follow up on this idea, the Institute of Management Accountants is located at, [161/191c]   **20**

10 Paragon Drive, Montvale, NJ 07645; the phone number is 800-638-4427. If you're not [161] [176a]   **21**

interested, just pitch this letter in the nearest circular file, which is where all of your father's [101c/148]   **22**

brilliant ideas typically wind up. I really don't care, as a matter of fact, what happens to your career. [122a/144a]   **23**

It's my grandchildren's future that I worry about. Give them all a hug for me.                     **24**

---

**Note to Instructor: There is a total of 30 errors in this material.**

Name _____ Date _____ Class _____     15

**Directions:** Supply missing punctuation and strike out or correct any inappropriate punctuation in the following **personal letter.** Change the capitalization as necessary. Circle all changes you make. **References:** Sections 1–2.

Dear Mary Lee, ¹⁹⁴ᵃ          **1**

    You've been working much too hard lately, don't you think? ¹¹⁴ᵃ I'd like to propose a three-day    **2**

getaway for the two of us—and maybe our husbands as well. The occasion? ¹¹¹ A conference    **3**

sponsored by the North Carolina Bed & Breakfast Association. ¹⁰² Friends of ours—Barbara and Gerry    **4**

Ryan ²⁰¹/²⁰⁶ tell me that the conference is designed to appeal not only to perspiring innkeepers (those    **5**

who are currently doing it) and expiring innkeepers (those who want to get out from under) but    **6**

also to aspiring innkeepers (namely ¹³⁸ᵃ you and me) ²²⁵ᵃ The conference formally begins on Saturday,    **7**

February 24 ¹⁴⁸ at 4 p.m., and it runs until 12:30 p.m. on Monday, the 26th. If we register for only    **8**

one day's series of meetings ¹³⁰ᵃ/¹³² the fee is $75; for all three days ¹⁷²ᵃ $125.    **9**

    It sounds a little crazy ¹²²ᵃ/¹⁴⁴ᵃ I know, but you and I are always talking about how much fun it would    **10**

be to move away from Washington, D.C. ¹⁶⁰ᵃ and set ourselves up as country innkeepers. Even if the    **11**

idea is only a pipe dream right now ¹²⁵ᶠ and can't be seriously pursued for another thirty years, it    **12**

would still be a lot of fun to find out what's involved from people who really know.    **13**

    The location of the conference alone makes the trip worthwhile—the Biltmore Estate in    **14**

Asheville, North Carolina. The Biltmore House itself is a national treasure ¹²²ᵇ/¹⁴⁴ᵃ I'm told. Commissioned    **15**

in 1887 by George Vanderbilt and modeled after elegant French chateaus ¹²⁴/¹³⁵ᵃ it remains the largest ¹⁶⁹    **16**

private home in this country today, with its 35 guest rooms, its banquet hall and library, its    **17**

handsome collection of sculpture and paintings ¹⁶²ᵃ and its extensive grounds. It will take us from six    **18**

to eight hours to get there ¹³⁷ depending on which of us does most of the driving.    **19**

    All the meetings will be held right on the grounds of the estate ¹²³ᵃ/¹²⁶ᵃ but there will be time each    **20**

day to work in as much exploring and sightseeing as we like. It may help you to know that ¹³⁰ᵈ If we    **21**

register by January 15, we can be sure of getting attractive accommodations at one of the local    **22**

inns ¹⁰¹ᶜ for only $50 a night.    **23**

    The conference offers formal presentations on virtually every topic you can think of. (For    **24**

example ¹³⁸ᵃ/¹³⁹ the title of one speech is ¹⁴⁵ "How to Handle Difficult Guests" ²⁴² ²²⁶ᵃ One especially nice feature of    **25**

the program ¹⁴⁵ Mary Lee is all the time set aside for networking. In that way we can talk with some    **26**

of the perspiring innkeepers, the ones who know what it's all about; ¹⁷⁸ [OR: ⊙ Moreover,…] moreover, we can meet some    **27**

of the expiring innkeepers, the ones who might have just the place you'd love to take over.    **28**

    One final thought. Why don't you persuade your husband ¹⁵⁰ Jeff to make the trip with you? ¹¹⁰ᵃ If    **29**

he says ²³³ yes I'm sure I could get Dave to come ¹⁴³ᵃ too. The only question is how ¹¹⁵ can you resist so    **30**

attractive a proposition? ¹¹⁵ Look ¹²⁴ᵃ why don't you talk this over with Jeff and get back to me? The    **31**

sooner I get a positive response from you ¹⁷²ᶜ the faster I can make all the necessary arrangements.    **32**

---

Note to Instructor: There is a total of 30 errors in this material.

# 8 Capitalization

**Directions:** If the boldface word or phrase is correctly capitalized, write *C* in the answer column. If not, correct it as follows: To change a capital letter to a small letter, draw a line through it /The. To change a small letter to a capital letter, draw three lines under it /the. Circle all changes you make. **References:** ¶¶301–330.

| | | | |
|---|---|---|---|
| 1. | Have you found the Pelikan **company** to be a dependable supplier? | 1. _____ | 309a 320a |
| 2. | Let's meet in the lobby of the **hotel** and then go on to the convention. | 2. C | 308 |
| 3. | **Attorney general** Harriet Cox has not yet issued an opinion. | 3. _____ | 312a |
| 4. | While you're in Washington, get a reaction from several **senators.** | 4. C | 307 314 |
| 5. | My **uncle** gave me his medical library when he closed his practice. | 5. C | 319a |
| 6. | Please ask the **legal department** to review the attached letter of agreement. | 6. _____ | 322 |
| 7. | That legislation was passed in 1986 by the **Ninety-Ninth Congress.** | 7. _____ | 325 |
| 8. | I seriously question whether the proposed bill is **constitutional.** | 8. C | 304 |
| 9. | Do you think the **governor** will support the antipollution measure? | 9. _____ | 313b |
| 10. | Our new offices are at the corner of Wilson and Sixth **streets.** | 10. _____ | 309a |
| 11. | I have applied for a fellowship at the **University Of The South.** | 11. _____ | 303 320 |
| 12. | Our aim is to set up a franchised operation in every state in the **union.** | 12. _____ | 330a |
| 13. | How do you plan to increase revenues, **governor,** without raising taxes? | 13. _____ | 315 |
| 14. | The people in **accounting** want us to cut 15 percent from our budgets. | 14. _____ | 323 |
| 15. | Should the chapter numbers go in **Roman** numerals or be spelled out? | 15. _____ | 306 |
| 16. | I think we ought to submit a bid on the **van Vleck** property along the river. | 16. _____ | 311e |
| 17. | The **president** of Benjamin Brothers has announced his resignation. | 17. C | 313d |
| 18. | I would like some more information about the **company's** health plan. | 18. C | 321 |
| 19. | All **Federal** and state funding for this training program will end on June 30. | 19. _____ | 328 |
| 20. | The flower garden was sponsored by the Belmont **chamber of commerce.** | 20. _____ | 309a 320a |
| 21. | Do you still have an opening for a **Systems Analyst?** | 21. _____ | 313e |
| 22. | The remaining question is, **how** will this new program be funded? | 22. _____ | 301d |
| 23. | Attending the conference was Watertown's **mayor,** Gilbert Kohlman. | 23. C | 312b |
| 24. | We had the premises inspected by someone from our local **Fire Department.** | 24. _____ | 327 |
| 25. | How do you think **Senator Elect** Coghill will vote on the bond issue? | 25. _____ | 317 |
| 26. | There has been some talk about an antitrust action by the **Federal Government.** | 26. _____ | 329 |
| 27. | Noel Byrd, **Vice President** of Milex Labs, will testify at an FDA hearing. | 27. _____ | 313d |
| 28. | A detailed analysis of the responses to our survey is given in Appendix A (**See** pages 216–224). | 28. _____ | 302a |
| 29. | The massive murals in the Metropolitan Opera House were done by **Painter** Marc Chagall. | 29. _____ | 312c |
| 30. | Someone in their **Accounting Department** should be able to explain. | 30. _____ | 322 |

Name _____ Date _____ Class _____

17

**Directions:** Correct the capitalization in the following sentences. If a sentence is correctly capitalized, write *C* in the answer column. Circle all changes you make. **References:** ¶¶301–330.

31. Ms. Eileen Kilmer, Executive Vice President of the Hampton real estate agency, says, "real estate prices are expected to remain stable for the rest of the year."   **31.** _____
313d<br>309a<br>320a<br>301c

32. The current Mayor, Walter Marx, will honor Former Mayor George Gille and Mayor Elect William Pavlick at a reception.   **32.** _____
312b<br>317

33. *In a company memo:* Janet Russo, Manager of the human resources department, has been named head of the equal employment opportunity committee.   **33.** _____
313d<br>322

34. This conflict between the U.S. department of the treasury and the federal reserve board dates back to the days of the Roosevelt administration. Although the board has brought the matter before the supreme court, the court feels that this is an administrative rather than a Constitutional issue.   **34.** _____
325<br>328<br>326<br>304

35. Leaders from both the republican and the democratic parties met today with the president at the white house. An announcement from the oval office will be sent shortly to the senate and the house.   **35.** _____
309a<br>313b<br>305<br>326

36. Dr. Wanda A. Jory, Research Director for Biogenetic labs, will be an adjunct professor at our local University for the coming academic year.   **36.** _____ *(capital letters are acceptable but not necessary)*
313d<br>309a<br>320a<br>308

37. I would like to apply for the job of Regional Manager in your sales department.   **37.** _____
313e<br>322

38. Your Uncle, John Traynor, was identified in *the Wall Street Journal* as the person behind the du Hamel takeover attempt.   **38.** _____
319a<br>324a<br>311e

39. *From a city agency's memo:* The mayor and the city council will meet tomorrow to discuss the Garvey company's application to construct a Shopping Mall on the block bounded by Summer, Marsh, Oak, and Maple streets.   **39.** _____
313c<br>327<br>307<br>309a

40. When Radical Author William Boynton accepted a two-year grant from the Huntington foundation, reporters asked this question: "Tell us, Sir, how does it feel to be supported by the establishment?"   **40.** _____
312c<br>309a<br>315<br>305

41. *From the Whitlock University course catalog:* The university offers a wide variety of courses to first-year students. However, for course titles marked with an asterisk, please get the approval of the Department Head before signing up.   **41.** _____
321<br>308

42. *From an educational journal:* Whitlock University has announced plans to establish a Medical School in the next three years. Details of the University's plans were released today by the President.   **42.** _____
307<br>321<br>313d

43. I want to apologize for the problems you had with our credit department. According to Ms. Marie Longo, the Manager of the Department, you now have a credit balance of $78.10.   **43.** _____
322<br>313d<br>321

18

C-32

# 9

# Capitalization (Continued)

**Directions:** If the boldface word or phrase is correctly capitalized, write C in the answer column. If not, correct it as follows: To change a capital letter to a small letter, draw a line through it The. To change a small letter to a capital letter, draw three lines under it the. Circle all changes you make. **References:** ¶¶331–366.

1. My investment portfolio is managed by a Manhattan brokerage house that has excellent contacts on the **Street.**

    1. **C**     332

2. Our business is targeted chiefly at the **Winter** tourist trade.

    2. \_\_\_\_ 343

3. Please read **"Sales Tax is Sure to be Reduced"** in today's newspaper.

    3. \_\_\_\_ 360

4. I used to stay at the Melrose Hotel, but the **Hotel** has gone downhill recently.

    4. \_\_\_\_ 331

5. Will we need a special charter to do business in the **State** of Georgia?

    5. \_\_\_\_ 335a

6. What undergraduate courses does the university offer in the area of **Western Civilization?**

                                                  340

    6. \_\_\_\_ 352

7. In the late **nineties** we had to shift our business to new product lines.

    7. **C**     345

8. You can quickly find the names of other suppliers in the **yellow pages.**

    8. **C**     356a

9. I'm still not happy with the wording in **Paragraph** 3.

    9. \_\_\_\_ 359

10. Bud's living in the **bay area,** but I can't tell you precisely where.

    10. \_\_\_\_ 333a

11. No **midwesterner** would know what you meant by an "egg cream."

    11. \_\_\_\_ 339

12. Ted's promotion is a perfect illustration of the Peter **principle.**

    12. \_\_\_\_ 346

13. At times like this, we could use a crash course in the **ten commandments.**

    13. \_\_\_\_ 350a

14. Please be sure to give your **social security** number along with your name.

    14. **C**     347a

15. I grew up in Ripley, a small town in **Western** Tennessee north of Memphis.

    15. \_\_\_\_ 341

16. When do you think the **City** of Clifton will change its zoning laws?

    16. \_\_\_\_ 334

17. This year we will work only a half day on Christmas **eye.**

    17. \_\_\_\_ 342

18. I remained in Santa Fe when my parents moved back **east.**

    18. \_\_\_\_ 338

19. I expect to receive my **Master's** degree next spring.

    19. \_\_\_\_ 353

20. *In a contract:* Roger L. Bork, hereinafter called the **buyer,** agrees to . . .

    20. \_\_\_\_ 358

21. My father foresaw the boom in residential real estate after **World War II.**

    21. **C**     344a

22. We'll be touring **northern** Vermont for much of our vacation.

    22. **C**     341
                              355

23. *In an advertisement:* Try Northridge's **All-Natural Wheat Bread** for a treat.

    23. **C**     357

24. Mrs. Fry said in her letter that she did not pretend to speak for all **Blacks.**

    24. \_\_\_\_ 348a

25. Our daughter Ellen is doing her **Junior** year of college abroad.

    25. \_\_\_\_ 354

26. *In a heading:* Twentieth-**century** Achievements in Civil Rights

    26. \_\_\_\_ 363

27. I'm taking courses in English **Literature** in a special weekend program.

    27. \_\_\_\_ 352

28. Mr. van Lieuw was originally a native of **the** Netherlands.

    28. **C**     337a

29. I just put my faith in the Lord and let **him** work things out for me.

    29. **C**     349b
                              360a

30. Under separate cover I'm sending you a copy of **Growing up at Last.**

    30. \_\_\_\_ 361c

Name _____ Date _____ Class _____     19

**Directions:** Correct the capitalization in the following sentences. If a sentence is correctly capitalized, write *C* in the answer column. Circle all changes you make. **References:** ¶¶301–366.

31. My family down south can't understand how I can enjoy living in the big Apple. Wait till they see my apartment in the village.

31. _____ | 338 333a 332

32. I will check with American airlines at Kennedy airport to see whether anyone has turned in the Manila envelope you lost.

32. _____ | 309a 331 306

33. You may get a laugh out of Ella's new article, "Nirvana is not as great a place as it's cracked up to be."

33. _____ | 360 361

34. The supporting data is presented in appendix 4. (See, in particular, chart 3 on page 514 and column 2 of table 14 on page 631.)

34. _____ | 359

35. Jennie Moore will be coming back east to serve as District Manager for all of New England plus the State of New York. All of her customers and business associates from the twin cities are going to miss her.

35. _____ | 338 313e 335a 333a 345

36. At the beginning of the Twentieth Century, my grandfather moved out west and founded a small seed business. By the late Nineteen-thirties, just before the start of the second world war, the company had annual sales of $3,000,000.

36. _____ | 319 338 345 344a 321 354 309a

37. I am now a senior at the university of Tennessee, majoring in Business Administration. I expect to get my Bachelor's degree this spring.

37. _____ | 352 353 343

38. The Mid-March reports indicate that sales are strong in the northeast but are faltering in the Farm Belt and the Sunbelt.

38. _____ | 363 338 333a

39. My brother-in-law works for the State as a Photographer in the department of travel and tourism.

39. _____ | 335b 313e 325

40. I have asked the reverend Frank Carleo, Pastor of St. Mark's roman catholic church, to give the invocation at the Lions club banquet on veterans day.

40. _____ | 312a 313a 320a 309a 342

41. When Bart Peterson returns to the States this spring, I will take over his job in the middle east.

41. _____ | 335a 343 338

42. We need stronger Environmental Protection Laws if we are to save the Earth from destructive pollution.

42. _____ | 346b 351

43. Wilma Cooley, the congresswoman from South Dakota, will head a house committee studying safety procedures in nuclear plants, especially those in earthquake-prone areas on the coast.

43. _____ | 313b 326 332

44. For our upcoming Computer Convention I think we ought to invite someone like Tracy Kidder as our keynote speaker. Among his impressive credentials is the fact that he won the Pulitzer prize for *The Soul Of A New Machine.*

44. _____ | 308 364 360a

20

C-34

# 10 Numbers

**Directions:** Circle all errors in number style, and write the correct forms in the answer column. Follow the **figure** style (¶¶401–403) unless another style is called for. If a sentence is correct as given, write *C* in the answer column.
**References:** ¶¶401–428, 461, 465.

| | | |
|---|---|---|
| 1. We'll be leaving in ⑧ days for a month's trip to Australia. | **1. eight** | 401a |
| 2. Last year we mailed ⑥ million fliers; this year, ⑧,000,000. | **8 million** OR<br>**2. 6,000,000** | 403b<br>461 |
| 3. I would like to respond to your letter dated May twenty-first. | **3. 21** | 407b<br>414 |
| 4. Our new van cost several $1000 dollars more than we had budgeted. | **4. thousand** | 423 |
| 5. Effective July 1, parkway tolls will be increased to 40¢. | **5. 40 cents** | 418 |
| 6. Nelson E. R. Dillon the third is forming his own law firm. | **6. III** OR **3d** | 426 |
| 7. I requisitioned ⑥ laptop computers but got approval to buy only two. | **7. six** | 402 |
| 8. The council consists of 11 Democrats, eight Republicans, and one Independent. | **8. 8, 1** | 402<br>404a |
| 9. *Word style:* We have invited 75 people to our daughter's wedding. | **9. seventy-five** | 404a<br>465a |
| 10. Please call the banquet manager and say we expect about 300 guests. | **10. C** | 401a |
| 11. We will celebrate the company's 150th anniversary next month. | **11. C** | 424 |
| 12. *Word style:* Over 21 million TV viewers saw our show last night. | **12. twenty-one** | 404a<br>465a-b |
| 13. A really good attaché case can cost $150.00 or more. | **13. $150** | 415 |
| 14. Eighty people out of 100 could not remember the advertiser's name. | **14. a hundred** | 421<br>404a |
| 15. *Word style:* Between 300 and 325 people responded to our ad. | **15. C** | 405 |
| 16. Pergola Industries stock was selling today at two dollars a share. | **16. $2** | 413a |
| 17. *Formal style:* We will arrive in Paris on the 6th of April. | **17. sixth** | 407a |
| 18. *Emphatic style:* Our Summer Sale will run until the 1st of September. | **18. C** | 407a |
| 19. The building will cost between $18 and $20 million to construct. | **19. $18 million** | 416d |
| 20. Nearly 2/3 of those surveyed preferred the package done in orange. | **20. two-thirds** | 427a |
| 21. The warehouse expansion is scheduled to begin July 1st, 2006. | **21. July 1, 2006** | 408 |
| 22. The cost of gas is now three and a half times what it was in 1970. | **22. 3½** | 428a |
| 23. The outside of the building has not been painted since June 2000. | **23. C** | 410 |
| 24. I found a printer who can do these brochures for only $.30 apiece. | **24. 30 cents** | 418a |
| 25. 64 pages of the book contain full-color illustrations. | **25. Sixty-four** | 421 |
| 26. Last year our sales were $3,574,119; this year we will do over $4 million. | **26. $4,000,000** | 403b<br>461a |
| | **$500,000** OR | 417 |
| 27. The owners of that office building have cut the price by $½ million. | **27. a half-million dollars** | 461 |
| 28. You may participate in the pension plan after your 30th birthday. | **28. thirtieth** | 424 |

Name _____ Date _____ Class _____ 21

29. Our semiannual sales meeting starts on the (2d) of March.     29. **2d** <sub></sub> 407a / 425a

30. Pay (one-half) of the balance now and the other half in six months.     30. **one half** 427c

31. Fran can give you (100) reasons why the report is not yet completed.     31. **a hundred** 401c

32. The variance is less than (three-sixteenths of an inch.)     32. **3/16 inch** 427a

33. The pattern calls for (7-3/8 yards of material.)     33. **7 3/8 OR 7⅜** 428b

34. Our chief competitor has just cut prices by (ten) percent.     34. **10** 401b

35. About (ten) to 15 callers mentioned the typo in last Sunday's ad.     35. **10** 402

36. *Word style:* Can your living room hold as many as 125 people?     36. **C** 404a

37. All I wanted was 50 (cents) worth of rubber bands.     37. **cents'** 418a

38. A good fax machine will run between $175 and (250.)     38. **$250** 419

39. (Four fifths) of our orders come from just three states.     39. **Four-fifths** 427b / 421

40. My bank statement shows a balance of only (six dollars and 14 cents.)     40. **$6.14** 413a

**Directions:** Rewrite the following sentences to correct errors in number style and related punctuation. Follow the **figure** style unless another style is called for. **References:** ¶¶401–428, 461, 465.

41. We sold eight refrigerators, 11 stoves, and three freezers in only two days.   **We sold 8 refrigerators, 11 stoves, and 3 freezers in only two days.**   402

42. Thank you for your letter of May 9th, in which you asked about a deed dated 3/3/01.   **Thank you for your letter of May 9, in which you asked about a deed dated March 3, 2001.**   407b / 408c

43. On July 10, we will submit the will dated August 11th, 2004 for probate.   **On July 10 we will submit the will dated August 11, 2004, for probate.**   410 / 408d

44. Allow $750,000 to $1 million for expenses plus another $100 thousand for fees.   **Allow $750,000 to $1,000,000 for expenses plus another $100,000 for fees.**   416c / 461

45. The unit cost of $1.71 represents 56 cents for parts, 93¢ for labor, and $0.22 for shipping.   **The unit cost of $1.71 represents $.56 for parts, $.93 for labor, and $.22 for shipping.**   418b

46. On the first of May, 2008 I promise to pay Six Thousand ($6000) Dollars . . .   **On May 1, 2008, I promise to pay Six Thousand Dollars ($6000) . . . [OR Six Thousand (6000) Dollars . . . ]**   408 / 410 / 420a

47. $325 seems to me to be a lot to charge for so small a repair job.   **It seems to me [OR I think] $325 is a lot to charge for so small a repair job.**   422

48. Join the 100s of voters in the 21st Ward who want to return Tim Bannigan for his 5th term in Congress.   **Join the hundreds of voters in the Twenty-first Ward who want to return Tim Bannigan for his fifth term in Congress.**   423 / 424

49. In ¼ of an hour we can show you how to cut your packaging costs in ½.   **In a quarter [OR one-quarter] of an hour we can show you how to cut your packaging costs in half.**   427

50. *Word style:* On the 25th of September we expect more than 20,000 residents will help to celebrate the 100th anniversary of the founding of the city.   **On the twenty-fifth of September we expect more than twenty thousand residents will help to celebrate the one hundredth anniversary of the founding of the city.**   407a / 404a / 427d

22

C-36

# 11

# Numbers (Continued)

**Directions:** Circle all errors in number style, and write the correct forms in the answer column. Follow the **figure** style (¶¶401–403) unless another style is called for. If a sentence is correct as given, write *C* in the answer column.
**References:** ¶¶429–470 plus the basic rules (¶¶401–406).

1. Take Route I-95 to Exit 69, go north on Route 9 to the Essex turnoff, and then go west for three miles to Ivoryton.

    **1.** 3    429a

2. Children who are not 5 years old by October 31 may not enter school this fall.

    **2.** C    433

3. A 48-month automobile loan might be easier for you to carry.

    **3.** C    436a

4. Why hasn't Bly & Bly reordered from us in the past 6 months?

    **4.** six    437

5. You can avoid the tunnel traffic if you leave home by 6 A.M.

    **5.** a.m.    440a / 440b

6. If you order by August 15, take an extra five percent off the total.

    **6.** 5    447a

7. Perhaps #78312 was voided and a new purchase order was issued.

    **7.** No.    455

8. Our markets expanded dramatically between 1995–2005.

    **8.** 1995 and 2005    459b

9. We are planning a first printing of 8000 copies.

    **9.** C    461a

10. Feel free to call me at home between 8:00 and 9:30 p.m.

    **10.** 8    440c

11. The table on page 1,157 shows the properties of the tested alloys.

    **11.** 1157    462

12. *General style:* The reception room needs only a 9- x 12-foot rug.

    **12.** by    432

13. We plan to fly to Bermuda to celebrate our 25th wedding anniversary.

    **13.** twenty-fifth    435

14. Our capital needs were far simpler in the early 1990's.

    **14.** 1990s    438 / 464

15. *Formal style:* The Ebert-Rogers reception will begin at 7 o'clock.

    **15.** seven    441a

16. The council approved the tax increase by a vote of eight to two.

    **16.** 8 to 2    451

17. There may be a 15–20° drop in temperature at night.

    **17.** 15°    453b

18. It's unheard of for someone in her early 30's to be made CEO.

    **18.** thirties    434

19. By the late 90's over half of our sales came from exports.

    **19.** '90s OR nineties    439a

20. *Formal style:* The awards ceremony will begin at eight thirty.

    **20.** eight-thirty    442a

21. In the markets we serve, women outnumber men on a ratio of 5 to 2°.

    **21.** C    450a / 418c

22. *Footnote in catalog:* *Add fifty ¢ to cover the cost of handling.

    **22.** 50¢    453a

23. *Footnote in a report:* *See pages 400–02.

    **23.** 402    460b

24. I can trace my family back almost three-hundred years.

    **24.** three hundred    465b / 437

25. To approximate our unit cost, divide the list price by 5.

    **25.** C    452

26. Let me give you my unlisted phone number—555/4989.

    **26.** 555-4989 OR 555.4989    454a

27. The year 2008 in roman numerals is MMVII.

    **27.** MMVIII    469

28. Maude is in her seventys but she doesn't look more than sixty.

    **28.** seventies    467 / 434

29. *In an ad:* Salary up to $50K to qualified person with solid experience.

    **29.** C    470

30. During the summer the temperature rarely goes above the low 80's.

    **30.** 80s    464

Name _____ Date _____ Class _____

**Directions:** Rewrite the following sentences to correct errors in number style and related punctuation. Follow the **figure** style unless another style is called for. **References:** ¶¶401–470.

**31.** I will be at the booth between 9:30 a.m. in the morning and 12 a.m. noon. **I will be at the booth between 9:30 a.m. and 12 noon.**

440h
440f

**32.** Mrs. Engle will get a finder's fee of $12000, or .5% of the price paid for the property. **Mrs. Engle will get a finder's fee of $12,000, or 0.5 percent of the price paid for the property.**

461a
448a
401a

**33.** I have 2 questions about Invoice No. 10,414 dated May 3rd, 2007. **I have two questions about Invoice 10414, dated May 3, 2007.**

455a
463
408d

**34.** In 1999, seventy percent of our revenues came from only eighteen items in our product line. **In 1999, 70 percent of our revenues came from only 18 items in our product line.**

456
447a
401a

**35.** 2,000 64-page booklets can be printed for about 90¢ each. **Two thousand 64-page booklets can be printed for about 90 cents each.**

421
457
418a

**36.** From 2005–2008 we plan to do an intensive study of 8th-grade students. **From 2005 to 2008 we plan to do an intensive study of eighth-grade students.**

459b
424

**37.** On January 1 2008 1 will be exactly 22 years, 4 months, and 7 days old. **On January 1, 2008, I will be exactly 22 years 4 months and 7 days old.**

410
433

**38.** I am five feet, five inches tall, and I weigh a hundred and forty-two pounds. **I am 5 feet 5 inches tall, and I weigh 142 pounds.**

430
429a

**39.** Since 2003, an employee with more than twenty years of service can get full retirement benefits at age sixty-two. **Since 2003 an employee with more than 20 years of service can get full retirement benefits at the age of 62.**

410
436a
433

**40.** On her 21st birthday Jane Best will inherit ¼ of a million dollars. **On her twenty-first birthday Jane Best will inherit one-quarter of a million dollars [OR $250,000].**

435
417
439a

**41.** Back in the 90's it was easy to get a thirty-year mortgage at six and a half %. **Back in the nineties [OR '90s] it was easy to get a 30-year mortgage at 6½ [OR 6½] percent.**

436a
448b
447a

**42.** I like to get to the office at 7 and leave early in the p.m. **I like to get to the office at 7:00 [OR seven] and leave early in the afternoon.**

442a
440d

**43.** *Formal style:* Let's meet on the 21st of June at 9:30 o'clock. **Let's meet on the twenty-first of June at half past nine o'clock [OR half after nine o'clock].**

407a
441b

**44.** *In an ad:* All inventory must be sold! Enjoy 50–70% price reductions! **All inventory must be sold! Enjoy 50%–70% price reductions!**

453b

**45.** Between 2005–2008 we plan to open three discount outlets in Ohio, one in Kentucky, and twelve in Indiana. **Between 2005 and 2008 we plan to open 3 discount outlets in Ohio, 1 in Kentucky, and 12 in Indiana.**

459b
402

**46.** *Formal style:* Over 1500 guests danced till 2 a.m. o'clock at the University Club. **Over fifteen hundred guests danced till two o'clock in the morning at the University Club.**

404a
466
440e

# 12 Abbreviations

**Directions:** Supply the correct abbreviation for each of the following terms. **References:** ¶¶501–550.

| # | Term | Abbrev. | Ref. |
|---|------|---------|------|
| 1. | Senior | **Sr.** | 506a 518 |
| 2. | Corporation | **Corp.** | 520b 541 |
| 3. | continued | **cont.** | 505a 541 |
| 4. | vice president | **VP** | 541 |
| 5. | Doctors | **Drs.** | 517a |
| 6. | Company | **Co.** | 520b 541 |
| 7. | Wednesday | **Wed.** | 532 |
| 8. | pounds | **lb** | 535a 541 |
| 9. | liter | **L** | 537a 541 |
| 10. | end of month | **e.o.m.** OR **EOM** | 541 542 |
| 11. | chief operating officer | **COO** | 541 |
| 12. | bulletin board service | **BBS** | 544a |
| 13. | bachelor of laws | **LL.B.** | 509 519a |
| 14. | Incorporated | **Inc.** | 520b 541 |
| 15. | United States | **U.S.** | 525 |
| 16. | south-southwest | **SSW** | 531b |
| 17. | miles per hour | **mph** | 535a 541 |
| 18. | kilometers per hour | **km/h** | 538a 541 |
| 19. | for example | **e.g.** | 545 |
| 20. | postage and handling | **P&H** | 541 |

| # | Term | Abbrev. | Ref. |
|---|------|---------|------|
| 21. | doctor of philosophy | **Ph.D.** | 509 519a |
| 22. | personal computer | **PC** | 541 544a |
| 23. | that is | **i.e.** | 507 545 |
| 24. | North Dakota | **N. Dak.** OR **ND** | 527 1334b |
| 25. | cubic centimeters | **cu cm** OR **cm³** | 509 538e |
| 26. | fiscal year | **FY** | 504 541 |
| 27. | kilogram | **kg** | 537a 541 |
| 28. | December | **Dec.** | 532 |
| 29. | year to date | **YTD** | 541 |
| 30. | modulator and demodulator | **modem** | 522c |
| 31. | not applicable | **NA** | 541 |
| 32. | input/output | **I/O** | 544a |
| 33. | digital video disc | **DVD** | 546 |
| 34. | facsimile | **fax** | 510 |
| 35. | [Jay Fenn] the third | **3d** OR **III** | 518d |
| 36. | and other people | **et al.** | 545 |
| 37. | not in my backyard | **NIMBY** | 522a |
| 38. | Felicity R. O'Malley | **FRO** | 516c |
| 39. | random-access memory | **RAM** | 544a |
| 40. | my eyes glaze over | **MEGO** | 522a |

**Directions:** Underline any word or abbreviation that is incorrectly styled, and write the correct form in the answer column. If a sentence is correct, write *C* in the answer column. **References:** ¶¶501–550.

41. When I next visit Mount Vernon, I hope to visit <u>Doctor</u> Cali.

**41. Dr.** 529a 517a

42. How long will it take to drive from Sandpoint, Idaho, to Eugene, <u>Ore.</u>?

**42. Oregon** 504 526

43. Samuel Potter <u>Junior</u> is expected to be named the new CEO.

**43. Jr.** 518a 541

44. Attached are copies of the following purchase orders: <u>Nos</u> 61715, 63821, and 64111.

**44. Nos.** 506a 455

45. We need another <u>Wats</u> line to handle the dramatic surge in orders.

**45. WATS** 522a

46. The best programming consultant I know is J. G. Head of <u>Saint Louis</u>.

**46. St. Louis** 516a 529b

Name _____ Date _____ Class _____   25

47. Either a tax lawyer or a <u>C.P.A.</u> could advise you on how to treat the proceeds of this sale for income tax purposes.

**47. CPA** — 519g, 541

48. Next year we plan to open more discount outlets throughout the <u>U.S.</u>

**48. United States** — 525

49. When the temperature reaches 30°<u>C.</u>, you'll want a bathing suit, not an overcoat.

**49. C (for Celsius)** — 537b, 505b

50. How do you feel about a breakfast meeting at 7 <u>oclock</u>?

**50. o'clock** — 533, 508

51. I need to get ready for a tax audit by the <u>I.R.S.</u>

**51. IRS** — 524

52. Top management wants a Harvard MBA to critique our long-range plans.

**52. C** — 519b

53. Representatives from the <u>Afl-Cio</u> are now evaluating the impact of automation on employment levels.

**53. AFL-CIO** — 520a, 527

54. Edna Helmstatter does liaison work for us in Washington, D.C.

**54. C** — 528a, 544a

55. Sales of our CD-ROM products have increased <u>22 %</u> this year.

**55. 22%** — 543d, 505a

56. *Note at the bottom of a page:* <u>Cont'd</u> on next page.

**56. Cont.** — 541

57. Would you be willing to serve on the <u>ad. hoc.</u> committee being set up to study alternative HMO plans?

**57. ad hoc** — 545, 541

58. The morning session begins at 9:30 a.m.; the afternoon session, at 1:30 <u>P.M.</u>

**58. p.m.** — 504, 533

59. Bette Dorsey will receive her <u>Ed. D.</u> this spring.

**59. Ed.D.** — 509, 519a

60. The next meeting of the Alumni Club is scheduled for the <u>14th.</u> of May.

**60. 14th** — 510

61. Why do our customers prefer Brand <u>X.</u> over our product line?

**61. X** — 547

62. Our uptown office is located at 4139 Burney Boulevard, SE.

**62. C** — 531a

63. We should be doubling our investment in <u>R & D</u> if we expect to grow.

**63. R&D** — 543c, 546

64. <u>Doctor Mark Duff, Ph.D.</u>, has been appointed to a federal advisory panel to study ways to boost the growth rate of our GDP.

**64. Mark Duff, Ph.D.** — 517a, 519c, 546

65. These relics must date back at least to 500 <u>BC</u>.

**65. B.C.** — 508

**Directions:** Rewrite the following sentences to correct any errors in abbreviation style. **References:** ¶¶501–550.

66. Mr. Morton Li, MBA, CPA, is an expert on L.B.O. strategies. **Morton Li, M.B.A., C.P.A., is an expert on LBO strategies.** — 519c, 519g, 541

67. The Hon. Frieda L. Goodman will speak tomorrow at 10 a.m. and at 3 o'clock. **The Honorable Frieda L. Goodman will speak tomorrow at 10 a.m. and at 3 p.m.** — 517e, 504

68. Ask Ed. whether he thinks Mr. G wants to sell his condo. in L.A. **Ask Ed whether he thinks Mr. G. wants to sell his condo in Los Angeles.** — 515, 516d, 510, 526

69. Messers Amory and Powell have talked with L.B. Kelley about a partnership. **Messrs. Amory and Powell have talked with L. B. Kelley about a partnership.** — 517a, 516a

70. Mister Rudolfi has OK'd your trip to Ft. Worth. **Mr. Rudolfi has okayed your trip to Fort Worth.** — 517a, 550, 548, 529a

# 13 Editing Survey B

**Directions:** Edit the following material (a draft of a news release) for capitalization, number, and abbreviation style. Circle all changes you make. **References:** Sections 3–5; pages 358–359 or the inside back cover for proofreaders' marks.

532  Dr. 517a  313d
~ptember~ Doctor Raymond Kaufman, President of Computer Concepts, Inc., has announced that on    **1**

Sep. 1 Frederick de Winter thirty-six will join the company as Executive Vice President in    **2**
36    433    313d

charge of special projects.    **3**

thirty 437
Mr. de Winter developed his passionate interest in computers over 30 years ago. During    **4**

354    508
his Junior year at M.I.T., this brilliant software engineer achieved his first commercial success    **5**

461a
with a spreadsheet program, which he sold to a major software publisher for $100,000 plus    **6**

352
royalties. Following his graduation with a degree in Computer Science, this computer whiz    **7**

devoted his newly won profits and his extraordinary talents to developing a machine that could    **8**

scan printed material and convert it into synthesized speech for the blind.    **9**

311e
It is de Winter's extensive background in synthesized speech that brings him to Computer    **10**

343    308/321
Concepts. Last Fall the Company announced plans to speed up its development of a voice-activated    **11**

computer. Dragon Systems and Lernout & Hauspie have already developed software that can    **12**

160    429a
recognize 250,000 words and convert speech to text at a rate of one hundred sixty words a minute.    **13**

508/520a  The progress made by these companies has attracted the interest of industry giants like    **14**

508/543b, note    #  516a    541
I.B.M. and A.T.& T. as well as smaller innovative firms. J.V. Terrant, the C.E.o, of Computer    **15**

544a    301c
Concepts and an expert on C.A.D. (computer-aided design), says, "voice-activated computers repre-    **16**

United States. 525
sent a potentially huge market in the U.S. industry analysts estimate that sales could easily    **17**

$2 billion
exceed $2,000,000,000." 416a    **18**

fifteen 421    101
The field has already come a long way from its early beginnings 15 years ago.    **19**

303
Parcel Services Of America was using a limited-vocabulary system that permitted workers to    **20**

call out routing and sorting directions for each package without physically handling it. The    **21**

latest software consists of continuous-speech recognition programs that allow you to dictate    **22**

to your computer in a relatively natural manner (without having to pause between words).    **23**

percent 447a
Yet the programs currently available have not yet achieved the 95% accuracy rate that    **24**

experts consider a critical standard. And that is the challenge facing Computer Concepts.    **25**

Fred de Winter recognizes the high risks entailed in his project, but he is eager to start    **26**

338
work as soon as he transplants his family from the West Coast. When interviewed at the    **27**

309a/331    338    four 401a/404a
Airport, he said, "My wife and I are excited about coming back east, and my 4 kids can't wait    **28**

340
to experience their first Northern winter. If you think developing a voice-activated computer    **29**

is a challenge, have you tried developing a voice-activated child?"    **30**

> **Note to Instructor: There is a total of 30 errors in this material.**

Name _____ Date _____ Class _____    27

**Directions:** Edit the following material (a draft of a term paper) for capitalization, number, and abbreviation style. Circle all changes you make. **References:** Sections 3–5; pages 358–359 or the inside back cover for proofreaders' marks.

Getting out the Vote: an Up-to-date Approach     1

My Grandfather recently recalled that when he was a young man, getting out the vote    2

usually meant that workers for each political machine went out and twisted a few arms. He    3

was reflecting on the fact that in the final decade of the Twentieth Century, the computer had    4

revolutionized the way politicians get people to vote for them.    5

Both the Republican and the Democratic parties are increasingly basing their strategies on    6

computer analyses. In a recent campaign for president, one election committee asked a computer    7

to match the names of all registered drivers against the names of all registered voters in a    8

particular State. The result was a list of unregistered voters, which was further analyzed so as    9

to identify those people most likely to vote for the Committee's candidate. The results on    10

election day were a dramatic vindication of this approach.    11

According to Pollster Norman Monagle of the Center For Public Research, "The election    12

game began to change in the Nineties. Candidates at all levels—Federal, state, and local—must    13

now find out all they can about the age, gender, and economic status of the voters." Even managers    14

of small-scale campaigns can now buy commercial software programs that sell for as little as    15

$75–100. (The cost of customized programs, of course, can run into the 1000's.) thousands    16

The computer can do more than target unregistered voters. One candidate from the    17

Western part of Washington state, running for a seat in the house, learned from computer    18

analyses about a dramatic increase in the number of 18- to 24-year-olds and those over sixty in    60   19

his district. He immediately started to call on more schools and strengthen his support for those    20

on Social Security. As a result, he won by a substantial margin.    21

A Senator from the nutmeg state, running for election for the 2nd time, had access to a    second   22

computerized file of past speeches of her opponent. Once she publicly compared his past    23

positions and his current promises—especially on the Environmental Protection Law—you    24

wouldn't have given 2¢ for her opponent's chances.    two cents   25

A recent article, entitled "The Powerful Machine On The Political Scene," noted that the    26

computer would continue to effect massive changes in the conduct of our political campaigns,    27

changes that our founding fathers could never have foreseen. Nevertheless, even with the ready    28

accessibility of $75.00 software, the skills of political pros will always be needed. Even though    29

we advance further into the Computer Age, the conduct of politics will always be an art.    30

Note to Instructor: There is a total of 30 errors in this material.

# 14 Plurals

**Directions:** Supply the correct plural form for each of the following items. **References:** ¶¶601–626; a dictionary (optional).

| | | | | | | | |
|---|---|---|---|---|---|---|---|
| 1. | area | **areas** | 601 | 31. | address | **addresses** | 602 |
| 2. | ability | **abilities** | 604 | 32. | day | **days** | 605 |
| 3. | memo | **memos** | 607a | 33. | shelf | **shelves** | 608b |
| 4. | business | **businesses** | 602 | 34. | sketch | **sketches** | 602 |
| 5. | belief | **beliefs** | 608a | 35. | company | **companies** | 604 |
| 6. | rule of thumb | **rules of thumb** | 612a | 36. | fee | **fees** | 601 |
| 7. | phenomenon | **phenomena** | 614 | 37. | trade-off | **trade-offs** | 612b |
| 8. | criticism | **criticisms** | 601 | 38. | stereo | **stereos** | 606 |
| 9. | printout | **printouts** | 611 | 39. | woman | **women** | 609 |
| 10. | agency | **agencies** | 604 | 40. | alumnus | **alumni** | 614 |
| 11. | crash | **crashes** | 602 | 41. | Mr. and Mrs. Gaines | the **Gaineses** | 615b |
| 12. | Mr. and Mrs. Duffy | the **Duffys** | 615c | 42. | contract | **contracts** | 601 |
| 13. | highway | **highways** | 605 | 43. | boy | **boys** | 605 |
| 14. | foot | **feet** | 609 | 44. | t | **t's** | 623 / 604 |
| 15. | vol. | **vols.** | 619 | 45. | photocopy | **photocopies** | 611 |
| 16. | byte | **bytes** | 601 | 46. | two | **twos** | 624b |
| 17. | hang-up | **hang-ups** | 612b | 47. | property | **properties** | 604 |
| 18. | apology | **apologies** | 604 | 48. | customer | **customers** | 601 |
| 19. | portfolio | **portfolios** | 606 | 49. | echo | **echoes** | 607b |
| 20. | child | **children** | 610 | 50. | traveler's check | **traveler's checks** | 612d |
| 21. | CEO | **CEOs** | 622a | 51. | graffito | **graffiti** | 614 |
| 22. | pro and con | **pros and cons** | 625 | 52. | witness | **witnesses** | 602 |
| 23. | tax | **taxes** | 602 | 53. | M.D. | **M.D.s** | 622a |
| 24. | taxi | **taxis** | 601 | 54. | Mr. and Mrs. Heinz | the **Heinzes** | 615b |
| 25. | index *(of a book)* | **indexes** | 614 | 55. | runner-up | **runners-up** | 612a |
| 26. | X | **Xs** | 622a | 56. | attorney | **attorneys** | 605 |
| 27. | inquiry | **inquiries** | 604 | 57. | lb | **lb** | 620 |
| 28. | the German | the **Germans** | 617a | 58. | Mr. and Mrs. Caro | the **Caros** | 615a |
| 29. | 1990 | **1990s** | 624a | 59. | basis | **bases** | 614 |
| 30. | menu | **menus** | 601 | 60. | fallacy | **fallacies** | 604 |

Name _____ Date _____ Class _____    29

**Directions:** Underline any word that is misspelled or misused, and write the correct form in the answer column. If a sentence is correct, write *C* in the answer column. **References:** ¶¶601–626; a dictionary (optional).

| | | | |
|---|---|---|---|
| 61. | In selecting projects, he has only one <u>criteria</u>: profit. | 61. criterion | 614 |
| 62. | Have the <u>Weaver's</u> moved out of the area? | 62. Weavers | 615a |
| 63. | Let's get bids from three or four <u>studioes</u> before we decide. | 63. studios | 606 |
| 64. | Hal likes to flash a wad of <u>twentys</u> and fifties. | 64. twenties | 624b |
| 65. | Attached is a list of <u>do's and don't's</u> for the newcomers. | 65. dos and don'ts | 625 |
| 66. | <u>The Miss Perry</u> are the sole heirs to their mother's estate. | 66. The Miss Perrys OR The Misses Perry | 618b |
| 67. | The two Terrys in our office keep getting each other's calls. | 67. C | 616 |
| 68. | I have had no response to the six <u>faxs</u> I sent to Ted. | 68. faxes | 602 |
| 69. | These drawings could become <u>collectors' items</u> in a few years. | 69. collector's items | 612d |
| 70. | My <u>sister-in-laws</u> will help me with the painting. | 70. sisters-in-law | 612a |
| 71. | Please give my best regards to the McNeelys and the <u>Welchs</u>. | 71. Welches | 615b |
| 72. | Economists are now analyzing the effects of globalization on international markets throughout the 1990s. | 72. C | 624a |
| 73. | We're looking for men and <u>woman</u> with financial backgrounds. | 73. women | 609 |
| 74. | As a result of the environmental damage, the company now faces a <u>crises</u> of confidence as well as numerous lawsuits. | 74. crisis | 614 |
| 75. | All those <u>editor in chiefs</u> have rejected my manuscript. | 75. editors in chief | 612a |
| 76. | Let's invite the Farleys, the McCoys, and the Tullys. | 76. C | 615c |
| 77. | It's hard to distinguish the *n*'s and *u*'s in his handwriting. | 77. C | 623 |
| 78. | Our <u>attornies</u> will send you a revised draft of the contract. | 78. attorneys | 605 |
| 79. | How soon can I get an <u>analyses</u> of our quarterly sales? | 79. analysis | 614 |
| 80. | Please make two photocopies of the attached <u>bill of ladings</u>. | 80. bills of lading | 611 612a |
| 81. | We hope to attract new customers from outlying <u>communitys</u>. | 81. communities | 604 |
| 82. | The supporting data is given in Appendix B (see <u>p.</u> 48–52). | 82. pp. | 621 |
| 83. | Our Februarys and <u>Marchs</u> are slow months as a rule. | 83. Marches | 617a |
| 84. | I am looking for results, not <u>alibies</u>. | 84. alibis | 601 |
| 85. | Our <u>wifes</u> have opened a real estate agency in Mill Valley. | 85. wives | 608b |
| 86. | He offered the cashier two handfuls of pennies. | 86. C | 613 |
| 87. | I have always considered myself a loyal <u>alumni</u> of Duke. | 87. alumnus | 614 |
| 88. | Have the <u>Romeroes</u> returned their proxies? | 88. Romeros | 615a 604 |
| 89. | We must devise more effective marketing <u>strategys</u>. | 89. strategies | 604 |
| 90. | Their field staff consists only of Ph.D.s. | 90. C | 622a |
| 91. | <u>Mme.</u> Lenard and Tremont will oversee the arrangements. | 91. Mmes. OR Mrs. Lenard and Mrs. Tremont | 618 |
| 92. | How many new <u>Macintosh's</u> have been requisitioned? | 92. Macintoshes | 617a |
| 93. | Four <u>agencys</u> are competing for the Longyear account. | 93. agencies | 604 |
| 94. | The <u>feetprint</u> outside the window prove there were two thieves. | 94. footprints | 611 |
| 95. | We have retained Messrs. Fina and Sternhagen to represent us. | 95. C OR Mr. Fina and Mr. Sternhagen | 618 |

# 15 Possessives

**Directions:** For each singular noun in the first column, supply the correct forms for the singular possessive, the plural, and the plural possessive. **References:** ¶¶630–638 for possessive forms; ¶¶601–626 for plural forms.

| | SINGULAR | SINGULAR POSSESSIVE | | PLURAL | | PLURAL POSSESSIVE | |
|---|---|---|---|---|---|---|---|
| 1. | contractor | contractor's | 630a | contractors | 601 | contractors' | 632a |
| 2. | boss | boss's | 631a | bosses | 602 | bosses' | 632a |
| 3. | Hirsch | Hirsch's | 631a | the Hirsches | 615b | the Hirsches' | 632a |
| 4. | attorney | attorney's | 630a | attorneys | 605 | attorneys' | 632a |
| 5. | child | child's | 630a | children | 610 | children's | 633 |
| 6. | Columbo | Columbo's | 630a | the Columbos | 615a | the Columbos' | 632a |
| 7. | lady | lady's | 630a | ladies | 604 | ladies' | 632a |
| 8. | file clerk | file clerk's | 634 | file clerks | 612a | file clerks' | 635a |
| 9. | woman | woman's | 630a | women | 609 | women's | 633 |
| 10. | Koontz | Koontz's | 631a | the Koontzes | 615b | the Koontzes' | 632a |
| 11. | wife | wife's | 630a | wives | 608b | wives' | 632a |
| 12. | son-in-law | son-in-law's | 634 | sons-in-law | 612a | sons-in-law's | 635b |
| 13. | shareholder | shareholder's | 634 | shareholders | 611 | shareholders' | 635a |
| 14. | alumna | alumna's | 630a | alumnae | 614 | alumnae's | 633 |
| 15. | Willis | Willis's | 631a | the Willises | 615b | the Willises' | 632a |
| 16. | hero | hero's | 630a | heroes | 607b | heroes' | 632a |
| 17. | Kennedy | Kennedy's | 630a | the Kennedys | 615c | the Kennedys' | 632a |
| 18. | CPA | CPA's | 638 | CPAs | 622 | CPAs' | 638 |
| 19. | emcee | emcee's | 630a | emcees | 623 | emcees' | 632a |
| 20. | secretary | secretary's | 630a | secretaries | 604 | secretaries' | 632a |

**Directions:** Underline all errors and write the correct forms in the answer column. If a sentence is correct, write _C_ in the answer column. **References:** ¶¶627–652.

21. Some changes in <u>worker's</u> compensation laws may be enacted this year.

    21. workers'   652 / 629

22. Mary Jo is applying for a six <u>month's</u> leave of absence.

    22. months'   646

23. They seem to have no respect for one <u>anothers'</u> viewpoint.

    23. another's   637

24. The <u>alumnis'</u> contributions to the Centennial Fund are 13 percent ahead of last year's figure.

    24. alumni's   633 / 632

25. It's hard to manage two <u>boss's</u> correspondence at the same time.

    25. bosses'   633

Name _____ Date _____ Class _____ 31

| | | |
|---|---|---|
| 26. Anyone on Mrs. <u>Adam's</u> staff can handle that kind of problem. | 26. **Adams'** OR **Adams's** | 631c |
| 27. Our division's <u>sale's</u> goal for the year is $3.2 million. | 27. **sales** | 628a |
| 28. The green binders are mine; the red binders are <u>her's</u>. | 28. **hers** | 636 |
| 29. Two <u>CPA's</u> audits have turned up no evidence of fraud. | 29. **CPAs'** | 638 |
| 30. Look for special discounts this month at your <u>dealer</u>. | 30. **dealer's** | 644 |
| 31. Lida Wolfe has had fifteen <u>years</u> experience in the office automation industry. | 31. **years'** | 629 / 646 |
| 32. The job offer depends on <u>him</u> being willing to travel. | 32. **his** | 647 |
| 33. Do you know <u>John</u> and Kathy's birthdays? | 33. **John's** | 642a |
| 34. You will need a <u>vice presidents'</u> signature on this invoice. | 34. **vice president's** | 634 |
| 35. We plan to enter the <u>childrens'</u> wear market next fall. | 35. **children's** | 633 |
| 36. Did you know that your favorite bakery has just lost <u>it's</u> lease? | 36. **its** | 636 |
| 37. The scholarship was given by the <u>Womens'</u> Union Club. | 37. **Women's** | 633 / 640a |
| 38. Were you impressed with Frank Parker Jr.'s new partner? | 38. **C** | 639 |
| 39. Was there a witness to <u>Ellis's</u> and Marsh's contract? | 39. **Ellis** | 643a |
| 40. What did you think of our <u>hostess'</u> comments last night about her guest of honor? | 40. **hostess's** | 631a |
| 41. We've been invited to the <u>Fergusons</u> after the banquet. | 41. **Fergusons'** | 644 |
| 42. All <u>manager's</u> travel plans may be curtailed for two months. | 42. **managers'** | 632 |
| 43. My surgeon was a college roommate of my <u>wife</u>. | 43. **wife's** | 648 |
| 44. Two <u>dollars</u> worth of oil could have prevented the problem. | 44. **dollars'** | 632 / 646 |
| 45. I have to admit that their catalog looks a lot nicer than <u>our's</u>. | 45. **ours** | 636 |
| 46. Next year the separate <u>men</u> and women's tournaments will be combined. | 46. **men's** | 633 / 642a |

**Directions:** Rewrite the following sentences to remove all errors and awkward expressions. **References:** ¶¶627–652.

47. I'm reluctant to put more money in my brothers-in-law's business. <u>**I'm reluctant to put more money in the business owned by my brothers-in-law.**</u>    635b

48. It was Wendy Donnelly, my lawyer's idea to insert that clause. <u>**It was the idea of Wendy Donnelly, my lawyer, to insert that clause.**</u>    641

49. This quarter's inventory turnover rate is much better than last quarter. <u>**This quarter's inventory turnover rate is much better than last quarter's [OR than it was last quarter].**</u>    644a

50. You'll find the quotation in the article's last paragraph. <u>**You'll find the quotation in the last paragraph of the article.**</u>    645

51. A friend of mine's sister has just joined our firm as a partner. <u>**The sister of a friend of mine has just joined our firm as a partner.**</u>    648c

52. The new ad grew out of the product manager's nine-year-old daughter's sketch. <u>**The new ad grew out of a sketch done by the product manager's nine-year-old daughter.**</u>    649

# 16

# Spelling

**Directions:** In the answer column write the correct form of each word given in parentheses. **References:** ¶¶701–711; a dictionary (optional).

| | |
|---|---|
| 1. We are now (ship + ing) over 2000 units a day. | **1.** shipping    701 |
| 2. They have not yet tracked down the missing (ship + ment). | **2.** shipment    703 |
| 3. I gather Frank was (offer + ed) the West Coast opening. | **3.** offered    704 |
| 4. Bart (refer + ed) to an earlier letter that I had never seen. | **4.** referred    702 |
| 5. Feel free to give my name as a (refer + ence). | **5.** reference    702 |
| 6. Sybil and I were shocked when the waiter (total + ed) our bill. | **6.** totaled    704 |
| 7. How has Kitchens Inc. (maintain + ed) so high a rate of growth? | **7.** maintained    705 |
| 8. I am currently (manage + ing) a retail jewelry store. | **8.** managing    707a |
| 9. This decision has to be approved by higher (manage + ment). | **9.** management    708 |
| 10. Please record your (mile + age) and any expenses for gas. | **10.** mileage    707a |
| 11. You used superb (judge + ment) in answering Roy's complaint. | **11.** judgment    708 |
| 12. We need to probe into the (underlie + ing) causes. | **12.** underlying    709 |
| 13. I have tried and will go on (try + ing) to get some response. | **13.** trying    710a |
| 14. You (display + ed) remarkable poise when you were challenged at the board meeting. | **14.** displayed    711 |
| 15. I (cancel + ed) the order on the basis of the first sample. | **15.** canceled    704 |
| 16. My assistant will be (record + ing) all the sessions. | **16.** recording    706 |
| 17. Do you think these new regulations will be (enforce + able)? | **17.** enforceable    707c |
| 18. We need a consultant with a (program + ing) background. | **18.** programming    704 |
| 19. (Equip + ing) a new research lab will not be cheap. | **19.** Equipping    705 |
| 20. Was Palmer (full + ly) aware of your feelings? | **20.** fully    706 |

**Directions:** Select the correct form in parentheses, and write your answer in the column at the right. **References:** ¶¶712–718; a dictionary (optional).

| | |
|---|---|
| 21. Property owners are hoping for some tax (releif, relief ) soon. | **21.** relief    712 |
| 22. You need to adopt a more (flexable, flexible) position. | **22.** flexible    713b |
| 23. We have to become less (dependant, dependent) on our domestic markets and give new emphasis to exports. | **23.** dependent    714 |
| 24. The Fox project is (proceding, proceeding) on schedule. | **24.** proceeding    716b |
| 25. Our research director will (analize, analyze) the government study and will report to the committee. | **25.** analyze    715c |
| 26. We have (received, recieved) over 250 answers to our ad. | **26.** received    712 |

Name _____ Date _____ Class _____    33

27. This memo (supercedes, supersedes) my earlier memo of May 4.

28. We had strong (resistance, resistence) to our price increases.

29. Baldwin does not (weild, wield) as much power as he thinks.

30. Could you please submit two copies of your (resumé, résumé).

31. This complaint is only an isolated (occurance, occurrence).

32. I do not think we should (intercede, interceed) in their dispute.

33. Ms. Karras is now (supervising, supervizing) a staff of twelve.

34. Is it (possable, possible) that Powers never saw the memo?

35. The acquisition rumors are making everyone (panicy, panicky).

| 27. | **supersedes** | 716a |
|-----|----------------|------|
| 28. | **resistance** | 714 |
| 29. | **wield** | 712 |
| 30. | **résumé** | 718a |
| 31. | **occurrence** | 714 |
| 32. | **intercede** | 716c |
| 33. | **supervising** | 715b |
| 34. | **possible** | 713b |
| 35. | **panicky** | 717 |

**Directions:** If the boldface word is correct as given, write *C* in the answer column. If the word is misspelled, supply the correct form. References: ¶¶719–720.

36. If you want to win Julie over, you need to take a different **tack**.

37. Please prepare a **seperate** memo of agreement for Mrs. Carey.

38. Negotiations have now broken down and are at an **impass**.

39. A corner office is one of the **prerequisites** of the CEO's job.

40. If you ask about the Taiwan incident, please be **discreet**.

41. Use the Farraday contract or something **similiar** as a model.

42. Your analysis is based on a number of **erronious** assumptions.

43. We can **accomodate** over 200 people in our meeting room.

44. I'm enclosing a copy of Mrs. Fonseca's **itinery**.

45. If Joe continues to **flaunt** the rules, he'll lose his job.

46. An analysis of last year's performance is due on **Febuary** 1.

47. According to our **personal** policy, you are entitled to two weeks' vacation after one year's employment.

48. I will have to **forego** your kind invitation to the theater.

49. We were given gold pins as a **momento** of the occasion.

50. Here's an **uninterested** appraisal of your investment portfolio.

51. **Basicly,** it is your unreasonable deadlines that are the problem.

52. It's hard to **guage** Marge's true feelings about the move.

53. When can we expect a **definate** answer from Ms. Russo?

54. Mr. Daumier has promised to **appraise** us of any new developments in the Busoni investigation.

55. This pamphlet will **aquaint** you with our discount policy.

56. How could such a **collossal** error get through undetected?

57. Kim's contribution to the success of the project was **miniscule**.

58. We need someone to act as **liasion** between the two committees.

59. Does Mark have the **temperment** to manage a staff of ten?

60. Thank you for responding so promptly to our **questionaire**.

| 36. | C | 719 |
|-----|---|-----|
| 37. | separate | 720 |
| 38. | impasse | 720 |
| 39. | perquisites | 719 |
| 40. | C | 719 |
| 41. | similar | 720 |
| 42. | erroneous | 720 |
| 43. | accommodate | 720 |
| 44. | itinerary | 720 |
| 45. | flout | 719 |
| 46. | February | 720 |
| 47. | personnel | 719 |
| 48. | forgo | 719 |
| 49. | memento | 720 |
| 50. | disinterested | 719 |
| 51. | Basically | 720 |
| 52. | gauge | 720 |
| 53. | definite | 720 |
| 54. | apprise | 719 |
| 55. | acquaint | 720 |
| 56. | colossal | 720 |
| 57. | minuscule | 720 |
| 58. | liaison | 720 |
| 59. | temperament | 720 |
| 60. | questionnaire | 720 |

34

# 17 Choosing the Right Word

**Directions:** Select the correct form in parentheses, and write your answer in the column at the right. **References:** ¶719.

1. How could these funds have been (disbursed, dispersed) without your okay?
2. It (may be, maybe) too late to prevent the loss of the Rexford account.
3. I could (cite, sight, site) numerous precedents for the court's ruling.
4. Mrs. Campo played the (principal, principle) role in the negotiations.
5. Please sign the (waver, waiver) of liability for your child's field trip.
6. Your policy makes you (liable, libel) for the first $500 in damages.
7. Our TV campaign has (peaked, piqued) the interest of many buyers.
8. I'll be happy to write the (foreword, forward) for your book.
9. The paint must be (especially, specially) mixed to match this chip.
10. I refuse to (accede, exceed) to the board's demands.
11. Many weeks have (passed, past) since you promised to write to us.
12. The uproar at yesterday's meeting didn't (faze, phase) me a bit.
13. We need to fight our competitors with all our (might, mite).
14. The actual figures don't (gibe, jibe) with the earlier estimates.
15. I will not comment out of (deference, difference) to Mrs. Cabot's views.
16. We can invalidate the contract on the grounds of (undo, undue) influence.
17. Cost overruns forced us to (expand, expend) more than we budgeted.
18. Thanks (a lot, allot, alot) for all your help.
19. These trays would (complement, compliment) your existing product line.
20. With the latest financial setback, bankruptcy is (eminent, imminent).
21. How can we (assure, ensure, insure) that the mistake will not recur?
22. Our only recourse will be to get a (lean, lien) on his property.
23. I am not (adverse, averse) to your getting a larger share of the profits.
24. How can we (affect, effect) the reorganization with minimum confusion?
25. Let's (adapt, adopt) the existing procedures rather than set up new ones.
26. We (cannot, can not) only sell you new photocopiers but also service the ones you have.
27. You must find some way to (brake, break) the sudden drop in sales.
28. Are you free on Monday to meet with a (perspective, prospective) buyer?
29. If you need help, Carole can (council, counsel, consul) you.
30. We plan to appeal the decision rather than (accept, except) it.

1. <u>disbursed</u>
2. <u>may be</u>
3. <u>cite</u>
4. <u>principal</u>
5. <u>waiver</u>
6. <u>liable</u>
7. <u>piqued</u>
8. <u>foreword</u>
9. <u>specially</u>
10. <u>accede</u>
11. <u>passed</u>
12. <u>faze</u>
13. <u>might</u>
14. <u>jibe</u>
15. <u>deference</u>
16. <u>undue</u>
17. <u>expend</u>
18. <u>a lot</u>
19. <u>complement</u>
20. <u>imminent</u>
21. <u>ensure</u>
22. <u>lien</u>
23. <u>averse</u>
24. <u>effect</u>
25. <u>adapt</u>
26. <u>can not</u>
27. <u>brake</u>
28. <u>prospective</u>
29. <u>counsel</u>
30. <u>accept</u>

Name _____ Date _____ Class _____ 35

**Directions:** Underline every word that is misspelled or misused, and write the correct form in the answer column. If a sentence is correct, write *C* in the answer column. **References:** ¶¶719–720; a dictionary (optional).

| # | Sentence | # | Answer | Ref |
|---|----------|---|--------|-----|
| 31. | There were a number of errors and <u>ommissions</u> in the minutes. | 31. | **omissions** | 720 |
| 32. | In what <u>catagory</u> should I record these miscellaneous sales? | 32. | **category** | 720 |
| 33. | Waxman's presentation was amateurish and <u>embarassing</u>. | 33. | **embarrassing** | 720 |
| 34. | Our attorney believes that a complaint should be <u>formerly</u> lodged. | 34. | **formally** | 719 |
| 35. | Ashberry's bankruptcy could put our own financial stability in <u>jepardy</u>. | 35. | **jeopardy** | 720 |
| 36. | We must insist on strict <u>temperture</u> controls in the laboratory. | 36. | **temperature** | 720 |
| 37. | Jon views each <u>aquisition</u> like a connoisseur eyeing a work of art. | 37. | **acquisition** | 720 |
| 38. | It's your <u>perogative</u> to demand better liaison between the two groups. | 38. | **prerogative** | 720 |
| 39. | <u>Curtesy</u> produces loyal customers and yields repeat business. | 39. | **Courtesy** | 719 |
| 40. | It was the consensus of the group that you proceed with your plan. | 40. | **C** | 720 |
| 41. | Mediocre products are never the <u>bargins</u> they are made out to be. | 41. | **bargains** | 720 |
| 42. | The <u>alledged</u> damage to the environment has been exaggerated. | 42. | **alleged** | 720 |
| 43. | Fewer <u>then</u> forty customers have returned our questionnaire. | 43. | **than** | 719 |
| 44. | You'll find a parking lot <u>ajacent</u> to our main entrance. | 44. | **adjacent** | 720 |
| 45. | We'll have to forgo the <u>priviledge</u> of hearing you speak. | 45. | **privilege** | 720 |
| 46. | The only way to <u>eliminate</u> the deficit is to cut back on spending. | 46. | **eliminate** | 720 |
| 47. | The directors will be arriving on the eighth or <u>nineth</u> of May. | 47. | **ninth** | 720 |
| 48. | This policy does not supersede <u>anyone</u> of the existing policies. | 48. | **any one** | 719 |
| 49. | We've had <u>phenominal</u> success in launching this year's models. | 49. | **phenomenal** | 720 |
| 50. | We need to issue a corporate policy statement on sexual <u>harrassment</u>. | 50. | **harassment** | 720 |
| 51. | Making prophecies about the bond market is not exactly my forte. | 51. | **C** | 719 |
| 52. | Will government regulation be a help or a <u>hinderance</u> in this case? | 52. | **hindrance** | 720 |
| 53. | Can you name any <u>uninterested</u> parties to serve as arbiters? | 53. | **disinterested** | 719 |
| 54. | I <u>implied</u> from what you said that I would not be affected. | 54. | **inferred** | 719 |
| 55. | Why do I always <u>mispell</u> the word *grammar?* | 55. | **misspell** | 720 |
| 56. | Judge Frazier is an <u>imminent</u> jurist, renowned for her legal opinions. | 56. | **eminent** | 719 |
| 57. | The only way out of the <u>dillemma</u> is to waive your rights. | 57. | **dilemma** | 720 |
| 58. | We can offer you a discount of 10 to 40 percent, depending on the <u>quanity</u> you order. | 58. | **quantity** | 720 |
| 59. | Frankly, I'm <u>loathe</u> to sponsor Halliday for reelection. | 59. | **loath** | 719 |
| 60. | <u>Entreprenuers</u> in search of funding often submit glamorous proposals. | 60. | **Entrepreneurs** | 720 |
| 61. | Our last mail <u>campain</u> did not pull very many orders. | 61. | **campaign** | 720 |
| 62. | Plagiarism is the only explanation for this amount of <u>parralel</u> wording. | 62. | **parallel** | 720 |
| 63. | It was <u>presumptious</u> of Vic to criticize the proposal. | 63. | **presumptuous** | 720 |
| 64. | The color of the <u>stationary</u> and the envelopes should be quite light. | 64. | **stationery** | 719 |
| 65. | We'll need to take out a second <u>morgage</u> to cover these expenses. | 65. | **mortgage** | 720 |

36

# 18

## Compound Words

**Directions:** Underline every word or phrase that is misspelled or misused, and write the correct form in the answer column. If a sentence is correct, write C in the answer column. **References:** ¶¶801–812.

1. We need to get some <u>feed-back</u> from our sales reps in the South.

2. Ellen Berkowitz has served as <u>secretary treasurer</u> for two years.

3. I prefer to have all my drafts typed <u>triple spaced.</u>

4. Simply place a <u>checkmark</u> next to each item you want to order.

5. Let's weed out the ones with real talent from the wannabes.

6. Sheila Grove, 37, has been named executive vice president of the Lombard-Rosetti Agency.

7. We need to hire more <u>salesmen</u> to handle this new product line.

8. When <u>air conditioning</u> an office, be sure to check the wiring.

9. Bev has a reputation for troubleshooting and problem solving.

10. Please <u>follow-up</u> with Bellows if he doesn't respond by Friday.

| | | |
|---|---|---|
| 1. | feedback | 803h |
| 2. | secretary-treasurer | 806 / 811 |
| 3. | triple-spaced | 812a |
| 4. | check mark | 801a |
| 5. | C | 804a |
| 6. | C | 808c |
| 7. | salespeople OR sales representatives | 809a |
| 8. | air-conditioning | 812a |
| 9. | C | 805a |
| 10. | follow up | 802 |

**Directions:** Insert hyphens as necessary in each boldface group of words. Circle all hyphens you insert. If a sentence is correct as given, write C in the answer column. **References:** ¶¶813–847. Give special attention to ¶¶813–815.

11. We are hoping to get a **30-year** mortgage on a Victorian farmhouse that is more than **100 years old**.

12. This **medical insurance** policy does not cover **preexisting** conditions.

13. We build **state-of-the-art turnkey** installations for public agencies.

14. The **pro- and antiunion** forces are each running a **hard-hitting** campaign.

15. I'd like you to recast the **five-year** sales figures in your **long-range** plan.

16. **Small business** owners are finding it hard to meet their **break-even** point.

17. Frank is **well known** for his **no-nonsense** approach to marketing.

18. Can we be sure these **cost-benefit** projections are **up to date**?

19. Call us **toll-free** on these **day- and** nighttime phone numbers.

20. The operating instructions are **well illustrated** and are **self-explanatory.**

21. Please be sure that all items on the form are properly **filled in**.

22. An **ad hoc** committee has been formed to make a **go/no-go** decision.

23. Where can I find some **time-tested** guidelines for **nonprofit** organizations?

24. Our **highest-priority** goal is to boost our **bottom-line** results by 12 percent.

25. All tickets will be sold on a **first-come**, **first-served** basis.

26. Please get me **up-to-date** costs on **off-the-shelf** financial software.

| | | |
|---|---|---|
| 11. | | 813 / 817a / 818a |
| 12. | C | 835a |
| 13. | | 831a / 830a / 833d |
| 14. | | 822a |
| 15. | | 817a / 816a |
| 16. | | 818c / 829a |
| 17. | | 824b / 815a |
| 18. | | 818b / 831a / 820a |
| 19. | | 832d / 824b |
| 20. | | 836a |
| 21. | C | 826 |
| 22. | | 831c / 831d |
| 23. | | 831a / 833a / 816a |
| 24. | | 814 |
| 25. | | 831d |
| 26. | | 831a |

27. You will be eligible for **social security** benefits in another six months.

27. **C**      818a
     824a

28. The **newly formed** division will focus exclusively on (high-tech) products.

28. _____    814

29. Even if we suffer a (short-term) loss, the (long-term) prospects are excellent.

29. _____    816a

30. Let's get a couple of bids on (recovering) the reception room furniture.

30. _____    837
     827b

31. There are no (hard-and-fast) rules for this type of **freewheeling** situation.

31. _____    824d
     833a

32. Our first hint of an **antitrust** suit came from a (high-ranking) source.

32. _____    822a
     831e

33. The company has a (rinky-dink) setup with a lot of **Mickey Mouse** procedures.

33. _____    819a

34. All contributions to Project Hope are (tax-deductible.)

34. _____    820a
     847f

35. Our new **Web site** design is (better-looking) than the old one.

35. _____    822b
     816a

36. Mr. Paley wants a (first-class) ticket on a **nonstop** flight to Singapore.

36. _____    833a
     832

37. There will be a (three-to four-month) delay until we get new **laptops.**

37. _____    847e
     828a

38. This (hit-or-miss) attitude toward quality is an **industrywide** problem.

38. _____    820c
     831b

39. Running a (mom-and-pop) kind of business can be quite (time-consuming.)

39. _____    821d

40. Sandy has a (part-time) job now but hopes to work (full-time) this spring.

40. _____    816a
     833a

41. The latest **semiannual** report shows a **steadily increasing** demand for VCRs.

41. **C**      824a
     819b

42. Please check the (Chicago-Phoenix) plane schedules and the (round-trip) fare.

42. _____    816a
     817a

43. Effective April 1, there will be a **13.5 percent** jump in **auto insurance** rates.

43. **C**      818a
     823a

44. These (high-priced,) (steel-belted) tires will last longer than your present tires.

44. _____    821a
     825b

45. Upon retirement I plan to follow a **less demanding,** (slower-paced) schedule.

45. _____    823b
     831a

46. We expect to have some (out-of-town) visitors in (mid-July.)

46. _____    838
     826

47. Our new contract with the company contains a (built-in) (cost-of-living) clause.

47. _____    831a

**Directions:** Rewrite the following sentences to correct all errors and remove sexist expressions. **References:** ¶¶801–847. For the rules on sexist expressions, see ¶¶809–810 and 840.

48. Businessmen need to follow-up with their sub-ordinates to avoid any break down in operations.

**Business managers need to follow up with their subordinates to avoid any breakdown in operations.**

   809a
   802
   833a
   802

49. Ethel Kaplan, the well known authoress, will embark on a six-weeks' tour of the Mid-West.

**Ethel Kaplan, the well-known author, will embark on a six-week [OR six weeks'] tour of the Midwest.**

   824b
   840a
   817a
   838

50. The chairman of every committee should spot check the on line records to ensure they are up-to-date. **The head of every committee should spot-check the online records to ensure they are up to date.**

   809d
   811
   847b
   831a

51. The woman surgeon who operated on my mother in law sees a 50 50 chance of a flare up in the pain. **The surgeon who operated on my mother-in-law sees a 50–50 chance of a flare-up in the pain.**

   810
   839
   817c
   802
   803a

52. Send your congressman an E mail to protest the state wide campaign to build on government owned land. **Send your representative in Congress an e-mail to protest the statewide campaign to build on government-owned land.**

   809d
   847d
   820c
   821a

38

# 19 Word Division

**Directions:** On each line below, there is one word that is *incorrectly* divided or that does *not* follow the preferred style of word division. Write the identifying letter for that word in the answer column. **References:** ¶¶901–922; a dictionary (optional).

| | | | | | |
|---|---|---|---|---|---|
| 1. **a.** prefer-/ ring | **b.** permit-/ ted | **c.** shun-/ ned | **d.** win-/ ner | 1. c | 902 922 |
| 2. **a.** pre-/ arranged | **b.** recre-/ ation | **c.** re-/ act | **d.** re-/ ach | 2. d | 901c 914 |
| 3. **a.** rebel-/ ling | **b.** clip-/ ping | **c.** confer-/ ring | **d.** surpas-/ sing | 3. d | 901c 922 |
| 4. **a.** up-/ on | **b.** up-/ per | **c.** up-/ roar | **d.** up-/ date | 4. a | 904 |
| 5. **a.** la-/ tent | **b.** par-/ ent | **c.** would-/ n't | **d.** war-/ rant | 5. c | 906 |
| 6. **a.** recall-/ ing | **b.** impell-/ ing | **c.** misspell-/ ing | **d.** pull-/ ing | 6. b | 922 |
| 7. **a.** a-/ broad | **b.** ab-/ duct | **c.** ab-/ sorb | **d.** ab-/ stract | 7. a | 903a |
| 8. **a.** re-/ cap | **b.** mad-/ cap | **c.** fools-/ cap | **d.** AS-/ CAP | 8. d | 905 |
| 9. **a.** mas-/ terpiece | **b.** weather-/ proof | **c.** time-/ saving | **d.** share-/ holder | 9. a | 907 |
| 10. **a.** para-/ legal | **b.** anti-/ septic | **c.** un-/ derneath | **d.** inter-/ office | 10. c | 909 |
| 11. **a.** air-/ conditioned | **b.** weather-/ beaten | **c.** old-/ fashioned | **d.** govern-/ ment-owned | 11. d | 908 |
| 12. **a.** in-/ terpret | **b.** in-/ ternal | **c.** super-/ fluous | **d.** ex-/ traordinary | 12. c | 909 |
| 13. **a.** buzz-/ ing | **b.** swell-/ ing | **c.** barr-/ ing | **d.** cross-/ ing | 13. c | 922 |
| 14. **a.** responsi-/ ble | **b.** prob-/ able | **c.** change-/ able | **d.** fea-/ sible | 14. a | 910 |
| 15. **a.** bat-/ tle | **b.** diff-/ ered | **c.** pas-/ senger | **d.** mar-/ ried | 15. b | 922 |
| 16. **a.** un-/ helpful | **b.** nonsmok-/ ing | **c.** retire-/ ment | **d.** prevail-/ ing | 16. b | 911 |
| 17. **a.** pay-/ off | **b.** print-/ out | **c.** check-/ up | **d.** break-/ down | 17. c | 904 |
| 18. **a.** continu-/ ation | **b.** patrio-/ tic | **c.** courte-/ ous | **d.** ingredi-/ ent | 18. b | 914 |
| 19. **a.** help-/ fulness | **b.** meaning-/ ful | **c.** hopeless-/ ness | **d.** sportsman-/ ship | 19. a | 911 |
| 20. **a.** break-/ up, | **b.** cave-/ in; | **c.** mark-/ down | **d.** mark-/ up | 20. d | 904 |
| 21. **a.** man-/ agement | **b.** inter-/ national | **c.** follow-/ ing | **d.** pre-/ occupied | 21. a | 912 |
| 22. **a.** para-/ lyze | **b.** log-/ ical | **c.** specu-/ late | **d.** ele-/ gant | 22. b | 913 |
| 23. **a.** unluck-/ y, | **b.** trade-/ in; | **c.** stand-/ by? | **d.** line-/ up: | 23. a | 903a |
| 24. **a.** cIan-/ nish | **b.** regret-/ table | **c.** control-/ ler | **d.** spel-/ ling | 24. d | 901c 922 |
| 25. **a.** be-/ lieve | **b.** soc-/ iety | **c.** vari-/ ety | **d.** pa-/ tience | 25. b | 901c 914 |
| 26. **a.** con-/ nect | **b.** cor-/ rect | **c.** col1-/ ect | **d.** cof-/ fee | 26. c | 922 |
| 27. **a.** micro-/ chip | **b.** eye-/ witness | **c.** paper-/ work | **d.** moneylend-/ ers | 27. d | 907 |
| 28. **a.** improve-/ ment | **b.** bor-/ rowing | **c.** hyper-/ active | **d.** under-/ developed | 28. b | 912 |
| 29. **a.** neg-/ ative | **b.** rele-/ vant | **c.** moni-/ tor | **d.** salu-/ tation | 29. a | 913 |
| 30. **a.** im-/ mobile | **b.** hum-/ ming | **c.** skim-/ med | **d.** ham-/ mer | 30. c | 902 922 |

Name _____  Date _____  Class _____   39

**Directions:** Rewrite each word in the answer column to indicate the preferred word division at the end of a line. If a word cannot be divided, put a dash in the answer column. **References:** ¶¶901–922; a dictionary (optional).

| | | | | | | | |
|---|---|---|---|---|---|---|---|
| 31. | similar | **simi-/ lar** | 913 | 41. | connection | **connec-/ tion** | 912 |
| 32. | thoughtfulness | **thoughtful-/ ness** | 911 | 42. | muffled | **muf-/ fled** | 922c |
| 33. | repayable | **repay-/ able** | 910 901c | 43. | markup | **–** | 904 |
| 34. | expressed | **ex-/ pressed** | 914 | 44. | $429,600 | **–** | 915 |
| 35. | straightforward | **straight-/ forward** | 907 | 45. | self-conscious | **self-/ conscious** | 908 |
| 36. | about | **–** | 903a | 46. | continuation | **continu-/ ation** | 914 |
| 37. | announce | **an-/ nounce** | 922c 903a | 47. | strength | **–** | 902 |
| 38. | piano | **pi-/ ano** | 914 903a | 48. | shouldn't | **–** | 906 901c |
| 39. | amusement | **amuse-/ ment** | 910 | 49. | addressed | **ad-/ dressed** | 922c |
| 40. | circumstances | **circum-/ stances** | 909 | 50. | UNICEF | **–** | 905 |

**Directions:** In the following entries a diagonal rule is used to suggest where one typed line ends and another begins. If the line ending does not reflect preferred style, draw a new diagonal line to indicate a better point of word division. (If there is more than one way to improve the word division, draw the new diagonal line as close as possible to the old one.) If the line ending is acceptable as given, write OK in the answer column. **References:** ¶¶915–920.

51. The reunion luncheon has been scheduled for June/ 4,/2007, at the Alumni
Club . . .     **51.** _____ 920a

52. We had hoped to raise $50,-/ 000/in this year's campaign for homeless shelters . . .     **52.** _____ 915

53. On the basis of the lab reports,/Dr./ Cortines recommends that . . .     **53.** _____ 919

54. Our main distribution center is only/14/ miles from . . .     **54.** _____ 919

55. This year's luncheon speaker is Attorney/ General Jane Minetta . . .     **55. OK** _____ 920g

56. You will have to ask Thomas Gilmartin/ Jr.,/who drafted the proposal . . .     **56.** _____ 919

57. The Fulton Literary Prize was awarded to Ms. Celia/ R./Gomez . . .     **57.** _____ 920d

58. The annotated bibliography on page/ 236/offers . . .     **58.** _____ 919

59. We have leased new offices at 680 Pennington/ Boulevard . . .     **59. OK** _____ 920b

60. Let's plan to get together in my office on May/ 2/at 3 o'clock . . .     **60.** _____ 919

61. You can send it to my summer home in Cohasset,/ Massachusetts 02025 . . .     **61. OK** _____ 920c

62. Let's talk with Bart Elliott/ —/he's the general manager of . . .     **62.** _____ 920k

63. I urge you to read Chapter/ 7/for its trenchant analysis of . . .     **63.** _____ 919

64. Total annual sales (domestic and foreign) now exceed $12,000,-/ 000,000 . . .     **64. OK** _____ 915

65. The meeting should end by 10/ p.m./at the latest . . .     **65.** _____ 919

66. . . . will have three main objectives:/(1)/ to determine how . . .     **66.** _____ 920j

67. Gateway Industries has announced the promotion of Jay Tracy/ II/to . . .     **67.** _____ 919

68.     We are pleased to announce that Janice Krauss will be join-/     **68.** _____ 917

69. ing/our staff as a senior account executive. She has previous-/     **69.** _____ 904

70. ly/served as a copywriter for several top-rated agencies, work-/
ing with such clients as . . .     **70. OK** _____ 916

40

# 20

# Editing Survey C

**Directions:** Supply missing punctuation and strike out or correct any inappropriate punctuation in the following material. Change the spelling as necessary. Circle all changes you make. **References:** Sections 6–9.

Since the 1990's users of personal computers have been quiet likely to encounter           **1**

computer viruses that have been concocted by mischievous hackers or malicious weirdoes to erase           **2**

computer data and software programs. A computer virus is actually a small program in itself           **3**

that manages to infiltrate other programs, data files, and operating systems. It typically spreads           **4**

ads as "infected" e-mail messages, documents, and programs are forwarded to different PC's.           **5**

One can readily conjure up a series of hair raising scenarios for disaster, but it's difficult           **6**

to conceive the motivation of the people who mastermind the creation of these viruses.           **7**

The problem was dramatically highlighted by the worldwide appearance of a virus named           **8**

Michelangelo. The virus was named for the fifteenth-century Italian artist, because on March 6, 1992           **9**

(the occasion of Michelangelo's 517th birthday), the virus, which had been quietly spreading           **10**

for a while, was designed to attack IBM computers as well as IBM-compatible equipment.           **11**

According to a news article that appeared on that day in *The New York Times*, this virus was           **12**

first detected in Germany in 1991. Because of the advance warning, most users succeded in           **13**

eliminating the virus before it could effect their programs. Indeed, manufacturers of antiviral           **14**

programs profited handsomely from the demand for devices that could protect equipment           **15**

otherwise susceptible to serious damage from the virus.           **16**

In August 2003 three powerful viruses spread over hundreds of thousands of computers.           **17**

The MSBlaster virus attacked 120,000 computers in one 24-hour period alone. This virus searched           **18**

the Internet for vulnerable computers, forcing many to shut down every time they reconnected to           **19**

the Internet.           **20**

There are several ways to fight computer viruses—each with it's own pro's and con's—           **21**

but many computer company's did not start to make use of their know-how until customers           **22**

began to demand this kind of security. There is now a concensus among knowledgable people           **23**

in the field, who say that personal computers must be redesigned to provide the neccessary           **24**

protection.           **25**

Lance J. Hoffman, a computer expert sited in the *Times* article, put the whole issue in           **26**

clear prospective: "It's just like automobiles. When people got tired of seeing people thrown           **27**

out on the highway after accidents, they began adding seat belts. We need the equivalent of           **28**

seat belts built into our computers."           **29**

---

**Note to Instructor: There is a total of 30 errors in this material.**

Name _____ Date _____ Class _____          41

**Directions:** Supply missing punctuation and strike out or correct any inappropriate punctuation in the following material. Change the spelling as necessary. Circle all changes you make. **References:** Sections 6–9.

If you often have material that needs to be copied—indeed, if you are running a home-based **1**
business—you are familiar with the frustration of continuously going out to the copy shop or waiting **2**
in line at the library. In that case, you're definitely going to welcome the news about the increased **3**
affordability of compact photocopiers designed specifically for home use. These home copiers **4**
have become so popular that they now sell well over 500,000 units a year in this country. **5**

Today's easy-to-use models can come in handy for a variety of purposes. You can conveniently **6**
ly reproduce legal documents, tax records, cancelled checks, notices, and receipts—and even your **7**
children's report cards. The equipment is so user-friendly that youngsters can copy their own **8**
homework and drawings. **9**

What has made these compact copiers feasable is a technology that eliminates the need for **10**
a service technician to replace the toner (a powder that melts to form images) and the photo- **11**
conducting element (typically a drum that transfers the toner onto the copy paper). These **12**
elements can now be supplied in no-muss, no-fuss cartridges. As a result, most small copiers **13**
will yield high-quality reproductions on almost any type of paper. **14**

You will find that prices for these desktop copiers are relatively low when they are compared **15**
ed with the prices for typical office equipment. The basic machine carries a list price of **16**
$150 to $300, but you can often get as much as a 60 percent discount. The replacable toner **17**
cartridges typically cost between $10 and $120; they usually make between 1000 and 3500 **18**
copies, and some make as many as 11,500. Replaceable drums cost between $120 and $140, **19**
and cartridges containing both the toner and the drum cost between $90 and $125. If you **20**
consider just the cost of the paper and the cartridges, the average cost for each copy can range **21**
from 3 to 14 cents. If you also figure in some tiny fraction of what it cost to purchase the copier **22**
itself, the cost for each copy is much higher. In other words, the cost of making copies at home **23**
is not exactly a bargain. **24**

Since capability's vary, you should carefully compare the pro's and con's of the different **25**
machines and pick the one that best fits your needs and your wallet. For example, some copiers **26**
can make legal-size copies; others can make only the standard 8½ by 11-inch copies. Some will **27**
make enlargements and reductions, some will accept computer print/outs, and some will **28**
copy pages strait from bound books. You should also consider differences in the copiers speed **29**
of operation. Some can produce as many as 10 or 11 copies a minute; others produce only 3 or **30**
4 copies a minute. In any case, it can take 10 to 30 seconds for the first copy to appear. **31**

Before you procede to buy a compact copier, you ought to way the investment in equipment **32**
and supplies against the cost of making copies commercially. In most large cities single-copy **33**
rates can range from 5 to 10 cents. If you will not be making a large number of copies at one time, **34**
consider a budget-priced machine with a minimum of controls and special features. **35**

**Note to Instructor: There is a total of 30 errors in this material.**

# 21

# Subjects and Verbs

**Directions:** Select the correct form in parentheses, and write your answer in the column at the right. **References:** ¶¶1001–1048.

| # | Sentence | Answer | Ref |
|---|----------|--------|-----|
| 1. | Every investor and saver (has, have) become more cautious recently. | 1. has | 1002c 1009b |
| 2. | Neither the directors nor the top executives (wants, want) to relocate. | 2. want | 1004 |
| 3. | Only one of the photocopiers (is, are) working properly. | 3. is | 1006a 1008a |
| 4. | One of the causes for the breakdowns (is, are) poor maintenance. | 4. is | 1006a 1008a |
| 5. | (Has, Have) any of your customers complained about deliveries? | 5. Have | 1013a |
| 6. | The criteria for paying bonuses (has, have) to be rethought. | 6. have | 1018a |
| 7. | *Changing Times* (is, are) offering subscribers a special renewal rate. | 7. is | 1022 |
| 8. | Over three-quarters of the draft (has, have) to be rewritten. | 8. has | 1025a |
| 9. | There (has, have) been no news from Frank in two months. | 9. has | 1014 1028a |
| 10. | Those who (did, done) the customer survey deserve much praise. | 10. did | 1032b |
| 11. | It is critical that this memo (is, be) distributed this afternoon. | 11. be | 1038a |
| 12. | More than one client (has, have) asked me whether Chris is leaving. | 12. has | 1013a |
| 13. | Neither management nor the union (likes, like) the settlement. | 13. likes | 1003 |
| 14. | Mr. Hall, along with his two partners, (is, are) going to Paris today. | 14. is | 1007 |
| 15. | (Has, Have) their board voted yet on the reorganization plan? | 15. Has | 1019a |
| 16. | The number of job openings (has, have) increased this month. | 16. has | 1023 |
| 17. | Many of our salespeople have (rose, risen) quickly to higher-level jobs. | 17. risen | 1033 |
| 18. | Paul said that he (will, would) debug the program over the weekend. | 18. would | 1047 |
| 19. | Kate is one of those people who (writes, write) well without effort. | 19. write | 1008b |
| 20. | None of the applicants (impress, impresses) either of us very much. | 20. impress | 1013b |
| 21. | I wish I (was, were) going to be considered for Larry's job. | 21. were | 1039a |
| 22. | Many on the sales staff (wants, want) to attend the seminar. | 22. want | 1012 |
| 23. | Either of the editors (is, are) willing to take on your manuscript. | 23. is | 1009a |
| 24. | Brooks Brothers (is, are) having its annual sale next week. | 24. is | 1020 |
| 25. | Twenty dollars (doesn't, don't) buy much these days. | 25. doesn't | 1024 |
| 26. | If I had heard, I would (tell, have told) you the news. | 26. have told | 1040 |
| 27. | One of the products we distribute (is, are) coffee grinders. | 27. is | 1008a 1029a |
| 28. | A number of my customers (has, have) asked for bigger discounts. | 28. have | 1023 |
| 29. | Attached (is, are) three layouts for you to evaluate and choose from. | 29. are | 1027a |
| 30. | Every one of us (hopes, hope) you will have a speedy recovery. | 30. hopes | 1010 |

Name _____  Date _____  Class _____  43

**Directions:** Underline all errors in the following sentences, and write the correct forms in the answer column. If a sentence is correct, write *C* in the answer column. **References:** ¶¶1001–1048.

31. Many a trainer and instructor <u>have</u> been helped by your techniques.    31. **has**    1002c 1009b
32. Not only the workers but also the management favors a four-day week.    32. **C**    1005
33. Our arrangements with the Dodd Service Agency <u>has</u> worked out quite well.    33. **have**    1006a
34. Your survey, along with Fox's study, <u>prove</u> that the supplier was at fault.    34. **proves**    1007
35. One of the factors we consider in choosing suppliers <u>are</u> fast service.    35. **is**    1008a 1029a
36. Olive is the only one of our employees who <u>are</u> consistently on time.    36. **is**    1008c
37. Every art director and designer on staff wants to work on the Athens account.    37. **C**    1002c 1009b
38. Few of the people I talked with actually <u>believes</u> the merger will occur.    38. **believe**    1012
39. More than six people have turned down the chance to work for Alix.    39. **C**    1013a
40. Although most of our stock is selling well, some of the goods <u>isn't</u> moving.    40. **aren't**    1013a 1015
41. A series of management seminars <u>have</u> been planned for the fall.    41. **has**    1016
42. With the right teacher, economics is a fascinating subject.    42. **C**    1017
43. The number of new competitors has <u>rose</u> at an alarming rate.    43. **risen**    1023 1033
44. That the HMO plan offers many advantages <u>are</u> not to be denied.    44. **is**    1026a
45. Yet only a small percentage of our employees <u>has</u> chosen the HMO plan.    45. **have**    1025a
46. <u>Here is</u> a descriptive brochure and a sample copy of the book.    46. **are**    1028a
47. The photocopying equipment on the seventh floor has <u>broke</u> down again.    47. **broken**    1033
48. It is urgent that Frank <u>responds</u> quickly to the job offer.    48. **respond**    1038b
49. I wish it <u>was</u> the end and not the start of the holiday rush.    49. **were**    1039a
50. It is the sales reps who want the pricing schedule adjusted.    50. **C**    1029a

**Directions:** Rewrite the following sentences to correct all errors and remove awkward expressions. **References:** ¶¶1005, 1007, 1010, 1018, 1019, 1032, 1033, 1037, 1046, and 1048.

51. Everyone of us want to thank you for all that you done. **Every one of us wants to thank you for**    1010 1032

 **all that you did [OR all that you have done].**    1033a

52. I have always thought and still do that our problems begun when the Troy plant was sold by us.
    **I have always thought and still do think that our problems began when we sold the Troy plant.**    1048 1032 1037b

53. The whole staff, including John and me, think the books should be audited by you at once.
    **The whole staff, including John and me, thinks you should audit the books at once.**    1019a 1007 1037b

54. The board is not able to agree on whether to immediately raise prices. **The members of the**    1019b

 **board are not able to agree on whether to raise prices immediately.**    1046

55. The criteria for acceptable performance has been established, but neither the employees nor the
    manager understands them. **The criteria for acceptable performance have been established,**    1018a

 **but neither the manager nor the employees understand them.**    1005

44

# 22 Pronouns and Other Grammar Problems

**Directions:** Select the correct form in parentheses, and write your answer in the column at the right. **References:** ¶¶1049–1088.

| | | |
|---|---|---|
| 1. The company has given (its, their) managers new productivity goals. | 1. **its** | 1049a |
| 2. A number of you have not yet signed (their, your) commission contracts. | 2. **your** | 1053d |
| 3. Bob can make the presentation a lot more effectively than (I, me). | 3. **I** | 1057 |
| 4. (Who, Whom) should we invite as the keynote speaker? | 4. **Whom** | 1061d |
| 5. This year's convention displays look (real, really) handsome. | 5. **really** | 1065 |
| 6. Given the two alternatives, I think you chose the (best, better) plan. | 6. **better** | 1071g |
| 7. They have asked for no discount (or, nor) any other special terms. | 7. **or** | 1076c |
| 8. These price increases are retroactive (to, from) October 15. | 8. **to** | 1077 |
| 9. Neither Bert nor Jerry can lend us (his, their) boat for the weekend. | 9. **his** | 1049c |
| 10. It was Jan and (me, I) who made all the arrangements for the banquet. | 10. **I** | 1054b |
| 11. Every company has (its, it's) own policy on promotions and transfers. | 11. **its** | 1056e |
| 12. This is the kind of case that (us, we) lawyers find truly challenging. | 12. **we** | 1058 |
| 13. We want to know (who, whom) you think will be appointed. | 13. **who** | 1061c |
| 14. We feel very (bad, badly) about your decision to move out of the area. | 14. **bad** | 1067 |
| 15. I have decided that I do not want (any, no) part of the money. | 15. **any** | 1076a |
| 16. The monitor you shipped us does not correspond (to, with) the one described in your brochure. | 16. **to** | 1077 |
| 17. Please let that be a private matter between you and (me, I). | 17. **me** | 1055b |
| 18. Jack is a person (who's, whose) reputation for fairness is well known. | 18. **whose** | 1063 |
| 19. This trip to Scandinavia will be a dream come true for my family and (me, myself). | 19. **me** | 1060d |
| 20. This is a problem every adult faces with (their, his or her) parents. | 20. **his or her** | 1050 / 1052a |

**Directions:** Underline all errors in the following sentences, and write the correct forms in the answer column. If a sentence is correct, write *C* in the answer column. **References:** ¶¶1049–1088.

| | | |
|---|---|---|
| 21. Either Lois or Pam can lend you <u>their</u> procedures manual. | 21. **her** | 1049c |
| 22. If anyone has already paid the fee, he or she should ask for a refund. | 22. **C** | 1053a |
| 23. Ball's use of company funds looks highly questionable to <u>we</u> auditors. | 23. **us** | 1058 |
| 24. I have no questions <u>nor</u> concerns about the terms of the contract. | 24. **or** | 1076c |
| 25. We can fill your orders just as quickly and as cheaply as <u>them</u>. | 25. **they** | 1057 |

Name _____  Date _____  Class _____  45

26. Rita considered you and <u>I</u> to be sisters or at least first cousins.    26. **me**      1064a

27. It is you who <u>has</u> to make the first move toward reconciliation.    27. **have**      1049a

28. No one will represent the firm at the trade fair except you and <u>I</u>.    28. **me**      1055b

29. George Fry and <u>myself</u> hosted the party for the Kennellys.    29. **I**      1060d

30. Please deliver these tapes to <u>whomever</u> is in charge of the studio.    30. **whoever**      1061c

31. It's clear that <u>they're</u> marketing strategy is more effective than ours.    31. **their**      1056e

32. <u>Whom</u> do you think will apply for Larry Kenilworth's job in Finance?    32. **Who**      1061c

33. The commission will issue <u>their</u> long-awaited ruling on Monday.    33. **its**      1049a

**Directions:** Rewrite the following sentences to correct all errors, fix awkward or ungrammatical constructions, and remove sexist expressions. **References:** ¶¶1049–1088. For the rules on sexist expressions, see ¶¶1050–1053.

34. Neither the sales representatives nor the sales manager has submitted his expense report.
    **Neither the sales manager nor the sales representatives have submitted their expense reports.**
    1049c

35. Everyone in Marketing should submit his catalog copy no later than July 20. **Everyone in Marketing should submit his or her catalog copy no later than July 20.**
    1053a

36. Rhode Island is smaller than any state in the Union. **Rhode Island is smaller than any other state in the Union.**
    1071h

37. To ensure a full refund, the original sales slip should be sent along with the merchandise.
    **To ensure a full refund, send [OR you should send] the original sales slip along with the merchandise.**
    1082b

38. If a customer asks for Model B-1101, tell him that we are out of stock. **If customers ask for Model B-1101, tell them that we are out of stock.**
    1050
    1052b

39. Randy only plans to take two courses next summer. **Randy plans to take only two courses next summer.**
    1072

40. We got off the plane at about 11:45 p.m. **We got off the plane at [OR about] 11:45 p.m.**
    1078

41. Your performance not only moved the audience but also the other members of the cast. **Your performance moved not only the audience but also the other members of the cast.**
    1081b

42. In auditing your account, two discrepancies were noted by my assistant. **In auditing your account, my assistant noted two discrepancies.**
    1082c

43. This year's profit goals are much higher than last year. **This year's profit goals are much higher than last year's [OR than they were last year].**
    1071i

44. We don't get many inquiries, or many requests for, these oil lamps. **We don't get many inquiries about, or many requests for, these oil lamps.**
    1079

# 23  Usage

**Directions:** Select the correct form in parentheses, and write your answer in the column at the right. **References:** Section 11. The individual entries are listed alphabetically. If you have difficulty in finding an entry, consult the list at the start of Section 11 (on pages 308–310 of *The Gregg Reference Manual*).

| | | | |
|---|---|---|---|
| 1. | (A, An) M.B.A. degree would surely bring you better job offers. | 1. | An |
| 2. | The loss of two programmers will greatly (affect, effect) our output. | 2. | affect |
| 3. | Mary Lee is (already, all ready) to take on her new assignment. | 3. | all ready |
| 4. | We'll be glad to help in (anyway, any way) that we can. | 4. | any way |
| 5. | A large (amount, number) of people visited our convention exhibit. | 5. | number |
| 6. | Simply ignore the problem for (awhile, a while) and see what happens. | 6. | a while |
| 7. | The reason we lost the deal is (because, that) our offer was topped. | 7. | that |
| 8. | If Frank (don't, doesn't) like the new procedure, he should say why. | 8. | doesn't |
| 9. | Does anyone (beside, besides) Bo know our CEO very well? | 9. | besides |
| 10. | Our sales have dropped (due to, because of) new competition. | 10. | because of |
| 11. | I urged Sam to delve (farther, further) into the reasons for heavy returns. | 11. | further |
| 12. | We've had (fewer, less) complaints since the product was redesigned. | 12. | fewer |
| 13. | (First, Firstly), you need to streamline your approval procedures. | 13. | First |
| 14. | You'll have to take another (tack, tact) if you want to change Ed's mind. | 14. | tack |
| 15. | I doubt (if, whether) we'll be able to make the party on the 15th. | 15. | whether |
| 16. | From what Sue said, I (implied, inferred) that she won't be back. | 16. | inferred |
| 17. | Fred has been (laying, lying) down on the job lately. | 17. | lying |
| 18. | There (maybe, may be) some truth to the story after all. | 18. | may be |
| 19. | More (important, importantly), this model carries a lower price tag. | 19. | important |
| 20. | Anyone could (of, have) seen through that ruse. | 20. | have |
| 21. | Bond prices have been (raising, rising) all this quarter. | 21. | rising |
| 22. | You can (set, sit) the easel in my office while I'm gone. | 22. | set |
| 23. | I will call Mary myself (so, so that) we can get to the bottom of this. | 23. | so that |
| 24. | Glen saw her at Lake Tahoe (sometime, some time) ago. | 24. | some time |
| 25. | We (sure, surely) appreciate all you have done for us. | 25. | surely |
| 26. | Most of our customers prefer (this, these) kind of printer. | 26. | this |
| 27. | If you (would have, had) told me your arrival time, I would have met you at the airport. | 27. | had |
| 28. | We are all (anxious, eager) to get the scoop on our merger with Cali Co. | 28. | anxious |
| 29. | I don't know (as, whether) I can reveal that information. | 29. | whether |
| 30. | I am writing (in regard to, in regards to) your order of April 12. | 30. | in regard to |

Name _____  Date _____  Class _____     47

C-61

**Directions:** If the boldface word or phrase is correct, write *C* in the answer column. If the word or phrase is incorrect, supply the correct form. **References:** Section 11.

| | | |
|---|---|---|
| 31. | My notes for the minutes of the meeting were **accidently** thrown out. | 31. accidentally |
| 32. | It has been taking us **all together** too long to get new products out in the marketplace. | 32. altogether |
| 33. | Mrs. Penney's estate will be equally split **between** her six children. | 33. among |
| 34. | Please keep me **appraised** of any falloff in our international sales. | 34. apprised |
| 35. | We all feel very **badly** about the way Ted has treated you. | 35. bad |
| 36. | Whatever information passes between you and **me** is confidential. | 36. C |
| 37. | In **less** than five years our firm has achieved a statewide reputation. | 37. C |
| 38. | Our new warehouse is **further** out from the downtown district. | 38. farther |
| 39. | I **graduated** from Emory University with a B.S. in economics. | 39. C |
| 40. | It looks **like** you may have a winner on your hands after all. | 40. as if |
| 41. | I feel my supervisor treats me **different** from the others on her staff. | 41. differently |
| 42. | What **kind of an** outcome do you want this letter to produce? | 42. kind of |
| 43. | Because of her asthma Jean needs to move to a **healthier** climate. | 43. more healthful |
| 44. | Please come **into** see me when you are next in town. | 44. in to |
| 45. | The new floor plan was **laying** on her desk where anyone could see it. | 45. lying |
| 46. | Will you please **leave** me see the summary of your report? | 46. let |
| 47. | I would like you to check **upon** our new customer service procedures. | 47. up on |
| 48. | The weather this winter has been **real** mild. | 48. really |
| 49. | I received your letter and will answer **same** next week. | 49. it |
| 50. | We try to **service** our customers efficiently and courteously. | 50. serve |
| 51. | Be **sure and** stop by when you next get to Nashville. | 51. sure to |
| 52. | Our market share is much greater **then** it was three years ago. | 52. than |
| 53. | Both sides in the dispute are slowly moving **towards** a compromise. | 53. C [OR toward] |
| 54. | Our partnership has come a long **ways** since we started in 1999. | 54. way |
| 55. | This new product line will put us **indirect** competition with Bascom. | 55. in direct |
| 56. | I think **this here** layout works better than anything else I've seen. | 56. this |
| 57. | Stan hopes that **a** M.B.A. degree will get him a better-paying job. | 57. an |
| 58. | Since you made the service call, everything has worked **alright.** | 58. all right |
| 59. | Please **bring** the contracts to Mr. Hellman when you go to visit him. | 59. take |
| 60. | I wish we knew who **done** the original construction. | 60. did |
| 61. | Will they be able to **learn** me how to improve my English? | 61. teach |
| 62. | Your procedure is different **than** the one I learned in school. | 62. from |
| 63. | The two of us need to sound out **one another's** ideas before we go to the conference. | 63. each other's |
| 64. | These power outages are becoming an **everyday** affair. | 64. C |
| 65. | **Everyone** of these customer complaints needs to be fully investigated. | 65. Every one |

48

C-62

# 24 Usage (Continued)

**Directions:** If the boldface word or phrase is correct as given, write *C* in the answer column. If the word or phrase is incorrect, supply the correct form in the answer column. **References:** Section 11. The individual entries are listed alphabetically. If you have difficulty in finding an entry, consult the full listing of entries at the start of Section 11 (on pages 308–310 of *The Gregg Reference Manual*).

1. What strategies are likely to have a significant **affect** on our output?     1. effect _____
2. We plan to mail this questionnaire to people **age** 55 and up.     2. aged _____
3. We were **almost** relieved to hear of your son's recovery from surgery.     3. all most _____
4. My husband is not doing too **bad** since he took early retirement.     4. badly _____
5. I'll make a point of seating you **besides** the speaker.     5. beside _____
6. The statements and the checks should be **altogether** in the red file folder.     6. all together _____
7. I don't doubt **but what** you'll get the fellowship you applied for.     7. that _____
8. I doubt **if** we can still make the target date for our fall ad campaign.     8. whether _____
9. Any success I've achieved has been largely **due to** the staff support I got.     9. C _____
10. We are willing to consider **always** of reducing our costs.     10. all ways _____
11. Len, Gary, and I will undertake identical research studies and then share the data with **each other**.     11. one another _____
12. **Everyone** has to work at the convention booth except you and me.     12. C _____
13. Let's not sell the condo for **awhile** in case prices start to go up again.     13. a while _____
14. The fabric comes in red, blue, and purple, but I prefer the **former.**     14. first _____
15. I bought a van with only 12,000 miles on it **off** a tennis partner of mine.     15. from _____
16. The noise was so loud that we **couldn't hardly** hear ourselves.     16. could hardly _____
17. In telling me about the reorganization, Frank **inferred** that he would be promoted to assistant vice president.     17. implied _____
18. **Incidently,** what more have you heard about the Kossoff investigation?     18. Incidentally _____
19. Andy seemed **in different** when I told him my plans.     19. indifferent _____
20. We can make no exceptions to this policy, **irregardless** of the situation.     20. regardless _____
21. You **can** take Monday off as long as you make up the time.     21. may _____
22. **Most all** of the backlog of orders has now been cleaned up.     22. Almost all _____
23. I know of **no body** on the staff with those qualifications.     23. nobody _____
24. Ben should **of** told us he was planning to sell his interest in the firm.     24. have _____
25. It's time for us to move **onto** a new topic for discussion.     25. on to _____
26. We have a real **dilemma** when it comes to dealing with the cost of health insurance.     26. problem _____
27. I was doing 78 miles **per** hour when the police pulled me over.     27. an _____

Name _____ Date _____ Class _____     49

28. I will try **and** get you price quotes from several suppliers by Friday.    28. to _____

29. **Who ever** heard of a top-quality DVD recorder for under $500?    29. c _____

30. It may be better, **than,** to put our decision off until next month.    30. then _____

**Directions:** Rewrite the following sentences to correct all errors in usage. **References:** Section 11.

31. The reason for our inventory problems is because a large percent of our product line is outmoded.

    **The reason for our inventory problems is that a large percentage of our product line is outmoded.**

32. We are cutting costs travelwise, per your mandate. **We are cutting travel costs in accordance with your mandate.**

33. I could not help from smiling at that kind of a snappy comeback. **I could not help smiling at that kind of snappy comeback.**

34. The reviews for both albums were equally as good, but we couldn't find copies of either, however.

    **The reviews for both albums were equally good, but we couldn't find copies of either.**

    **[OR The reviews for both albums were equally good; however, we couldn't find copies of either.]**

35. The amount of compliments we received on our new showroom was kind of impressive.

    **The number of compliments we received on our new showroom was rather impressive.**

36. Everyone of us enthused over the way the play ended up. **Every one of us was enthusiastic about the way the play ended.**

37. I cannot help but remember my one encounter with former President Carter. **I cannot help remembering my one encounter with former President Carter.**

38. Television is the one media that we don't scarcely use for our ad campaigns. **Television is the one medium that we scarcely use for our ad campaigns.**

39. Being that we both like these kind of mineral water, why don't we split a case among us? **Since we both like this kind [OR these kinds] of mineral water, why don't we split a case between us?**

40. The latest train leaves the main terminal at about 11:30 p.m. **The last train leaves the main terminal at [OR about] 11:30 p.m.**

41. Incidently, yesterday Joe served us an excellent breakfast of melon, cereal, bacon and eggs.

    **Incidentally, yesterday Joe served us an excellent breakfast of melon, cereal, and bacon and eggs.**

42. Less men these days are buying items such as hats and ties, etc. **Fewer men these days are buying items such as hats and ties.**

43. Please lie the sketch down carefully so it doesn't smudge. **Please lay the sketch down carefully so that it doesn't smudge.**

44. Like I warned you before, your failure to pay these bills will seriously effect your credit rating. **As I warned you before, your failure to pay these bills will seriously affect your credit rating.**

45. Come and see me, Ed, when you have sometime to review my investment portfolio. **Come to see me, Ed, when you have some time to review my investment portfolio.**

# 25 Editing Survey D

**Directions:** Edit the following material for errors in grammar and usage. Circle any changes you make. **References:** Sections 10–11.

*The New York Times* reports regularly on new developments in computer technology. According **1**

to a recent column by Peter H. Lewis, "As a drawing or painting tool, the computer mouse is only **2**

slightly less effective than a potato." The limitations of the mouse have created special problems for **3**

a large number of people whose goal is to draw, paint, or trace images by means of a personal **4**

computer. **5**

A solution to the problem has been around for awhile in the form of graphics tablets that make **6**

use of a cordless electronic stylus. This stylus is a kind of a pen that is pressure-sensitive. As a result, **7**

the more pressure you apply, the thicker the line you create. In most cases, when you use this **8**

stylus, the image shows up on the screen but not on the graphics tablet; however, for people who **9**

are used to working on paper, there are electronic pens (and pencils) that write simultaneously **10**

with real ink (or lead) and with electrons. In that way you can create images on paper and on the **11**

screen at the same time. **12**

Now comes an innovation that takes this technology further. Who could have imagined an **13**

electronic pen *with an eraser?* Well, it's happened. Like the pen itself, the eraser is pressure- **14**

sensitive. Thus the harder you bear down on the tablet with the eraser, the more thorough **15**

the erasing effect will be on the electronic image. **16**

More important, you don't have to be an artist to appreciate the merits of an electronic pen **17**

with an electronic eraser. The pen not only works with graphics programs but also with word **18**

processing programs and other types of applications. More than one expert has noted that the pen **19**

is actually more effective than a mouse in moving a cursor around on the screen, and it can be used **20**

to initiate the commands needed to delete words, paragraphs, cells, and other items on the screen. **21**

What's more, by using this type of electronic pen, you're likely to develop fewer injuries, such as **22**

mouse elbow (a repetitive strain injury very much like tennis elbow). The worst that can happen **23**

when you use an electronic pen for a long period of time is an everyday case of writer's cramp. **24**

Maybe that's why a lot of people are really eager to get their hands on this new technological **25**

marvel. **26**

Personal digital assistants (PDAs) and tablet PCs allow you to write text with the pen. The **27**

software interprets the handwritten letters and converts them into typed characters on the screen. **28**

> **Note to Instructor: There is a total of 30 errors in this material.**

Name _____ Date _____ Class _____ 51

**Directions:** Edit the following material for errors in grammar and usage. Circle any changes you make. **References:** Sections 1–11.

If you are buying your first personal computer, there ~~is~~ (are) [1028a/1023] a number of devices you also need to  **1**

buy. One purchase that requires (real) ~~ly~~ [1101] careful thought ~~are~~ (is) [1001a/1029a] printers. When considering which type (of) [1079]  **2**

printer to buy, one key criterion ~~should be kept~~ (keep) [1028a] in mind: Do you want to print in color? Or are  **3**

you content with black-~~and~~-white [827b] results?  **4**

If you work mainly with black-and-white text pages and high quality has to be (e) [1101] ~~insured~~, con-  **5**

sider laser printers. This kind of (a) [1101] printer (provides) not only [1081b] sharp, clear text but also turns  **6**

out pages quickly and quietly. Laser printers (use) ~~d~~ (to) [1101] cost thousands of dollars but now cost no  **7**

more (th~~e~~n) (a) [719/1101] $200 to $400.  **8**

If the use of color is important in the ~~work~~ you do, consider buying (an) [1101] ~~a~~ ink-jet printer.  **9**

Good ink-jets are typically priced between $150 (and) [459b] $400, but some can be found for as little as  **10**

$50. Color laser printers are also available, but they are much too expensive (about $1000) for  **11**

most home users. When you consider that (1) ink-jets provide excellent color printing, (2) in  **12**

some cases they produce black-and-white pages as good as what you'd get from laser printers,  **13**

and (3) they cost about the same as laser printers, you'd be tempted to conclude that ink-jets  **14**

are the only smart choice. Yet there are other factors you need to take into account.  **15**

1. *Speed. Consumer Reports* (state) (s) [1022] that the laser printers its staff recently tested pro-  **16**

   duce 9 to 15 black-and-white pages a minute, (,) [101c] Whereas the ink-jets with  **17**

   the best-looking black-and-white pages turn out between 2.5 and 9.5 pages a  **18**

   minute. Good color printing takes much longer—2 to 18 minutes (a) [1101] ~~per~~ page.  **19**

2. *Quality.* Laser printers excel in producing black-and-white text at high speed (,) [127b]  **20**

   but do less well with black-and-white graphics and photos. Ink-jets excel in  **21**

   color work. (⊙) [1081a, note]  **22**

3. ~~What About Cost?~~ The cost of a black-and-white page produced by an ink-jet  **23**

   can range from 3 to 9 cents, compared ~~to a~~ (with) [1077] cost of 2 to 4 cents for a simi-  **24**

   lar page produced by a laser printer. Color printing is quite expensive: 8  **25**

   to 32 cents for color graphics and as much as $1.10 for co~~lor photos~~ (his or her) OR (a) [1052]  **26**

At one time, when a computer user wanted ~~to buy~~ a printer for ~~their~~ home office and a major  **27**

consideration (were) (was) [1029a] costs, the only real choice would ~~of~~ (have) [1101] been a dot matrix printer. However, with the  **28**

significant advances in technology, buying dot matrix printers no longer (make) (s) [1026a] sense. A large (per-  **29**

cent, of) [1101] these users now (recognize) (s) [1025] that laser and ink-jet printers provide superior performance on a  **30**

cost-effective basis. Because of heavy competition the prices of printers have not ~~rose~~ (risen) [1033, note/1101] lately. In  **31**

fact, the prices of many models have ~~fell~~ (fallen) [1033, note] this year, and next year's prices are expected to be lower  **32**

than this (year) (is) [1071i] Moreover, a new generation of printers ~~are~~ (is) [1006a] now being developed. With this  **33**

continuing advance in technology (comes) [1027] new opportunities for high-quality printers at lower  **34**

cost.  **35**

---

**Note to Instructor: There is a total of 30 errors in this material.**

52

# 26

## Letters

**Directions:** For each of the following sentences choose the phrase that best completes the meaning of the sentence. Then in the answer column record the identifying letter for the phrase you selected. **References:** ¶¶1301–1341.

1. In what letter style do the date line, the complimentary closing, and the writer's identification start at center and all other lines start at the left margin: **(a)** the block style; **(b)** the simplified styles; **(c)** the modified-block style—standard format?  **1. c** ____ 1302a

2. What are the dimensions of *letter (standard)* stationery: **(a)** 8" × 11"; **(b)** 8½" × 11; **(c)** 8½" × 11½"?  **2. b** ____ 1303

3. To create a top margin of 2 inches, **(a)** space down 12 times from the top of the sheet; **(b)** space down 9 times; **(c)** space down 6 times from the default top margin of 1 inch.  **3. c** ____ 1304a

4. If you are using *letter (standard)* stationery and want to use a text line that is shorter than the standard, you can increase the default side margins up to **(a)** 1.5 inches; **(b)** 1.75 inches; **(c)** 2 inches.  **4. b** ____ 1305b

5. If you are writing to someone who rents a mailbox from a private company, place the private mailbox number **(a)** on the line above the name of the person; **(b)** on the line above the street address; **(c)** on the same line preceding the street address.  **5. b** ____ 1338d

6. *Standard* punctuation calls for **(a)** a comma or period at the end of each displayed line; **(b)** only a colon after the salutation and a comma after the complimentary closing; **(c)** no punctuation after any displayed line.  **6. b** ____ 1308a

7. Where should a personal or confidential notation be typed: **(a)** on the second line below the date, beginning at center; **(b)** on the second line below the date, beginning at the left margin; **(c)** on the second line below the date, ending at the right margin?  **7. b** ____ 1314

8. If there are no special notations following the date, then on what line below the date should the inside address begin: **(a)** on the fourth line; **(b)** on the fifth line; **(c)** on the sixth line?  **8. a** ____ 1318a

9. When a person's name ends with *Jr.,* **(a)** insert a comma before *Jr.;* **(b)** do not insert a comma before *Jr.;* **(c)** do not insert a comma before *Jr.* unless you know that is the person's preference.  **9. c** ____ 1324a

10. If an apartment number or a room number appears in an inside address, it should be typed **(a)** after the street address or on the line above; **(b)** after the street address or on the line below; **(c)** in the lower left corner of the envelope.  **10. a** ____ 1316b 1317b

11. You must always show the state name in an inside address as a two-letter abbreviation—**(a)** true; **(b)** false.  **11. b** ____ 1341a

12. Which of the following date line styles is *not* acceptable: **(a)** August 12, 2008; **(b)** 12 August 2008; **(c)** 8/12/08?  **12. c** ____ 1313a

13. When a company name ends with *Inc.,* **(a)** insert a comma before *Inc.;* **(b)** do not insert a comma before *Inc.;* **(c)** do not insert a comma before *Inc.,* unless you know that it is the company's preference.  **13. c** ____ 1328 1329b

Name _____ Date _____ Class _____

53

**Directions:** Each of the items at the left represents an element in a business letter. If the item is correctly styled, write *C* in the answer column. If not, rewrite the item to make it correct. Assume the use of a **modified-block style—standard format** (¶1302a), **standard punctuation** (¶1308a), and **single spacing**. **References:** ¶¶1301–1341, plus ¶462 and ¶517a.

| | | |
|---|---|---|
| **14.** Jan. 29, 2007 | **14.** January 29, 2007 | 1313a |
| **15.** Confidential | **15.** CONFIDENTIAL | 1314 |

Treat items 16–31 as they should appear in an **inside address.**

| | | |
|---|---|---|
| **16.** Ralph G. Ferrara, Jr.<br>*(agrees with signature)* | **16.** Mr. Ralph G. Ferrara, Jr. | 1322a<br>1324a |
| **17.** Kathleen A. Koch<br>*(title preference unknown)* | **17.** C **OR** Ms. Kathleen A. Koch | 1322b |
| **18.** N. J. Harper | **18.** C | 1322c |
| **19.** Mr. & Mrs. Lloyd Welsh | **19.** Mr. and Mrs. Lloyd Welsh | 1323a |
| **20.** Doctor Nancy Fordyce | **20.** Dr. Nancy Fordyce | 517a<br>1322a |
| **21.** Mr. Royce Mead Esq. | **21.** Royce Mead, Esq. | 1323b |
| **22.** Dr. Sally Eng, M.D. | **22.** Sally Eng, M.D. | 1323c |
| **23.** Ms. Jan Corey, Director of<br>Research and development | **23.** Ms. Jan Corey<br>Director of Research and Development | 1325 |
| **24.** Marketing Department, Beta<br>Aerospace Corporation | **24.** Marketing Department<br>Beta Aerospace Corporation | 1327 |
| **25.** Capp & Rollins Co., Inc.<br>*(no letterhead available)* | **25.** Capp and Rollins Company Inc. | 1329 |
| **26.** 764 Haskell St. N.E. | **26.** 764 Haskell Street, NE | 1335a<br>1337 |
| **27.** No. 163, 9th Avenue | **27.** 163 Ninth Avenue | 1332<br>1333a |
| **28.** #1 West Eleventh Street | **28.** One West 11th Street | 1332<br>1333b |
| **29.** 1,616 S. Fuller Blvd. | **29.** 1616 South Fuller Boulevard | 462<br>1334<br>1337 |
| **30.** Ft. Lauderdale, FL, 33315 | **30.** Fort Lauderdale, FL 33315 | 1340c<br>1339 |
| **31.** Pittsburgh P.A. 15234 | **31.** Pittsburgh, PA 15234 | 1339<br>1341a |
| **32.** Dear Jane Reddy:<br>*(title preference unknown)* | **32.** C **OR** Dear Ms. Reddy: | 1339a |
| **33.** Dear Prof. Simcoe, | **33.** Dear Professor Simcoe: | 1338d<br>1338b |
| **34.** Gentlemen: | **34.** Ladies and Gentlemen: **OR** Gentlemen and Ladies: | 1340a |
| **35.** Australia | **35.** AUSTRALIA | 1336a |

# 27 Letters, Memos, and E-Mail

**Directions:** Choose the phrase that best completes the meaning of each of the following sentences. Then in the answer column record the identifying letter for the phrase you selected. Assume the use of a **modified-block style–standard format** (¶1302a), **standard punctuation** (¶1308a), and **single spacing**. **References:** Section 13.

1. A subject line, if used, should be typed **(a)** on the third line below the inside address; **(b)** on the third line below the salutation; **(c)** on the second line below the salutation.

   1. **c**    1343a

2. Begin the message of the letter **(a)** on the third line below the salutation (or subject line) at the left margin; **(b)** on the second line below the salutation (or subject line) at the left margin; **(c)** on the second line below the salutation (or subject line) indented 5 spaces.

   2. **b**    1344a

3. How many blank lines should be left between paragraphs: **(a)** 1; **(b)** 2; **(c)** none?

   3. **a**    1344e

4. When a three-line paragraph falls at the bottom of a page that is running long, you can carry one or two lines over to the top of the next page—**(a)** true; **(b)** false.

   4. **b**    1344i

5. Type the complimentary closing **(a)** on the second line below the message, starting at the left margin; **(b)** on the second line below the message, starting at the center; **(c)** on the third line below the message, starting at the center.

   5. **b**    1346a

6. How many lines below the complimentary closing or the company signature should the writer's name ordinarily be typed: **(a)** 4; **(b)** 5; **(c)** 6?

   6. **a**    1348a

7. How should an 8½" × 11" sheet of stationery be folded for insertion in a No. 10 envelope: **(a)** in half; **(b)** in thirds; **(c)** in half, then in thirds?

   7. **b**    1367a

8. To hold the length of a memo to one page, you can reduce the top margin to **(a)** 1 inch; **(b)** 1.5 inches; **(c)** 1.75 inches.

   8. **a**    1374b

9. In a memo, a salutation should **(a)** always be used; **(b)** never be used; **(c)** be used whenever you want to keep the memo from seeming cold or impersonal.

   9. **c**    1374l, note

10. It is not necessary for e-mail messages to comply with the normal rules of written English—**(a)** true; **(b)** false.

    10. **b**    1376a, d

11. When you are sending an e-mail message to people who do not know each other, enter their names in **(a)** the *To* box; **(b)** the *Cc* box; **(c)** the *Bcc* box.

    11. **c**    1379b

**Directions:** Most of the items in the next exercise represent elements in a business letter. If the item is correctly styled, write *C* in the answer column. If not, rewrite the item to make it correct. Assume the use of a **modified-block style—standard format** (¶1302a), **standard punctuation** (¶1308a), and **single spacing** unless otherwise indicated. **References:** Section 13, plus ¶363, ¶455a, and ¶503.

12. Inside address and salutation: rewrite to avoid the use of an attention line and *Gentlemen*.

    Ace Programming Associates
    221 Jefferson Street, NE
    Albany, Oregon 97321-2717

    Attention: Ms. Wanda Lee Belcher

    Gentlemen:

    12. Ms. Wanda Lee Belcher

    Ace Programming Associates

    221 Jefferson Street, NE

    Albany, Oregon 97321-2717

    Dear Ms. Belcher:

    1337a
    1339a
    1340
    1341b

Name _____ Date _____ Class _____

**13.** Subject.   Long-range plans

**14.** We have two options to consider:


    1.   Rent the VCR for one month
and see how well it works.

**15.** Cordially Yours:

**16.** *Ms. Joanna Wall*

   (Ms.) Joanna Wall

**17.** *Rae H. Zion*

   Mrs. Gerard U. Zion

**18.** Writer's identification:

   Dr. Henry Greco, Ph.D., Professor
      of Economics

**19.** fgc:ssh
   Encs. 3
   cc. Ms. Wing
   Certified


**20.** PS:   All best regards to Pat.

**21.** Page 2
   Miss Selma L. Pomfret
   11/7/07


**22.** Address block typed on an envelope:

   Dwight G. Thorvald, Executive
      Vice President
   Winger Corp., Inc. *(official form not known)*
   651 East Neversink Rd.
   Suite 302
   Reading, Pa.  19606 3208


**23.** Heading typed on a memo:

   **TO:** Linda Lopez

   **DEPARTMENT:** Accounting

   **SUBJECT:** Invoice No. 24396

**24.** Salutation in a social-business letter:

   Dear Jennifer:


---

**13.** Subject:   Long-Range Plans    1343c / 363

**14.** We have two options to consider:

   1.   Rent the VCR for one month
       and see how well it works.    1344f / 1345c

**15.** Cordially yours,    1346b

**16.** (Ms.) *Joanna Wall*    *Joanna Wall*
   Joanna Wall **OR**   Ms. Joanna Wall    1352b

**17.** (Mrs.) *Rae H. Zion*    *Rae H. Zion*
   Rae H. Zion **OR**   Mrs. Rae H. Zion    1352e

**18.** Henry Greco, Ph.D.    1350a
   Professor of Economics    1350b / 1349b

**19.** ssh **OR** fgc/ssh **OR** FGC:SSH
   Enc. 3    1355a–c
   By certified mail    1358b / 503
   cc: Ms. Wing **OR** c: Ms. Wing    1359a / 1361a–f

**20.** C    1365b

**21.** Miss Selma L. Pomfret
   Page 2
   November 7, 2007    1366

**22.** Mr. Dwight G. Thorvald
   Executive Vice President    1368a / 1322a
   Winger Corporation Inc.    1325a / 1329b
   Suite 302    1317b / 1337
   651 East Neversink Road    1368f / 1368c
   Reading, PA 19606-3208    1341a / 1368d

**23.** TO:    Linda Lopez
   DEPARTMENT:   Accounting
   SUBJECT:    Invoice 24396    1393f / 455a

**24.** Dear Jennifer,    1372b

# 28

## Looking Things Up

**Directions:** Choose the phrase that best completes the meaning of the sentence. Then in the answer column record the identifying letter for the phrase you selected. **References:** Sections 12–18 and Appendixes A, B, C, and D.

1. When preparing a résumé, you should always indicate your age, your marital status, your height and weight, and your hobbies—**(a)** true; **(b)** false.

   1. **b**  ———  1708k

2. When breaking a paragraph at the bottom of a page in a report, what is the minimum number of lines you must leave at the bottom of one page and carry over to the top of the next: **(a)** one; **(b)** two; **(c)** three?

   2. **b**  ———  1407d / 1407e

3. When you discover that you have a large number of e-mail messages that require a response, answer them in the order in which they were received, starting with the earliest—**(a)** true; **(b)** false.

   3. **b**  ———  1387

4. Which is the best way to indicate that an apostrophe should be inserted in typed copy: **(a)** womens; **(b)** womens; **(c)** womens? *Insert apostrophe*

   4. **b**  ———  1206

5. If it is not possible to communicate a negative assessment to a person face to face, it is acceptable to do so in an e-mail message—**(a)** true; **(b)** false.

   5. **b**  ———  1382i–j

6. Which is the preferred pronunciation for *liaison:* **(a)** lee-YAY-zahn; **(b)** LAY-uh-zahn; **(c)** LEE-uh-zahn?

   6. **c**  ———  App. B

7. What is the most formal salutation you can use when writing to a woman you do not know: **(a)** Madam:; **(b)** Dear Madam:; **(c)** To whom it may concern:?

   7. **a**  ———  1801e

8. If the column heads in a table do not all take the same number of lines, align the column heads **(a)** at the top; **(b)** at the bottom.

   8. **b**  ———  1621g

9. Type quoted material as a displayed, single-spaced extract when it will make at least **(a)** four typed lines; **(b)** six; **(c)** eight.

   9. **a**  ———  1424d / 265a

10. When starting the first page of a new chapter, a table of contents, or a bibliography in a manuscript or a report, leave a top margin of **(a)** 1 inch; **(b)** 1.5 inches; **(c)** 2 inches.

    10. **c**  ———  1405a / 1415b / 1548a

11. When a column of figures represents percentages, type a percent sign (%) after **(a)** the first percentage only; **(b)** each percentage.

    11. **b**  ———  1630a

12. Which of the following represents an elliptical sentence: **(a)** Why not? **(b)** Drive slow. **(c)** Who cares?

    12. **a**  ———  App. D

13. In an e-mail message, the abbreviation *BTW* stands for **(a)** before the Web; **(b)** big time waster; **(c)** by the way.

    13. **c**  ———  1382m

14. When typing a report that will be bound, leave a left margin of **(a)** 1 inch; **(b)** 1.5 inches; **(c)** 2 inches.

    14. **b**  ———  1404b

Name ——————————————  Date ——————————  Class ——————

57

**Directions:** In the spaces provided, construct endnotes or bibliographic entries—as directed—for a specific book, using the following information: the title is *Safe Strategies for Financial Freedom;* the author is Van K. Tharp; the book was published in New York in 2004 by McGraw-Hill; the page numbers to be cited are 88, 89, 90, and 91; the price is $24.95.

**15.** Construct a business-style endnote referring to the Tharp book, and assign it the number 4.

    4. Van K. Tharp, *Safe Strategies for Financial Freedom*, McGraw-Hill, New York, 2004, pp. 88-91.

1513a
1526a
1529b
460d

**16.** Recast the endnote above to agree with the typical academic style.

    4. Van K. Tharp, *Safe Strategies for Financial Freedom* (New York: McGraw-Hill, 2004), pp. 88-91.

1513b
1536b

**17.** Make a subsequent reference in business style to the Tharp book in endnote 7. Cite page 104.

    7. Tharp, p. 104.

1531a

**18.** Recast the subsequent reference above, using a formal academic style.

    7. Tharp, op. cit., p. 104.

1531d

**19.** Construct an appropriate entry for the Tharp book in a business-style bibliography.

Tharp, Van K., *Safe Strategies for Financial Freedom*, McGraw-Hill, New York, 2004.

1551a

**20.** Recast the entry above, using an academic style.

Tharp, Van K. *Safe Strategies for Financial Freedom.* New York: McGraw-Hill, 2004.

1551c

**Directions:** For each group of names or abbreviations given below, give the two-letter Postal Service abbreviations. (Study the chart on page 388 or the inside back cover of *The Gregg Reference Manual* ahead of time, and complete this exercise from memory.)

**21.**

| | | | | | | | |
|---|---|---|---|---|---|---|---|
| Calif. | **CA** | Ala. | **AL** | Del. | **DE** | Ind. | **IN** |
| Fla. | **FL** | Colo. | **CO** | Okla. | **OK** | Oreg. | **OR** |
| Mass. | **MA** | Ill. | **IL** | Idaho | **ID** | Wis. | **WI** |
| Ohio | **OH** | Nebr. | **NE** | Mich. | **MI** | Wyo. | **WY** |
| Utah | **UT** | Wash. | **WA** | Ark. | **AR** | Guam | **GU** |

**22.**

| | | | | | | | |
|---|---|---|---|---|---|---|---|
| D.C. | **DC** | S. Dak. | **SD** | N.J. | **NJ** | N.C. | **NC** |
| N. Mex. | **NM** | N.H. | **NH** | S.C. | **SC** | W. Va. | **WV** |
| R.I. | **RI** | P.R. | **PR** | N. Dak. | **ND** | N.Y. | **NY** |

**23.**

| | | | | | | | |
|---|---|---|---|---|---|---|---|
| Conn. | **CT** | La. | **LA** | Maine | **ME** | Hawaii | **HI** |
| Iowa | **IA** | Ga. | **GA** | Ky. | **KY** | Kans. | **KS** |
| Va. | **VA** | Pa. | **PA** | Md. | **MD** | Vt. | **VT** |

**24.**

| | | | | | | | |
|---|---|---|---|---|---|---|---|
| Ariz. | **AZ** | Nev. | **NV** | Minn. | **MN** | Alaska | **AK** |
| Tex. | **TX** | Tenn. | **TN** | Mont. | **MT** | Mo. | **MO** |
| Miss. | **MS** | | | | | | |

# 29

# Editing Practice A

**Directions:** Edit the following letter (typed in modified-block style—standard format with standard punctuation). Correct any errors in style, grammar, usage, spelling, content, and format. Circle any changes you make within the lines or out in the margin; if you prefer, show all changes on a separate sheet, identified by line number. If time permits, retype the corrected letter on a plain sheet of paper, using 1.25-inch side margins. (Assume you are using a printed letterhead, and leave a 2-inch top margin.) Use today's date and address the letter to *Lloyd I. Poindexter, Chief Executive Officer, Beck & McCall Advertising Agency, 3017 East Wacker Drive, Chicago, Illinois 60601*. **References:** Sections 1–13.

```
Dear Mister Poindexter                                              17
                                                                   18
A few days ago you asked me to recommend a qualified candidate to become   19
director of client services. I can readily suggest Douglas Dichter.        20
                                                                   21
Doug majored in marketing at Northwestern and recieved an MBA from Stanford  22
in 1996. He worked for awhile as a management consultant in the Pittsburgh    23
office of Lyon & Waite Associates, but he found few opportunities to put his  24
creative talents to use. In 2000 he joined Belles and Vissels, a small        25
advertising agency in Cincinatti, as a copywriter. In that capacity he was    26
responsible for coming up with the brand name Scratch for a new line of       27
cake mixs. (Remember the slogan? "It's not store-bought. I made it from       28
Scratch.") Among his other creative achievements were the name Pit Stop       29
for an underarm deodorant. Doug was also responsible for The Inside           30
Scoop (a profitable chain of stores selling ice cream and frozen yogurt)      31
and The Emotional Outlet (a successful department store that has attracted    32
a large amount of impulsive shoppers). After 7 years he became an account     33
executive and brought in 1,000,000's of dollars in new business. As a re-     34
sult, the agency's reputation and size has undergone extraordinary growth.    35
Doug's boss gives him the lions share of the credit.                          36
                                                                   37
Doug is now ready to move on to more bigger challenges. Because of his        38
in-depth experience in keeping a wide range of clients happy, his proven      39
skill in generating new business and his demonstrated maturity of judg-       40
ment, I think Doug would be well qualified for the job you have in mind.       41
                                                                   42
I should note that Doug is married to my oldest daughter, but that does       43
not affect my ability to be objective about my son-in-laws qualifications.    44
However if you would like another opinion, why don't you write to Doug's      45
boss, Ms. Rhoda Colt? She knows of his eagerness to move to a higher level    46
position and can give you her own assessment of his past performance and      47
his future potential. If I can be of any further assistance, let me know.     48
                                                                   49
                        Sincerely yours                                       50
                                                                   51
                                                                   52
                                                                   53
                        Mr. Buford J. Bellows                                  54
```

> **Note to Instructor:** See page C-74 for notes and rule references for this editing practice.

**Directions:** On the reverse side of this sheet you will find a letter to **Mr. Anthony J. Leonardo** (typed in modified-block style—standard format with standard punctuation). Correct any errors in style, grammar, usage, spelling, content, and format. Make the corrections as you did in the letter above. If time permits, retype the corrected letter on a plain sheet of paper, using 1.25-inch side margins and positioning the date on the first line below a 2-inch top margin. **References:** Sections 1–13.

Name _____ Date _____ Class _____      59

# NOTES ON WORKSHEET 29, PAGE 59

**Line 17:**
1. Abbreviate *Mr.* [517a, 1338d]
2. Use a colon after the salutation. [194a, 1338b]

**Line 19:**
3. Spell *recommend* with one *c*. [720]

**Line 20:**
4. Do not capitalize *director of client services*. [313e]

**Line 22:**
5. Omit the comma after *Northwestern* (so as not to separate a compound predicate). [127b]
6. The letter *e* comes before *i* in *received*. [712, 1203a]
7. Insert periods in *M.B.A.* [519a–b]

**Line 23:**
8. Spell *a while* as two words. [1101]
9. Spell *Pittsburgh* with an *h*. [720]

**Line 24:**
10. Change *opportunitys* to *opportunities*. [604]

**Line 25:**
11. Omit the comma after *2000*. [135c, 410]

**Line 26:**
12. Change *Cincinatti* to *Cincinnati*. [720]

**Line 28:**
13. Change *mixs* to *mixes*. [602]
14. Hyphenate *store-bought*. [821a]

**Line 29:**
15. The closing quotation mark should follow the exclamation point. [249a, 252]
16. Change *were* to *was* (to agree with the singular subject *name*). [1027a]

**Line 30:**
17. Change *under-arm* to *underarm*. [833a]

**Line 31:**
18. Insert a closing parenthesis after *yogurt*. [224, 1203b]

**Line 33:**
19. Change *amount* to *number*. [1101]
20. Spell out *two*. [401a, 404a]

**Line 34:**
21. Change *1,000,000's* to *millions*. [414]

**Line 35:**
22. Do not capitalize *agency's*. [309a, 321]
23. Change *has* to *have* (to agree with the plural subject *reputation and size*). [1002a]
24. Change *extraordinary* to *extraordinary*. [720]

**Line 36:**
25. Change *lions share* to *lion's share*. [627a, 630a]

**Line 38:**
26. Change *more bigger* to *bigger* (to avoid a double comparison). [1071b]

**Line 39:**
27. Hyphenate *in-depth*. [831a]

**Line 40:**
28. Insert a series comma after *business*. [123b, 162a]

**Lines 40–41:**
29. Change *judge-/ment* to *judg-/ment*. [708, 720]

**Line 41:**
30. Do not hyphenate *well qualified*. [824b]

**Line 44:**
31. Change *effect* to *affect*. [719, 1101]
32. Hyphenate *son-in-law's*. [804c]

**Line 45:**
33. Insert a comma after *However* (following an introductory transitional expression). [138a, 139a]

**Line 46:**
34. Change the period after *Colt* to a question mark. [110a]
35. Hyphenate *higher-level*. [816a]

**Line 48:**
36. Change *farther* to *further*. [719, 1101]
37. Change *assistence* to *assistance*. [714]

**Line 50:**
38. Do not capitalize *yours*. [1359]
39. Insert a comma after the complimentary closing. [1346c]

**Line 54:**
40. Omit *Mr.* preceding the name. [1351]

*Final copy with 1.25" side margins*

Today's Date

Mr. Lloyd I. Poindexter
Chief Executive Officer
Beck & McCall Advertising Agency
3017 East Wacker Drive
Chicago, Illinois 60601

Dear Mr. Poindexter:

A few days ago you asked me to recommend a qualified candidate to become director of client services.  I can readily suggest Douglas Dichter.

Doug majored in marketing at Northwestern and received an M.B.A. from Stanford
in 1996.  He worked for a while as a management consultant in the Pittsburgh
office of Lyon & Waite Associates, but he found few opportunities to put his
creative talents to use.  In 2000 he joined Belles and Vissels, a small advertising agency in Cincinnati, as a copywriter.  In that capacity he was responsible for coming up with the brand name Scratch for a new line of cake mixes.
(Remember the slogan?  "It's not store-bought.  I made it from Scratch!")
Among his other creative achievements was the name Pit Stop for an underarm
deodorant.  Doug was also responsible for The Inside Scoop (a profitable chain
of stores selling ice cream and frozen yogurt) and The Emotional Outlet (a
successful department store that has attracted a large number of impulse shop-
pers).  After two years he became an account executive and brought in millions
of dollars in new business.  As a result, the agency's reputation and size
have undergone extraordinary growth.  Doug's boss gives him the lion's share
of the credit.

Doug is now ready to move on to bigger challenges.  Because of his in-depth
experience in keeping a wide range of clients happy, his proven skill in gen-
erating new business, and his demonstrated maturity of judgment, I think Doug
would be well qualified for the job you have in mind.

I should note that Doug is married to my oldest daughter, but that does not
affect my ability to be objective about my son-in-law's qualifications.  However, if you would like another opinion, why don't you write to Doug's boss,
Ms. Rhoda Colt?  She knows of his eagerness to move to a higher-level position
and can give you her own assessment of his past performance and his future
potential.  If I can be of any further assistance, let me know.

Sincerely yours,

Buford J. Bellows

**February 7,**

Feb. 7th, 2007

Mr. Anthony J. Leonardo
111 Horton Rd. **Road**
Durham, NC, 27712

Dear Mr. Lenardo:

I'd like to respond to your telephone message of Febuary forth in which
you asked for help in selecting a facsimile machine for you're home
office. Enclosed is a brochure that announces a one months sale on
all of the fax equipment that we have available for immediate delivery.
Let me highlight a few items in that brochure.

1. Our most popular fax machine—the Faxiomatic 2000 (Model FA4098—
has a 30-page automatic document feeder, and a transmission speed
of 4 seconds a page. Normally listed at $499, it is available during
the month of February for $179, a saving of $320.00!

2. An even more versatile machine is the Artifax 777, which has a three
second transmission speed and a 256-shade gray scale. Thanks to a
58 1/4% discount, the price of this machine (Model A777-2F) has been
slashed from $475 to $198.

3. Other models provide extra features such as automatic redialing and
delayed transmission (to let you take advantage of lower phone rates).
Sale prices range from $249 299.

Come into see these models by February 28 the last day you can enjoy
these special prices. Anyone of our salespeople can help you select the
equipment that's right for your home office and does not exceed your bud-
budget. Of course if you prefer, you can ask for Stephen Burgos, our Sales
Manager, or for myself. We'll be glad to help you in anyway that we can.

Sincerely,

Note to Instructor: See page C-77
for notes and rule references for
this editing practice.

Julia G. Hough
Vice President of Sales

ybj
Enclosure

60

# NOTES ON WORKSHEET 29, PAGE 60

**Line 13:**
1. *February* should be spelled out. [1313a]
2. Delete the *th* following *7*. [1313a]
3. Insert a comma between the day and the year *(February 7, 2007)*. [1313a]

**Line 17:**
4. Insert *Mr.* before *Anthony J. Leonardo.* [1322a]

**Line 18:**
5. Spell out *Road.* [1337]

**Line 19:**
6. Omit the comma before the ZIP Code. [1339]

**Line 21:**
7. Change *Lenardo* to *Leonardo* (as in the inside address and the directions). [1202c, 1338f]

**Line 23:**
8. Change *you* to *your* (a typographical error). [1202b]
9. Insert the missing *r* in *February.* [720]
10. Change *forth* to *4* (not *fourth*). [407b]
11. Insert a comma before *in which* (which introduces a nonessential clause). [122d, 152]

**Line 24:**
12. Change *you're* to *your.* [1056e]

**Line 25:**
13. Change *months'* to *month's* [632a, 646]

**Lines 29, 34, 39:**
14. Insert a period after *1, 2,* and *3* in the displayed enumeration. [106, 1345d]

**Line 29:**
15. Omit the space on either side of the first dash. [216a]
16. Insert a closing parenthesis before the second dash. [224a]

**Lines 30–32, 35–37, 40–41:**
17. Align turnovers in a displayed enumeration with the first word in the first line. [1345d]

**Line 30:**
18. Hyphenate *30-page.* [817a]
19. Omit the comma after *feeder;* it incorrectly separates two objects of the verb *has.* [125f]

**Line 32:**
20. Drop the *.00* from the whole dollar amount. [415]

**Line 34:**
21. Change *three* to *3.* [436a]

**Lines 34–35:**
22. Hyphenate *3-second.* [817a]

**Line 36:**
23. Omit the hyphen in *58 1/4.* [428b]
24. Spell out *percent.* [447a]

**Line 41:**
25. Replace the hyphen with *to.* [459b]
26. Insert the missing dollar sign *(from $249 to $299).* [453b]

**Line 43:**
27. Do not indent the first line of a paragraph in a letter done in the modified-block style—standard format. [1302a(1), 1344f]
28. Spell *in to* as two words. [1101]
29. Insert a comma after *28* (before an appositive expression). [148]

**Line 44:**
30. Spell *Any one* as two words. [719, 1010]

**Line 45:**
31. Change *excede* to *exceed.* [716b]
32. Omit *bud-* at the end of the line; the word *budget* is given in full on the next line. [1202a]

**Line 46:**
33. Insert a comma after *Of course* (an introductory expression). [124b, 138b, 139a]
34. Insert a comma after *prefer* (following an interrupting expression). [122a, 144a]

**Lines 46–47:**
35. Insert two commas to set off *our sales manager* (an appositive). [148]
36. Do not capitalize *sales manager* (a title following a name). [313d]

**Line 47:**
37. Change *myself* to *me.* [1060]
38. Spell *any way* as two words. [1101]

**Lines 49–54:**
39. Begin the closing at center, aligned with the date line. [1346a]

**Line 49:**
40. Insert a comma after *Sincerely* (the complimentary closing). [1346c]

*Final copy with 1.25" side margins*

February 7, 2007

Mr. Anthony J. Leonardo
111 Horton Road
Durham, NC 27712

Dear Mr. Leonardo:

I'd like to respond to your telephone message of February 4, in which you asked for help in selecting a facsimile machine for your home office. Enclosed is a brochure that announces a one month's sale on all of the fax equipment that we have available for immediate delivery. Let me highlight a few items in that brochure.

1. Our most popular fax machine—the Faxiomatic 2000 (Model FA4098)—has a 30-page automatic document feeder and a transmission speed of 15 seconds a page. Normally listed at $499, it is available during the month of February for $179, a saving of $320!

2. An even more versatile machine is the Artifax 777, which has a 3-second transmission speed and a 256-shade gray scale. Thanks to a 58 1/4 percent discount, the price of this machine (Model A777-2F) has been slashed from $475 to $198.

3. Other models provide extra features such as automatic redialing and delayed transmission (to let you take advantage of lower phone rates). Sale prices range from $249 to $299.

Come in to see these models by February 28, the last day you can enjoy these special prices. Any one of our salespeople can help you select the equipment that's right for your home office and does not exceed your budget. Of course, if you prefer, you can ask for Stephen Burgos, our sales manager, or for me. We'll be glad to help you in any way that we can.

Sincerely,

Julia G. Hough
Vice President of Sales

ybj
Enclosure

# 30 Editing Practice B

**Directions:** Edit the following letter (typed in modified-block style—with indented paragraphs and standard punctuation). Correct any errors in style, grammar, usage, spelling, content, and format. Circle any changes you make within the lines or out in the margin; if you prefer, show all changes on a separate sheet, identified by line number. If time permits, retype the corrected letter on a plain sheet of paper, using 1.25-inch side margins and starting on the first line below a 2-inch top margin. Use *Sincerely* for the complimentary closing, and type an appropriate signature line for *Ms. Angela R. Terlizzi*. **References:** Sections 1–13.

```
                              328 Linden Street            13
                              Winnetka, IL 60093           14
                              October 23, 2007             15
                                                           16
                                                           17
                                                           18
President North                                            19
New Computer Technologie Inc.                              20
5120 N Northwest Highway                                   21
Chicago, IL   60631                                        22
                                                           23
Dear Sir or Madam:                                         24
                                                           25
   Can you please help me? During your semiannual sale last summer, a   26
   pleasant salesman named Nick Fry helped me select a computer and      27
   persuaded me to order a specially priced high-speed printer that was  28
   not on display in your showroom. What sold me on his recommendation   29
   was Mr. Fry's claim that this printer could turn out 40 pages a min-   30
   minute. The computer was delivered in a few days, but it took more    31
   than five weeks for the printer to arrive. When I hooked it up, I made 32
   the shocking discovery that this printer actually turns out only 10 pages 33
   a minute.                                               34
                                                           35
   I immediately called Mr. Fry to tell him that the printer was not      36
   acceptable, but he was reluctant to take it back because he said it had 37
   been specially ordered for me. He offered to sell me a special attach- 38
   ment that would increase the speed of the printer, but I refused to spend 39
   any more money on it. He finally agreed to take the printer back but said 40
   he would have to impose an $85 100 "restocking charge" against my refund 41
   because I had removed the printer from the carton and used it. I pointed 42
   out that (1) it was his misrepresentation that had caused the problem, I (2) 43
   had relied on his know-how, and (3) the charge was totally unjustified.  44
   I still don't have my money back, and I still don't have a usable printer. 45
   Would you be able to follow up with the appropriate people to get this  46
   problem promptly resolved? I sincerely hope so.         47
```

**Directions:** On the reverse side of this sheet you will find the second page of a letter to **Mr. Richard L. Booker Jr.** (typed in modified-block style—standard format with standard punctuation) and the No. 6¾ envelope that accompanies it. Correct any errors in style, grammar, usage, spelling, content, and format. Make the corrections as you did in the letter above. If time permits, retype the letter on a plain sheet of paper, using 1.25-inch side margins and starting the heading for the second page on the first line below a 1-inch top margin. Retype the envelope copy on a No. 6¾ envelope or on a sheet of paper trimmed or ruled off to the same dimensions. **References:** Sections 1–13.

Note to Instructor: See page C-80 for notes and rule references for this editing practice.

Name _____ Date _____ Class _____      61

# Notes on Worksheet 30, Page 61

**Line 14:** 1. Insert a comma after *Winnetka*. [161]

**Line 15:** 2. Insert a comma after *23*. [1313a]

**Line 20:** 3. Change *Technologys* to *Technologies*. [604]

**Line 21:** 4. Omit the comma from *5120*. [462]
5. Spell out *North*. [1334]

**Line 22:** 6. Change *ILL* to *IL*. [1341a]
7. Leave only 1 space before the ZIP Code. [1339]

**Line 24:** 8. Change the salutation to *Dear Sir or Madam:* or *Dear Madam or Sir:*. [1339a, 1340b]

**Line 26:** 9. Indent the first line of the paragraph (as called for in the directions). [1302a(2)]
10. Change the period to a question mark (following a polite request that asks a favor). [103b]
11. Do not hyphenate *semiannual*. [833a]
12. Do not capitalize *summer*. [343]

**Line 27:** 13. Omit the comma after *computer* (to avoid separating a compound predicate). [125f, 127b]

**Line 28:** 14. Do not hyphenate *specially priced*. [824a]
15. Hyphenate *high-speed*. [814, 816a]

**Line 29:** 16. Spell *recommendation* with only one *c*. [720]

**Line 30:** 17. Change *Frys'* to *Fry's*. [630a]

**Lines 30–31:** 18. Omit *min* at the beginning of line 31 (see the end of line 30). [1202a]

**Line 32:** 19. Change *then* to *than*. [719]

**Line 38:** 20. Change *offerred* to *offered*. [704]

**Line 40:** 21. Change *finely* to *finally*. [719]

**Line 41:** 22. Omit *.00* from *$85*. [415]

**Lines 43–44:** 23. Insert an opening parenthesis before the numbers *1* and *3*. [222a]

**Line 43:** 24. Change *cause* to *caused*. [1033b, 1203d]
25. Insert *(2)* before *I*. [1203e]

**Line 44:** 26. Hyphenate *know-how*. [804a]

**Line 45:** 27. Spell *money back* as two words (a typographical error). [1202e]
28. Change *useable* to *usable*. [707a]

**Line 46:** 29. Do not hyphenate *follow up* when used as a verb. [802]

**Line 47:** 30. Change *sincerly* to *sincerely*. [708, 720, 1203a]

328 Linden Street
Winnetka, IL 60093
October 23, 2007

President
New Computer Technologies Inc.
5120 North Northwest Highway
Chicago, IL 60631

Dear Sir or Madam:

Can you please help me? During your semiannual sale last summer, a pleasant salesman named Nick Fry helped me select a computer and persuaded me to order a specially priced high-speed printer that was not on display in your showroom. What sold me on his recommendation was Mr. Fry's claim that this printer could turn out 40 pages a minute. The computer was delivered in a few days, but it took more than five weeks for the printer to arrive. When I hooked it up, I made the shocking discovery that this printer actually turns out only 10 pages a minute.

I immediately called Mr. Fry to tell him that the printer was not acceptable, but he was reluctant to take it back because he said it had been specially ordered for me. He offered to sell me a special attachment that would increase the speed of the printer, but I refused to spend any more money on it. He finally agreed to take the printer back but said he would have to impose an $85 "restocking charge" against my refund because I had removed the printer from the carton and used it. I pointed out that (1) it was his misrepresentation that had caused the problem, (2) I had relied on his know-how, and (3) the charge was totally unjustified. I still don't have my money back, and I still don't have a usable printer. Would you be able to follow up with the appropriate people to get this problem promptly resolved? I sincerely hope so.

Sincerely,

Ms. Angela R. Terlizzi

understanding of the different kinds of businesses that this organization    10
has acquired or built from the ground up.    11

12

In short, within the next three months we need to hire a Director of Corporate    13
Planning and Development with at least ten years' experience in a large    14
industrial corporation. Because of our need to compete more effectively    15
in global markets, we would give preference to a candidate who (1) has    16
worked for a multinational organization, (2) adjusts easily to a variety    17
of corporate cultures, and (3) is proficient in one or more foreign lan-    18
guages (particularly Japanese, German, and French). The successful candi-    19
date will report directly to the CEO, but he or she must be a bright, energetic    20
self-starter who does not need others to set goals and priorities. It's    21
not going to be easy to find someone who meets all the qualifications in    22
the enclosed job description, Rich, but if anyone can locate the ideal    23
person, you're the one who can do it.    24

25

Sincerely,    26

27
28
29

P. J. McInerny    30
Executive Vice President    31

32

pac    33
By certified mail    34
Enclosure    35

---

P. J. ~~Macinery~~ McInerny    2
    3
    4
CHESHIRE INDUSTRIES INC.    5
1200 North Market Street    6
Wilmington, Delaware 19801    7
    8
Personal    9
←    10
    11
    12
Mr. Richard L. Booker, Jr.    13
Kopf-Jaeger International    14
Suite 450    15
1150 Connecticut Avenue, N.W.    16
Washington, D.C. 20036    17

---

**Note to Instructor:** See page C-83 for notes and rule references for this editing practice.

# Notes on Worksheet 30, Page 62

*Letter*

**Line 7:**   1. Transpose the date and the page number. [1366c]
2. Omit the word *page.* [1366c]
3. Spell out *February.* [1313a]
4. Change *23rd* (followed by a period) to *23* (followed by a comma). [1313]

**Line 10:**   5. Change the partial word *derstanding* to *understanding* (to avoid breaking the final word on the preceding page). [918, 1366k]

**Line 11:**   6. Change *aquired* to *acquired.* [720]

**Line 13:**   7. Insert a comma after *In short.* [124b, 138a, 139a]
8. Spell out *three.* [401a, 404a]

**Lines 13–14:**   9. Do not capitalize *director of corporate planning and development.* [313e]

**Line 14:**   10. Change *year's* to *years'.* [646]
11. Omit the comma after *large.* (*Large* modifies *industrial corporation.*) [169]

**Line 16:**   12. Insert a comma after *markets* (following an introductory phrase). [124, 135c]
13. Change *preferrence* to *preference.* [704]
14. Omit the colon after *who.* [191c]

**Lines 16, 17, 18:**   15. Insert an opening parenthesis before the numbers *1, 2,* and *3.* [222a]

**Line 17:**   16. Change the word *multi-national* to *multinational.* [833a]

**Line 19:**   17. Insert a series comma after the word *German.* [162a]
18. Place the period outside the closing parenthesis. [225a]

**Line 20:**   19. Change *he* to *he or she.* [1052a]

**Line 21:**   20. Hyphenate *self-starter.* [836a]
21. Change *priority̓s* to *priorities.* [604]

**Line 23:**   22. Insert a comma after *description* (to set off the name *Rich*). [145]

**Line 24:**   23. Change *your* to *you're.* [1056e]

**Line 30:**   24. Insert space between the initials *P. J.* [516a]

**Lines 34–35:**   25. The enclosure notation should come before the delivery notation. [1359a]

*Envelope*

**Line 3:**   26. Change *Macinery* to *McInerny* (to agree with the writer's name in the signature block). [1368p]

**Line 9:**   27. Type *Personal* (in caps and lowercase, underlined) aligned at the left with the return address. [1368m]

**Line 13:**   28. Omit the comma before *Jr.* (to agree with the treatment of the name in the continuation-page heading and in the directions). [1368p]

**Line 16:**   29. Change *N. W.* to *NW* (without space or periods). [1335a]

**Line 17:**   30. Change *D.C.* to *DC* (without periods). [1341]

*Final copy with 1.25" side margins*

understanding of the different kinds of businesses that this organization has acquired or built from the ground up.

In short, within the next three months we need to hire a director of corporate planning and development with at least ten years' experience in a large industrial corporation.  Because of our need to compete more effectively in global markets, we would give preference to a candidate who (1) has worked for a multinational organization, (2) adjusts easily to a variety of corporate cultures, and (3) is proficient in one or more foreign languages (particularly Japanese, German, and French).  The successful candidate will report directly to the CEO, but he or she must be a bright, energetic self-starter who does not need others to set goals and priorities.  It's not going to be easy to find someone who meets all the qualifications in the enclosed job description, Rich, but if anyone can locate the ideal person, you're the one who can do it.

                         Sincerely,


                         P. J. McInerny
                         Executive Vice President


pac
Enclosure
By certified mail


P. J. McInerny

### CHESHIRE INDUSTRIES INC.

1200 North Market Street
Wilmington, Delaware 19801


Personal


                         Mr. Richard L. Booker Jr.
                         Kopf-Jaeger International
                         Suite 450
                         1150 Connecticut Avenue, NW
                         Washington, DC 20036

# 31 Editing Practice C

**Directions:** Read the following letter (typed in **block style** with standard punctuation). Correct any errors in style, grammar, usage, spelling, content, and format. Circle any changes you make within the lines or out in the margins; if you prefer, show all changes on a separate sheet, identified by line number. If time permits, retype the corrected letter on a plain sheet of paper, using 1.25-inch side margins. Use *Jennifer A. Warren* for the writer's typed signature. (Assume you are using a computer-generated letterhead, and type today's date on the first line below a top margin of 2 inches.)
**References:** Sections 1–13.

```
Mr. Peter Q. Dorian                                        17
1 Eagle Sq.                                                18
Concord, N.H. 03301                                        19
                                                           20
Dear Pete:                                                 21
                                                           22
George and I are now ready to go forward with the vacation house we    23
discussed with you last spring. You'll recall that our hideaway is to  24
be built on a 1½ acre plot atop Mt. Waumbeck. It's not an easy place   25
to get to, because the unpaved road that leads from the highway to our 26
property is a narrow, twisting lane. We're planning to name our        27
mountain retreat Great Lengths, so if any of our children and their    28
families want to visit us there, they'll have to go to . . . I think you 29
get the point.                                             30
                                                           31
Can you design a log cabin for George and I? I don't know whether you  32
have worked with logs before, but a recent Smithsonian article says that 33
the log cabin is making a real comeback, largely as a result of the    34
back-to-the-earth movement that started in the 1960's. Then the fuel   35
crisis in the 70's prompted the development of new types of sealants   36
and caulkings. This means that the log cabins being built today can    37
project the pioneer look of the past and meet the energy-efficient     38
needs of the future at the same time.                      39
                                                           40
Once we get the plans from you, we are thinking of building the cabin  41
ourselves. It doesn't sound too hard. In fact, one person referred to  42
in the Smithsonian article made this comment: "To build a log cabin,   43
all you need are a good chain saw and a good chiropractor."            44
                                                           45
We weren't planning to cut the logs ourselves. There are kits you can  46
buy, but the logs we looked at seemed too uniform in appearance. We    47
have found a great sawmill in nearby Jefferson that has offered to     48
cut the logs in accordance with your plans.                49
                                                           50
When can we get together with you to discuss the rough sketches we have 51
made? We'll be glad to drive into your office in Concord or if you pre- 52
fer to your studio in Hopkinton. We are free most Wednesdays from 7:30 to 53
9 p.m. Just say the word and we'll be there.               54
                                                           55
                        Sincerely,                         56
```

**Note to Instructor:** See page C-86 for notes and rule references for this editing practice.

**Directions:** On the reverse side of this sheet you will find a memo concerning an upcoming sales conference at **The Homestead in Hot Springs, Virginia.** Correct any errors in style, grammar, usage, spelling, and format. Make the corrections as you did in the letter above. If time permits, retype the corrected memo on a plain sheet of paper, using 1-inch side margins and starting on the first line below a 1-inch top margin. **References:** ¶¶1373–1374 (on memos), Section 16 (on tables), plus Sections 1–12.

Name _____ Date _____ Class _____  63

# NOTES ON WORKSHEET 31, PAGE 63

**Line 18:**
1. Change *1* to *One.* [1332]
2. Spell out *Square.* [1337]

**Line 19:**
3. Omit the periods in *NH.* [1341]

**Line 23:**
4. Change *foreword* to *forward.* [719]

**Line 24:**
5. Do not capitalize *spring.* [343]

**Line 25:**
6. Hyphenate *1½-acre.* [817a]
7. Change *Mt.* to *Mount.* [529a]

**Line 27:**
8. Insert a comma between the adjectives *narrow, twisting.* [123c, 168a]

**Lines 27–28:**
9. Either omit *moun-* at the end of line 27, or omit *moun* at the start of line 28. [1202a]

**Line 29:**
10. Change *familys* to *families.* [604]

**Line 32:**
11. Change *George and I* to *George and me.* [1055b]
12. Insert a question mark after *me.* [110a]

**Line 33:**
13. Insert a comma after *before.* [123a, 126a]

**Line 34:**
14. Do not hyphenate *comeback.* [803h]
15. Change the period after *comeback* to a comma and do not capitalize *largely.* (The phrase beginning with *largely* cannot stand alone as a separate sentence and should be treated as an afterthought.) [122b, 144a, 101c]

**Line 35:**
16. Hyphenate the compound adjective *back-to-the-earth.* [831a]
17. Change *1960's* to *1960s.* [624a]

**Line 36:**
18. Change *70's* to *'70s.* [439a]

**Line 38:**
19. Hyphenate *energy-efficient.* [820a]

**Line 41:**
20. Insert a comma after *you* (following an introductory clause). [124, 130a]

**Line 42:**
21. Change *to hard* to *too hard.* [719]
22. Change *refered* to *referred.* [702]

**Line 48:**
23. Change *offerred* to *offered.* [704]

**Line 52:**
24. Change *into* to *in to.* (*To drive [one's car] into an office* would be very destructive.) [1101]

**Lines 52–53:**
25. Set off the interrupting phrase *if you prefer* with commas. [122a, 144a]

**Line 53:**
26. Change *Wensdays* to *Wednesdays.* [720]

**Lines 53–54:**
27. Change *from 7:30–* to *from 7:30 to.* [459b]

**Line 54:**
28. Change *9:00* to *9.* [440c]
29. Use *p.m.* or *in the evening* but not both. [440f]

**Line 56:**
30. The blocked style requires this line to begin at the left margin. [1302a(3)]

Today's Date

*Final copy with 1.25" side margins*

Mr. Peter Q. Dorian
One Eagle Square
Concord, NH 03301

Dear Pete:

George and I are now ready to go forward with the vacation house we discussed with you last spring. You'll recall that our hideaway is to be built on a 1½-acre plot atop Mount Waumbeck. It's not an easy place to get to, because the unpaved road that leads from the highway to our property is a narrow, twisting lane. We're planning to name our mountain retreat Great Lengths, so if any of our children and their families want to visit us there, they'll have to go to . . . I think you get the point.

Can you design a log cabin for George and me? I don't know whether you have worked with logs before, but a recent _Smithsonian_ article says that the log cabin is making a real comeback, largely as a result of the back-to-the-earth movement that started in the 1960s. Then the fuel crisis in the '70s prompted the development of new types of sealants and caulkings. This means that the log cabins being built today can project the pioneer look of the past and meet the energy-efficient needs of the future at the same time.

Once we get the plans from you, we are thinking of building the cabin ourselves. It doesn't sound too hard. In fact, one person referred to in the _Smithsonian_ article made this comment: "To build a log cabin, all you need are a good chain saw and a good chiropractor."

We weren't planning to cut the logs ourselves. There are kits you can buy, but the logs we looked at seemed too uniform in appearance. We have found a great sawmill in nearby Jefferson that has offered to cut the logs in accordance with your plans.

When can we get together with you to discuss the rough sketches we have made? We'll be glad to drive in to your office in Concord or, if you prefer, to your studio in Hopkinton. We are free most Wednesdays from 7:30 to 9 p.m. Just say the word and we'll be there.

Sincerely,


Jennifer A. Warren

# INTEROFFICE MEMORANDUM

**To:** Tiffany N. Cartier      **From:** Ben G. Opalewski

**Department:** Conference Services     **Department:** Southern Region

**Subject:** Southern Sales Conference     **Date:** June 14, 2007

Dear Tiffany:

This is a follow-up to my memo of June 6th. The site for the Southern Regional sales conference has now been selected: a five-star hotel in Hot Springs, Virginia, called The Homestead. The conference will start at 7:00 P.M. on Tuesday, August 7, with a formal dinner on the terrace (weather permitting). The meeting will end at 12 noon on Saturday, the 11th; we'll skip the closing luncheon this year so that everyone can get an earlier start for home. Sounds all right so far, doesn't it?

Here comes the fun part. In addition to the handouts that should be run off (we discussed these last week), about 65 slides need to be made up. Could you get Jenny Ziff in graphic arts to do these for us? She did a first-rate job on slides for our February meeting.

At the August meeting we'll have to supply our own AV equipment, I'm sorry to say. The conference director at The Homestead has told me that almost all their equipment is committed to two other groups meeting during the same week. Therefore, I'd appreciate it if you could have the following items delivered to the hotel and if you could be on hand to help the speakers at the conference.

| Schedule | AV Equipment | Speaker |
|---|---|---|
| Wednesday, Session 1 | DVD player and VCR; 3 color monitors (largest size available) | Oberholtzer |
| Thursday, Session 5 | Computer projector plus screen* | Potterfield |
| Friday, Session 9 | Wireless microphone plus speakers; easel with pad | Velasquez |

*Potterfield may also want a digital camcorder to record some role-playing situations; he'll let us know by July 20.

The other speakers all say they need no equipment, so be prepared for last-minute requests. Thanks, Tiffany, for your help and your patience.

BGO

lcd

Note to Instructor: See page C-89 for notes and rule references for this editing practice.

64

C-88

# Notes on Worksheet 31, Page 64

**Line 9:** 1. Change *Southren* to *Southern* (a typographical error). [1202d]

**Line 14:** 2. Spell *Tiffany* with two *f*'s. [1202c]

**Line 16:** 3. Hyphenate *follow-up* as a noun. [802, 803a]

4. Change *6th* to *6*. [407b]

**Line 17:** 5. Change *Regions'* to *Region's*. [630a, 632b]

6. Hyphenate the compound adjective *five-star*. [817a]

**Line 18:** 7. Set off *Virginia* with commas. [160a]

**Line 19:** 8. Change *7:00* to *7*. [440c]

9. Change *P.M.* to *p.m.* [440b]

10. Insert a comma after *7* (to set off an appositive). [148]

**Line 20:** 11. Spell *permitting* with two *t*'s. [702]

12. The period should follow the closing parenthesis. [225a]

**Line 21:** 13. Change the comma following *11th* to a semicolon. (The comma may also be changed to a period; in that case capitalize *We'll*.) [176]

**Line 22:** 14. Change *alright* to *all right*. [1101]

15. Change the period after *it* to a question mark. [114a]

**Line 24:** 16. Omit the comma after *In addition*. [139a]

**Line 25:** 17. The comma before the opening parenthesis should follow the closing parenthesis. [224a]

18. Express *65* in figures. [401a]

**Line 26:** 19. Capitalize *Graphic Arts* (the name of a department). [323]

**Line 27:** 20. Change the period after *us* to a question mark. [110a]

21. Hyphenate the compound adjective *first-rate*. [817a]

22. Insert a hyphen after *mid*. [838]

23. Change *Febuary* to *February*. [720]

**Line 29:** 24. Insert a comma after *equipment*. [144a, 173]

**Line 30:** 25. Do not capitalize *conference director*. [313d]

**Line 31:** 26. Change *most* to *almost*. [1101]

27. Change *are* to *is* (to agree with *equipment*). [1013]

**Line 32:** 28. Insert a comma after *Therefore*. [138a, 139a]

29. Insert *it* after *appreciate*. [1101]

**Line 33:** 30. Spell *delivered* with only one *r*. [704]

31. Omit the comma after *hotel*. [125f]

**Line 35:** 32. There should be 2 blank lines above a table with column heads. [1611c(3)]

**Lines 39–41:** 33. Indent the turnovers ¼-inch. [1626c]

**Line 41:** 34. Insert a closing parenthesis after *available*. [1203b]

**Line 51:** 35. When a table footnote turns over onto a second line, *indent* the first line of the footnote ½ or ¼ inch. [1634d]

36. Change *Potterfeld* to *Potterfield* (to agree with the spelling in the table above). [1202c]

**Line 52:** 37. Hyphenate the compound adjective *role-playing*. [821a]

38. Change the comma after *situations* to a semicolon. [128]

**Line 56:** 39. Set off *Tiffany* with commas. [145]

40. Change *patients* to *patience*. [719]

*Final copy with 1.25" side margins*

| | | | |
|---|---|---|---|
| **To:** | Tiffany N. Cartier | **From:** | Ben G. Opalewski |
| **Department:** | Conference Services | **Department:** | Southern Region |
| **Subject:** | Southern Sales Conference | **Date:** | June 14, 2007 |

Dear Tiffany:

This is a follow-up to my memo of June 6. The site for the Southern Region's sales conference has now been selected: a five-star hotel in Hot Springs, Virginia, called The Homestead. The conference will start at 7 p.m. on Tuesday, August 7, with a formal dinner on the terrace (weather permitting). The meeting will end at 12 noon on Saturday, the 11th; we'll skip the closing luncheon this year so that everyone can get an earlier start for home. Sounds all right so far, doesn't it?

Here comes the fun part. In addition to the handouts that should be run off (we discussed these last week), about 65 slides need to be made up. Could you get Jenny Ziff in Graphic Arts to do these for us? She did a first-rate job on slides for our mid-February meeting.

At the August meeting we'll have to supply our own AV equipment, I'm sorry to say. The conference director at The Homestead has told me that almost all their equipment is committed to two other groups meeting during the same week. Therefore, I'd appreciate it if you could have the following items delivered to the hotel and if you could be on hand to help the speakers at the conference.

| Schedule | AV Equipment | Speaker |
|---|---|---|
| Wednesday, Session 1 | DVD player and VCR; 3 color monitors (largest size available) | Oberholtzer |
| Thursday, Session 5 | Computer projector plus screen* | Potterfield |
| Friday, Session 9 | Wireless microphone plus speakers; easel with pad | Velasquez |

*Potterfield may also want a digital camcorder to record some role-playing situations; he'll let us know by July 20.

The other speakers all say they need no equipment, so be prepared for last-minute requests. Thanks, Tiffany, for your help and your patience.

BGO

lcd

C-90

# 32  Editing Practice D

**Directions:** Edit the following letter to **Dr. Prescott T. Daley** (typed in modified-block style—standard format with standard punctuation). Correct any errors in style, grammar, usage, spelling, content, and format. Circle any changes you make within the lines or out in the margin; if you prefer, show all changes on a separate sheet, identified by line number. If time permits, retype the corrected letter on a plain sheet of paper, using 1.25-inch side margins. (Assume you are using a printed letterhead, and leave a 2-inch top margin.) Use the current date, use *Sincerely* as the complimentary closing, and prepare an appropriate signature block for *Ms. Joyce L. Givens, director of alumni programs.* Supply reference initials and any other notations that may be appropriate. **References:** Section 1–13.

```
                  North
Dr. Prescott T. Daley, M.D.                                    17
                      enue
2901 N. Central Ave.                                           18
Phoenix, AR  85012                                            19
        AZ                                                     20
                 e
Dear Dr. Daly:                                                21
                                                              22
             d                          and
We are pleased to announce a special alumni program that offers unusual   23
                                                     eighteenth
travel and study opportunities. Between June 3 13 Cary O. Neilson, a      24
professor of English who specializes in English literature of the 18th    25
century will lead a tour through the western counties of England. An      26
engaging and entertaining lecturer, Professor Neilson will help you see   27
the land and its people through the eyes of Jane Austen, William Shake-   28
speare and other great English writers.                                   29
                                          United States        30
              four
The trip begins on Wednesday, June 3 with a departure from the U.S. on    31
a regularly scheduled flight to Heathrow airport. You will then travel    32
                                                   m
by motor coach to Bath, where you will have accommodations at the elegant 33
Francis Hotel for the first 4 nights. The mineral springs at Bath have    34
made this a fashionable gathering place since roman times. From Bath      35
you will embark on a full-day excursion to the cathedral town of Salis-   36
bury. You will continue onto Stonehenge, the 4000-year-old circle of      37
massive stones that draw all visitors into the continuing debate about    38
the original purpose of this monument. Your itinerary will next take you  39
to Stratford, the site of William Shakespeare's home. On the morning of   40
June 13 you will be taken back to Heathrow for a return flight to the     41
United States. Throughout your trip Professor Neilson will offer an       42
educational program of lectures and reading materials that make signifi-  43
cant references to all the places you will visit.                         44
                                                              45
The enclosed brochure provides a detailed description of the itinerary,   46
                                                 n                        47
the rate schedules, and the activities planned by Professor Neilson.
Because I made the trip last year I think I can answer any questions      48
you may have about the trip. May we reserve a place for you?              49
```

> **Note to Instructor: See page C-92 for notes and rule references for this editing practice.**

**Directions:** On the reverse side of this sheet you will find a page taken from a business report on information processing (with business-style footnotes). Correct any errors in style, grammar, usage, spelling, content, and format (including spacing). Make the corrections as you did in the letter above. If time permits, retype the corrected page on a plain sheet of paper, using 1.25-inch side margins and starting on the first line below a 1-inch top margin. **References:** Sections 14–15 plus Sections 1–12.

Name _____  Date _____  Class _____     65

# Notes on Worksheet 32, Page 65

**Line 17:** 1. Omit *Dr.* (since *M.D.* follows the name). [519c, 1324c]

**Line 18:** 2. Omit the comma in *2901*. [462]
3. Spell out *North*. [1334]
4. Spell out *Avenue*. [1337]

**Line 19:** 5. Change *AR* (the abbreviation for *Arkansas*) to *AZ* (the correct abbreviation for *Arizona*). [1203c, 1341]
6. Omit the comma before the ZIP Code. [161, 1339]

**Line 21:** 7. Change *Daly* to *Daley* (to match the spelling in the inside address and in the directions). [1202c, 1338f]

**Line 23:** 8. Change *please* to *pleased*. [1202b]

**Line 24:** 9. Replace the hyphen with *and (Between June 3 and 13)*. [459b]

**Line 25:** 10. Do not capitalize *professor* (following a name). [313a]
11. Do not capitalize *literature*. [352]
12. Spell out *eighteenth*. [424, 438]

**Line 26:** 13. Insert a comma after *century* (to set off a long appositive expression). [148]
14. Do not capitalize *western*. [340]

**Line 29:** 15. Insert a series comma after *Shakespeare*. [123b, 162a]

**Line 31:** 16. Insert a comma after *3* (to set off an appositive expression). [148]
17. Spell out *United States*. [525]

**Line 32:** 18. Do not hyphenate *regularly scheduled*. [824a]
19. Capitalize *Airport*. [309a, 331]

**Line 33:** 20. Spell *accommodations* with two *m*'s. [720]

**Line 34:** 21. Spell out *four*. [401a, 404a]

**Line 35:** 22. Capitalize *Roman*. [304, 306]

**Line 36:** 23. Hyphenate *full-day*. [816a]

**Line 37:** 24. Spell *on to* as two words. [1101]
25. Hyphenate the compound adjective *4000-year-old*. [817a]

**Line 38:** 26. Change *draw* to *draws* (to agree with the singular antecedent *circle*). [1063c]

**Line 39:** 27. Change *itinery* to *itinerary*. [720]

**Line 40:** 28. Change *Shakespeares'* to *Shakespeare's*. [630a]

**Line 47:** 29. Change *planed* to *planned*. [701]

**Line 48:** 30. Insert a comma after *year* (following an introductory independent clause). [130a]

*Final copy with*
*1.25" side margins*

Today's Date

Prescott T. Daley, M.D.
2901 North Central Avenue
Phoenix, AZ 85012

Dear Dr. Daley:

We are pleased to announce a special alumni program that offers unusual travel
and study opportunities. Between June 3 and 13 Cary O. Neilson, a professor
of English who specializes in English literature of the eighteenth century,
will lead a tour through the western counties of England. An engaging and
entertaining lecturer, Professor Neilson will help you see the land and its
people through the eyes of Jane Austen, William Shakespeare, and other great
English writers.

The trip begins on Wednesday, June 3, with a departure from the United States
on a regularly scheduled flight to Heathrow Airport. You will then travel by
motor coach to Bath, where you will have accommodations at the elegant Francis
Hotel for the first four nights. The mineral springs at Bath have made this a
fashionable gathering place since Roman times. From Bath you will embark on a
full-day excursion to the cathedral town of Salisbury. You will continue on to
Stonehenge, the 4000-year-old circle of massive stones that draws all visitors
into the continuing debate about the original purpose of this monument. Your
itinerary will next take you to Stratford, the site of William Shakespeare's
home. On the morning of June 13 you will be taken back to Heathrow for a return
flight to the United States. Throughout your trip Professor Neilson will offer
an educational program of lectures and reading materials that make significant
references to all the places you will visit.

The enclosed brochure provides a detailed description of the itinerary, the
rate schedules, and the activities planned by Professor Neilson. Because I
made the trip last year, I think I can answer any questions you may have about
the trip. May we reserve a place for you?

Sincerely,

Ms. Joyce L. Givens
Director of Alumni Programs

def
Enclosure

opportunities will always be available in the field of information processing

for those who have good skills and can adapt to continual changes in the

workplace. According to one authority:

*-1 l #*

Most people will change careers two to four times within their working lifetimes—and that statistic does not include job changes. The average working person . . . will make five, six, or even more job changes in addition to career changes.[4]

Moreover, within the next ten to fifteen years, between 20 and 50 percent of the available

jobs will have titles and descriptions that do not now exist.[5] In other

words, not only will you be changing jobs in the course of your career,

but the jobs themselves may be changing as well. For that reason it is

critical to develop skills that are transferable from one job to another

and are not likely to become obsolete.

CAREERS IN INFORMATION PROCESSING

Within an organization there are typically three levels of jobs: opera-

tors, assistants, and managers. In addition, there are a number of re-

lated opportunities outside the organization.[6]

Operators

*-1 l #*

Operators jobs are usually classified according to the level of

skill and experience required.

**Information Processing Trainee.** This is an entry-level job that

requires good keyboarding and formatting skills but no experience. Un-

Move to next page

---

4. Sharon Lund O'Neil, *Office Information Systems: Concepts and Applications*, 3d ed., Glencoe, Westerville, Ohio, 1999, p. 292.

*+1 l #* 5. O'Neil, p. 300, C-301

6. See appendix A for a full list of job titles and descriptions.

Note to Instructor: See page C-95 for notes and rule references for this editing practice.

# NOTES ON WORKSHEET 32, PAGE 66

**Line 10:**
1. Change *portunities* to *opportunities* (to avoid dividing a word between one page and the next). [918]
2. Change *feild* to *field.* [712, 1202d]

**Lines 15–16:**
3. Leave only 1 blank line above a displayed quotation. [1424d]

**Line 17:**
4. Omit the quotation mark at the start of a displayed quotation. [265a]

**Line 19:**
5. Use only three periods to signify an omission within a quoted sentence. [274]

**Line 22:**
6. In the phrase *ten to 15 years,* put both numbers either in figures or in words. In this context words are preferred. [402, 405, 436a, 437]
7. Change *between 20–50* to *between 20 and 50.* [459b]
8. Spell out *percent.* [447a]

**Line 24:**
9. Make the *5* a superior number, and omit the space between the period and the superior number. [1502b]

**Line 26:**
10. Insert a comma after *words* (following an introductory phrase). [124b, 138a, 139a]

**Line 28:**
11. Change *maybe* to *may be.* [719]

**Line 30:**
12. Change *transferrable* to *transferable.* [704, 713a]
13. Omit the comma after *another* (to avoid separating two predicates in a *that* clause). [125f]

**Line 32:**
14. Change *be come* to *become.* [1202, 1203a]

**Line 35:**
15. Spell *PROCESSING* with only one *C.* [1203a]

**Line 37:**
16. Indent the first line of a paragraph ½ inch. [1424c]

**Line 39:**
17. Change *is* to *are* (to agree with the plural subject *a number*). [1028a, 1023]

**Line 41:**
18. Change *opportunitys* to *opportunities.* [604]
19. Change the superior number from *7* to *6.* [1203e]

**Lines 45–46:**
20. Leave only 1 blank line below a side head. [1426]

**Line 47:**
21. Change *Operator's* to *Operators'.* [632]

**Line 51:**
22. Hyphenate the compound adjective *entry-level.* [816a]

**Line 53:**
23. Change *formating* to *formatting.* [704]
24. Move *Un-* from the end of the line to the first line on the next page. [918]

**Line 56:**
25. Do not capitalize *and* in the subtitle. [360]

**Line 57:**
26. Do not italicize *3d ed.* [1514]

**Line 59:**
27. Change *p.* to *pp.* (since more than one page number is involved). [621a, 1529a]
28. Change *300–1* to *300–301.* [460b]
29. Leave a blank line between footnotes 5 and 6. [1503c]

**Line 60:**
30. Capitalize *Appendix.* [359]

opportunities will always be available in the field of information processing for those who have good skills and can adapt to continual changes in the workplace. According to one authority:

> Most people will change careers two to four times within their working lifetimes—and that statistic does not include job changes. The average working person . . . will make five, six, or even more job changes in addition to career changes.[4]

Moreover, within the next ten to fifteen years, between 20 and 50 percent of the available jobs will have titles and descriptions that do not now exist.[5] In other words, not only will you be changing jobs in the course of your career, but the jobs themselves may be changing as well. For that reason it is critical to develop skills that are transferable from one job to another and are not likely to become obsolete.

## CAREERS IN INFORMATION PROCESSING

Within an organization there are typically three levels of jobs: operators, assistants, and managers. In addition, there are a number of related opportunities outside the organization.[6]

### Operators

Operators' jobs are usually classified according to the level of skill and experience required.

**Information Processing Trainee.** This is an entry-level job that requires good keyboarding and formatting skills but no experience.

---

4. Sharon Lund O'Neil, *Office Information Systems: Concepts and Applications*, 3d ed., Glencoe, Westerville, Ohio, 1999, p. 292.

5. O'Neil, pp. 300–301.

6. See Appendix A for a full list of job titles and descriptions.

# 33

*Key*

# Final Survey

**Directions:** Correct the punctuation and capitalization in each sentence below. If the punctuation is incorrect, draw a line through it: *an old winter coat.* If new punctuation is to be inserted, circle it: *I too hope so.* To change a small letter to a capital letter, draw three lines under it: *Christmas.* To change a capital letter to a small letter, draw a line through it: *Enough.* If a sentence is correct as given, write *C* in the answer column. **References:** Sections 1–3.

1. Bob, Lois, and I want to find small, aggressive companies we can invest in.    1. _____
2. May I please have two hours of your time on Monday, May 6, to get some advice?    2. _____
3. Thanks for sending me a copy of your letter of March 4, in which you take the directors to task for approving excessive pay for top executives, what a mess. [OR: (!)]    3. _____
4. The President of Gage seminars has asked how many managers you plan to send.    4. _____
5. Did you really exceed your sales goal by 40 percent? Unbelievable!    5. _____
6. It's odd, isn't it, how some people will buy a pre-owned vehicle but not a used car?    6. _____
7. Did the supplier who called on us last friday send the additional data I asked for?    7. _____
8. In my judgment, his son Ted lacks the managerial skills needed to run the Division.    8. _____
9. If your assistant is not that busy, could she please help us with our backlog?    9. _____
10. We could rendezvous in Amherst, New York, or if you prefer, in London, Ontario.    10. _____
11. It is urgent, therefore, that we make a counteroffer to their President, Fay Perry.    11. _____
12. Please supply the following data: Purpose of loan, amount needed, duration of loan.    12. _____
13. Liza Lotte, Ph.D., is writing the Company's history and will be done this Fall.    13. _____
14. The transaction meets State laws, but will it satisfy Federal regulations?    14. _____
15. Before I came back east last Winter, I worked for a large, mining company in Utah.    15. _____
16. You don't think our profit shortfall will go as high as $1,000,000, do you?    16. _____
17. We must therefore ask for a deposit, even though your credit rating is good.    17. _____
18. We can't find the will, but we do have the codicil dated december 6, 2004.    18. _____
19. Paul, do you think Dan Peters, the President of NDG, would be a good CEO for us?    19. _____
20. In 2004, Farley Mudge, Jr., made a substantial investment in Ariel, Inc. *(commas not needed)*    20. **C**
21. To enter a subscription, call 1-800-555-0600, to renew one, call 1-800-555-0602.    21. _____
22. Whenever I tell Charlie that I need his help, he says, can it wait? ☺    22. _____
23. (See section 2.4) and to be fought for in exodus from the desert.)    23. _____
24. The demonstration sites are Ames, Iowa; Bath, Maine; and Logan, Utah.    24. _____
*[OR: ...me. However, ask...]*
25. The layouts look great to me, however, ask the marketing department to okay them.    25. _____
26. Could someone from the Center For Auto Safety pick me up at Reagan airport?    26. _____
27. He teaches french history and is an authority on the eighteenth century, for *[OR: ...century. For...]* example, he did a book on the Seventeen Nineties and the french revolution.    27. _____
28. After I graduated, I left Knoxville, but I'm still fond of Eastern Tennessee.    28. _____
29. The CEO, along with his staff, will host a party on the fourth of July.    29. _____
30. An ad hoc committee was set up in July 2005, or was it August?    30. _____

Name _____ Date _____ Class _____    67

   C-97

# 33

## *Rule Numbers*
## Final Survey

**Directions:** Correct the punctuation and capitalization in each sentence below. If the punctuation is incorrect, draw a line through it: *an old winter coat*. If new punctuation is to be inserted, circle it: *I too hope so.* To change a small letter to a capital letter, draw three lines under it: *christmas*. To change a capital letter to a small letter, draw a line through it: *Enough*. If a sentence is correct as given, write *C* in the answer column. **References:** Sections 1–3.

1. Bob Lois and I want to find small aggressive companies we can invest in $^{101a}$ $^{168a}$ $^{123b/162a}$    1. _____

2. May I please have two hours of your time on Monday May 6 to get some advice $^{148}$ $^{103b}$    2. _____

3. Thanks for sending me a copy of your letter of March 4 in which you take the $^{131b/152}$ directors to task for approving excessive pay for top executives what a mess $^{101a/301b}$ $^{101b}$    3. _____

4. The President of Gage seminars has asked how many managers you plan to send $^{313d}$ $^{309/320a}$ $^{104}$    4. _____

5. Did you really exceed your sales goal by 40 percent unbelievable $^{110a}$ $^{301b}$ $^{119}$    5. _____

6. It's odd, isn't it, how some people will buy a pre-owned vehicle but not a used car $^{114a/122a}$ $^{114a}$    6. _____

7. Did the supplier who called on us last friday, send the additional data I asked for $^{342}$ $^{131a}$ $^{110a}$    7. _____

8. In my judgment his son Ted lacks the managerial skills needed to run the Division $^{124b/139a}$ $^{149/150}$ $^{309}$ $^{101a}$    8. _____

9. If your assistant is not that busy could she please help us with our backlog $^{130a}$ $^{103b}$    9. _____

10. We could rendezvous in Amherst New York or if you prefer in London Ontario $^{160a}$ $^{122a/144a}$ $^{160a}$ $^{101a}$    10. _____

11. It is urgent therefore that we make a counteroffer to their President Fay Perry $^{122c/141}$ $^{312b/148}$ $^{101a}$    11. _____

12. Please supply the following data Purpose of loan amount needed duration of loan $^{189}$ $^{196}$ $^{123b/162}$ $^{101a}$    12. _____

13. Liza Lotte Ph.D. is writing the Company's history, and will be done this Fall $^{157}$ $^{309/321}$ $^{127b}$ $^{343}$ $^{101a}$    13. _____

14. The transaction meets State laws but will it satisfy Federal regulations $^{335b}$ $^{123/126a}$ $^{328}$ $^{110a}$    14. _____

15. Before I came back east last Winter I worked for a large, mining company in Utah. $^{338}$ $^{343}$ $^{130a}$ $^{169}$ $^{101a}$    15. _____

16. You don't think our profit shortfall will go as high as $1000000 do you $^{123}$ $^{114a/122b}$ $^{114a}$    16. _____

17. We must therefore ask for a deposit even though your credit rating is good $^{122c/141}$ $^{131b/132}$ $^{101a}$    17. _____

18. We can't find the will but we do have the codicil dated december 6 2004 $^{123a/126a}$ $^{342}$ $^{154a}$ $^{101a}$    18. _____

19. Paul do you think Dan Peters the President of NDG would be a good CEO for us $^{145}$ $^{148}$ $^{313b}$ $^{148}$ $^{110a}$    19. _____

20. In 2004 Farley Mudge Jr. made a substantial investment in Ariel Inc. $^{135c}$ $^{156}$ $^{159}$ $^{101a}$    20. _____

21. To enter a subscription call 1-800-555-0600 to renew one call 1-800-555-0602 $^{135b}$ $^{128/176a}$ $^{136a}$ $^{101a}$    21. _____

22. Whenever I tell Charlie that I need his help he says can it wait $^{130a/256a/227/301c}$ $^{249a/227/257}$    22. _____

23. (See section 2 a land to be fought for in exodus from the desert $^{359}$ $^{148/242}$ $^{360}$ $^{148/247}$ $^{289a/290/360}$ $^{101a/220}$    23. _____

24. The demonstration sites are: Ames Iowa Bath Maine and Logan Utah $^{191c}$ $^{148}$ $^{184}$ $^{148}$ $^{184}$ $^{148}$ $^{101a}$    24. _____

25. The layouts look great to me however ask the marketing department to okay them $^{178}$ $^{142a}$ $^{322}$ $^{101a}$    25. _____

26. Could someone from the Center For Auto Safety pick me up at Reagan airport $^{303}$ $^{331}$ $^{110a}$    26. _____

27. He teaches french history, and is an authority on the eighteenth century for $^{304}$ $^{352}$ $^{127b}$ $^{345}$ $^{181a}$ example he did a book on the Seventeen-Nineties and the french revolution $^{142/181a}$ $^{345}$ $^{344a}$ $^{101a}$    27. _____

28. After I graduated I left Knoxville but I'm still fond of Eastern Tennessee $^{130a}$ $^{133/177c}$ $^{341}$ $^{101a}$    28. _____

29. The CEO along with his staff will host a party on the fourth of July $^{146}$ $^{342}$ $^{101a}$    29. _____

30. An "ad hoc" committee was set up in July 2005 or was it August $^{287}$ $^{155a}$ $^{207}$ $^{110a}$    30. _____

Name _____ Date _____ Class _____    67

**Directions:** The following items deal with problems in number style, abbreviations, plural and possessive forms, spelling, compound words, and word division. (*Note:* The symbol / is used in items 96–100 to show word division at the end of a line.) If an item is correct as given, write *C* in the answer column. If an item is incorrect, circle the error and show the correct form in the answer column. **References:** Sections 4–9.

| # | Item | Answer | Ref |
|---|------|--------|-----|
| 31. | got 12 PCs (6 are laptops) | C | 402 |
| 32. | after July 31st | 31 | 407b |
| 33. | had to pay over $200.00 | $200 | 415 |
| 34. | with a unit cost of $.86 | 86 cents | 418 |
| 35. | for now 20 years ago . . . | Twenty | 421 / 424 |
| 36. | before the 20th century | twentieth | 438 |
| 37. | is more than 1/2 done | half | 427 |
| 38. | in two-liter containers | 2-liter | 429a |
| 39. | reduced benefits before 65 | C | 433 |
| 40. | a thirty-day grace period | 30-day | 436a |
| 41. | almost fifty years ago | C | 437 / 440 |
| 42. | opens at nine A.M. | 9 a.m. | 453a |
| 43. | consulted R.M. Siu | R. M. | 516a |
| 44. | Doctor Baldwin's opinion | Dr. | 517a |
| 45. | an S.E.C. ruling | SEC | 524a |
| 46. | US Department of Energy | U.S. | 525 |
| 47. | a trip to Washington, D.C. | C | 527 |
| 48. | 6 lbs. @ $8.25 | lb | 535 |
| 49. | only a 100-km drive | 100-km | 538b |
| 50. | entertain a VIP. | VIP | 546 |
| 51. | unexpected tendencys | tendencies | 604 |
| 52. | when the attornies meet | attorneys | 605 |
| 53. | invite husbands and wifes | wives | 608b |
| 54. | console the runner-ups | runners-up | 612a |
| 55. | a strange phenomena | phenomenon | 614 |
| 56. | sold by the Connollys | C | 615c |
| 57. | back in the 1990's | 1990s | 624a |
| 58. | the witness's account | C | 631a |
| 59. | took Jo Barne's place | Barnes's | 631a |
| 60. | both agencies' accounts | C | 632a |
| 61. | a sale on womens' coats | women's | 633 |
| 62. | it's Harry's, not their's | theirs | 636 |
| 63. | Ed and Fran's signatures | Ed's | 642a |
| 64. | need two dollars worth | dollars' | 646 |
| 65. | ask about me getting a job | my | 647a |
| 66. | defered this payment | deferred | 702 |
| 67. | a cancelled check | canceled | 704 |
| 68. | an acknowledgment | C | 708 |
| 69. | quite an acheivement | achievement | 712 |
| 70. | very persistant | persistent | 714 |
| 71. | may now procede | proceed | 716b |
| 72. | submit your resume | résumé | 718a |
| 73. | our principle goal | principal | 719 |
| 74. | to forego an increase | forgo | 719 |
| 75. | can't except his excuse | accept | 719 |
| 76. | to wave one's rights | waive | 719 |
| 77. | was basicly correct | basically | 720 |
| 78. | try to accomodate | accommodate | 720 |
| 79. | it looks familar | familiar | 720 |
| 80. | highly reccommended | recommended | 720 |
| 81. | need your good will | goodwill | 801a |
| 82. | let's check-up on it | check up | 802 |
| 83. | read the print-outs | printouts | 803d |
| 84. | good at problem solving | C | 805a |
| 85. | wants it triple spaced | triple-spaced | 812 / 813 |
| 86. | a high pressure job | high-pressure | 816a |
| 87. | a three-year's lease | three-year OR three years' | 817a |
| 88. | my income-tax return | income tax | 818a |
| 89. | our toll free number | toll-free | 820a |
| 90. | found it nerve racking | nerve-racking | 821a |
| 91. | was too fast paced | fast-paced | 823a |
| 92. | a newly decorated office | C | 824a |
| 93. | bring me up-to-date | up to date | 831a |
| 94. | let's re-elect her | reelect | 835a |
| 95. | much too self confident | self-confident | 836a |
| 96. | we stop-/ped going | stopped | 902 |
| 97. | on sep-/arate checks | sepa-/rate | 913 |
| 98. | an exped-/ient action | expedi-/ent OR expe-/dient | 914 |
| 99. | was transferr-/ing | transfer-/ring | 922b |
| 100. | sell-/ing at a loss | C | 922a |

68

**Directions:** Underline all errors and write the correct forms in the answer column. If a sentence is correct as given, write *C* in the answer column. **References:** Sections 10–11.

| | | | | |
|---|---|---|---|---|
| 101. | Every sales rep and field manager <u>have</u> to be notified at once. | 101. | has | 1002c 1009b |
| 102. | Only one of the fax machines <u>are</u> in service right now. | 102. | is | 1006a 1008a |
| 103. | <u>Was</u> any of the incoming phone calls from Mrs. Malifitano? | 103. | Were | 1013a |
| 104. | Our criteria for establishing a customer's creditworthiness <u>has</u> changed. | 104. | have | 1018a |
| 105. | The number of calls about equipment breakdowns is unacceptable. | 105. | C | 1023 |
| 106. | Bob is one of those people who <u>assumes</u> you always have time to talk. | 106. | assume | 1008b |
| 107. | None of the position papers deal with the impact on employee morale. | 107. | C | 1013a |
| 108. | I wish I <u>was</u> able to devote time to the company's tutoring program. | 108. | were | 1039a |
| 109. | When will the company update <u>their</u> policy on environmental issues? | 109. | its | 1020 1049a |
| 110. | Between you and <u>I</u>, the board isn't very happy with the new CEO. | 110. | me | 1055b |
| 111. | Moira seems to think she's better qualified to do my job than <u>me</u>. | 111. | I | 1057 |
| 112. | Mike and <u>myself</u> expect our funding proposal to be approved. | 112. | I | 1060d |
| 113. | <u>Whom</u> do you think is the leading authority on artificial intelligence? | 113. | Who | 1061 |
| 114. | We had a <u>real</u> nice time at the Benzingers' reception. | 114. | really | 1065 |
| 115. | I feel very bad about losing the lease on my store. | 115. | C | 1067 |
| 116. | We never participated in <u>no</u> meetings with the Finley brothers. | 116. | any | 1076 |
| 117. | It's too early to tell whether the rail strike will <u>effect</u> us. | 117. | affect | 1101 |
| 118. | We've had an excessive <u>amount</u> of complaints on those bearings. | 118. | number | 1101 |
| 119. | Business was slow for <u>awhile</u>, but orders are starting to pick up. | 119. | a while | 1101 |
| 120. | In recent weeks I've made <u>less</u> mistakes. | 120. | fewer | 1101 |

**Directions:** Rewrite the following sentences to correct all errors. **References:** Primarily Sections 10–11.

121. Every salesman should continuously monitor his travel expenses.  **All sales representatives [OR salespersons] should continually monitor their travel expenses.**

122. We not only reviewed this years' sales patterns but also last year.  **We reviewed not only this year's sales patterns but also last year's.**

123. Neither the employees nor the supervisor has met his production quota.  **Neither the supervisor nor the employees have met their production quotas.**

124. To open an account, this card should be filled out. And returned to us.  **To open an account, fill out this card and return it to us.**

125. The will's provisions have been challenged by everyone of us relatives.  **Every one of us relatives has challenged the provisions of the will.**

**Directions:** On the reverse side of this sheet you will find a letter to **Mr. Ferris G. Hartmann** (typed in modified-block style—standard format with standard punctuation). Correct all errors in style, grammar, and format; also look for errors in typing and content. Circle all changes you make within the lines or out in the margins; if you prefer, show all changes on a separate sheet, identified by line number. If time permits, retype the corrected letter on a plain sheet of paper, using 1.25-inch side margins and positioning the date on the first line below a 2-inch top margin. **References:** Section 13 plus Sections 1–12. See also pages 358–359 or the inside back cover of *The Gregg Reference Manual* for a chart showing how to indicate corrections on typed material.

Name _____ Date _____ Class _____ 69

# Highlawn Hills

P.O. Box 455 Sparta, NJ 07871  Phone: 973.555-5675  Fax: 973.555-5890  Web: www.hhills.com

February Feb. 10, 2007

Mr. Ferris G. Hartmann
12516 S.W. 10th St. (Southwest Tenth Street)
Topeka, KS 66604

Dear Mr. Hartman:

Thank you for your letter of February sixth (6) in which you expressed some interest in acquiring a one-family home in Highlawn Hills. Since you and your wife will not be visiting the Sparta area until later in the spring, let me try to answer some of your questions now.

1. The community consists entirely of custom-crafted two, three, and four bedroom houses, artfully blended into an 800-acre hilltop setting and priced from $335,000 to $595,000. In short, every house enjoys a million-dollar view without the million-dollar price tag.

2. Highlawn Hills has been created by the Saroyan Brothers Development Company, master builders of award-winning communities with more than thirty years' experience. Every house contains such amenities as a wood-burning fireplace, a sundeck, sun-filled skylights, and 2 1/2 bathrooms (including a jacuzzi in the master bathroom).

3. Every family in Highlawn Hills can enjoy the following on-site facilities: an 18-hole golf course, tennis courts, an Olympic-size swimming pool, jogging trails, and a clubhouse with a fitness center. At a nearby shopping center are a gourmet supermarket, two department stores, and a number of elegant boutiques. Moreover, your children will have access to a school district that is rated one of the best in the state.

I'm enclosing a prospectus that describes all the properties now being offered for sale. Also enclosed are a booklet about Sparta and a brochure describing the lovely, unspoiled setting of Highlawn Hills. When you do come to Sparta, why don't you give me a call? Either Farley Fox, our Sales Manager, or I would be pleased to help you in anyway we can.

Cordially yours,

Paula B. Sharpe
Associate Sales Manager

Enclosures 3

Note to Instructor: See page C-102 for notes and rule references for this editing practice.

70

**Line 13:** 1. Change *Feb.* to *February.* [1313a]
2. Separate the day and the year with a comma *(February 16, 2007).* [1313a]

**Line 17:** 3. Insert *Mr.* before *Ferris G. Hartmann.* [1322a]

**Line 18:** 4. Omit the comma in the house number *(1516).* [462]
5. Spell out *Southwest.* [1334]
6. Spell out *Tenth.* [1333a]
7. Spell out *Street.* [1337]

**Line 21:** 8. Change *Hartman* to *Hartmann* (as in the inside address and the directions). [1202c, 1338f]

**Line 23:** 9. Do not indent the first line of a paragraph when a letter is typed in modified-block style—standard format. [1302a, 1344f–i]
10. Change *sixth* to *6* in the date. [407b]
11. Insert a comma after *6* (a nonessential clause follows). [122d, 152]

**Line 24:** 12. Hyphenate *one-family* [814, 817a]

**Line 26:** 13. Do not capitalize *spring.* [343]
14. Insert a comma after *spring* (following an introductory dependent clause). [124, 130a]

**Lines 28, 33, 39:** 15. Insert a period after *1, 2,* and *3* in the enumeration. [106, 1345d]

**Line 28:** 16. Spell out the numbers *two, three,* and *four.* [401a, 404a]
17. Insert a suspending hyphen after *two* and *three (two-, three-,* and *four-bedroom houses).* [832]

**Lines 29–31, 34–37, 40–44:** 18. Align the turnovers in the displayed enumeration with the first word in the first line. [1345d]

**Line 29:** 19. Do not hyphenate *artfully blended.* [824a]

**Line 30:** 20. Replace the hyphen with *to* in the phrase *from $335,000 to $595,000.* [459b]
21. Insert a comma after *In short* (an introductory transitional expression). [138a]

**Line 35:** 22. Insert an apostrophe after *years (years').* [646]

**Lines 35–36:** 23. Hyphenate *wood-burning.* [821a]

**Line 36:** 24. Insert a series comma after *skylights.* [123b, 184]
25. Change *2-½* to *2½.* [428]

**Line 37:** 26. Capitalize *Jacuzzi.* [356]
27. Insert a closing parenthesis after *bathroom* and before the period. [225a, 1203b]

**Line 40:** 28. Change the semicolon to a colon. [189]
29. Spell *swimming* with two *m*'s. [701]

**Lines 41–42:** 30. Do not divide *nearby* (with only two letters carried to the next line). [904]

**Line 43:** 31. Change *excess* to *access.* [719]

**Line 44:** 32. Do not capitalize *state.* [335]

**Line 46:** 33. Omit the comma before *that* (introducing an essential clause). [131a, 132]
34. Change *propertys* to *properties.* [604]

**Line 47:** 35. Change *offerred* to *offered.* [704]
36. Change *is* to *are* to agree with the plural subject that follows (*booklet* and *brochure*). [1027a]
37. Omit the comma after *Sparta* to avoid separating two subjects (*a booklet about Sparta* and *a brochure . . .* ). [125f]

**Line 48:** 38. Insert a comma after *lovely.* [168a]

**Line 49:** 39. Change the period to a question mark. [110a]

**Line 50:** 40. Do not capitalize *sales manager* (following a name). [313d]
41. Insert a comma after *manager.* [148]
42. Change *please* to *pleased* (a typographical error). [1202b]
43. Spell *any way* as two words. [1101]

**Lines 52, 56–57:** 44. Begin the closing at center, aligned with the date line. [1346a]

**Line 52:** 45. Spell *Cordially* with two *l*'s. [1203a, 1346a]
46. Do not capitalize *yours.* [1346b]
47. Insert a comma after *Cordially yours.* [1346c]

**Line 57:** 48. Capitalize *Sales Manager.* [1349, 1325a]

**Line 59:** 49. Change *Enclosures 2* to *Enclosures 3* (to agree with lines 46–48). [1203e, 1358a]

**Line 60:** 50. The reference initials should precede the enclosure notation. [1355b, 1358a]

February 16, 2007

Mr. Ferris G. Hartmann
1516 Southwest Tenth Street
Topeka, KS 66604

Dear Mr. Hartmann:

Thank you for your letter of February 6, in which you expressed some interest in acquiring a one-family home in Highlawn Hills. Since you and your wife will not be visiting the Sparta area until later in the spring, let me try to answer some of your questions now.

1. The community consists entirely of custom-crafted two-, three-, and four-bedroom houses, artfully blended into an 800-acre hilltop setting and priced from $335,000 to $595,000. In short, every house enjoys a million-dollar view without the million-dollar price tag.

2. Highlawn Hills has been created by the Saroyan Brothers Development Company, master builders of award-winning communities with more than thirty years' experience. Every house contains such amenities as a wood-burning fire-place, a sundeck, sun-filled skylights, and 2½ bathrooms (including a Jacuzzi in the master bathroom).

3. Every family in Highlawn Hills can enjoy the following on-site facilities: an 18-hole golf course, tennis courts, an Olympic-sized swimming pool, jogging trails, and a clubhouse with a fitness center. At a nearby shopping center are a gourmet supermarket, two department stores, and a number of elegant boutiques. Moreover, your children will have access to a school district that is rated one of the best in the state.

I'm enclosing a prospectus that describes all the properties now being offered for sale. Also enclosed are a booklet about Sparta and a brochure describing the lovely, unspoiled setting of Highlawn Hills. When you do come to Sparta, why don't you give me a call? Either Farley Fox, our sales manager, or I would be pleased to help you in any way we can.

Cordially yours,

Paula B. Sharpe
Associate Sales Manager

was
Enclosures 3

# 34

*Key*
# Final Survey

**Directions:** Correct the punctuation and capitalization in each sentence below. If the punctuation is incorrect, draw a line through it: *an old/winter coat.* If new punctuation is to be inserted, circle it: *I too hope so.* To change a small letter to a capital letter, draw three lines under it: *christmas.* To change a capital letter to a small letter, draw a line through it: *Enough.* If a sentence is correct as given, write *C* in the answer column. **References:** Sections 1–3.

1. Carole, Paula, and I have rented a handsome, sun-filled house for the summer.      1. _____
2. May I please use your transparencies for my presentation next Tuesday, May 9?      2. _____
3. I've just received your note of May 1, in which you asked whether you could
   borrow my transparencies of course.      3. _____
4. The Marketing Director of Galway industries asked how much the demo cost.      4. _____
5. Did you really take top honors in the photo competition, my warmest congratulations!      5. _____
6. It's strange, isn't it, that so many nice people turn into ogres when they drive?      6. _____
7. Did the person whom I interviewed last monday submit samples of her work?      7. _____
8. In my opinion, the company's stock will not split before the year 2008.      8. _____
9. If you have some free time, would you please comment on the attached proposal?      9. _____
10. We could stop in Hampton, New Hampshire, and if you like, go on to Camden, Maine.      10. _____
11. It is essential, therefore, that we notify their Treasurer, Tom Bray, of the new plan.      11. _____
12. Please fill in the following boxes: Your date of birth, your address, your phone number.      12. _____
13. Ken Foy, LL.D., spoke today to the company's managers, and will return this Spring.      13. _____
14. Did last week's oil spill draw the attention of Federal and State regulators?      14. _____
15. After we moved down south last Winter, we decided to open a small antique shop.      15. _____
16. Forrest's investment in Apple must be over $2,000,000 by now, don't you think?      16. _____
17. We must therefore reject your buyout offer, even though your terms are attractive.      17. _____
18. The lawsuit was filed last May, but the case will not be tried until june 3, 2008.      18. _____
19. Phil, have you heard that Jane Seidel, the Mayor of Warren, will not run again?      19. _____
20. In 2004, Ray Twomey, Jr., stepped down as the head of Zodiac Creations, Inc.  [commas not needed]      20. C
21. To leave a message, record after the tone; to speak with an operator, dial 0.  [OR: O To:...]      21. _____
22. If you ask Mona for help, she always smiles and says what needs to be done.      22. _____
23. (See chapter 4a) time to be born in going with the flow.      23. _____
24. The locations of our stores are: Tulsa, Oklahoma; Tyler, Texas; and Tempe, Arizona.  [OR: O However...]      24. _____
25. I like the overall design, however, the Marketing Director wants a brighter color.      25. _____
26. Is the Television Bureau of Advertising really located on Madison avenue?  [OR: O for...]      26. _____
27. Nan's field is european history, and literature in the twentieth century, for example,
    she has taught courses on the Nineteen Forties and the holocaust.      27. _____
28. After I retired, I moved to Northern Vermont, but I miss my house in Rye, New York.      28. _____
29. Martha, along with her children, is taking a cruise to celebrate mother's day.      29. _____
30. An ad hoc committee was created in April 2002, or was it 2003?      30. _____

Name _____ Date _____ Class _____      71

**Directions:** Correct the punctuation and capitalization in each sentence below. If the punctuation is incorrect, draw a line through it: *an old winter coat.* If new punctuation is to be inserted, circle it: *I too hope so.* To change a small letter to a capital letter, draw three lines under it: *christmas.* To change a capital letter to a small letter, draw a line through it: *Enough.* If a sentence is correct as given, write *C* in the answer column. **References:** Sections 1–3.

1. Carole Paula and I have rented a handsome sun-filled house for the summer    1. _____

2. May I please use your transparencies for my presentation next Tuesday May 9    2. _____

3. I've just received your note of May 1 in which you asked whether you could borrow my transparencies of course    3. _____

4. The Marketing Director of Galway industries asked how much the demo cost    4. _____

5. Did you really take top honors in the photo competition my warmest congratulations    5. _____

6. It's strange isn't it that so many nice people turn into ogres when they drive    6. _____

7. Did the person whom I interviewed last monday, submit samples of her work    7. _____

8. In my opinion the Company's stock will not split before the year 2008    8. _____

9. If you have some free time would you please comment on the attached proposal    9. _____

10. We could stop in Hampton New Hampshire and if you like go on to Camden Maine    10. _____

11. It is essential therefore that we notify their Treasurer Tom Bray of the new plan    11. _____

12. Please fill in the following boxes Your date of birth your address your phone number    12. _____

13. Ken Foy LL.D. spoke today to the Company's managers, and will return this Spring    13. _____

14. Did last week's oil spill draw the attention of Federal, and State, regulators    14. _____

15. After we moved down south last Winter we decided to open a small, antique shop    15. _____

16. Forrest's investment in Apple must be over $2000000 by now don't you think    16. _____

17. We must therefore reject your buyout offer even though your terms are attractive    17. _____

18. The lawsuit was filed last May but the case will not be tried until june 3 2008    18. _____

19. Phil have you heard that Jane Seidel the Mayor of Warren will not run again    19. _____

20. In 2004 Ray Twomey Jr. stepped down as the head of Zodiac Creations Inc.    20. _____

21. To leave a message record after the tone, to speak with an operator dial 0    21. _____

22. If you ask Mona for help she always smiles and says what needs to be done    22. _____

23. (See chapter 4 a time to be born in going with the flow    23. _____

24. The locations of our stores are: Tulsa Oklahoma Tyler Texas and Tempe Arizona    24. _____

25. I like the overall design however the Marketing Director wants a brighter color    25. _____

26. Is the Television Bureau Of Advertising really located on Madison avenue    26. _____

27. Nan's field is european history, and literature in the twentieth century for example she has taught courses on the Nineteen-Forties and the holocaust    27. _____

28. After I retired I moved to Northern Vermont but I miss my house in Rye New York    28. _____

29. Martha along with her children is taking a cruise to celebrate mother's day    29. _____

30. An ad hoc committee was created in April 2002 or was it 2003    30. _____

Name _____ Date _____ Class _____

71

C-105

**Directions:** The following items deal with problems in number style, abbreviations, plural and possessive forms, spelling, compound words, and word division. (*Note:* The symbol / is used in items 96–100 to show word division at the end of a line.) If an item is correct as given, write C in the answer column. If an item is incorrect, circle the error and show the correct form in the answer column. **References:** Sections 4–9.

| # | Item | Answer | Ref |
|---|------|--------|-----|
| 31. | 18 yeses and six noes | 6 | 402 |
| 32. | before December 15th | 15 | 407b |
| 33. | on sale for only $99.00 | $99 | 415 |
| 34. | cost only $.79 apiece | 79 cents | 418 |
| 35. . . . | our ad. 16 callers | Sixteen | 421 424 |
| 36. | in the 19th century | nineteenth | 438 |
| 37. | 1/3 of the way through | one-third | 427 |
| 38. | in fifty-gallon drums | 50-gallon | 429a |
| 39. | my son turned three | C | 434 |
| 40. | a ninety-day warranty | 90-day | 436a |
| 41. | nearly 30 years ago | thirty | 437 440 |
| 42. | closes at five P.M. | 5 p.m. | 453a |
| 43. | wrote to H.H. Green | H. H. | 516a |
| 44. | Doctor Singh's visit | Dr. | 517a |
| 45. | approved by the F.D.A. | FDA | 524a |
| 46. | US State Department | U.S. | 525 |
| 47. | lives in Washington, D.C. | C | 527 |
| 48. | 200 bbls @ $85 | bbl | 535 |
| 49. | weighed about 75 km. | km | 538b |
| 50. | found a good H.M.O. | HMO | 546 |
| 51. | too many liabilitys | liabilities | 604 |
| 52. | made many journies | journeys | 605 |
| 53. | a cat with nine lifes | lives | 608b |
| 54. | my two son-in-laws | sons-in-law | 612a |
| 55. | more than one criteria | criterion | 614 |
| 56. | visited the Kennedies | Kennedys | 615c |
| 57. | throughout the 1990's | 1990s | 624a |
| 58. | an actress' ambition | actress's | 631a |
| 59. | bought Ella James's car | James's | 631a |
| 60. | both company's CEOs | companies' | 632a |
| 61. | mens' suits are on sale | men's | 633 |
| 62. | it's ours, not your's | yours | 636 |
| 63. | Ed and Jan's shoes | Ed's | 642a |
| 64. | several dollars worth | dollars' | 646 |
| 65. | do you mind me asking | my | 647a |

| # | Item | Answer | Ref |
|---|------|--------|-----|
| 66. | transfered the deed | transferred | 702 |
| 67. | profitted from the sale | profited | 704 |
| 68. | used good judgment | C | 708 |
| 69. | whatever I recieved | received | 712 |
| 70. | resistent to infection | resistant | 714 |
| 71. | will not interceed | intercede | 716c |
| 72. | copy my resume | résumé | 718a |
| 73. | this passed week | past | 719 |
| 74. | I can not tell you why | cannot | 719 |
| 75. | that maybe impossible | may be | 719 |
| 76. | was accidently broken | accidentally | 720 |
| 77. | in a large quanity | quantity | 720 |
| 78. | on the nineth or tenth | ninth | 720 |
| 79. | something similar | similar | 720 |
| 80. | was a real privaledge | privilege | 720 |
| 81. | a true master piece | masterpiece | 801a |
| 82. | to cover-up mistakes | cover up | 802 |
| 83. | over 200 hand-outs | handouts | 803d |
| 84. | needs skill-building | skill building | 805a |
| 85. | type it double spaced | double-spaced | 812a 813 |
| 86. | a high level meeting | high-level | 816a |
| 87. | a ten-year's loan | ten-year OR ten years' | 817a note |
| 88. | word-processing center | word processing | 818a |
| 89. | a cost effective plan | cost-effective | 820a |
| 90. | very eye catching | eye-catching | 821a |
| 91. | looks old fashioned | old-fashioned | 823a |
| 92. | a highly deserved raise | C | 824a |
| 93. | brought me up to date | C | 831a |
| 94. | would re-employ him | reemploy | 835a |
| 95. | the fact is self evident | self-evident | 836a |
| 96. | I plan-/ ned to leave | planned | 902 |
| 97. | it is imper-/ ative | impera-/ tive | 913 |
| 98. | try media-/ tion | medi-/ ation | 914 |
| 99. | retell-/ ing an old story | C | 922a |
| 100. | controll-/ ing our costs | control-/ ling | 922b |

**Directions:** Underline all errors and write the correct forms in the answer column. If a sentence is correct as given, write *C* in the answer column. **References:** Sections 10–11.

| | | | |
|---|---|---|---|
| 101. | Every marketing manager and copywriter <u>have</u> seen the new logo. | **101.** has | 1002c 1009b |
| 102. | Only one of the service representatives <u>are</u> available on weekends. | **102.** is | 1006a 1008a |
| 103. | <u>Does</u> any of the plans meet the goal of higher sales and lower costs? | **103.** Do | 1013a |
| 104. | Our criteria for granting parental leave <u>needs</u> to be updated. | **104.** need | 1018a |
| 105. | The number of uninsured drivers <u>are</u> high and continuing to grow. | **105.** is | 1023 |
| 106. | Nora is one of those people who <u>spends</u> time to say they have no time. | **106.** spend | 1008b |
| 107. | None of the passengers <u>was</u> seriously injured, but the car was totaled. | **107.** were | 1013a |
| 108. | I wish I <u>was</u> going to the convention in Bermuda with the rest of you. | **108.** were | 1039a 1020 |
| 109. | How long can the company maintain <u>their</u> share of the market? | **109.** its | 1049a |
| 110. | Attendance is mandatory for everyone except you and <u>I</u>. | **110.** me | 1055b |
| 111. | Maria is so much better at dealing with angry customers than <u>me</u>. | **111.** I | 1057 |
| 112. | Jan and <u>myself</u> will move to Utah, even if my transfer is not okayed. | **112.** I | 1060d |
| 113. | <u>Whom</u> do you think will get the Oscar this year for best actress? | **113.** Who | 1061 |
| 114. | It was <u>real</u> nice of you to cover for me while I was in the hospital. | **114.** really | 1065 |
| 115. | We feel very bad about your decision to take early retirement. | **115.** C | 1067 |
| 116. | I've reviewed your proposal carefully, and I don't have <u>nothing</u> to add. | **116.** don't . . . anything OR ~~don't~~ | 1076 |
| 117. | How will the proposed increase in the sales tax <u>effect</u> your business? | **117.** affect | 1101 |
| 118. | Mayor Fry's budget cuts have angered a large <u>amount</u> of voters. | **118.** number | 1101 |
| 119. | I need to consider my options for <u>awhile</u> before I make my next move. | **119.** a while | 1101 |
| 120. | Why do <u>less</u> people attend the Friday concerts than those on Monday? | **120.** fewer | 1101 |

**Directions:** Rewrite the following sentences to correct all errors. **References:** Primarily Sections 10–11.

121. Every congressman should continuously monitor the views of his constituents. **Every member of**
*(1053a   809a   719   1052/1053a)*
**Congress should continually monitor the views of his or her constituents. (OR All members . . . their)**

122. We not only discussed this years' sales projections but also next year. **We discussed not only this**
*(1081b   630a   644/1071i)*
**year's sales projections but also next year's.**

123. Neither the professors nor the dean is happy about the impact of funding cuts on his programs. _____
*(1005   1049c)*
**Neither the dean nor the professors are happy about the impact of funding cuts on their programs.**

124. When applying for a loan, this form should be filled out and brought back. When you come for an
*(1082d   101c)*
interview. **When applying for a loan, fill out this form and bring it back when you come for an interview.**

125. The new law's provisions have been reviewed by everyone of us lawyers. **Every one of us lawyers**
*(645   1037b   1010, note)*
**has reviewed the provisions of the new law.**

**Directions:** On the reverse side of this sheet you will find a letter to **Dr. Margaret P. Jensen** (typed in modified-block style—standard format with standard punctuation). Correct all errors in style, grammar, and format; also look for errors in typing and content. Circle all changes you make within the lines or out in the margins; if you prefer, show all changes on a separate sheet, identified by line number. If time permits, retype the corrected letter on a plain sheet of paper, using 1.25-inch side margins and positioning the date on the first line below a 2-inch top margin. **References:** Section 13 plus Sections 1–12. See also pages 358–359 and the inside back cover of *The Gregg Reference Manual* for a chart showing how to indicate corrections on typed material.

Name _____ Date _____ Class _____   73

# Caribbean Cruises

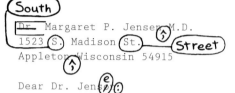

**1200 BISCAYNE BOULEVARD**
**MIAMI, FLORIDA 33132**
**(305) 555-2800**

October 14th, 2008

South
Dr. Margaret P. Jensen, M.D.
1523 S. Madison St. — Street
Appleton, Wisconsin 54915

Dear Dr. Jensen:

Thank you for your letter of October seventh in which you asked for
for information about our winter cruises to the Caribbean. I can well
understand of course why you are thinking about a warmer place a few months
from now, since I grew up in Northern Minnesota. Let me try to provide
some answers to the questions you raised in your letter.

1. From December 15 to March 21 we are offering a wide selection of cruises.
There are frequent sailing dates to fit every schedule, and prices to fit
every budget.

2. If your time is limited, you maybe most interested in our seven-day
cruises, which stop in 3 ports (for example, Nassau, San Juan and Antigua.
three

3. If you're in a position to take a longer voyage, you might consider our
16-day cruises which stop in six ports. Better yet, our 16-day cruise sails
from Miami through the Panama Canal to Los Angeles.

4. Prices start at $1950.00 and includes round trip airfare between
Chicago and Miami (and Los Angeles if you decide on our longest cruise).

I'm enclosing three brochures that describe in detail each of our three
types of cruises. Regardless of the one you choose, you can expect gourmet
dining, oversized cabins, and an attentive crew to spoil you. If you want
to escape this winter into a warm wonderful world of luxury and excitement,
why not ask your travel agent about reservations?

Sincerely yours,

Mr. Edward J. Cantwell,
Director of Customer Services

aem
Enclosures 3

> **Note to Instructor:** See page C-109
> for notes and rule references for
> this editing practice.

74

# NOTES ON WORKSHEET 34, PAGE 74

**Line 13:**
1. Change *14th* to *14*. [1313a]
2. Separate the day and the year with a comma *(October 14, 2008)*. [1313a]

**Line 17:**
3. Delete *Dr.* (since *M.D.* follows). [519c, 1324c]
4. Insert a comma before *M.D.* [1324c]

**Line 18:**
5. Spell out *South*. [1334]
6. Spell out *Street*. [1337]

**Line 19:**
7. Insert a comma after *Appleton* (but not after *Wisconsin*). [161, 1339]

**Line 21:**
8. Change *Jenson* to *Jensen* (as in the inside address and the directions). [1338f]
9. Insert a colon after *Jensen* [194a, 1338b]

**Line 23:**
10. Do not indent the first line of a paragraph in a letter typed in modified-block style—standard format. [1302a(1), 1344f]
11. Change *seventh* to *7*. [407b]
12. Insert a comma before a nonessential clause (*in which . . .* ). [122d, 152]

**Line 24:**
13. Omit *for* (a repetition of the last word in line 26). [1202a]
14. Do not capitalize *winter*. [343]
15. Correct the spelling of *Caribbean* (which is shown properly in the letterhead). [720]

**Line 25:**
16. Set off *of course* with commas. [122c, 141]

**Line 26:**
17. Change the period after *now* to a comma and do not capitalize *since*. (*Since* introduces a nonessential dependent clause that should be treated as part of the preceding sentence.) [101b, 131b, 132]
18. Do not capitalize *northern*. [341]

**Line 27:**
19. Change the second *you* to *your*. [1202b]

**Line 29:**
20. Change the dash between dates to the word *to* (*From December 15 to March 21*). [459b]
21. Change *offering* to *offering*. [704]

**Lines 30–31, 34, 37–38, 41:**
22. Align the turnovers in the displayed enumeration with the first word in the first line. [1345d]

**Line 30:**
23. Omit the comma before *and*. (Do not separate two items joined by *and*.) [125f]

**Line 33:**
24. Change *maybe* to *may be*. [1101]

**Line 34:**
25. Change *3* to *three*. [401a]
26. Insert a comma after *San Juan* (the second of three items in a series). [123b, 162a]
27. Insert a closing parenthesis before the period at the end of the sentence. [225a]

**Line 36:**
28. Change *your* to *you're* (or *you are*). [1056e]
29. Insert a comma after *voyage* (following an introductory clause). [124, 130a]

**Line 37:**
30. Hyphenate the compound adjective *11-day*. [817a]
31. Insert a comma before a nonessential *which* clause. [131b]
32. Insert a comma after the introductory phrase *Better yet*. [124b, 138b, 139a]

**Line 38:**
33. Capitalize *Canal*. [331]
34. Insert a period at the end of the sentence. [101a]

**Line 40:**
35. Omit the *.00* from a whole dollar amount (*$1950*). [415]
36. Omit the comma before *and* to avoid separating a compound predicate. [127b]
37. Change *includes* to *include* to agree with the subject *Prices*. [1001a]
38. Hyphenate the compound adjective *round-trip*. [816a]

**Line 41:**
39. Place the closing parenthesis before the period. [225a]

**Line 43:**
40. Omit the comma before *that* (introducing an essential clause). [131a, 132]
41. Change *there* to *three*. [1202d]

**Line 44:**
42. Insert a comma after *choose* (following an introductory element). [124, 135c]

**Line 46:**
43. Insert a comma between the adjectives *warm* and *wonderful*. [168a]

**Line 47:**
44. Change the period at the end of the sentence to a question mark. [110]

**Line 49:**
45. Do not capitalize *yours*. [1346b]
46. Insert a comma after *yours*. [1346c]

**Line 53:**
47. Omit *Mr.* before a man's typed signature. [1351]
48. Omit the comma after *Cantwell*. [1349a]

**Line 54:**
49. Do not capitalize *of*. [1349b, 1325a]

**Line 57:**
50. Change *Enclosure 1* to *Enclosures 3* (to agree with line 43 in the body of the letter). [1358a]

*Final copy with 1.25" side margins*

October 14, 2008


Margaret P. Jensen, M.D.
1523 South Madison Street
Appleton, Wisconsin 54915

Dear Dr. Jensen:

Thank you for your letter of October 7, in which you asked for information about our winter cruises to the Caribbean. I can well understand, of course, why you are thinking about a warmer place a few months from now, since I grew up in northern Minnesota. Let me try to provide some answers to the questions you raised in your letter.

1. From December 15 to March 21 we are offering a wide selection of cruises. There are frequent sailing dates to fit every schedule and prices to fit every budget.

2. If your time is limited, you may be most interested in our seven-day cruises, which stop in three ports (for example, Nassau, San Juan, and Antigua).

3. If you're in a position to take a longer voyage, you might consider our 11-day cruises, which stop in six ports. Better yet, our 16-day cruise sails from Miami through the Panama Canal to Los Angeles.

4. Prices start at $1950 and include round-trip airfare between Chicago and Miami (and Los Angeles if you decide on our longest cruise).

I'm enclosing three brochures that describe in detail each of our three types of cruises. Regardless of the one you choose, you can expect gourmet dining, oversized cabins, and an attentive crew to spoil you. If you want to escape this winter into a warm, wonderful world of luxury and excitement, why not ask your travel agent about reservations?

Sincerely yours,


Edward J. Cantwell
Director of Customer Services


aem
Enclosures 3

# CLASSROOM PRESENTATIONS

# Strategies for Using PowerPoint Slides and Transparencies With *The Gregg Reference Manual* and the *Worksheets*

**Transparencies H-1 to H-6.** Use these transparencies to introduce (or reteach) *how to look things up* in *The Gregg Reference Manual.* These transparencies use a problem-and-solution approach to explain how to look thinks up.

Display Transparencies H-1 and H-2 to emphasize using the index of *The Gregg Reference Manual.* After you have led your students through Transparency H-1, have them consult ¶103 to determine that a question mark is the right punctuation for this sentence. In the same way, have them consult page 317 to determine that *among* is the right word to use in the example depicted on Transparency H-2.

Display Transparency H-3 to present *consulting lists of topics* in *The Gregg Reference Manual* for solutions to problems. Obscure ¶328 at the bottom of the transparency until your students have determined for themselves that *federal* is the correct form.

Display Transparencies H-4 and H-5 to present *playing the numbers.* For the first problem, ask your students to consult ¶¶421–422 to determine that *Forty* is the correct form. For the second problem, ask your students to explain why ¶¶429–431 and 535–538 are irrelevant. Then ask them to consult ¶620 to determine that *lb* is the correct plural form.

Display Transparency H-6 to present *looking for specific words.* When discussing the index entries under *Commas,* point out grammatical terms they may not understand (for example, *transitional expressions*). Ask them to consult Appendix D to find the definition of such terms.

**Slides 1-1 to 1-40.** Use these slides to introduce (or reteach) the basic rules for the *major punctuation marks.*

Display Slides 1-1 to 1-9 to introduce (or reteach) the three marks of *terminal punctuation* (the period, the question mark, and the exclamation point). Display Slides 1-1 to 1-4 to discuss ¶¶101a, 110a, 104, 119a, and 103. Note that the first example on Slide 1-1 makes a statement about the writer's views, even though it begins with the words *I question.* Use the second example to point out when a sentence ends with an abbreviation, the period that marks the end of the abbreviation also serves to mark the end of the statement. In Slide 1-2, which provides examples of direct and indirect questions for ¶110a and ¶104, point out the difference in word order. In a direct question, the

verb typically precedes the subject; in this case, *is* precedes the subject *policy.* In an indirect question, the verb follows the subject; in this case, *is* follows *policy.* In Slide 1-3, which presents an example for ¶119a, an exclamation expresses strong feeling and requires an exclamation point. In Slide 1-4, which presents two examples from ¶103, point out that both make polite requests. However, the first example asks someone a favor and requires that person to give a yes-or-no response. The second example does not call for a yes-or-no answer; it requires someone (*you*) to take action (in this case, letting another person know whether you are planning to stay overnight or not).

Display Slide 1-5 to introduce (or reteach) ¶¶101b, 111, and 119a. In these examples underlining is used to highlight the elliptical expressions. Ask students to explain why a period, a question mark, or an exclamation point is used in each case. Display Slides 1-6 and 1-7 to introduce (or reteach) ¶107a and b. Use the example on Slide 1-6 to point out that the three numbered elements are needed to complete the introductory statement, whereas in the example of a displayed list on Slide 1-7, the introductory statement is complete by itself.

Display Slides 1-8 and 1-9 to illustrate the difference between using 1 or 2 spaces after a period (or any other punctuation mark) at the end of a sentence. Explain that the use of 1 space is now the general standard but the use of 2 spaces is not incorrect and should be used whenever necessary to maintain a strong visual break between the sentences.

Display Slides 1-10 to 1-17 to introduce (or reteach) ¶122, the basic rule for using *commas that set off nonessential expressions,* and to present examples of various types of nonessential expressions.

Display Slides 1-18 to 1-27 to introduce (or reteach) ¶¶123–124, the basic rules for using *commas that separate elements within a sentence* to clarify their relationship to one another. Discuss the examples that require a comma to separate elements within a sentence.

Display Slides 1-28 to 1-31 to introduce (or reteach) ¶¶126–132, the basic rules for using *commas within a sentence.*

Display Slides 1-32 and 1-33 to introduce (or reteach) ¶¶176 and 178, the basic rules for using the *semicolon.* Explain that a period may be preferable to a semicolon when the independent clauses are long and would make an extremely long sentence. Also explain that a period is preferable when the clauses are not closely related. (See ¶176b in the manual for an example.) Also point out that a comma follows the transitional expression when it introduces the second independent clause.

Display Slides 1-34 and 1-35 to introduce (or reteach) ¶187, the basic rule for using the *colon.* If your students have difficulty grasping when to use a colon or a semicolon in sentences like those provided on this transparency, encourage them to take the sure way out and treat the clauses as independent sentences.

Display Slides 1-36 to 1-40 to introduce (or reteach) ¶¶181 and 182, the basic rules for using a *semicolon or a colon with for example, namely, and that is.* Here again, point out that a comma follows these transitional expressions when they introduce the second clause in the sentence.

**Slides 2-1 to 2-18.** Use these slides to introduce (or reteach) the basic rules for *other marks of punctuation.*

Display Slides 2-1 to 2-3 to introduce (or reteach) ¶¶183, 201, and 219, the basic rules for using *dashes, parentheses, and commas to set off expressions introduced by for example, namely, and that is.*

Display Slides 2-4 to 2-15 to introduce (or reteach) the basic rules for using *quotation marks.* Display Slide 2-4 and the example for ¶227 to point out that when a quoted statement falls at the end of a larger statement, the period goes *inside* the closing quotation mark. Also note that a comma typically separates the introductory words from the quoted material that follows. Display Slide 2-5 to show how the direct question illustrated on Slide 2-4 is transformed here into an indirect question.

Display Slide 2-6 and use the example for ¶253a to explain that when a quoted statement falls at the beginning of a sentence, the period that normally ends a statement is in this case replaced by a comma. Then display Slide 2-7 and use the example for ¶254 to highlight the difference when a quoted question falls at the beginning of a statement. In this case the quoted question retains the question mark.

Display Slide 2-8 to explain that when a quoted exclamation falls at the beginning of a sentence, the quoted exclamation retains the exclamation point.

Display Slides 2-9 and 2-10 to illustrate the use of a comma or a colon before a quoted sentence that falls at the end of a larger sentence.

Display Slide 2-11 to explain that when a quotation falls at the end of a sentence, a period always goes inside the closing quotation mark.

Display Slides 2-12 to 2-14 to explain that the placement of a question mark depends on whether the quotation is a question embedded in a statement or a statement embedded in a question. When the quoted

material is a question at the end of a statement (as in Slide 2-12), the question mark goes *inside.* If the quoted material is a statement at the end of a question (as in Slide 2-13), the question mark goes *outside.* If students should ask what happens when a quoted question falls at the end of a question (as in Slide 2-14), explain that the question mark in that case would fall *inside* and refer the students to ¶257.

Display Slides 2-15 to 2-18 to introduce (or reteach) the basic rules for using *quotation marks, italics, and underlining.* Refer students to ¶287 in the manual for a list of the most commonly used foreign expressions that are now considered part of the English language. If students ask what the term *mouse potato* means (in the example on Slide 2-17), ask them to consult the glossary of computer terms for the definition at <http://www.gregg.com>.

**Slides 3-1 to 3-24.** Use these slides to introduce (or reteach) the basic rules for *capitalization.*

Display Slides 3-1 to 3-6 to explain the *function of capitalization*—namely, to give distinction, importance, and emphasis to words (see the introduction to Section 3 on page 93 of the manual). That is why the first word of a sentence is capitalized: to indicate distinctively and emphatically that a new sentence has begun.

Display Slides 3-7 to 3-13 to introduce (or reteach) the basic rules for the *capitalization of proper nouns.* Note that here again these terms are capitalized to convey the special importance and distinction of the persons, places, and things that they refer to. Point out that the term *federal government* (on Slide 3-8) is not typically capitalized except by federal employees, who as insiders would assign the term a special significance that outsiders would not. Make use of the insider-outsider concept to explain why the rules of capitalization vary from one style manual to another. The differences arise because the authors of these manuals assign or withhold importance, emphasis, and distinction depending on where they stand in relation to the thing being named.

Display Slides 3-14 to 3-18 to introduce (or reteach) the basic rules for the *capitalization of common nouns.* To help your students grasp the difference between proper and common nouns, you might explain that the expression *the White House* (the home of the U.S. President) is capitalized to indicate its special importance and to distinguish it from *the white house next door* or *any white house.* You might also warn your students about the Tarzan Syndrome, the tendency to capitalize words that do not deserve this special distinction or emphasis. Explain that when Jane gave birth to a son, she told Tarzan that they were now the parents of a *boy* (using a common noun). Tarzan, misunderstanding, thought she was giving a formal name to the child and thereafter called

D-2

him *Boy.* Urge your students to be more like Jane and less like Tarzan.

You might also point out that short forms such as *company* (on Slide 3-16) and *university* (on Slide 3-17) are capitalized in formal or legal writing when the short form is intended to evoke the full authority of the full official name.

Display Slides 3-19 to 3-24 to introduce (or reteach) the basic rules for *capitalization of titles.* When displaying Slide 3-24, explain that the titles of local officials (such as *mayor*) are often capitalized in internal documents and even in the local newspaper, because within that limited context *the Mayor* is viewed as a very important person. Similarly, the titles of company officials are often capitalized in internal documents because of the importance that these people have within their organization. By the same token, organizational terms such as *the board of directors* or *the advertising department* are usually capitalized in internal documents because of the importance they have from an insider's perspective; they would be lowercased when viewed from an outsider's perspective.

**Slides 4-1 to 4-14.** Use these slides to introduce (or reteach) the basic rules for *expressing numbers.* Explain that two sets of basic rules are in wide use: the *figure style* (which uses figures for most numbers above 10) and the *word style* (which uses figures for most numbers above 100). Students need to be familiar with both styles and be prepared to use each appropriately as the situation demands.

Display Slides 4-1 to 4-12 to introduce (or reteach) the *figure style of numbers.* Stress that the figure style is most commonly used in business documents and technical material. In this kind of writing, most numbers represent significant quantities or measurements that need to stand out for emphasis or quick comprehension. If students inquire why the numbers *1* through *10* are expressed in figures in the statement of the basic rule in Slide 4-1, explain that these numbers should be in figures when they need to stand out for quick comprehension.

Display Slides 4-2 to 4-12 for additional rules and examples for the figure style. In Slide 4-7 the examples that illustrate the treatment of numbers in dates can be used to illustrate the use of commas in dates. In Slide 4-8 use the example *from $4.95 to $9* to point out that it is not necessary to add a decimal point and two zeros to *$9* except in a column of figures. Use the examples in Slides 4-10 to 4-12 to explain that numbers used in *technical* references to age, periods of time, and measurements are expressed in figures even when they are below 11, whereas numbers used in *nontechnical* references to these elements are expressed in words even when they are above 10. To make this point, compare the technical references to *a 20-year mortgage* and *packages over 5 pounds* with the nontechnical reference to *over twenty years ago* and *need to lose five pounds.*

Display Slides 4-13 and 4-14 to introduce (or reteach) the *word style of numbers.* Point out that the word style is used chiefly in nontechnical material and certain high-level executive communication where the writing is of a more formal nature and the use of figures would give numbers an undesired emphasis and obtrusiveness. Also use the examples to explain that numbers like *three hundred* and *ninety-five million* may be spelled out when they appear alone in a sentence but should be put in figures when they appear together with numbers like *350* and *125 million.* Refer to ¶¶407–470 in *The Gregg Reference Manual* for rules covering those situations that require special handling.

**Slides 5-1 to 5-15.** Use these slides to introduce (or reteach) several rules for *abbreviations.* Define abbreviation as a shortened form of a word or phrase used primarily to save space. Explain that abbreviations occur most frequently in technical writing, statistical material, tables, and notes. As you discuss each of the basic rules on these slides, ask the students to identify the meaning of each abbreviation. Ask students to identify other abbreviations for each rule. Stress the importance of following company standards and using a dictionary. To review punctuation and spacing rules for abbreviations, display Slides 5-7 to 5-15 and refer students to ¶¶506–513 in the manual. Refer students to the remaining rules in Section 5 for special rules on abbreviations (especially ¶541 regarding abbreviations for business expressions).

**Slides 6-1 to 6-19.** Use these slides to introduce (or reteach) basic rules for *forming plurals.* Refer to *The Gregg Reference Manual* for additional examples for each rule. Ask students to identify other examples as you discuss each rule. Stress the importance of referring to a dictionary whenever they are uncertain about the plural form of a word.

Refer to the remaining rules in Section 6 (¶¶601–626) for special cases for forming plurals. Ask students to critique realistic business documents for the correct forms of plurals.

**Slides 6-20 to 6-33.** Use these slides to introduce (or reteach) basic rules for *forming possessives.* Display Slides 6-20 to 6-23 to discuss possessives of singular nouns, Slides 6-24 to 6-27 to discuss possessives of plural nouns, and Slides 6-28 to 6-33 to discuss possessive pronouns.

On Slide 6-20 note that words like *Illinois* and *Arkansas* end with a *s* but not with a *s* sound. It is for that reason these words require an apostrophe plus *s.* On Slide 6-21, point out that some people spell *boss's* without the final *s.* Ask your students to try saying *your boss' approval* aloud (without the extra *s* sound), and they'll quickly understand why the correct form is *boss's*. Display Slide 6-22 and ask your students to try pronouncing *goodness's, Massachusetts's, New Orleans's,* and *Los Angeles's* with the extra *s* sound. That will help them understand why these words require only an apostrophe to form the possessive.

On Slide 6-24, call attention to the use of an apostrophe in *ten dollars' worth*. Omitting the apostrophe before *worth* is a common error.

On Slide 6-27, note that the two examples—*the editors in chief's judgments* and *my sons-in-law's Internet start-up*—are correct but extremely awkward. Ask students to revise the two examples to avoid the possessive form: for example, *the judgments of the editors in chief* and *the Internet start-up of my sons-in law.*

On Slides 6-28 to 6-31 caution students never to use an apostrophe with the possessive forms of *personal pronouns*. On Slides 6-32 and 6-33 note that an apostrophe plus *s* is used to form the possessive of *singular indefinite pronouns*.

Use Slides 10-54 to 10-57 to help students identify the possessive forms for *I, you, he, she, it, we,* and *they*. To reinforce the difference between possessive forms and contractions that sound like them, display Slides 10-58 to 10-61.

For a discussion of the difference between *who's* and *whose*, display Slide 10-83. Refer students to ¶¶627–652 in the manual for other special rules for forming possessives.

**Slides 6-34 to 6-41.** Use these slides to discuss *forming plural and possessive forms of surnames.* Stress the importance of never changing the spelling of names.

**Slides 7-1 to 7-19.** Use these slides to introduce (or reteach) basic *spelling rules.* Emphasize that the authority for spelling in *The Gregg Reference Manual* is the 2003 printing of *Merriam-Webster's Collegiate Dictionary,* Eleventh Edition. Point out that the rules in Section 7 are only guides and many exceptions to the rules do exist. Using an up-to-date dictionary is critical when in doubt regarding the spelling of a word.

Display Slides 7-1 to 7-4 to introduce (or reteach) ¶¶701–704—spelling guides that indicate when a final consonant should or should not be doubled. Ask students to identify other words as examples or exceptions for these rules.

Display Slides 7-5 to 7-10 to introduce (or reteach) ¶¶705–708 and 710. Ask students to identify other words as examples or exceptions for these rules.

Display Slides 7-11 to 7-13 to introduce (or reteach) ¶712—spelling guides for *ie* and *ei* words. Refer students to the rhyme for the i-before-e rule on page 197 of the manual. Ask students to identify other examples or exceptions for this rule.

Display Slides 7-14 to 7-19 to introduce (or reteach) ¶¶715 and 716—spelling guides for words ending in *ize, ise,* and *yze* and words ending in *cede, ceed,* and *sede*.

As a classroom exercise, ask students to critique realistic business documents for spelling errors. Discuss the nonverbal message of spelling errors in business documents and potential risks in terms of present and future business. Ask students to identify how spelling errors can be avoided: spell checkers, careful proofreading, verification against a dictionary, proofreading with the help of another person. Instruct students to always proofread documents carefully, even if they have used a spell checker to verify the spellings. Emphasize that spell checkers do not catch words that are spelled correctly but used incorrectly in context.

Ask students to review ¶719 in the manual for commonly confused words. Note that a spell checker would not catch an instance where the incorrect word was used. Ask students to review ¶720 for troublesome words that are often misspelled. Discuss ways students can use the two lists to reduce spelling errors.

**Slides 8-1 to 8-29.** Use these slides to introduce (or reteach) the basic rules for *compound words*. Explain that some compound words are written as solid words, some are written as separate words, and some are hyphenated. Remind your students that the only way to be sure of the spelling of a compound noun is to check a manual or a dictionary.

Display Slides 8-1 to 8-4 to introduce (or reteach) ¶¶801, 802, and 811—basic rules for *compound nouns and verbs*. Demonstrate that compound nouns and verbs follow no set pattern in the way they are written. When displaying Slides 8-2 to 8-3, emphasize the need to distinguish a compound noun from a verb phrase that consists of the same elements. Note the slight difference in wording that distinguishes *a get-together* from *to get together.*

Display Slides 8-5 to 8-7 to introduce (or reteach) ¶¶809 and 840—the basic rules for *gender-free nouns*. Ask students to identify other examples for the two rules. Ask students to critique realistic business documents for the use of gender-free nouns. You may also want to use this transparency in conjunction with a discussion of ¶¶1050–1053 (which deal with the agreement of pronouns with common-gender antecedents and indefinite-pronoun antecedents).

Display Slides 8-8 to 8-24 to introduce (or reteach) basic rules for *compound adjectives*. Display Slides 8-8 to 8-13 to present ¶¶813, 814, and 815—three basic rules for compound adjectives. As you discuss each rule, ask students to identify other examples. Discuss ¶813 and the accompanying examples to demonstrate what happens when an adjective phrase or clause in converted to a compound adjective.

D-4

In many cases (like the examples on Slide 8-8), the phrase or clause is simply condensed to a few essential words *(long-term, well-known)*. Sometimes they undergo a change in word order *(exempt from taxes* becomes *tax-exempt)*. Sometimes (like the examples on Slide 8-9), they undergo a change in form *(for two weeks* becomes *two-week, who speaks softly* becomes *soft-spoken)*. In the examples on Slide 8-12, the first two display normal form and normal word order when they occur elsewhere in a sentence *(that lasts all day, part of the time)*. However, in the final example *(I work part-time), part-time* retains the condensed form: as a result, it must also retain the hyphen.

Display Slides 8-14 to 8-17 to introduce (or reteach) ¶¶816 through 819—additional basic rules for *compound adjectives*. As you discuss each rule, ask students to identify other examples. On Slide 8-14 note that *high-speed* and *red-carpet* are not hyphenated in the *after* examples because they are in normal form and normal word order. On Slide 8-15 *three-hour* and *20-year* are not hyphenated in the *after* examples because they appear in normal form *(three hours* and *20 years)*. When compound nouns (see Slide 8-16) and proper names (see Slide 8-17) are used as adjectives, they are not hyphenated because they can be readily grasped as a unit in each case.

Display Slides 8-18 to 8-24 to introduce (or reteach) ¶¶820, 821, 822, 823, 826, and 831—additional basic rules for *compound adjectives*. Explain that the examples on Slides 8-18 to 8-21 are hyphenated *before* and *after* because in either position the elements are not in normal word order *(is friendly-looking* rather than *looks friendly)*. Note that the *after* examples on Slides 8-22 to 8-24 are not hyphenated because the elements are in normal word order. Ask students to identify other examples for these rules.

Display Slides 8-25 to 8-29 to introduce (or reteach) ¶¶833 through 836—basic rules for *hyphenation with prefixes* and *suffixes*. Note the exceptions on Slides 8-27 and 8-28 where a few *co* words and one *de* word require a hyphen. Ask students to identify other examples for these rules.

**Slides 9-1 to 9-14.** Use these slides to introduce (or reteach) the basic rules for *word division*. Many word processing programs provide automatic hyphenation. As a result, some students may feel that word division at the end of a line will take care of itself. However, certain situations exist in which judgment is required. Emphasize the importance of referring to a dictionary. Ask students to identify other examples for each rule.

**Slides 10-1 to 10-5.** Use Slide 10-1 to introduce (or reteach) the *principal parts of common* **regular** *verbs* (¶1030a). Explain that the principal parts of a verb are the four simple forms upon which all tenses and other modifications of the verb are based.

On Slides 10-1 and 10-2 note that the first six words—*ask, confirm, need, reveal, maintain,* and *taxi*—simply add *ed* or *ing* to the root word (present form).

On Slide 10-2, explain also that some verbs require a minor change in the ending of the present form before *ed* and *ing* (for example, *planned* and *shipped)*.

On Slide 10-3 use *occur* and *compel* to explain that a *two-syllable* root word ending in a vowel plus a consonant *with the accent on the second syllable* must double the final consonant before *ed* and *ing*. Explain that similar words with the accent on the first syllable (like *offer* and *travel)* require no change in the root word.

On Slide 10-4 use *receive, agree, die,* and *tie* to show that only *d* (rather than *ed*) is added, and note the change of *ie* to *y* (in *die* and *tie)* before *ing*.

On Slide 10-5 use *carry* and *hurry* to show that *y* changes to *i* before *ed (carried, hurried)* but does not change before *ing (carrying, hurrying)*. Use *obey* and *annoy* to show that there is no change in a root word ending in a vowel plus *y*.

**Slides 10-6 to 10-20.**   Use these slides to introduce (or reteach) the *principal parts of common* **irregular** *verbs* (¶1030b). Point out that there is no rule for forming the past and the past participle for many verbs; that is why they are called irregular. The present participle is formed regularly except for the doubling of the final consonant in certain root words before *ing* (for example, *beginning, forgetting, getting, running, setting, sitting,* and *swimming)* and the dropping of the final *e* from other root words before *ing* (for example, *choosing, coming, driving, giving, losing, shaking,* and *writing)*. Also note that the word *lie* (like *die* and *tie)* changes *ie* to *y* before *ing (lying, dying,* and *tying)*.

**Transparencies 10-1 to 10-6.**   Use these transparencies to introduce (or reteach) the formation of *verb tenses*, using *to see* as a model (¶¶1031–1034 and 1036). Also refer your students to the chart on pages 274–275 in the manual so that they can clearly see how the verbs *to be* and *to have* are used in the formation of verb tenses. As you discuss the conjugation of *to see,* you may want to display selected slides from the sequence 10-1 through 10-15 again and ask your students to use the principal parts of some of these regular and irregular verbs to form the tenses under discussion (following the pattern of *to see)*.

Display Transparency 10-1 to introduce (or reteach) the *present, past, and future tenses* (¶¶1031–1032). After you review the conjugation of *to see* in the present, past, and future tenses, note that the use of *shall* in the first person *(I, we)* is limited these days to the most formal speech and writing. (Under ordinary circumstances, *will* is used with all three persons.) For full discussion of the use of *shall* and *will,* refer your students to the entry *Shall-will* in Section 11.

Display Transparency 10-2 to introduce (or reteach) *the perfect tenses* (¶1033). Present the conjugation of *to have* (the helping verb) in the present, past, and future tenses. Also note that the past participle of the main verb *(seen)* remains unchanged in all three perfect tenses.

Display Transparencies 10-3 and 10-4 to present the *progressive tenses* (¶1034). Use Transparency 10-3 to present the conjugation of *to be* (the helping verb) in the present, past, and future progressive tenses. Note that the present participle of the main verb *(seeing)* remains unchanged in all three tenses. Use Transparency 10-4 to present the conjugation of *to be* in the present perfect, the past perfect, and the future perfect progressive tenses. Also note that the present participle of the main verb *(seeing)* remains unchanged in all six progressive tenses.

Display Transparencies 10-5 and 10-6 to introduce (or reteach) *passive* and *perfect passive tenses* (¶1036). Review the conjugation of *to be* (the helping verb) in the present, past, and future passive tenses as well as in the three perfect passive tenses. You may also want to emphasize that these passive forms use *to be* plus the *past* participle, whereas the progressive forms use *to be* plus the *present* participle.

**Slides 10-21 to 10-45.** Use these slides to introduce (or reteach) the basic rules of *subject-verb agreement.*

Display Slides 10-21 to 10-23 to present ¶¶1001 and 1002. If your students are not familiar with the concepts of number and person, use Transparencies 10-1 to 10-6 (showing the conjugation of a verb) and Slide 10-46 (showing personal pronouns in all three persons in the singular and plural).

Display Slides 10-24 to 10-27 to introduce (or reteach) ¶¶1003 through 1005. In discussing the related examples on Slides 10-26 and 10-27, point out that sentences of this type usually sound better if the second subject is plural; then the verb can be made plural as well.

Display Slides 10-28 to 10-30 to introduce (or reteach) ¶¶1006 through 1008. Encourage your students to read the examples without the intervening phrases or clauses so that they can make sure the subjects and verbs agree.

Display Slides 10-31 to 10-34 to introduce (or reteach) ¶¶ 1009, 1010, 1012, and 1013.

Display Slides 10-35 to 10-38 to introduce (or reteach) ¶¶1018 and 1019. Point out that *The jury have not yet agreed* is grammatically correct but sounds funny nonetheless. For that reason, inserting a phrase such as *the members of* before *the jury* better conveys the idea that the jury is not acting as a unit.

Display Slides 10-39 to 10-42 to introduce (or reteach) ¶¶1023, 1025, and 1027.

Display Slides 10-43 to 10-45 to introduce (or reteach) ¶¶1028 and 1029.

**Slides 10-46 to 10-61.** Use these slides to introduce (or reteach) the basic rules for *personal pronouns* (¶¶1054–1056).

**Slides 10-62 to 10-70.** Use these slides to introduce (or reteach) ¶¶1049–1053, the rules for *pronoun-antecedent agreement.* If a question comes up concerning how to choose a pronoun when the antecedent consists of two nouns—one singular and one plural—that are joined by *or* or *nor,* refer your students to ¶1049c, note. Also use Slides 10-69 and 10-70 to discuss ways to avoid an awkward sentence that results from the use of *he* or *she* (or a similar expression). Refer your students to ¶1053a, note, in the manual for further details.

**Slides 10-71 to 10-83.** Use these slides to introduce (or reteach) ¶¶1060, 1061, and 1063, the basic rules for *compound personal pronouns* and *interrogative and relative pronouns.*

**Slides 10-84 to 10-101.** Use these slides to introduce (or reteach) the basic rules for *adjectives and adverbs.*

Display Slides 10-84 to 10-86 to define an *adjective.* In discussing adjectives, point out that a compound modifier such as *power-hungry* (on Slide 10-85) is a stripped-down version of a relative clause (as in the example directly above—*who hungers for power*).

Display Slides 10-87 to 10-89 to define an *adverb.*

Display Slides 10-90 to 10-93 to introduce (or reteach) ¶¶1065 through 1067. Use the example *Joe seemed friendly* (on Slide 10-93) to make an observation embodied in ¶1069a: although the *ly* ending usually signifies an adverb, a few adjectives also end in *ly*—for example, *friendly, costly, lively, lovely, lonely.* With respect to the incorrect example *I feel badly* (on Slide 10-92) explain that the only way you can feel badly is to have your fingertips cut off.

Display Slides 10-94 to 10-101 to introduce (or reteach) ¶1071. On Slide 10-94 note that a word like *thin* doubles the *n* before adding *er and est.* Also note on Slide 10-96 that a word like *happy* changes the *y* to *i* before adding *er* and *est.* Warn students about not making *double comparisons;* for example, *more better, less thinner.* In the second Jim example on Slide 10-98, explain that the comparative form *taller* is correct because Jim is being compared with his two brothers one at a time. In the second Trudy example on Slide 10-99, explain that without the word *else* it would appear that Trudy is not on the staff. Similarly, in the second Chicago example on Slide 10-100, explain that without the word *other* it would appear that Chicago is not in Illinois.

**Slides 10-102 to 10-109.** Use these slides to introduce (or reteach) the basic rules for *prepositions.*

Display Slides 10-102 to 10-106 to present a list of common prepositions. Note that the object of a preposition needs to be in the objective case. By way of example, point to *between you and me* on Slide 10-103 and indicate why *between you and I* is wrong. You could also display Slide 10-50 and point to the example *They gave Jim and me free tickets.* Note that the preposition *to* is understood (though not expressed) and requires a pronoun in the objective case *(me).*

Use Slides 10-107 to 10-109 to introduce (or reteach) ¶¶1078 and 1079. Ask your students to say these sentences out loud. In that way they may develop some real sense of why some prepositions are unnecessary and why some prepositions need to be retained.

**Slides 10-110 to 10-113.** Use these slides to introduce (or reteach) parallelism in *sentence construction* (¶1081). In the wrong example on Slide 10-110 point out that *stimulating* is an adjective and *challenge* is a noun. The corrected version uses two adjectives— *stimulating* and *challenging.*

The wrong example on Slide 10-111 uses two adjectives *(easy* and *efficient)* and an independent clause *(it is relatively inexpensive).* The corrected version uses three adjectives—*easy, efficient,* and *inexpensive.*

In the wrong example on Slide 10-112 the enumerated items consists of an infinitive phrase *(how to deal . . . ),* a participial phrase *(coping with . . .),* and a dependent *clause (what the . . .).* The corrected version on Slide 10-113 uses three nouns—*ways, techniques,* and *role.*

**Slides 10-114 to 10-116.** Use these slides to introduce (or reteach) *dangling constructions* (¶1082). To help your students understand what makes a phrase dangle, explain that in the wrong example on Slide 10-114, it would seem that the *questions* had studied the cost estimates. In the corrected version, the doer of the action of *studying* is the subject of the sentence—*I.*

In the wrong example on Slide 10-115, it would seem that the *coupon* was obtaining the booklet. In the corrected version, the doer of the action of *obtaining* is the subject of the sentence—*you.*

In the wrong example, on Slide 10-116, the *errors* seem to be analyzing the data. In the corrected version, the doer of the action of *analyzing* is the subject of the sentence—*I.*

**Slides 11-1 to 11-12.** Use these slides to introduce (or reteach) *usage* (¶1101). For reasons of space these slides provide only examples without explanatory text. Thus, for example, when discussing the entry for *between-among,* explain that *between* is used when referring to two things and *among* when referring to three or more things.

**Transparency 12-1.** Discuss the definition of *proofreading* (¶1201a). Point out that a spell checker will not catch all errors; ask students to identify the types of errors that a spell checker will not catch. (Refer them to pages 350–351 in the manual.) Remind students that they must read carefully and thoughtfully. Discuss the different types of mistakes to watch for in the proofreading process. Use Transparency 12-1 to illustrate ¶1202b.

**Transparency 12-2.** Discuss the definition of *editing* (¶1201b). Use Transparency 12-2 to introduce (or reteach) the factors to consider in the editing process (¶1203a–h). Use this transparency in conjunction with Transparencies 12-3 through 12-8, which show the most commonly used proofreaders' marks. You could also ask your students to look at the charts on pages 358–359 (which show the same proofreaders' marks) as you discuss each correction on this transparency.

**Transparencies 12-3 to 12-8.** Use these transparencies to introduce (or reteach) the *proofreaders' marks.* Emphasize the importance of using proofreaders' marks in the editing and proofreading process. When you introduce the worksheets, display Transparencies 12-3 through 12-8 so that your students will know how to correct the errors they find in the editing exercises. You may also want to prepare transparencies showing an edited document and the final version. (See, for example, pages C-16 and C-18.)

**Transparencies 13-1 to 13-4.** Use these transparencies to illustrate four *letter styles:* modified-block letter style—standard format (Transparency 13-1), modified-block letter style—with indented paragraphs (Transparency 13-2), block letter style (Transparency 13-3), and simplified letter style (Transparency 13-4). You may also want to discuss letter templates available with word processing programs (see the introduction to Section 13, pages 363–364).

Display Transparency 13-1 to introduce (or reteach) the *modified-block letter style—standard format,* still the most commonly used letter style. Ask students to identify the features of this style: (1) the date line, the complimentary closing, the company signature, and the writer's identification all begin at center; (2) all other lines begin at the left margin. Ask students to identify the letter parts illustrated in this letter (and discussed in the specified paragraphs):

A  Letterhead (¶¶1310–1311)
B  Date Line (¶1313d–f)
C  Inside Address (¶¶1316–1336)
D  Salutation (¶¶1338–1341)
E  Message (¶¶1344–1345)
F  Complimentary Closing (¶1346)
G  Company Signature (¶1347)
H  Writer's Signature Block (¶¶1348–1354)
I  Reference Initials (¶1355)
J  File Name Notation (¶¶1356–1357)
K  Enclosure Notation (¶1358)
L  Delivery Notation (¶1359)
M  Copy Notation (¶¶1361–1364)

Display Transparency 13-2 to introduce (or reteach) the *modified-block letter style with indented paragraphs*. Ask students to identify the features of this style: (1) the date line, the complimentary closing, the company signature, and the writer's identification all begin at center; (2) all other lines begin at the left margin except the first line of each paragraph, which is indented 0.5 inch. Ask students to identify the letter parts illustrated in this letter (and discussed in the specified paragraphs):

N    Return Address (¶1312)
O    Reference Notation (¶1315)
P    Attention Line (¶1337)
Q    Paragraph Indentions (¶1344f)
R    Postscript (¶1365)

Display Transparency 13-3 to introduce (or reteach) the *block letter style*. Ask students to identify the key feature of this style: all lines begin at the left margin. Ask students to identify the letter parts illustrated in this letter (and discussed in the specified paragraphs):

S    Confidential Notation (¶1314)
T    International Address (¶1336)
U    Subject Line (¶¶1342–1343)
V    Displayed Extract (¶1345a)

Display Transparency 13-4 to introduce (or reteach) the *simplified letter style*. Ask students to identify the features of this style: (1) all lines begin at the left margin, (2) the salutation is replaced by an all-capital subject line, (3) the complimentary closing is omitted, (4) the writer's identification is typed in all-capital letters on one line, and (5) open punctuation is always used. Ask students to identify the letter parts illustrated in this letter (and discussed in the specified paragraphs):

W    Subject Line (in place of a salutation) (¶1342)
X    Complimentary Closing (¶1346)
Y    Writer's Signature Block (¶1349a)
Z    Justified Right Margin (¶1344g)

**Transparency 13-5.** Use Transparency 13-5 to introduce (or reteach) the placement of the return address, the name of the writer, the confidential notation, and the mailing address on an *envelope* (see ¶1368). Note the use of capital and small letters in the mailing address, the same style that is used for the inside address. Note the advantage for computer users of being able to use the envelope feature of a word processing program to reproduce the inside address on the envelope without any retyping. Also note that the state name may be spelled out or presented as a two-letter abbreviation. Either style is acceptable to the U.S. Postal Service.

**Transparency 13-6.** Use Transparency 13-6 to introduce (or reteach) the *all-cap style for a mailing address on an envelope* (see ¶1369). This style uses no punctuation and many abbreviations. Explain that this style was developed primarily for the use of mass mailers. While the U.S. Postal Service (USPS) encourages the use of this style for envelopes individually prepared, note that the OCR equipment used by the USPS can read the "inside address" style just as well. Since this all-cap style is not suitable for use in the inside address, anyone who follows this style will have to type the envelope address anew.

**Transparencies 13-7 to 13-8.** Use these transparencies to illustrate two formats for *memos:* a memo with a block-style heading (Transparency 13-7) and a memo with an alternative block-style heading (Transparency 13-8). You may also want to discuss memo templates available on word processing programs (¶1374).

Display Transparency 13-7 to introduce (or reteach) a *memo with a block-style heading* format. In this format, *all* the elements in the memo heading and the memo itself are blocked at the left margin. Also note that the use of a typed signature line or initials is optional. If the writer of the memo intends to insert a handwritten signature or initials above the typed signature line, leave 3 blank lines for the insertion; otherwise, leave only 1 blank line. Also note that 1 or 2 blank lines may be used to separate the heading from the text. This transparency (like the illustration on page 422 of the manual) uses 2 blank lines. The illustration on page 425 of the manual uses only 1 blank line.

Display Transparency 13-8 to introduce (or reteach) an *alternative memo format*. In this format, the word *MEMORANDUM* (or *MEMO*) appears on a line by itself; the first guide word in the heading simply reads *TO:* (instead of *MEMO TO:*, as on Transparency 13-7). Also note that the writer of this memo chooses to write her initials next to her typed name in the heading. In this case no typed signature line appears below the memo message.

**Transparencies 13-9 to 13-13.** Display Transparency 13-9 to introduce (or reteach) the formatting of e-mail headings. Use Transparencies 13-10 and 13-11 to illustrate how an e-mail message looks before it is sent and after it is received. Display Transparency 13-12 to show how to refer to attachments. Use Transparency 13-13 to illustrate one way of responding to an e-mail message; point out how all the short responses are embedded (using boldface type) in the original message. Indicate that using a color such as red would make the responses stand out more clearly from the original message.

**Transparencies 14-1 and 14-2.** Use these transparencies to illustrate an informal business report and an academic report. Display Transparencies 15-2 and

15-4 to illustrate quoted material displayed as an extract (¶1424d).

Display Transparency 14-1 to introduce (or reteach) the format of an *informal business report*. What distinguishes an *informal* report from a *formal* report is that the informal report has no front matter. The information that would go on a separate title page in a formal report appears at the top of the first page in an informal report and is immediately followed by the body of the report. Note that this transparency illustrates only two levels of text headings: side heads and run-in heads. However, other heading arrangements may be used. (See ¶¶1425–1426.)

Note that 1 or 2 blank lines may separate the title from the body of the report. This transparency (like the illustration on page 453 in the manual) uses 2 blank lines to achieve a more open look.

Display Transparency 14-2 to introduce (or reteach) the format of an *academic report*. Ask students to identify the differences between the format of an academic report and the format of an informal business report: (1) the first page uses a top margin of 1 inch (rather than 2 inches) and (2) a block of copy (including the writer's name) goes in the upper right corner.

**Transparencies 15-1 to 15-4.** Use these transparencies to introduce (or reteach) functions of *notes*: (1) they provide *comments* and (2) they serve as *source references*. Emphasize that many variations for notes exist, but indicate that the business style featured in *The Gregg Reference Manual* employs the simplest punctuation and the most straightforward presentation of the necessary data without any sacrifice in clarity or completeness.

Display Transparency 15-1 to present two format styles of a *source reference note* for a *book title*. Note that the book title may be italicized or underlined. Point out that the only difference between the *business* and the *academic* styles occurs in the treatment of three elements; the name of the publisher, the place of publication, and the year of publication. Also note that the number at the start of the note should be on the line for endnotes, but a superscript (raised) figure is now commonly used in footnotes. Mention that ¶¶1513–1535 discuss how to construct notes for all types of material. You may also want to discuss executing notes using the footnote and endnote features of word processing software (¶¶1503b, 1505b).

Display Transparency 15-2 to present the format for *footnotes*. Note the use of superscript (raised) figures in the text to refer to the numbered footnotes at the bottom of the page. Point out that the second footnote in this illustration reflects the format shown on Transparency 15-1 for a reference to a book title. You may also want to discuss executing footnotes using the footnote feature of word processing software

(¶1503b). You may also want to point out the format for a displayed extract (¶1424d) as illustrated in Transparencies 15-2 and 15-4.

Display Transparency 15-3 to present the format for *endnotes*. Point out that endnotes are becoming more popular because they leave the text pages looking less cluttered. However, until the reader turns to the endnotes section, the reader will not know whether the endnote contains a comment of substance (as in the first endnote on this transparency) or simply a source reference (as in the second endnote on this transparency). You may also want to discuss executing endnotes using the endnote feature of word processing software (¶1506).

Display Transparency 15-4 to present the format for a *textnote*. Note that the textnote in this illustration reflects the business-style format for a reference to a book title (shown in Transparency 15-1) except in one respect: no number is needed to introduce the textnote since it appears in the text at the point where it is needed. You may also want to point out the format for a displayed extract (¶1424d) as illustrated in Transparencies 15-2 and 15-4.

**Transparency 15-5.** Use Transparency 15-5 to illustrate how notes based on Web and e-mail sources may be formed. Call attention to the use of angle brackets (< >) to set off a URL or an e-mail address; this permits other punctuation to be used before and after the URL without any danger that this punctuation will be mistakenly considered part of the URL or e-mail address.

To help your students learn how to decode URLs and e-mail addresses, refer them to the discussion in ¶¶1508–1509. To show them how to divide a URL or e-mail address at the end of a line, refer them to ¶1510.

**Transparency 15-6.** Use Transparency 15-6 to introduce (or reteach) the format for a *bibliography*. Ask students to identify how the style for the entries in a bibliography differs from the style for entries in a list of endnotes: (1) the name of the first author is inverted (last name first) and (2) page numbers are not used unless the work being cited is part of a larger work. Also note that the entries in Transparency 15-6 reflect the business style. For the academic style, see ¶1549c. Mention that when a state name (such as *Massachusetts*) is used to identify the place of publication (as in the second entry), it is abbreviated in the traditional style *(Mass.)* and not in the two-letter style used in mailing addresses *(MA)*.

Display Transparency 15-3 again to point out how the formatting of an endnote differs from the formatting of an entry in a bibliography.

**Transparencies 17-1 to 17-5.** Use these transparencies to introduce (or reteach) the overall content for a résumé and the various formats for résumés. Emphasize that there is no one correct format; individuals must select a format that best presents their qualifications for the job they want to get. You may also want to discuss résumé templates available with some word processing programs.

Display Transparencies 17-1 and 17-2 to introduce (or reteach) the *chronological-style résumé emphasizing dates.* The chronological style is the most widely used résumé style and presents a person's employment history sequenced by date, starting with the most current job and working backward. On Transparency 17-1 call attention to the following features on this opening page: the heading (A), the objective statement (B), and experience (C). Note in particular that in this sample résumé, the dates for each job are featured in the left column, starting with the most recent job. The listing of jobs continues on the second page of the résumé (see Transparency 17-2). Generate a class discussion on when this style would be most effective.

Display Transparency 17-2 to introduce (or reteach) the remaining sections of a *chronological-style résumé.* Note the continuation of the Experience section, with the jobs listed in reverse chronological order. Also call attention to the following features on this page: education (H), continuing education (I), computer skills (J), and community service (K). Note that other sections can be added to this résumé (using such headings as professional affiliations, professional activities, military service, and special interests) if they will provide job-related information.

Display Transparency 17-3 to introduce (or reteach) a *chronological-style résumé emphasizing job titles.* Note the use of job titles (A) rather than dates in the first column. Also note the arrangement of specific achievements for each job in a single paragraph (C), and compare it with the bulleted format used on Transparency 17-1. Generate a class discussion on when this style would be most effective.

Display Transparencies 17-4 and 17-5 to introduce (or reteach) the *functional-style résumé.* Note on these transparencies that the achievements of this person have been grouped under four functional headings (B): marketing experience, administrative experience, writing skills, and computer skills. Note further that these four headings are closely tied into the wording of the objective statement *(in which marketing and administrative experience plus strong writing and computer skills can be used).* Generate a class discussion on when this style would be most effective.

**Transparency 17-6.** Use Transparency 17-6 to illustrate a one-page résumé for a person recently out of school or soon to graduate. Point out that this format is appropriate for a person without a great deal of job experience. Note that the educational background is presented first and in much greater detail than would usually be the case.

**Transparencies 17-7 and 17-8.** Use Transparencies 17-7 and 17-8 to illustrate the format for a résumé that can be scanned by an optical character reader. Point out that boldface, italics, underlining, bullets, and other graphic devices are not used in order to ensure that the résumé will be scannable. Also point out that an OCR will be searching the résumé for certain keywords related to the job opening. The more keywords located in the résumé, the more likely the résumé will be selected for further evaluation.

Use Transparency 17-8 to point out that asterisks (but not bullets) may be used to introduce items in a displayed list. Also point out that turnover lines must be flush left rather than indented.

**Transparencies 17-9 to 17-11.** Use these transparencies to introduce (or reteach) three other employment documents: *application letter, follow-up letter after an interview,* and *acceptance letter.* Mention that the general guidelines in ¶1708 in the manual apply to all employment communications.

Display Transparency 17-9 to introduce (or reteach) the *application letter.* Call attention to the two-column arrangements in the body of the letter (C) which relates the writer's qualifications to the job requirements stated in the ad for the organization. You may also want to discuss how an application letter and a résumé should be correlated: same type and color of paper, same font for heading on both documents, same font for text, most important details from résumé repeated on letter in appropriate manner. You may also want to discuss the importance of the application letter in terms of the initial contact with a potential employer.

Display Transparency 17-10 to introduce (or reteach) the *follow-up letter.* Ask students to identify the significance of a follow-up letter: (1) to thank the interviewer for meeting with you, giving you better insight into the available job and the organization you would be working for, and considering your qualifications in light of the available job; (2) a means to remind the potential employer why you would be an asset to the organization; (3) a means to offer additional information about your qualifications if they were not fully discussed during the interview; and (4) a means to address questions that arose during the interview that you were not fully prepared to answer at the time. Discuss the importance of using the same letter style, type elements, and stationery as was used for the application letter and résumé.

Display Transparency 17-11 to introduce (or reteach) the *acceptance letter.* Ask students to identify the significance of an acceptance letter: (1) to formally accept the job, (2) to confirm the key details of your working arrangements, and (3) to express your pleasure in coming to work for the organization and the person who has offered you the job. Discuss the importance of using the same letter style, type elements, and stationery as was used for the application letter and résumé.

**Transparency 18-1.** Use Transparency 18-1 to introduce (or reteach) *forms of address*. This transparency is intended only as a sample of what appears in Section 18. Because of space limitations in that section, only the masculine forms of address have been given in some categories. Call attention to an important note that appears in the introduction to Section 18 (page 579). This note shows how to adapt the masculine forms of address for use with women's names.

Transparency 18-1 shows what the feminine forms will look like when the appropriate substitutions are made. Discuss the relationship of the inside address and the salutation in a letter.

For additional examples of forms of address and matching the inside address and salutation in a letter, display Transparency 13-1 (modified-block letter style—standard format), Transparency 13-2 (modified-block letter style—with indented paragraphs), Transparency 13-3 (block letter style), Transparency 17-9 (application letter), and Transparency 17-11 (acceptance letter).

# How To Look Things Up: Use the Index

**Problem:** Will you please let me borrow your BMW convertible this weekend [. or ?]

**Solution:** Consult the detailed index at the back of the manual.

Boldface numbers
refer to rule
numbers.

*The Gregg Reference Manual*

**Transparency H–1**

# How to Look Things Up: Use the Index (continued)

**Problem:** His estate will be evenly divided [between? among?] his five children.

**Solution:** Consult the detailed index.

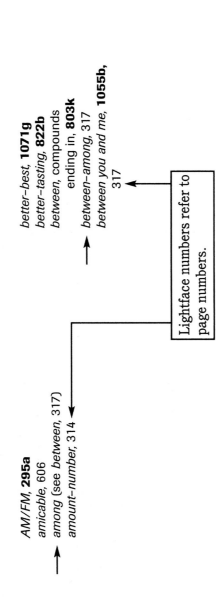

*AM/FM,* **295a**
*amicable,* 606
→ *among* [see *between,* 317]
*amount–number,* 314

*better–best,* **1071g**
*better–tasting,* **822b**
*between,* compounds
    ending in, **803k**
→ *between–among,* 317
*between you and me,* **1055b,**
    317

Lightface numbers refer to page numbers.

# How to Look Things Up: Consult Lists of Topics

**Problem:** These transactions must comply with [Federal? federal?] regulations.

**Solution:** Check the topical index on the inside front cover.

Business organizations, **320–324, 520–521, 1020, 1326, Appendix C: Rules 6–11**

→ Capitalization, **196–199, 272–273, 301–366, 514**

Charts and graphs, **1642**

Check the list of topics at the start of the appropriate section.

**Special Rules (¶¶311–366)**
Personal Names (¶311)
Titles With Personal Names (¶¶312–317)
Family Titles (¶¶318–319)
Names of Organizations (¶¶320–324)
→ Names of Government Bodies (¶¶325–330)

Check the appropriate sequence of rules to find the answer.

**328** Capitalize *federal* only when it is part of the official name of a federal agency, a federal act, or some other proper noun.

the *Federal* Reserve Board     the *Federal* Insurance Contributions Act

**BUT:** . . . subject to *federal*, state, and local laws.

**Transparency H–3**

# How To Look Things Up: Play the Numbers

**Learn what each section number stands for. For example:**

The 300 series of rules refers to CAPITALIZATION.

The 400 series of rules refers to NUMBERS.

The 500 series of rules refers to ABBREVIATIONS.

The 600 series of rules refers to PLURALS and POSSESSIVES.

**Problem:** [40? Forty?] percent of our employees are over 50 years old.

**Solution:** Check the list of topics at the start of Section 4 (Numbers).

**Special Rules (¶¶407–470)**
Dates (¶¶407–412)
Money (¶¶413–420)
→ At the Beginning of a Sentence (¶¶421–422)

D-16   **Transparency H–4**

# How to Look Things Up: Play the Numbers (continued)

**Problem:** 5 lbs? 5 lb?

**Solution:** Consult the detailed index and select the most appropriate rule numbers.

*weekly,* **1069b**
*weigh* (see *way,* 210)
*weight* (see *wait,* 210)
*weight* (*wt.*), **541**
→ Weights, **429–431, 535–538, 620**

As an alternative, consult the list of topics at the start of Section 6.

**Forming Plurals (¶¶601–626)**
Basic Rule (¶601)
Nouns Ending in *S, X, CH, SH,* or *Z* (¶¶ 602–603)

. . .

Proper Names (¶¶615–617)
Titles With Personal Names (¶618)
Abbreviations, Letters, Numbers, Words, and Symbols (¶¶619–625)
→ Plural Endings in Parentheses (¶626)

# How To Look Things Up: Look Up Specific Words

**?        ?**

**Problem:** It is (,) therefore (,) essential that we meet next Wednesday.

**Solution:** First, consult the detailed index for the specific word.

*theoretically,* **138b**
*there* (see *their,* 209)
→ *therefore,* **122, 124b, 138–142, 178, 290f,** 328, 343

If the word is not listed, check another entry in the index.

Commas, **122–175,** 14
  with academic abbreviations, **122f, 157**
  :
→   with essential expressions, **122,**
    **131–132, 137, 139–142, 149–150**
  :
→   with nonessential expressions,
    **122, 127d, 131–132, 137–153**
  :
→   with transitional expressions,
    **122c, 135c, 138–143, 178–183**

For words that look alike or sound alike, see ¶719.
For words that are commonly misspelled, see ¶720.
For usage problems involving specific words, see Section 11.

*The Gregg Reference Manual*

     **Transparency H–6**

# PRESENT, PAST, AND FUTURE TENSES (¶¶1031–1032)

| INFINITIVE | | to see |
|---|---|---|
| **PRESENT TENSE** | I | see |
| First Principal Part | you | see |
| | he or she | *sees* |
| | we | see |
| | you | see |
| | they | see |
| **PAST TENSE** | I | saw |
| Second Principal Part | you | saw |
| | he or she | saw |
| | we | saw |
| | you | saw |
| | they | saw |
| **FUTURE TENSE** | I *shall* | see |
| Helping Verb (*shall* OR *will*) | you will | see |
| | he or she will | see |
| + | | |
| Main Verb (first principal part) | we *shall* | see |
| | you will | see |
| | they will | see |

*The Gregg Reference Manual*

**Transparency 10–1**

# PERFECT TENSES (¶1033)

| INFINITIVE | to see |
|---|---|

**PRESENT PERFECT TENSE**
  Helping Verb (present tense of *have*)

  +

  Main Verb (past participle)

| | |
|---|---|
| I have | seen |
| you have | seen |
| he or she *has* | seen |
| we have | seen |
| you have | seen |
| they have | seen |

**PAST PERFECT TENSE**
  Helping Verb (past tense of *have*)

  +

  Main Verb (past participle)

| | |
|---|---|
| I had | seen |
| you had | seen |
| he or she had | seen |
| we had | seen |
| you had | seen |
| they had | seen |

**FUTURE PERFECT TENSE**
  Helping Verb (future tense of *have*)

  +

  Main Verb (past participle)

| | |
|---|---|
| I *shall* have | seen |
| you will have | seen |
| he or she will have | seen |
| we *shall* have | seen |
| you will have | seen |
| they will have | seen |

*The Gregg Reference Manual*

# PROGRESSIVE TENSES (¶1034)

| INFINITIVE | | to see |
|---|---|---|

**PRESENT PROGRESSIVE TENSE**
  Helping Verb (present tense of *be*)

  \+

  Main Verb (present participle)

| | |
|---|---|
| I *am* | seeing |
| you are | seeing |
| he or she *is* | seeing |
| we are | seeing |
| you are | seeing |
| they are | seeing |

**PAST PROGRESSIVE TENSE**
  Helping Verb (past tense of *be*)

  \+

  Main Verb (present participle)

| | |
|---|---|
| I *was* | seeing |
| you were | seeing |
| he or she *was* | seeing |
| we were | seeing |
| you were | seeing |
| they were | seeing |

**FUTURE PROGRESSIVE TENSE**
  Helping Verb (future tense of *be*)

  \+

  Main Verb (present participle)

| | |
|---|---|
| I *shall* be | seeing |
| you will be | seeing |
| he or she will be | seeing |
| we *shall* be | seeing |
| you will be | seeing |
| they will be | seeing |

*The Gregg Reference Manual*

# PROGRESSIVE TENSES (¶1034)

| INFINITIVE | to see | |
|---|---|---|

**PRESENT PERFECT PROGRESSIVE TENSE**
Helping Verb
(present perfect of *be*)

+

Main Verb (present participle)

| | |
|---|---|
| I have been | seeing |
| you have been | seeing |
| he or she *has* been | seeing |
| | |
| we have been | seeing |
| you have been | seeing |
| they have been | seeing |

**PAST PERFECT PROGRESSIVE TENSE**
Helping Verb
(past perfect of *be*)

+

Main Verb (present participle)

| | |
|---|---|
| I had been | seeing |
| you had been | seeing |
| he or she had been | seeing |
| | |
| we had been | seeing |
| you had been | seeing |
| they had been | seeing |

**FUTURE PERFECT PROGRESSIVE TENSE**
Helping Verb
(future perfect of *be*)

+

Main Verb (present participle)

| | |
|---|---|
| I *shall* have been | seeing |
| you will have been | seeing |
| he or she will have been | seeing |
| | |
| we *shall* have been | seeing |
| you will have been | seeing |
| they will have been | seeing |

*The Gregg Reference Manual*

# PASSIVE TENSES (¶1036)

| INFINITIVE | | to see | |
|---|---|---|---|

## PRESENT PASSIVE TENSE
Helping Verb (present tense of *be*)

\+

Main Verb (past participle)

|  | I *am* | seen |
|---|---|---|
|  | you are | seen |
|  | he or she *is* | seen |
|  | we are | seen |
|  | you are | seen |
|  | they are | seen |

## PAST PASSIVE TENSE
Helping Verb (past tense of *be*)

\+

Main Verb (past participle)

|  | I *was* | seen |
|---|---|---|
|  | you were | seen |
|  | he or she *was* | seen |
|  | we were | seen |
|  | you were | seen |
|  | they were | seen |

## FUTURE PASSIVE TENSE
Helping Verb (future tense of *be*)

\+

Main Verb (past participle)

|  | I *shall* be | seen |
|---|---|---|
|  | you will be | seen |
|  | he or she will be | seen |
|  | we *shall* be | seen |
|  | you will be | seen |
|  | they will be | seen |

*The Gregg Reference Manual*

# PERFECT PASSIVE TENSES (¶1036)

| INFINITIVE | to see |
|---|---|

**PRESENT PERFECT PASSIVE TENSE**
Helping Verb
(present perfect of *be*)

    +

Main Verb (past participle)

|  |  |
|---:|:---|
| I have been | seen |
| you have been | seen |
| he or she *has* been | seen |
| we have been | seen |
| you have been | seen |
| they have been | seen |

**PAST PERFECT PASSIVE TENSE**
Helping Verb
(past perfect of *be*)

    +

Main Verb (past participle)

|  |  |
|---:|:---|
| I had been | seen |
| you had been | seen |
| he or she had been | seen |
| we had been | seen |
| you had been | seen |
| they had been | seen |

**FUTURE PERFECT PASSIVE TENSE**
Helping Verb
(future perfect of *be*)

    +

Main Verb (past participle)

|  |  |
|---:|:---|
| I *shall* have been | seen |
| you will have been | seen |
| he or she will have been | seen |
| we *shall* have been | seen |
| you will have been | seen |
| they will have been | seen |

*The Gregg Reference Manual*

# PROOFREADING (¶1202)

**¶1202b. Watch out for substitutions and omissions that change the meaning of the original material.**

**Original:** This kind of transaction is <u>not</u> legal.
**Copy:** This kind of transaction is <u>now</u> legal.

**Original:** Tom has reached the <u>acme</u> of his career.
**Copy:** Tom has reached the <u>acne</u> of his career.

**Original:** Our workers should <u>live</u> near their jobs.
**Copy:** Our workers should <u>lie</u> near their jobs.

**Original:** I was ticketed for <u>reckless</u> driving.
**Copy:** I was ticketed for <u>wreckless</u> driving.

**Original:** He's proud of his <u>flat</u> stomach.
**Copy:** He's proud of his <u>fat</u> stomach.

**Original:** There is <u>no</u> room for you in the van.
**Copy:** There is room for you in the van.

*The Gregg Reference Manual*

¶1203.   Watch out for errors in grammar, usage, spelling, punctuation, capitalization, and other matters of style.

Every one of the sales reps ~~have~~ *has* made ~~less~~ *fewer* calls in the past six months ~~then~~ *a* they did in the previous six months.

Our company's attorneys ~~have~~ advised us to proceed with the negotiations.

Why is it that/whenever we launch a new product, the company cuts our marketing dollars?

Please attend the Managers' meeting on monday, May 3rd, at ~~two~~ p. m.

*The Gregg Reference Manual*

# PROOFREADERS' MARKS (¶1206)

| PROOFREADERS' MARK | DRAFT | FINAL COPY |
|---|---|---|
| **SS** ⌐Single-space | **SS** ⌐ I have heard<br>└ he is leaving. | I have heard<br>he is leaving. |
| **ds** ⌐Double-space | **ds** ⌐ When will you<br>└ have a decision? | When will you<br><br>have a decision? |
| +lℓ# → Insert 1 line space | +lℓ# ——→ Percent of Change<br>16.25 | Percent of Change<br><br>16.25 |
| −lℓ# → Delete (remove) 1 line space | Northeastern<br>−lℓ# ——→<br>regional sales | Northeastern<br>regional sales |

*The Gregg Reference Manual*

# PROOFREADERS' MARKS (¶1206)

| PROOFREADERS' MARK | | DRAFT | FINAL COPY |
|---|---|---|---|
| ⌒⌣ | Delete space | to gether | together |
| #⟩⟨ | Insert space | It may be | It may not be |
| | Move as shown | it is (not) true | it is true |
| ∽ | Transpose | believable | believable |
| | | is it so | it is so |
| ◯ | Spell out | ② years ago | two years ago |
| | | 16 Elm (St.) | 16 Elm Street |
| ∧ OR ⟋ | Insert a word | How much it? | How much is it? |
| ⟍ OR — | Delete a word or a punctuation mark | it may not be true. | it may be true |

# Proofreaders' Marks (¶1206)

| PROOFREADERS' MARK | | DRAFT | FINAL COPY |
|---|---|---|---|
| ∧ or ⋏ | Insert a letter | temper_a_ture | temperature |
| ⪫ or ⟋ | Delete a letter and close up | commit~~t~~ment to buy~~y~~ | commitment to buy |
| ⌣ | Add on to a word | a real_ly_ good day | a really good day |
| ⋏ or ⟋ | Change a letter | this super_s_edes | this supersedes |
| ⋏ or ⌃ | Change a word | _But if_ and if you _can't_ ~~won't~~ | but if you can't |
| •••• | Stet (don't delete) | I was ~~very~~ glad | I was very glad |
| ⟋ | Lowercase a letter (make it a small letter) | ꟼederal ꟼovernment | federal government |
| ≡ | Capitalize | Janet L. g̲reyston | Janet L. Greyston |

*The Gregg Reference Manual*

# Proofreaders' Marks (¶1206)

| PROOFREADERS' MARK | DRAFT | FINAL COPY |
|---|---|---|
| ∨ Raise above the line | in her new book2 | in her new book[2] |
| ∧ Drop below the line | H2SO4 | $H_2SO_4$ |
| ⊙ Insert a period | Mr Henry Grenada | Mr. Henry Grenada |
| ⋏ Insert a comma | a large old house | a large, old house |
| ⋎ Insert an apostrophe | my childrens car | my children's car |
| Insert quotation marks | he wants a loan | he wants a "loan" |
| = Insert a hyphen | a first rate job | a first-rate job |
| | ask the coowner | ask the co-owner |
| Insert a one-em dash or change a hyphen to a one-em dash | Success at last! | Success—at last! |
| | Here it is cash! | Here it is—cash! |

# PROOFREADERS' MARKS (¶1206)

| PROOFREADERS' MARK | DRAFT | FINAL COPY |
|---|---|---|
| ——— Insert italics | Do it <u>now</u>, Bill! | Do it *now*, Bill! |
| *no ital* (Delete italics) | Do it (*now!*) *no ital* | Do it now! |
| ∿∿∿ Change to boldface | CONFIDENTIAL | **CONFIDENTIAL** |
| *no bf* (Delete boldface) | Ship by **June 1** *no bf* | Ship by June 1 |
| *no bf* Change to lightface | Ship by (**June 1**) *no bf* | Ship by June 1 |
| U/L Insert underline | an issue of (Time) U/L | an issue of <u>Time</u> |
| ↳↦ Delete underline | a <u>very</u> long day | a very long day |
| ( ) Insert parentheses | left today (May 3) | left today (May 3) |
| ¶ Start a new paragraph | ¶If that is so | If that is so |

*The Gregg Reference Manual*

# PROOFREADERS' MARKS (¶1206)

| PROOFREADERS' MARK | DRAFT | FINAL COPY |
|---|---|---|
| ⅀ Indent 2 spaces | Net investment in ⅀tangible assets | Net investment in tangible assets |
| ½" Indent 0.5 inch | ½"As a general rule, leave a top margin | As a general rule, leave a top margin |
| ⊐ Move to the right | $38,367,000⊐ | $38,367,000 |
| ⊏ Move to the left | ⊏Anyone can win! | Anyone can win! |
| ⊐⊏ Center | ⊐Table A-15⊏ | Table A-15 |
| = Align horizontally | Bob Muller<br>TO:⌐ | TO: Bob Muller |
| ‖ Align vertically | ‖ Jon Peters<br>‖ Ellen March | Jon Peters<br>Ellen March |

*The Gregg Reference Manual*

# MODIFIED-BLOCK LETTER STYLE—STANDARD FORMAT (PAGE 366)

**A** **Compudata Consultants Inc.**
600 East Algonquin Road
Arlington Heights, IL 60005-4332
Telephone: 847-555-4605
Fax: 847-555-5236
Web: www.comp-con.com

**6x**

**B** December 4, 2006

**4x**

**HEADING**

**C** Ms. Susan W. Morales
2839 Clary Street
Fort Worth, Texas 76111-4326

**↓2x**

**OPENING**

**D** Dear Ms. Morales: **↓2x**

**E** We were pleased to receive your letter of application for a sales position with Compudata Consultants. **↓2x**

At the moment we do not have an opening in the Fort Worth area, but we do need a field representative who is based in Lubbock and can cover the northwestern part of the state. If you would like to be considered for this position, please complete the enclosed application and return it to me. **↓2x**

**BODY**

As it happens, I will be attending a convention in Fort Worth next month. I would be delighted to meet with you while I'm in town and describe the job that is available. **↓2x**

When you return your completed application, please let me know whether you would be free to meet me at 4 p.m. on Wednesday or Thursday of the first week of January. I look forward to hearing from you. **↓2x**

**F** Sincerely, **↓2x**

**G** COMPUDATA CONSULTANTS INC.

**4x** **CLOSING**

*Kenneth R. Willmott*

**H** Kenneth R. Willmott
National Sales Manager **↓2x**

**I** bjn
**J** jobapp6d4
**K** Enclosure
**L** By FedEx
**M** cc: Ms. A. Rossi

*The Gregg Reference Manual*

# MODIFIED-BLOCK LETTER STYLE— WITH INDENTED PARAGRAPHS (PAGE 368)

**Center vertically**

**N**   1600 Fulton Road
Cleveland, OH 44113-3003
November 20, 2006   ↓**2x**

**O**   In reply to:  Invoice 57389

↓**4x**

**HEADING**

**P**   Accounting Department
Byfield & Duff
Post Office Box 268
Freeport, ME 04032-0268   ↓**2x**

Dear Byfield & Duff:   ↓**2x**

**OPENING**

**Q**       Over two months ago I ordered a pair of hiking boots, size 5.  You acknowledged my order, informed me that you were temporarily out of stock, and told me I could expect delivery within four weeks.   ↓**2x**

        Today I received Invoice 57389, billing me for two log carriers that I did not order and have not received.  May I ask that you cancel this invoice.  If the log carriers arrive, I will refuse delivery and have them shipped back to you at once.   ↓**2x**

**BODY**

        Sincerely,   ↓**4x**

*(Mrs.) Doris T. Hagerty*
Doris T. Hagerty   ↓**2x**

**CLOSING**

**R**       PS:  I'm still eager to have those boots. When may I expect to receive them?

*The Gregg Reference Manual*

# BLOCK LETTER STYLE (PAGE 369)

**Satellite Traders Inc.**
1500 Balboa Street
San Francisco, CA 94118-3519
Phone: +1-415-555-6000          www.sateltrade.com
Fax: +1-415-555-6143          jpgage@sateltrade.com

John P. Gage
President

**0.5 inch**

October 2, 2007

**2x**

**S**     CONFIDENTIAL

**4x**

Mr. Philip Wurlitzer Jr.
Executive Vice President
Satellite Traders Inc.
Apartado Aero 11255
Bogota, D.E.
**T**     COLOMBIA

**2x**

Dear Phil:

**2x**

**U**     Subject:  Your Request for Early Retirement

**2x**

I presented your request to the Board of Directors last Friday.  They were entirely sympathetic to your reasons for wanting to take early retirement, but they did express concern over the timing.  Al Barnes, in particular, raised the following points in a memo he sent me today.

**2x**

**V**          Ask Phil to identify people in the Bogota office he considers prospective candidates for his position.  Please ask him to spell out their present qualifications and estimate the time it would take to groom any one of these people for his job.

**2x**

If you and I can identify at least one qualified candidate acceptable to Al and the other directors, I know they will move quickly to honor your request.

**2x**

Sincerely,

**4x**

*John*

John P. Gage

**2x**

npl
wurltzrp071002
c:  A. J. Barnes
     C. L. Florio
     R. T. Washington

**HEADING**

**OPENING**

**BODY**

**CLOSING**

*The Gregg Reference Manual*

**Transparency 13–3**          D-35

# SIMPLIFIED LETTER STYLE (PAGE 370)

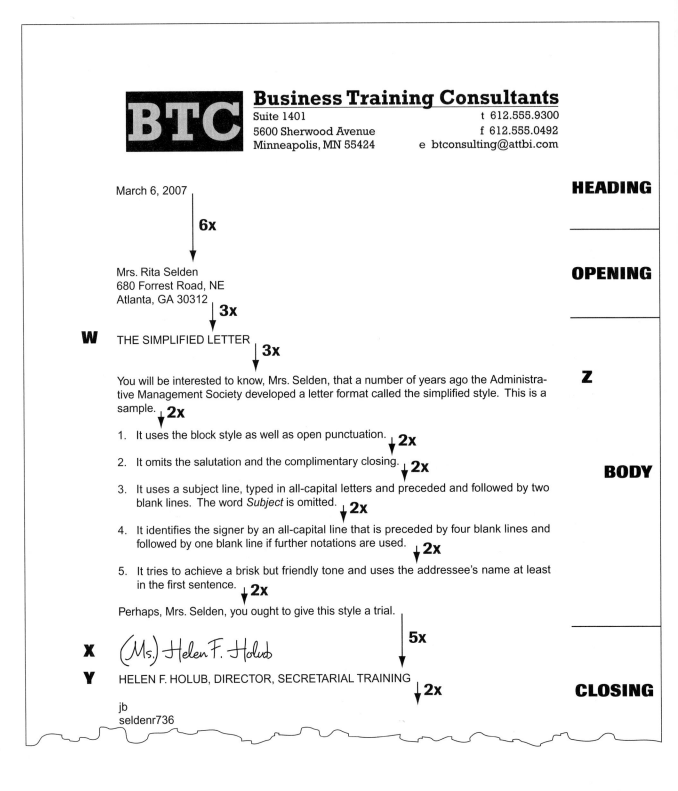

**Business Training Consultants**
Suite 1401
5600 Sherwood Avenue
Minneapolis, MN 55424

t 612.555.9300
f 612.555.0492
e btconsulting@attbi.com

**HEADING**

March 6, 2007

**6x**

Mrs. Rita Selden
680 Forrest Road, NE
Atlanta, GA 30312

**3x**

**OPENING**

**W**  THE SIMPLIFIED LETTER

**3x**

**Z**

You will be interested to know, Mrs. Selden, that a number of years ago the Administrative Management Society developed a letter format called the simplified style. This is a sample.

**2x**

1. It uses the block style as well as open punctuation.

**2x**

2. It omits the salutation and the complimentary closing.

**2x**

**BODY**

3. It uses a subject line, typed in all-capital letters and preceded and followed by two blank lines. The word *Subject* is omitted.

**2x**

4. It identifies the signer by an all-capital line that is preceded by four blank lines and followed by one blank line if further notations are used.

**2x**

5. It tries to achieve a brisk but friendly tone and uses the addressee's name at least in the first sentence.

**2x**

Perhaps, Mrs. Selden, you ought to give this style a trial.

**5x**

**X**  (Ms.) Helen F. Holub

**Y**  HELEN F. HOLUB, DIRECTOR, SECRETARIAL TRAINING

**2x**

**CLOSING**

jb
seldenr736

*The Gregg Reference Manual*

**Transparency 13–4**

# "Inside Address" Style for a Mailing Address on an Envelope (Page 414)

½ inch

Edgar Gardner
Evans & Massey Inc.
129 East Carlisle Avenue
Chicago, Illinois 60616

3x

CONFIDENTIAL

2 inches

Mrs. Susan Costello
Manager, Housewares Division
Lewis & Erickson Products Inc.
398 North Michigan Avenue
Chicago, Illinois 60603

4 inches

# ALL-CAP STYLE FOR A MAILING ADDRESS ON AN ENVELOPE (PAGE 416)

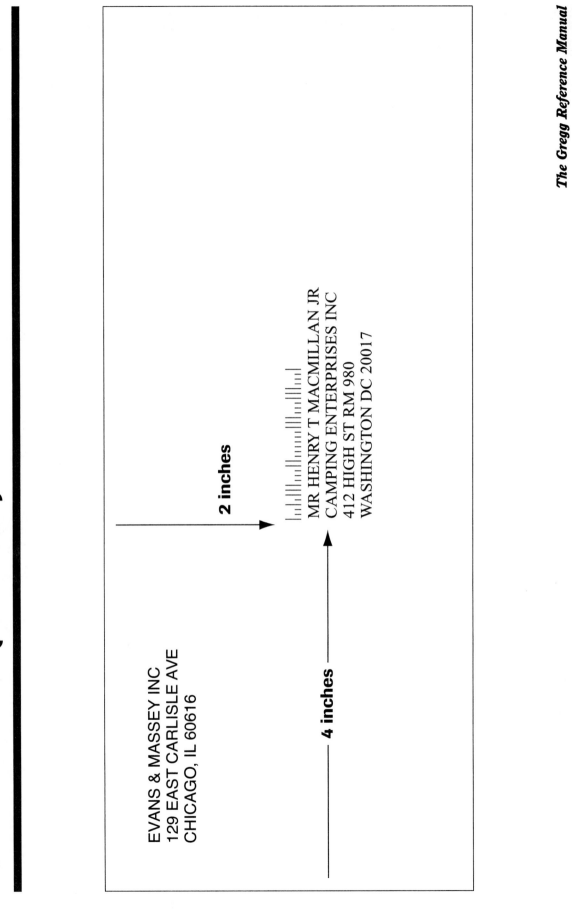

EVANS & MASSEY INC
129 EAST CARLISLE AVE
CHICAGO, IL 60616

2 inches

4 inches

MR HENRY T MACMILLAN JR
CAMPING ENTERPRISES INC
412 HIGH ST RM 980
WASHINGTON DC 20017

**Transparency 13–6**

# MEMO WITH A BLOCK-STYLE HEADING FORMAT (PAGE 422)

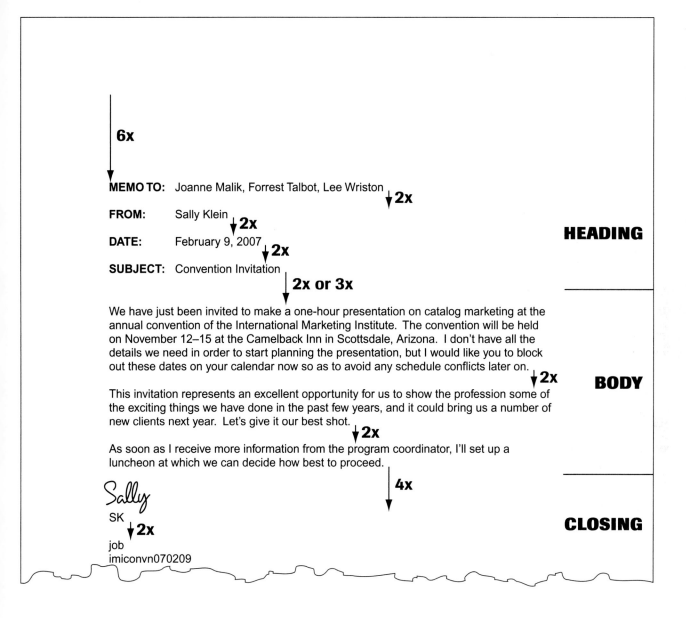

**6x**

**MEMO TO:**   Joanne Malik, Forrest Talbot, Lee Wriston
**↓2x**

**FROM:**   Sally Klein   **↓2x**

**DATE:**   February 9, 2007   **↓2x**

**SUBJECT:**   Convention Invitation

**↓2x or 3x**

We have just been invited to make a one-hour presentation on catalog marketing at the annual convention of the International Marketing Institute. The convention will be held on November 12–15 at the Camelback Inn in Scottsdale, Arizona. I don't have all the details we need in order to start planning the presentation, but I would like you to block out these dates on your calendar now so as to avoid any schedule conflicts later on.
**↓2x**

This invitation represents an excellent opportunity for us to show the profession some of the exciting things we have done in the past few years, and it could bring us a number of new clients next year. Let's give it our best shot.
**↓2x**

As soon as I receive more information from the program coordinator, I'll set up a luncheon at which we can decide how best to proceed.

**↓4x**

*Sally*

SK   **↓2x**

job
imiconvn070209

**HEADING**

**BODY**

**CLOSING**

*The Gregg Reference Manual*

**Transparency 13–7**

# Memo With a Block-Style Heading Format (Page 423)

MEMORANDUM

**TO:**         Bernard O'Kelly  ↓**2x**

**COPIES TO:**  Steve Kubat, Pat Rosario

**FROM:**       Janet R. Wiley *JRW*

**DATE:**       April 7, 2006

**SUBJECT:**    Test Marketing Arrangements  ↓**2 or 3x**

Dear Bernie:  ↓**2x**

Let me try to summarize the outcome of our excellent meeting last Friday, in which we discussed how your group might sell our product lines to the markets you serve.  ↓**2x**

1. Steve Kubat, chief product manager for my group, will provide you with product descriptions, catalog sheets, ad mats, and current price lists. If you need additional information, just call Steve (or me in his absence) and we'll be glad to help in any way that we can.  ↓**2x**

2. We will pay you an 18 percent commission on all orders you generate for our products. Please forward a copy of these orders to Steve, who will arrange to have the commission credited to your account.  ↓**2x**

3. We very much appreciate your offer to give us three hours at your weeklong sales meeting next month to present our products to your field staff. We'll be there.  ↓**2x**

4. We have agreed to give this new arrangement a six-month test to determine (a) how much additional sales revenue you and your people can produce with our products and (b) what effect, if any, this special marketing effort will have on your sales of other products. At the end of the test period, we will analyze the results and decide whether to continue the arrangement, modify it in some way, or abandon it altogether.  ↓**2x**

I don't think we'll be abandoning it, Bernie. In fact, I feel quite confident that this new arrangement is going to produce significant gains in sales and profits for both of us. I look forward to working with you to make it all happen.  ↓**2x**

imm
okellyb647

# E-MAIL HEADING (PAGE 430)

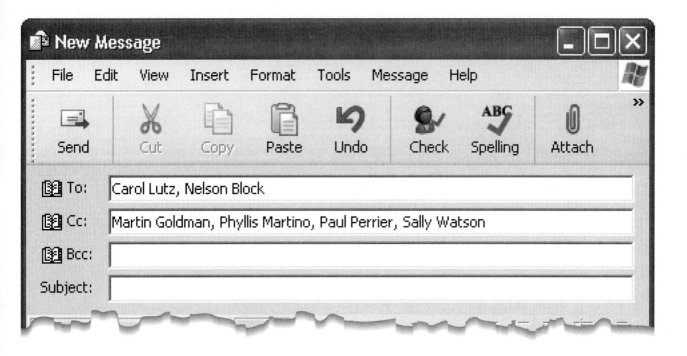

# E-Mail Message Sent (Page 434)

**Setting Up a Sub S Corporation**

File   Edit   View   Insert   Format   Tools   Message   Help

Send    Cut    Copy    Paste    Undo    Check    Spelling    Attach

**To:** Jack Lynch

**Cc:** Beverly Adler

**Bcc:**

**Subject:** Setting Up a Sub S Corporation

Times New Roman   12   **B** *I* U A

Hi Jack,

Bev and I have decided to take your advice and set up a Sub S corporation. I'll be in town next Thursday and Friday. Can you spare me a little time either afternoon?

All the best,

Margaret

*The Gregg Reference Manual*

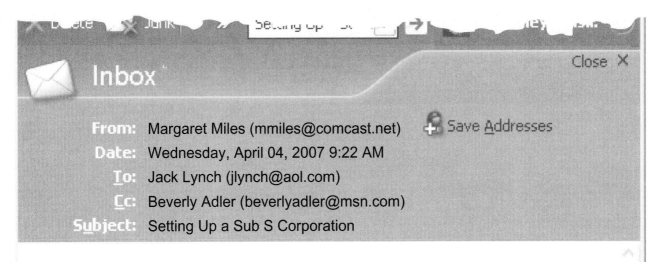

Hi Jack,

Bev and I have decided to take your advice and set up a Sub S corporation. I'll be in town next Thursday and Friday. Can you spare me a little time either afternoon?

All the best,

Margaret

*The Gregg Reference Manual*

# E-MAIL ATTACHMENT (PAGE 437)

**Regional Sales Patterns**

File  Edit  View  Insert  Format  Tools  Message  Help

Send | Cut | Copy | Paste | Undo | Check | Spelling | Attach

To: Craig Sanchez

Cc:

Subject: Regional Sales Patterns

Attach: Statistical Analysis.doc (23.5 KB)

Arial  10  B  I  U  A

Craig,

In the interest of time, I'm attaching a draft of the statistical analysis you asked me to do. I'll also put a hard copy in the mail today.

Bobby

*The Gregg Reference Manual*

# Academic Report (Page 453)

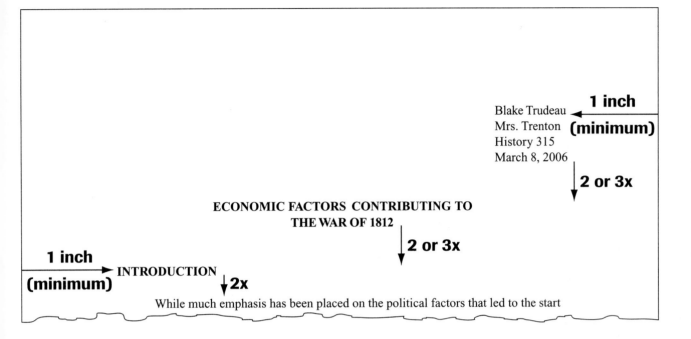

Blake Trudeau
Mrs. Trenton
History 315
March 8, 2006

**1 inch**
**(minimum)**

**2 or 3x**

ECONOMIC FACTORS CONTRIBUTING TO
THE WAR OF 1812

**2 or 3x**

**1 inch**
**(minimum)**

INTRODUCTION

**2x**

While much emphasis has been placed on the political factors that led to the start

*The Gregg Reference Manual*

**Transparency 14–2**

# How to Cite a Printed Book (Page 491)

## BUSINESS STYLE

[1]Author, *book title*, publisher, place of publication, year of publication, page number [if reference is being made to a specific page].

[1]Bill Bryson, *A Short History of Nearly Everything*, Broadway Books, New York, 2003, p. 384.

## ACADEMIC STYLE

[1]Author, *book title* (place of publication: publisher, year of publication), page number [if reference is being made to a specific page].

[1]Bill Bryson, *A Short History of Nearly Everything* (New York: Broadway Books, 2003), p. 384.

**BUSINESS STYLE:** . . . publisher, place of publication, year of publication . . .

**ACADEMIC STYLE:** . . . (place of publication: publisher, year of publication) . . .

*The Gregg Reference Manual*

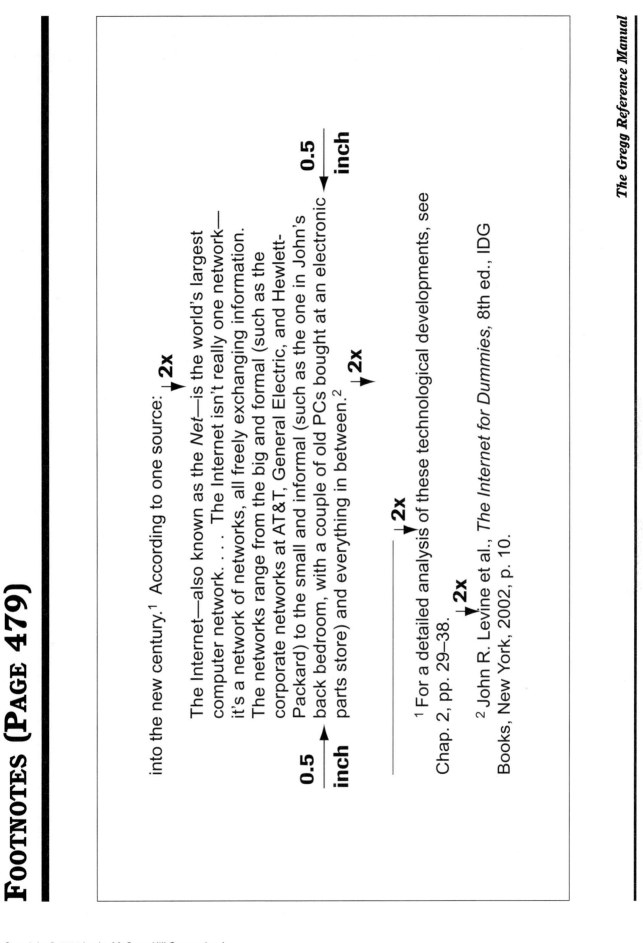

into the new century.[1]  According to one source:

The Internet—also known as the *Net*—is the world's largest computer network. . . .  The Internet isn't really one network—it's a network of networks, all freely exchanging information. The networks range from the big and formal (such as the corporate networks at AT&T, General Electric, and Hewlett-Packard) to the small and informal (such as the one in John's back bedroom, with a couple of old PCs bought at an electronic parts store) and everything in between.[2]

**0.5 inch** **2x**

**2x**

**2x**

---

[1] For a detailed analysis of these technological developments, see Chap. 2, pp. 29–38.

**2x**

[2] John R. Levine et al., *The Internet for Dummies*, 8th ed., IDG Books, New York, 2002, p. 10.

**0.5 inch**

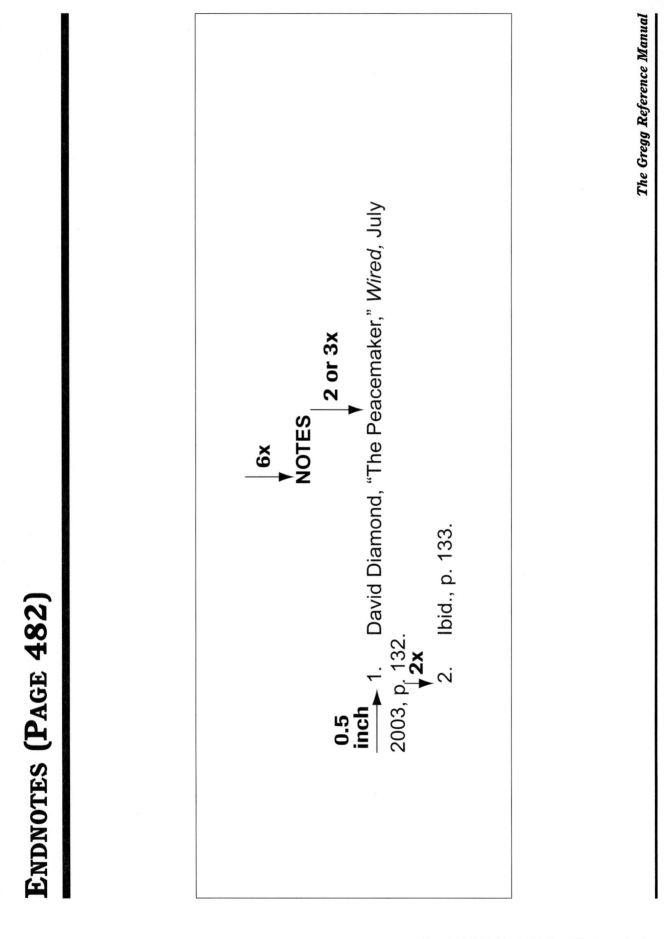

**0.5 inch**

1. David Diamond, "The Peacemaker," *Wired*, July 2003, p. 132.

**2x**

2. Ibid., p. 133.

**6x**

**NOTES**

**2 or 3x**

**Transparency 15–3**

recommended by the U.S. Postal Service. As for the abbreviations devised to hold down the length of place names in addresses, here is what one authority had to say:

And all you people with beautiful words in your addresses: Cut 'em down. There's a bright golden haze on the MDWS; a fairy dancing in your GDNS; and a safe HBR past the happy LNDG at the XING, where no hope SPGS. Environmentalists are now GRN, as in how GRN was my VLY. . . . Is the language not lessened when words like *meadow, gardens, harbor, landing, crossing, green, valley*—even *islands* (ISS)—are disemvoweled? (William Safire, *In Love With Norma Loquendi*, Random House, New York, 1994, p. 166.)

# HOW TO CITE ONLINE MATERIALS (PAGES 492, 495, 496, 498)

## ONLINE BOOK

[1]Author, *book title*, publisher, place of publication, year of publication, page number (if needed), <URL>, **accessed on** date.

[1]William Still, *The Underground Railroad*, Porter & Coates, Philadelphia, 1872, <http://invictus.quinnipiac.edu/ugrrmain.html>, accessed on May 28, 2007.

## ONLINE MAGAZINE ARTICLE

[2]Author [if known], "article title," *name of magazine*, date, <URL>, **accessed on** date.

[2]"Know Your Digital Parasites," *Slate*, August 12, 2003, <http://slate.msn.com/id/2086911>, accessed on September 14, 2007.

## ONLINE NEWSLETTER

[3]Author [if known], "article title" [if appropriate], *title of publication*, series title and series number [if appropriate], volume number and issue number [if appropriate], sponsoring organization, place [may be omitted], date, page number.

[3]Barbara Wallraff, "The State of Our Art," *Copy Editor*, August–September 2003, pp. 1, 6–7.

## E-MAIL MESSAGE

[4]Name of author, "subject line," **e-mail message,** date.

[4]Ann Valdez, "Taking the Spin Out of Corporate Communications," e-mail message, July 9, 2007.

# BIBLIOGRAPHY (PAGE 506)

6x

**BIBLIOGRAPHY**

2 or 3x

1 inch
(minimum)

1 inch
(minimum)

Buffett, Warren, et al., *The Essays of Warren Buffett,* rev. ed., Lawrence A. Cunningham, New York, 2001.

0.5 inch

2x

*A Critical Guide to Management Training Media,* Harvard Business School Press, Cambridge, Mass., 1997.

The Economist, *Guide to Economic Indicators: Making Sense of Economics,* 5th ed., Bloomberg, New York, 2003.

"Executive Pay: Revolting Shareholders," *The Economist,* May 24, 2003, p. 13.

Galbraith, Jay R., *Designing Organizations: An Executive Guide to Strategy, Structure, and Process,* 2d ed., Jossey-Bass, San Francisco, 2001.

Galbraith, John Kenneth, *The Affluent Society,* 4th ed., Houghton Mifflin, Boston, 1998.

————, *American Capitalism: The Concept of Countervailing Power,* rev. ed., Transaction Publishers, New Brunswick, N.J., 1993.

————, *The Good Society: The Humane Agenda,* Mariner, Boston, 1997.

————, *The Great Crash: 1929,* Mariner, Boston, 1997.

————, *A Short History of Financial Euphoria,* Penguin, New York, 1994.

———— and Andrea D. Williams, *A View From the Stands: Of People, Politics, Military Power, and the Arts*, Houghton Mifflin, Boston, November 1986.

Gerstner, Louis V., Jr., *Who Says Elephants Can't Dance?: Inside IBM's Turnaround,* HarperBusiness, New York, 2002.

*A Guide to the Project Management Body of Knowledge,* 2000 ed., Project Management Institute, Philadelphia, 2001.

Sigerman, Harriet (ed.), *The Columbia Documentary History of American Women Since 1941,* Columbia Univ. Press, New York, 2003.

*The Gregg Reference Manual*

**Transparency 15–6**

**A** **ALISON L. BUMBRY**

*AB* Apartment 145
395 West Center College Street
Yellow Springs, Ohio 45387

Phone: 937-555-7944
Fax: 937-555-8341
E-mail: albumbry@aol.com

**B** **OBJECTIVE:** A marketing management position in which marketing and administrative experience plus strong writing and computer skills can be used to maximize sales and profitability of one or more product lines.

**C** **EXPERIENCE:**

July 2001–Present

**ADMINISTRATIVE COORDINATOR FOR DIRECTOR OF** **D**
MARKETING, Zimmer & Boyle Inc., Dayton, Ohio

**E** • Created and managed a database to control budgeted expenses for advertising and promotion.
**F** • Participated in designing and implementing market research studies **G**
to determine potential size of market for new product lines.
• Coordinated focus group sessions to determine customer attitudes toward our product lines and those of competitors.
• Initiated desktop publishing program to create space ads, catalogs, and mailing pieces. Saved the company over $50,000 in the first year of operation.

February 1999–
June 2001

**ADMINISTRATIVE ASSISTANT TO SALES MANAGER**
Zimmer & Boyle Inc., Dayton, Ohio

• Analyzed field sales reports and wrote summaries highlighting problems requiring immediate action and those suggesting need for changes in product design, order fulfillment procedures, and customer service.
• Resolved customer complaints by taking direct action whenever possible or by routing the complaint to the appropriate person. Followed up to ensure complaint was properly handled.
• Supervised a secretary who handled all correspondence and clerical tasks.

May 1997–
January 1999

**SECRETARY TO MARKETING MANAGER**
Crouch and Cowar Incorporated, Toledo, Ohio

• Developed detailed marketing plans, working from rough outlines provided by marketing manager.
• Created and managed a segmented database of names of customers and qualified prospects for direct marketing campaigns.
• Wrote copy for mail campaigns and catalogs.
• Established media contacts to obtain free publicity for new products and special offers.

*The Gregg Reference Manual*

**ALISON L. BUMBRY** Page 2

| September 1995– April 1997 | ASSISTANT TO DIRECTOR OF PUBLIC RELATIONS The Toledo Museum of Art, Toledo, Ohio |
|---|---|

- Wrote news releases for new exhibits and special events.
- Wrote, designed, and laid out fund-raising brochures.
- Established and maintained effective media contacts with regional newspapers and TV and radio stations.

**H EDUCATION:** B.S. in marketing, 1995; minor in English
Arizona State University, Tempe, Arizona

- Wrote feature articles for *The Arizona Sundial* during sophomore and junior years.
**G** - Created (with two partners) an on-campus birthday celebration service. Managed the service during junior and senior years. Tested various direct marketing techniques to solicit orders from parents of students.

**I CONTINUING EDUCATION:** Courses in copywriting, telemarketing techniques, niche marketing, and computer graphics, Wright State University, Dayton, Ohio, 2001–2003.

**J COMPUTER SKILLS:** Microsoft Office XP Pro, Microsoft Word 2002, Corel WordPerfect Office 2002, CorelDRAW Graphics Suite 11, Adobe PageMaker 7.0, Adobe Illustrator 10.0, Adobe Photoshop 7.0, Microsoft PowerPoint 2002, QuarkXPress 5.01, Peachtree Accounting 2002 9.0, Microsoft Money 2003.

**K COMMUNITY SERVICE:** Wrote, designed, and laid out annual fund-raising brochures (since 2001) for the Dayton Homeless Shelter Coalition, using desktop publishing and computer graphics software.

*The Gregg Reference Manual*

**ALISON L. BUMBRY**

*AB*    Apartment 145                        Phone: 937-555-7944
        395 West Center College Street         Fax: 937-555-8341
        Yellow Springs, Ohio 45387      E-mail: albumbry@aol.com

OBJECTIVE:        A marketing management position in which marketing and admin-
                  istrative experience plus strong writing and computer skills can be
                  used to maximize sales and profitability of one or more product
                  lines.

EXPERIENCE:

**A** Administrative Coordinator    ZIMMER & BOYLE INC., Dayton, Ohio, July 2001–Present    **B**
      for Director of Marketing

                  **C** Created and managed a database to control budgeted expenses for
                  advertising and promotion. Participated in designing and imple-
                  menting market research studies to determine the potential size of
                  market for new product lines. Coordinated focus group sessions to
                  determine customer attitudes toward our product lines and those of
                  competitors. Initiated desktop publishing program to create space
                  ads, catalogs, and mailing pieces; saved the company over $50,000
                  in the first year of operation.

Administrative Assistant to    ZIMMER & BOYLE INC., Dayton, Ohio, February 1999–June 2001
Sales Manager

                  Analyzed field sales reports and wrote summaries highlighting
                  problems requiring immediate action and those suggesting a need
                  for changes in product design, order fulfillment procedures, and
                  customer service. Resolved customer complaints by taking direct
                  action whenever possible or by routing the complaint to the appro-
                  priate person; followed up to ensure the complaint was properly
                  handled. Supervised a secretary who handled all correspondence
                  and clerical tasks.

Secretary to Marketing    CROUCH AND COWAR INCORPORATED, Toledo, Ohio,
Manager                   May 1997–January 1999

                  Developed detailed marketing plans, working from rough outlines
                  provided by the marketing manager. Created and managed a seg-
                  mented database of names of customers and qualified prospects
                  for direct marketing campaigns. Wrote copy for mail campaigns
                  and catalogs. Established media contacts to obtain free publicity
                  for new products and special offers.

*The Gregg Reference Manual*

**ALISON L. BUMBRY**

*AB*

Apartment 145
395 West Center College Street
Yellow Springs, Ohio 45387

Phone: 937-555-7944
Fax: 937-555-8341
E-mail: albumbry@aol.com

**OBJECTIVE:**   A marketing management position in which marketing and administrative experience plus strong writing and computer skills can be used to maximize sales and profitability of one or more product lines.   **B**

**A**   **ACHIEVEMENTS:**   **MARKETING EXPERIENCE**   **B**

**C**
- Participated in designing and implementing market research studies to determine potential size of market for new product line.
- Coordinated focus group sessions to determine customer attitudes toward our product lines and those of competitors.
- Analyzed field sales reports and wrote summaries highlighting problems requiring immediate action and those suggesting need for changes in product design, order fulfillment procedures, and customer service.
- Developed detailed marketing plans, working from rough outlines provided by marketing manager.

**ADMINISTRATIVE EXPERIENCE**   **B**

**C**
- Controlled budgeted expenses for advertising and promotion.
- Resolved customer complaints by taking direct action whenever possible or by routing the complaint to an appropriate person.  Followed up to ensure complaint was properly handled.
- Established and maintained effective media contacts with regional newspapers and TV and radio stations to obtain free publicity for new products and special offers.
- Supervised a secretary who handled all correspondence and clerical tasks.

**WRITING SKILLS**   **B**

**C**
- Wrote copy for mail campaigns and catalogs.
- Wrote summaries of field sales reports to underscore need for immediate action.
- Wrote copy for fund-raising brochures for art museum.

*The Gregg Reference Manual*

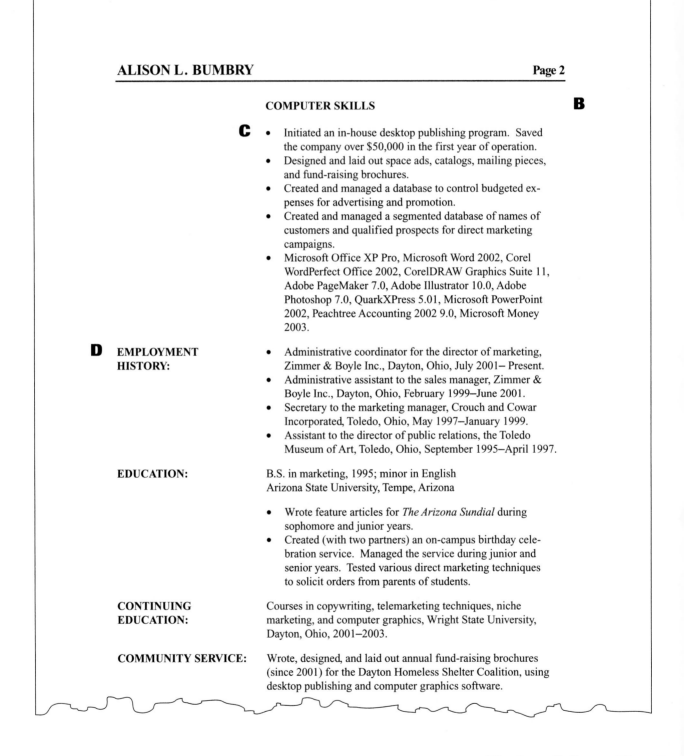

**ALISON L. BUMBRY**                                                            **Page 2**

**COMPUTER SKILLS**                                                    **B**

**C**
- Initiated an in-house desktop publishing program. Saved the company over $50,000 in the first year of operation.
- Designed and laid out space ads, catalogs, mailing pieces, and fund-raising brochures.
- Created and managed a database to control budgeted expenses for advertising and promotion.
- Created and managed a segmented database of names of customers and qualified prospects for direct marketing campaigns.
- Microsoft Office XP Pro, Microsoft Word 2002, Corel WordPerfect Office 2002, CorelDRAW Graphics Suite 11, Adobe PageMaker 7.0, Adobe Illustrator 10.0, Adobe Photoshop 7.0, QuarkXPress 5.01, Microsoft PowerPoint 2002, Peachtree Accounting 2002 9.0, Microsoft Money 2003.

**D EMPLOYMENT HISTORY:**
- Administrative coordinator for the director of marketing, Zimmer & Boyle Inc., Dayton, Ohio, July 2001– Present.
- Administrative assistant to the sales manager, Zimmer & Boyle Inc., Dayton, Ohio, February 1999–June 2001.
- Secretary to the marketing manager, Crouch and Cowar Incorporated, Toledo, Ohio, May 1997–January 1999.
- Assistant to the director of public relations, the Toledo Museum of Art, Toledo, Ohio, September 1995–April 1997.

**EDUCATION:**
B.S. in marketing, 1995; minor in English
Arizona State University, Tempe, Arizona

- Wrote feature articles for *The Arizona Sundial* during sophomore and junior years.
- Created (with two partners) an on-campus birthday celebration service. Managed the service during junior and senior years. Tested various direct marketing techniques to solicit orders from parents of students.

**CONTINUING EDUCATION:**
Courses in copywriting, telemarketing techniques, niche marketing, and computer graphics, Wright State University, Dayton, Ohio, 2001–2003.

**COMMUNITY SERVICE:**
Wrote, designed, and laid out annual fund-raising brochures (since 2001) for the Dayton Homeless Shelter Coalition, using desktop publishing and computer graphics software.

*The Gregg Reference Manual*

**RALPH A. PINKHAM**
148 Biscay Road
Damariscotta, Maine 04543
207-555-3266

**OBJECTIVE:** To gain experience as a bank teller as a first step toward a career in banking.

**A**    **EDUCATION:** *A.A. in business management, 2005*
*University of Maine, Augusta, Maine*

Courses in accounting, business communication, business management, finance, and office technology.   **E**

**B**   Academic scholarships, 2003–2005. Member of the intramural wrestling team, 2003–2004. Tutor in a university-sponsored community literacy program, 2004–2005.   **E**

**C**    **EXPERIENCE:** *Sales associate, Reny's, Damariscotta, Maine, June 2005–Present*

Handled cash and credit card transactions, using electronic cash register. Helped customers with product selections and suggested tie-in purchases. Resolved customer problems. Assisted in taking inventory and restocking shelves. Suggested special promotions and helped design merchandise displays.   **E**

*Cashier, Pinkham's Plantation, Damariscotta, Maine, May 2000–August 2003*

Worked part-time in family-owned business. Handled cash and credit card transactions. Advised customers on planting and care of purchased items. Set up special seasonal displays and recommended special pricing arrangements to boost sales.   **E**

**D**    **SKILLS:** Strong number sense and quick mastery of electronic cash register and calculators. Proven ability to handle large amounts of money accurately. Outgoing personality with the ability to grasp and respond to customers' needs and concerns. Excellent communication skills in writing, over the phone, and face to face. Mastery of Microsoft Office and Lotus Notes software. Facility in the use of e-mail and accessing information on the Web.   **E**

*The Gregg Reference Manual*

**A**    ALISON L. BUMBRY
Apartment 145
395 West Center College Street
Yellow Springs, Ohio 45387
Phone: 937-555-7944
Fax: 937-555-8341
E-mail: albumbry@aol.com

**B**  OBJECTIVE

A position in marketing management in which marketing experience and administrative expertise plus writing skills and computer skills can be used to promote sales growth and exceed profit goals for one or more product lines.

**B**  MARKETING SKILLS

**C**  Design and implementation of market research studies. Assessment of potential market size for new product lines. Coordination of focus group sessions. Assessment of customer attitudes toward product lines. Analysis of field sales reports. Pinpointing of problems for immediate action. Pinpointing of need for changes in product design, order fulfillment procedures, and customer service. Development of detailed marketing plans based on input from marketing manager.

**B**  ADMINISTRATIVE SKILLS

**C**  Control of advertising and promotion expense budgets. Resolution of customer complaints. Contacts with newspapers, TV stations, and radio stations for free publicity. Supervision of secretary.

**B**  WRITING SKILLS

**C**  Preparation of copy for mail campaigns, catalogs, and fund-raising brochures. Summaries of field sales reports.

**B**  COMPUTER SKILLS

**C**  Start-up of in-house desktop publishing program, with first-year savings of $50,000. Design and layout of space ads, catalogs, mailing pieces, and fund-raising brochures. Creation and management of database for control of advertising and promotion expense budgets. Creation and management of segmented database of customers and qualified

*The Gregg Reference Manual*

**H**    ALISON L. BUMBRY        Page 2

**B**    EMPLOYMENT HISTORY

**D**    * Administrative coordinator for director of marketing, Zimmer and Boyle Inc., Dayton, Ohio, July 2001–Present. **I**
* Administrative assistant to sales manager, Zimmer and Boyle Inc., Dayton, Ohio, February 1999–June 2001. **I**
* Secretary to marketing manager, Crouch and Cowar Incorporated, Toledo, Ohio, May 1997–January 1999.
* Assistant to director of public relations, the Toledo Museum of Art, Toledo, Ohio, September 1995–April 1997.

**B**    EDUCATION

**E**    B.S. in marketing, 1995, minor in English, Arizona State University, Tempe, Arizona.

Writer of feature articles for The Arizona Sundial during sophomore and junior years. Cofounder and manager of on-campus birthday service. Testing of various direct marketing techniques to solicit orders. **I**

**B**    CONTINUING EDUCATION

**F**    Courses in copywriting, telemarketing techniques, niche marketing, and computer graphics, Wright State University, Dayton, Ohio, 2001–2003.

**B**    COMMUNITY SERVICE

**G**    Writing, design, and layout of annual fund-raising brochures for the Dayton Homeless Shelter Coalition.

*The Gregg Reference Manual*

   **Transparency 17–8**     

**A**  **ALISON L. BUMBRY**

Apartment 145
395 West Center College Street
Yellow Springs, Ohio 45387

Phone: 937-555-7944
Fax: 937-555-8341
E-mail: albumbry@aol.com

March 3, 2005

Mr. Oliver Digby
Director of Human Resources
Hunt and Ketcham Inc.
1228 Euclid Avenue
Cleveland, Ohio 44115

Dear Mr. Digby:

**B** You advertised for a marketing manager in the March 2 *Plain Dealer*. I have used many Hunt and Ketcham texts in my computer courses, so I know that your company publishes books of consistently high quality. As the following comparison shows, my experience and background come close to satisfying all of the requirements stated in your ad.

**C**

| Your Requirements | My Qualifications |
|---|---|
| College degree | B.S. in marketing plus continuing education courses in marketing and computer software applications |
| Knowledge of technical publishing market | Over six years' experience in sales and marketing divisions of two educational publishing companies |
| Field sales experience | Extensive contact with field sales reps and customers, resolving a wide range of sales support and customer service problems |

The enclosed résumé will provide additional information about my marketing experience.

**D** I would appreciate the chance to meet with you and discuss the ways in which I can help Hunt and Ketcham achieve its marketing objectives and its profit goals. I will call your office on March 14 to determine whether there is a convenient time for you to see me.

Sincerely,

*The Gregg Reference Manual*

# Follow-Up Letter (Page 571)

**ALISON L. BUMBRY**
Apartment 145
395 West Center College Street
Yellow Springs, Ohio 45387

Phone: 937-555-7944
Fax: 937-555-8341
E-mail: albumbry@aol.com

March 25, 2005

Mr. Oliver Digby
Director of Human Resources
Hunt and Ketcham Inc.
1228 Euclid Avenue
Cleveland, Ohio 44115

Dear Mr. Digby:

**A** Thank you for taking the time last Friday to explain why my lack of field sales experience in the technical publishing market prevents me from being considered for the marketing manager's position at Hunt and Ketcham.

**B** Thank you, moreover, for arranging an interview that same day with your director of sales. Ms. Cantrell gave me a very detailed picture of a field rep's responsibilities. She also stated that in light of all my prior experience in educational publishing, I ought to make the transition to technical publishing very easily. I was encouraged to learn that after a year or two of experience in the field, I would be a strong candidate for any marketing manager's position that might open at that time.

**C** Ms. Cantrell has promised to let me know within the next four weeks whether she is in a position to offer me a field rep's job. If she does, I very much look forward to seeing you again. In any event, thank you for all the help you have given me.

Sincerely,

*Alison L. Bumbry*

Alison L. Bumbry

*The Gregg Reference Manual*

**Transparency 17–10**

**ALISON L. BUMBRY**

*AB*  Apartment 145
395 West Center College Street
Yellow Springs, Ohio 45387

Phone: 937-555-7944
Fax: 937-555-8341
E-mail: albumbry@aol.com

April 29, 2005

Ms. Jennifer Cantrell
Director of Sales
Hunt and Ketcham Inc.
1228 Euclid Avenue
Cleveland, Ohio 44115

Dear Jennifer:

**A** I am very pleased to accept the job of field sales representative, with the state of Ohio as my territory. What especially appeals to me is that this job not only represents an excellent opportunity in itself; it provides a springboard for higher-level marketing jobs with Hunt and Ketcham.

**B** The materials that Oliver Digby sent me answered all my questions about compensation arrangements and company policies. All the necessary paperwork has now been completed and returned. As I understand it, you want me to start work on June 6, spending the month in Cleveland for orientation and training. I assume that someone in your department will provide me with information about my accommodations during the month of June.

**C** I am genuinely excited about the prospect of working with you and for you. From our conversations I can tell how supportive you are of the people who report to you. When I think of how much I will learn under your supervision, I realize just how lucky I am to be joining Hunt and Ketcham.

**D** If there is anything you think I should be reading or doing in the next month, please let me know. I would welcome the chance to get a head start on the job before I actually report for work on June 6.

Sincerely,

*Alison L. Bumbry*

Alison L. Bumbry

# Forms of Address—For a Mayor (¶¶1801–1811)

**Inside Address:**       The Honorable . . . (*full name*)
                          Mayor of . . . (*city*)
                          City, State    ZIP Code

OR:       The Mayor of the City of . . .
          City, State    ZIP Code


**Salutation:**       Dear Mr. Mayor:      OR:    Dear Madam Mayor:

OR:       Dear Mayor . . . (*last name*):

*The Gregg Reference Manual*